FIGHTING FOR THE AMERICAN DREAM

FIGHTING FOR THE AMERICAN DREAM

From Blue-Collar Kid to Maverick Economist, The Battle to Defend Working Families

Charles J. Whalen

BLOOMSBURY ACADEMIC
NEW YORK • LONDON • OXFORD • NEW DELHI • SYDNEY

BLOOMSBURY ACADEMIC
Bloomsbury Publishing Inc, 1359 Broadway, New York, NY 10018, USA
Bloomsbury Publishing Plc, 50 Bedford Square, London, WC1B 3DP, UK
Bloomsbury Publishing Ireland, 29 Earlsfort Terrace, Dublin 2, D02 AY28, Ireland

First published in the United States of America 2026

Cover image: Aerial view of the historic Watch City industrial complex mirrored in the tranquil Charles River under a twilight sky. Waltham, Massachusetts, USA. © Amazing Aerial Premium/Shutterstock

Library of Congress Control Number: 2026941916

ISBN: HB: 979-8-216-39429-7
ePDF: 979-8-216-39430-3
eBook: 979-8-216-39431-0

Typeset by Integra Software Services Pvt. Ltd.
Printed and bound in the United States of America

For product safety related questions contact productsafety@bloomsbury.com.

To my family, and to all who pursue cooperation over predation

CONTENTS

PREFACE

A decades-long erosion of the American Dream has inflicted pain on workers, families, and communities. It has also sapped our economic strength, and deepened income and wealth inequality. Today, it even imperils our democracy and prospects for international peace and security.

Widespread worker insecurity and downward mobility in our current era contrast sharply with expanding prosperity and opportunity in the optimistic postwar era that extended into the mid-1970s. What happened? And what can we do to revitalize the American Dream, reduce worker precarity, and foster broadly shared prosperity? Those questions are at the heart of *Fighting for the American Dream*.

This book explores both questions from my perspective as a blue-collar kid (the son of a factory worker dad and first-generation Italian American mom) who became a maverick economist to advance the interests of working families like the one that raised me. It's a historical account of a national crisis long in the making, presented through the lens of a personal story about growing up in a work-obsessed family and pursuing a career devoted to addressing that crisis. It's also about coming to grips with the prejudices and other social forces that can sever the link between hard work and employment success, and about getting caught in the same currents as the workers I aimed to defend. A dozen years ago, President Barack Obama described the erosion of the American Dream as "the defining challenge of our time"; since then, the problem has continued to worsen and is now linked to the threat of authoritarianism and an erosion of the rule of law.

The book exposes obstacles that have always marred the paths of many seeking job opportunities, but it also traces the prolonged fading of the American Dream to the emergence of investor-driven predatory capitalism, a transformation that began a half century ago. Since the 1970s, no groups in society have shaped economic life more than the institutional investors who demand a relentless business focus on shareholder gains, and the policymakers who ignore or cynically manipulate the worker insecurity it produces. But another sort of capitalism, in which a rising tide truly does lift all boats, is possible: one that treats workers as a source of competitive advantage, not a cost to be minimized, and that recognizes nations advance by making strategic public investments, not by building tariff walls and recklessly dismantling public agencies and institutions.

The American Dream must be revitalized for the sake of working families, the nation, and the world. That will require economic reform driven by pro-worker policies and an innovation-oriented industrial strategy that appreciates the vital economic role of government. Motivated by a search for lessons from the past, this book recounts four decades of personal and persistent efforts on behalf of working families. But its aim is forward-looking: pointing a distressed nation in the direction of constructive—and long overdue—social change.

Charles J. Whalen

ACKNOWLEDGMENTS

This book benefits from recollections my parents shared with me during several interviews and discussions over the span of about a dozen years. More recently, my brother Frank provided valuable input and reviewed the manuscript, as did Guy Burns, Jim Peach, and Linda, my wife, without whose support it would have never been written. In addition, Kate Kelly (a friend, former colleague, and terrific editor) responded constructively and cheerfully to queries on word choice and sentence structure over many months. I'm grateful to each of them for their contributions.

I'm also grateful to Lilith Dorko, senior editor at Bloomsbury, who saw the merits of this project and worked with me to move smoothly from proposal to publication. In the process, I benefited from the comments and suggestions of three referees, as well as from the work of Saville Bloxham at Bloomsbury. Kudos and thanks to the publisher's entire production team, including Brigham Narins, who provided exceptional copy editing.

In addition, the author and publishers wish to thank the following publisher, which has kindly given permission to use excerpts of copyrighted material: The Society for the Advancement of Education, for Charles J. Whalen, "The Age of Anxiety: Erosion of the American Dream," *USA Today: The Magazine of the American Scene* (September 1996), 14–16.

ABBREVIATIONS

AACSB	Association to Advance Collegiate Schools of Business
AALS	Association of American Law Schools
AARP	American Association of Retired Persons
AAUP	American Association of University Professors
AFEE	Association for Evolutionary Economics
AFL-CIO	American Federation of Labor and Congress of Industrial Organizations
AIS	Automotive Industry Studies
ASSA	Allied Social Science Associations
BMC	Boston Manufacturing Company
BNE	Buffalo Niagara Enterprise
BRB	Big Red Band (Cornell University)
BU	Boston University
CBO	Congressional Budget Office
CLB	China Labour Bulletin
CNP	Center for National Policy
Cornell ILR	Cornell University School of Industrial and Labor Relations
EDG	Economic Development Group (WNY AFL-CIO)
EPI	Economic Policy Institute
FEC	Federal Election Commission
Fed	Federal Reserve
GDP	gross domestic product
GITIC	Guangdong International Trust and Investment Corporation
HWS	Hobart and William Smith Colleges
IACBE	International Accreditation Council for Business Education
IF	Interactivity Foundation
IFDP	Interactivity Foundation Discussion Process
IIS	Institute for Industry Studies (Cornell University)
ILR	industrial and labor relations

ILR Extension	Division of Extension and Public Service at Cornell ILR
ILR School	Cornell University School of Industrial and Labor Relations
INET	Institute for New Economic Thinking
IRRA	Industrial Relations Research Association
JEI	*Journal of Economic Issues*
LBJ School	Lyndon B. Johnson School of Public Affairs
LERA	Labor and Employment Relations Association
MAD	Macroeconomic Analysis Division (Congressional Budget Office)
MIT	Massachusetts Institute of Technology
NAFTA	North American Free Trade Agreement
NLRB	National Labor Relations Board
NPP	Niagara Power Project
OAB	Outokumpu American Brass
OECD	Organisation for Economic Cooperation and Development
OMB	Office of Management and Budget
PATCO	Professional Air Traffic Controllers Organization
PBGC	Pension Benefit Guaranty Corporation
PKI	post-Keynesian institutionalism
PoW	*Perspectives on Work*
ROTC	Reserve Officers' Training Corps
SAC	Student Advisory Council (Massachusetts)
SAT	Scholastic Aptitude Test
UAL	United Airlines
UAW	United Auto Workers
UT	University of Texas
WIC	Women, Infants, and Children
WNY	Western New York
WTC	World Trade Center
WTO	World Trade Organization

PROLOGUE: THE AMERICAN DREAM IN 100 BOXES

"You have had a good start. Work harder!" That's the command, now barely legible but printed originally in scolding red ink, constantly glaring at me from a fortune-cookie strip I taped to the wall facing my desk over thirty years ago. Looking beyond that faded fortune, I scan a home office ringed with overstuffed bookshelves and stacks of about 100 cardboard boxes, each nearly bursting with news clippings, letters, research reports, lecture notes, academic papers, and other documents accumulated since the 1970s. The collection includes more than four decades of my own work, but I've seldom considered much of it more than a good start. What's next has always been obvious—in fact, staring me in the face: "Work harder!"

Surrounded by all the paper I've collected and produced, I now realize just how much a focus on work shaped my identity and ambition since an early age. My parents, children of the Great Depression for whom college was an unthinkable luxury, obsessed over working "to put food on the table"—and did their best to instill in me the same preoccupation. They also stressed the belief that academic achievement and a university education would be essential to job-market security for baby boomers. That meant my work began at least as early as kindergarten. In fact, from what I can recall it's *always* been about work.

There's really no surprise, then, that I chose an undergraduate major devoted to the world of work (labor-management relations) and pursued graduate studies leading to a career as a labor economist. Mom thought I should become an accountant—professional, practical, business oriented, and far more financially secure than a factory worker like my dad. But watching my parents strive to simply make ends meet and wanting to make a modest difference to the struggles of working families, I attended Cornell University with ideas that included becoming a labor arbitrator or perhaps an expert in labor market policies. Then I learned that professors of labor economics often did both sorts of work, so in the 1980s I earned a PhD in economics from The University of Texas at Austin, where I focused on labor markets and national economic policy, studying with Ray Marshall, Secretary of Labor for President Jimmy Carter.

As a close observer of the US economy during the 1970s and 1980s, I understood that more and more workers strained mightily to preserve even a modest version of the American Dream—one centered on working to attain financial security and gradually improving economic well-being, not wealth and fame.[1] It was a tough period, during which millions of working families felt the squeeze of rapidly rising living expenses, widespread plant closings and workforce reductions, and aggressive business efforts to contain wages and benefits. Even worse, nothing on the horizon suggested the situation would improve any time soon. President Ronald Reagan and many other political leaders even argued that government and labor unions were main sources of the nation's problems, which left struggling workers with nowhere to turn. In response, I searched for new ideas; I was convinced that practical changes to government, business, and labor would foster greater security for the countless American workers wanting little more from the economy than robust job opportunities, a worry-free retirement, and a reasonable chance to see the next generation lead a somewhat better life.

Time has shown I was right to worry about the nation's workforce challenges—and well ahead of the crowd in identifying elements of a constructive path forward. But I failed to anticipate that my own professional life would be caught in the same currents as the workers whose interests I aimed to defend. I believed that hard work and an advanced degree with real-world relevance would set me on a solid career path and allow me to address the enormously important national problem of rising worker insecurity. But there was no solid path; the bulk of my career has involved swimming against a riptide and trying to keep my head above water.

My own employment insecurity only strengthened my resolve to fight for workers. And the upside to my job-search difficulties and unusual occupational path was an opportunity to see what's happened to the American workforce over the past few decades from several vantage points. Along the way, I've been privileged to assist working men and women in efforts to save family-supporting jobs—and create new ones—in their workplaces and communities. I've also had the opportunity to write timely *BusinessWeek* commentaries that reached a wide readership, and to produce economic analyses for federal lawmakers and the public through work at the Congressional Budget Office, doing my best in both cases to bolster economic well-being for workers and their families by helping the nation enact sensible policies.

This book explains, chronicles, and reflects on my career-long battle on behalf of working families, a mission that began as a public-service tribute to the people who raised me but quickly became also a fight for the financial security of my own family. It's a personal story, told with the aid of 100 boxes, about gradually accepting the limited role that hard work plays in shaping one's destiny. It's also a historical account of the slow erosion of the American Dream for many and its consequences for us all, combined with attention to the possibility of an alternative direction for public policy.

In the years ahead, policymakers will continue to struggle with the task of shoring up the American Dream. And I'll continue to grapple with the substantial limits to what can be accomplished through tenacity and working harder. Learning to accept those limits has been difficult, but I think I've made a good start.

BOOK I

MOONSHOT AND HARD LANDING

PART ONE

WORKING-CLASS ORIGINS

1 CONFIDENT, OPTIMISTIC, AND TENACIOUS

Sue Winterkorn sat directly behind me during the homeroom period that began each day at the public high school in Waltham, Massachusetts. It was an early hour for teens—school began at 7:30 a.m.—so most students arrived drowsy and subdued. A few days before graduation in June 1978, I greeted Sue while settling into my seat and, in mock exasperation, she replied: "You drive me crazy. Every day, for three years, you've come in happy, full of energy, with a big 'Good Morning!' I can't understand how you do it."

It was a compliment. And she was right: I did come to school each day wide awake, cheerful, and eager to start the day. I knew I'd have to work hard and there would be challenges, but I was confident, optimistic, and tenacious. I wasn't afraid of competition; after all, I was in constant competition with myself—always aiming to maximize my effort, boost my skills, and improve my results—especially in academic pursuits.

I inherited much of the drive to work hard from my parents, who were born into immigrant families during the Great Depression and watched the Second World War play out during their formative years.[1] Both sets of families came to America in search of work that would let them escape grinding poverty. These immigrants found jobs that didn't pay well, and working conditions were often hazardous; but modest expectations, a strong work ethic, and steady employment enabled them to provide for their children. In a similar manner, my parents experienced a better life for themselves and their own children thanks to frugality, relentless work, and a prosperous postwar economy. At the same time, vivid memories of their early years meant they didn't allow themselves—or their children—either a sense of entitlement or an opportunity to slack off.

From a young age, I saw perseverance as both a necessity and moral obligation—and the drive to work hard soon dovetailed with the lure of public service. As a result, I came to thrive on the striving. After all, despite occasional setbacks that tended to serve only as a source of further motivation, the hard work did often get results—at least during my days as a student. The ambitious, career-driven moonshot project of my adolescence ("Shoot for the moon!") would eventually return to earth for a hard landing, but in 1978 it seemed to be "all systems go." And that, Ms. Winterkorn, is how I did it.

2 WORK—AND THE LURE OF PUBLIC SERVICE

In 1860, John Brockman of Springfield, Illinois, wrote to Abraham Lincoln asking the best way to obtain a thorough knowledge of the law. Lincoln responded with a short note about the necessity of committing oneself to tedious study, in which he concluded: "Work, work, work, is the main thing."[1] My parents didn't know the law, but they certainly believed that work is the main thing. They saw a solid work ethic as essential for survival and imparted the same outlook to their children. They also enrolled me (and my brothers) in a Catholic elementary school that not only reinforced the value of hard work but also emphasized the importance of service to others. My career-long fight for working families was a personal choice, but there's no question the path I chose was influenced by both my family history and that early schooling.

"La Merica"

Thirteen-year-old Angelina Galluzzo entered the United States through the Ellis Island Immigration Station in New York Harbor on March 25, 1920. Angie—the Americanized nickname she preferred throughout adulthood—arrived from her hometown of Aragona, Sicily, accompanied by her mother and two older sisters. Their destination was Waltham, Massachusetts, an industrial city along the Charles River, about 10 miles west of Boston.[2] Waiting for them in Waltham was Angie's father, who emigrated to the United States a decade earlier to work and save enough money for the family to join him.

Angie was one of the millions of European immigrants to America who endured the ocean crossing in cramped and unsanitary quarters, often with more than a thousand other travelers.[3] Between 1880 and 1920, the United States received over 20 million immigrants, including more than 4 million from Italy.[4] Most of those Italian arrivals were different from their compatriots who made the journey before the US Civil War. The early arrivals were primarily northern Italian artisans and merchants seeking new markets; the new generation consisted mostly of southern Italian farmers and laborers looking to escape rural poverty and violence. To be sure, some in that second wave came to "La Merica" (America) in the hope of becoming rich, but according to historians the vast majority were looking for "a steady source of work—any work."[5]

Angie's dad, Giuseppe, eventually found a steady job as a janitor for the Waltham Police Department. He also raised chickens and grew vegetables behind the family's rented apartment in an immigrant neighborhood within the shadow of what was once the largest factory anywhere—a textile mill constructed a century earlier to house the world's first integrated spinning and weaving factory. Angie's mom, Antonina, sold eggs, tomatoes, and squash from home; she also worked as a midwife and was the neighborhood's go-to provider of care for minor injuries and illnesses. Angie and her sisters also earned money; Angie, for example, worked for a few years at a mill that processed cotton in Watertown, just east of Waltham.

Angie's mill work ended in 1925, when, at age 18, she married Vincenzo Cannistraro, a 26-year-old upholstery worker. He was also from Sicily, having arrived in the United States a few years before Angie. During their first six years of marriage, they shared an apartment with Vincenzo's younger brother, enabling them to save for the down payment on a duplex in an Italian neighborhood on Waltham's southeast side.

Vincenzo and Angie had seven children—four boys and three girls—and the entire family managed with only three bedrooms.[6] My mother, Madeline, born in 1935, was the second youngest. In 1951, Vincenzo fell ill and was diagnosed with a brain tumor. He died two years later, at age 54, just a couple of months following my mother's high-school graduation.

Vincenzo never aspired to run his own upholstery shop. From his perspective, starting such a business was too risky and expensive for a Sicilian-speaking worker with seven children. (Angie learned to read and write English by taking afternoon courses at a local public school after her youngest child began kindergarten, but her husband never participated in English classes because he was "too busy working to support the family."[7]) According to my mother, Vincenzo focused on "putting food on the table" by working his job and growing tomatoes in a small backyard garden on a hillside ledge overlooking a rail yard and train maintenance shed.

When Vincenzo became ill, his son Joseph ("Joe") stepped in with extra financial support for Angie, even though all the family's children were already working and contributing a share of their earnings to the household (those still in school worked part-time jobs).[8] Joe, then in his mid-20s, wasn't the eldest child (another son, Francis, was a couple of years older) but had already served in the US Army's military police (during the occupation of Japan at the end of the Second World War) and held an assembly-line job with decent pay at General Motors in nearby Framingham.[9] In the end, Joe never married and continued to live at home with Angie; she passed away in 1987, and Joe resided at the duplex until his death two decades later.

Ballroom Dancing

During high school, Madeline combined courses from the general curriculum with business-oriented courses such as typing and bookkeeping. Upon graduation, she worked in the accounting department at the Raytheon Company, an electronics and defense corporation that had a presence in Waltham since the 1930s when it purchased the facilities of a struggling button factory—a move that, in retrospect, signaled the end of the textile era and the start of the high-technology age for Waltham and the surrounding area.[10] In 1951, to accommodate a further expansion of business operations into areas including radar technologies and missile-guidance systems, Raytheon bought the sprawling Waltham Bleachery and Dye Works complex, a short distance downriver from the city's textile mill, which shuttered during the Great Depression. Madeline worked at that Raytheon site from 1953 until mid-1961, processing countless vendor accounts and invoices for the rapidly growing firm.

Attracted by the opportunity to learn ballroom dancing and meet other young adults, Madeline and her sister Anna traveled to Boston in March 1956 for a Saturday evening dance at the Arthur Murray Studio. That's where Madeline met Charles ("Charlie") Whalen, a machinist who just completed two years of service in the Marine Corps and took part in weekly classes at the studio. It turned out that he too grew up, lived, and worked in Waltham; in fact, their workplaces were only a few blocks away.[11] After seeing each other at a few Saturday dances, the couple began dating that summer and were married two years later, on September 6, 1958.

In many respects, Madeline and Charlie, who was a year older, made an odd couple. Like most Sicilians, Madeline's features included dark brown hair, brown eyes, an oval face, and olive complexion. In contrast, Charlie—whose grandparents were Irish immigrants—had blond hair, blue eyes, a square jaw, light complexion, and, at just over six feet tall, stood a foot above his wife. In addition, Charlie was born and raised in rural, northwest Waltham, the opposite side of town from Madeline's heavily populated Italian neighborhood; and he attended the vocational branch of the high school, while Madeline attended the main high school. Although both were devout Catholics, Charlie's church served mainly Irish immigrants and Madeline's parish was created to serve Italian immigrants, so there were language and cultural differences even when it came to practicing their faith.

Still, the immigrant experience of their families was similar. Both sets of families crossed the Atlantic and settled in the Greater Boston area to escape severe economic hardship and support their children by working hard. And despite their surface differences, Madeline and Charlie were similarly shaped by the experience of growing up in large, financially strapped families during hard times caused by the Great Depression and the Second World War.

In fact, Charlie's childhood was in some ways even more austere than that of Madeline. He was the fifth of six children raised by John and Helena Whalen.[12] The family lived on the outskirts of town in what was originally a two-room bungalow owned by Boston residents as a summer cottage near Hardy Pond, a popular destination for swimmers and campers beginning in the 1910s. Most of the children slept in the home's only bedroom, while John and Helena slept in an enclosed porch.[13] Years later, Charlie looked back in amazement at how everyone fit into such a tiny house: "Some of us must have slept in the living room." It wasn't until just before he entered the military that the family raised the roof to create space for a second-floor bedroom—a room that didn't receive drywall, a finished ceiling, or heat until after he was married.[14]

Charlie's father worked first at the Quincy Shipyard, which built battleships for the US Navy, and later, until age 65, operated a vulcanizing machine at the Hood Rubber plant in Watertown—a factory that employed 9000 people.[15] The largest footwear plant in the world during the mid-twentieth century, Hood's factory produced rubber-soled shoes such as combat boots and sneakers, including the once highly popular "P.F. Flyers." For decades, his workday began with a 40-minute walk from his home to downtown Waltham, where he caught a streetcar to the factory; when his shift ended, he took the same route in reverse.[16] The work was dangerous, the pace was grueling, and the air in and around the plant contained many hazardous substances. But according to a documentary film on Hood Rubber workers, the most important thing the factory offered was a steady paycheck. As one of the plant's former conveyor-belt operators described it, "It was important to have that money because we had to eat."[17]

New Frontier

On July 15, 1960, Senator John F. Kennedy, an Irish Catholic from Massachusetts, accepted the Democratic nomination for president of the United States. His address to the nominating convention quickly became known as the "New Frontier" speech, and although the days of the Kennedy campaign and early presidency are often portrayed as a time of unbridled optimism, his speech was more nuanced. The address was certainly forward looking, describing the nation and the world as standing on the edge of a New Frontier and insisting it was time for a new generation of leadership. But Kennedy also stressed there were serious challenges to confront; in fact, he emphasized that the New Frontier presented not only new opportunities, but also new problems, perils, and threats—including those posed by the development and spread of increasingly devastating weapons. Rather than encourage irrepressible optimism, Kennedy inspired Americans by challenging them to have the faith and commitment to meet the difficulties ahead.[18]

As Kennedy's address reverberated across the nation, Charlie and Madeline stood on the edge of their own "New Frontier." They were living in the rental portion of Angie's duplex (with only a wall separating them from where Madeline was born and raised and where her mother and several siblings still resided), and Madeline, due to deliver her first child, had just started unpaid maternity leave from Raytheon. On an exceptionally hot afternoon in late August, Madeline went into labor. Since Charlie was at work, Madeline's brother Joe, who happened to have the day off, drove her to the Waltham Hospital, where I was born later that night and named Charles Joseph Whalen.[19]

Within two months of my birth, Madeline was back to work and Angie cared for me each weekday. That arrangement continued for almost a year. In summer 1961, my mom left Raytheon because Angie said she didn't want to look after me as I began to walk, although Madeline also admits Angie probably hadn't fully accepted the idea of my mom working outside the home while I was very young.

More changes soon followed. In summer 1962, Madeline gave birth to my brother, Francis ("Frank"). A few months later, Charlie and Madeline purchased a modest 3-bedroom Cape Cod style house in the Waltham Highlands, a suburban neighborhood on the city's west side, and moved there shortly after New Year's Day in 1963.[20] The next year, Madeline and Charlie enrolled in local square-dance classes and met Lewis and Lela MacLeod, who worked at Polaroid Corporation, a Massachusetts-based company best known for its instant film and cameras. Lela held a position in the personnel department and encouraged Charlie to apply with the burgeoning company, which offered better pay and benefits than his current employer. In April 1965, Charlie left his job at a small machine shop on the Newton-Waltham border and began what would be a thirty-year Polaroid career as a tool and die maker, a highly skilled and specialized type of machinist.

Madeline and Charlie bought the Highlands home for $19,300. Monthly mortgage payments for the house, which had been built a decade earlier (but still contained some unfinished rooms), were about $120—one quarter of my dad's income.[21] The home's small lot was carved out of a hillside, with stone retaining walls marking the property line on three sides. Above the back wall was (and still is) a road with a sharp turn and steep slope, leading to the city-owned, wooded hilltop known as Prospect Hill Park. I always thought we'd someday find a car in our backyard, but my family lived there until 1983 and can recall only one close call.

From the mid-1950s until the first decade of the 2000s, Polaroid operated a 94-acre campus of offices and manufacturing facilities along the western edge of Prospect Hill Park. The Polaroid campus sat only a half mile over the crest of the hill from my boyhood home, but it was unreachable from the park owing to a fence and roads that to this day allow only seasonal access. Along the opposite side of the Polaroid site runs a stretch of Interstate 95 that area residents still call "Route 128," a highway that opened in the 1950s and emerged in the 1960s as the nation's first high-technology corridor. At its peak in 1978, Polaroid employed nearly 21,000 workers and was one of the largest employers in Massachusetts; over the course of his career, my dad worked at three Polaroid locations, but the first was the Waltham site overlooking Route 128.[22]

Heigh-Ho, Heigh-Ho ...

By summer 1964, Frank could keep up with me on foot and together we'd parade around the house to 7-inch records from films including *The Music Man* and *Snow White and the Seven Dwarfs*. "Heigh-Ho" was one of our favorites, a catchy tune perfect for marching and singing along.[23] It also reminded us of our parents, who both seemed to work "the whole day through."

Madeline, who remained out of the workforce until Frank began kindergarten in 1967 (and then returned to bookkeeping work until just before another son was born in 1970), was active each day from early in the morning until well after dark.[24] She seemed always in motion—preparing meals, washing clothes and dishes, cleaning the house, grocery shopping, organizing the family's schedule, and managing its finances. She was also an expert at finding (often with two children in tow) high-quality clothes at rock-bottom prices in the discount basements of department stores such as Grover Cronin in Waltham and Filene's in Boston.

Meanwhile, Charlie clocked as much overtime as possible at Polaroid, and for many years worked the second shift (3:00 p.m. until 11:30 p.m.) or even the overnight "graveyard" shift because the hourly pay rate for those periods was slightly higher than for the day shift. In addition, on weekends—and sometimes on weekdays before a Polaroid shift—he would stuff into the family station wagon a sturdy mop, a large metal pail with wheels and a wringer, and an industrial-size floor buffer, and then spend several hours making extra money by washing and waxing floors at local beauty salons and other businesses. He also found time not only to convert the unfinished basement of our house into an all-purpose room and workspace for home repair projects, but also to design and construct a large backyard shed—and read bedtime stories to his boys on a regular basis.

Madeline and Charlie made no secret of their strong work ethic. It had become second nature for them to work almost all the time. Even the square dancing stopped not long after Charlie began working at Polaroid, and our rare camping vacations didn't provide much rest; instead, those excursions always meant a lot of work for them both.[25] Given their upbringing in an era of depression and war, it's perhaps not surprising they often spoke of the need to work to "support the family," "pay the bills and put food on the table," or simply "make ends meet."

My parents also made no secret of their expectation that Frank and I also had to work—and that began with being a serious student and bringing home "good grades." It may have been mere coincidence that the bedroom I shared with my brother featured a pair of built-in desks, but for our early schoolwork my parents quite deliberately placed another pair of desks (each with its own book box) in the first-floor den, allowing Madeline to supervise us while working in the kitchen. And, from the start, "good grades" meant the best grades possible: "gold stars" in kindergarten, "check pluses" in elementary school, and "Straight A's" (A+'s, in fact) thereafter. Indeed, a perfect score of 100 percent on coursework was usually met with the question: "No extra credit?"

Madeline and Charlie—especially Madeline—were particularly determined to see that we made it to college. Their experience in the workplace taught them that the higher-paid workers—the managers, accountants, and engineers—had college degrees, which for my parents had been unaffordable. (In addition, Sicilian sexism meant higher education wasn't considered appropriate for women under any circumstances in my mom's family.) They learned quickly that employees couldn't advance far without such a degree and wanted to ensure their children didn't face the same constraint, especially having been born at the tail end of the nation's baby boom, which suggested we'd meet considerable competition ahead in the job market.[26] In an attempt to give us a leg up on that competition, Madeline enrolled me for kindergarten—and Frank two years later—in a small parochial school run by the Dominican Sisters of St. Catharine.

Catholic School

Dominican nuns operated Rosary Academy as an elementary school, high school, and convent in Watertown from 1911 until 1986. Originally a boarding school for girls, it later expanded enrollment to female day students and eventually to elementary-school boys.[27] I was a student at Rosary in kindergarten through second grade (fall 1965 through spring 1968). The school was four miles from my home, but since my dad often relied on the family's only car to get to Polaroid in the afternoon, I came home on a school bus that covered a much longer route and took nearly an hour to get me to the house. The bus ride was so long that my parents eventually arranged for me and Frank (a mere kindergartener) to take a public bus—which still meant at least a 20-minute ride and required a considerable walk at both ends—accompanied by a Rosary Academy high-school student who lived in our neighborhood.

In fall 1968, my brother and I transferred to the parish school of Our Lady Help of Christians Church in Newton. Both Rosary Academy and "Our Lady's" School were considered college-preparatory schools, but Our Lady's had the advantage of being an entirely coeducational institution through high school. The commute to Our Lady's was about a half hour, with a public bus stop just a block from home and another stop in front of the school. Because of the bus schedule, however, we arrived more than 30 minutes before classes began and there was no before-school program—so each day Frank and I attended morning mass at the adjacent church.

It turned out that I attended Our Lady's only for grades three and four (fall 1968 through spring 1970). That's because Madeline was pregnant and back out of the labor force in 1970, which meant the household budget required additional belt-tightening. In September 1970, Frank and I were enrolled in the local public school, and a month later John arrived, the third child of Madeline and Charlie.

Five years in Catholic school (followed by several years of participating in church youth programs and serving as an altar boy) provided not only a solid academic foundation, but also a religious education that taught the core beliefs and practices of Roman Catholicism. Over time, I gradually drifted away from the Catholic Church, yet it's clear that I absorbed at least three ethical principles that significantly shaped my thinking: an obligation to develop one's natural abilities; the commandment to "love thy neighbor"; and a duty to serve society.

The first of those principles dovetails with the work ethic taught by my parents. Since Catholics view one's talents and capacities as gifts from God, I was taught that those gifts must not be squandered. As a youngster, I interpreted that to mean I had the responsibility to be a diligent and attentive student and always strive for excellence in my schoolwork.

The other two principles are interconnected. The Great Commandment of "love thy neighbor" is, of course, related to the Golden Rule—"do unto others as you would have them do unto you"—and both call on us to treat others with respect, kindness, and understanding, including those holding views that differ from our own. I also consider that commandment a foundation of the Catholic emphasis on service. As a catechism from the mid-1960s states, "The Catholic commitment to Christ must be broad; it must be a commitment to … [all] people and Christ's world."[28] For example, that catechism stresses the need for Christians to care for the sick and others in need, counteract poverty and discrimination, engage in political life (starting with becoming familiar with the issues and problems of the day and voting in political elections), and commit—more urgent than ever in the nuclear age—to the pursuit of world peace.

Reflections

As a young student, I had no clear idea what career I would pursue. Yet, because of the influence of my Catholic education, I always envisioned that I'd find a way to meld professional work with public service. Of course, in 1970, the need to sort that out was still a long way off. And I would soon learn that public school, at least in a town with sizable income disparities and a large blue-collar population, was quite different from parochial school.

In time, I would also understand how my hometown and family reflected the broader narrative of economic history in the United States. In the colonial era and the early days of independence from Britain, American economic life depended heavily on farming, logging, trapping, and fishing; most of the country's population worked the land. That was certainly true of my hometown's earliest residents; in fact, when the western precinct of Watertown incorporated as a town in 1738, its farmers named their new community Waltham, a Saxon word meaning "forest home."

Merchants and port cities played a strategic role in the new nation's first decades, the era of *merchant* capitalism. Although most merchants were little more than country storekeepers, others coordinated the flow of commerce between towns and ports as well as the trade between ports and foreign nations, and they "prospered accordingly."[29] Affluent merchant traders also helped usher in the next economic era, *industrial* capitalism, by financing the introduction of expensive machinery and construction of factories (powered first by water, then steam, and eventually electricity).

Waltham played a pivotal role in the evolution from merchant to industrial capitalism. In the 1810s, Francis Cabot Lowell and other Boston merchants formed the Boston Manufacturing Company (BMC). It brought the Industrial Revolution to the United States by building a textile mill in Waltham along a stretch of the Charles River. The result was a large water-powered cotton mill that, "for the first time anywhere in the world," combined labor and machinery "to perform all the steps necessary to manufacture cloth under one roof."[30] According to the Waltham Museum, located today near a renovated portion of the mill, "BMC permanently changed Waltham from an agricultural to an industrial community"—and helped transform the nation "from an agrarian to an industrial society."[31]

The large factories and industrial facilities that sprang up in the following decades helped attract immigrants to the United States, including my Irish and Italian forebearers. The Waltham mill continued to operate when my grandmother Angie arrived in Waltham from Sicily, but that factory—unable to compete with newer, much larger mills in the Northeast and lower-cost facilities in the South—didn't survive the Great Depression. The Second World War provided steady work for many, including my grandfather Whalen (who supported his family by making army boots, after years of battleship-related work); but when the war ended, an economy organized around large-scale industrial production had to be paired with a mass-consumption society—and that's exactly what emerged in the postwar era known as *managerial* capitalism.

At the start of the managerial era, large American corporations dominated not only domestic markets but also global markets in many industries. Because only a few firms tended to dominate any specific product market (such as General

Motors, Ford, and Chrysler in the case of motor vehicles), the nation's top corporate executives didn't need to worry much about competitors, bankers, or stockholders as long as business profits and growth remained steady. Even national economic policies added to the power of that era's corporate managers by protecting profits through timely tax breaks, jolts of public spending, and financial assistance (via monetary policy) as needed.

Corporate personnel policies and labor relations practices made vital contributions to the prosperity of the managerial era. Business leaders secured labor peace and a committed workforce by taking an accommodative (but not capitulatory) stance toward unions as well as by offering career-long employment, employer-funded medical insurance, defined-benefit pensions, and job ladders that provided opportunities for advancement. Corporations also rewarded workers with rising incomes as workplace productivity increased, a practice that not only contributed to worker morale but also helped ensure consumer demand kept pace with business production.

In the month I was born, nearly 20 million Americans—one in three nonfarm workers—held jobs in goods-producing industries.[32] Throughout the 1960s, the work of my parents and other family members mirrored that employment distribution, especially the emphasis on production of consumer goods.[33] But the Greater Boston area also had a sizable defense and aerospace-oriented workforce in the 1960s, and the work done by members of my family reflected that as well.

Over time, the defense and space-related jobs would contribute to the emergence of Massachusetts as a center for computer-oriented companies and other businesses linked to high-technology innovation. However, ahead was also a reckoning for most other goods-producing parts of the economy across the state and the nation, especially in the Northeast and Midwest. Cracks in the economic framework of the managerial era spread throughout the 1970s and became so severe that a new era called *money manager* capitalism took root in the 1980s.[34] That new economy appeared to offer a bright future for highly educated workers, particularly those trained in engineering, science, and finance (especially the asset managers and other institutional investors for whom the new era was named). But many residents of my hometown and other blue-collar communities, especially those without college degrees, were in for a wrenching transition—and many young adults found it impossible to find affordable housing in their childhood neighborhoods following an influx of top-flight talent from elite universities around the world.

With the benefit of hindsight, the economic transformation of the past several decades takes the shape of a coherent process. Yet the path of economic evolution is never preordained. And at 10 years of age, I could certainly be excused for not anticipating any of it—after all, many of the postwar era's leading economic observers also failed to see what was coming.

3 "WHO THE HELL DO YOU THINK YOU ARE?"

From fifth grade through high school, I was a student in the Waltham public schools.[1] The first couple of years weren't very challenging, but from grade seven onward I believe I received a high-quality education, not only in mandatory subjects like English, math, and the sciences, but also in music. Public school also introduced me to the unpleasantness of bullying as well as to the prejudices of a stratified society. In the face of both sorts of intimidation, I did my best to stick to my principles, follow my interests, and carve out my own path forward.

Transition to Public School

Thanks in large part to having attended Catholic school since kindergarten, I seemed to have better academic preparation than my fifth-grade classmates—and much better study habits. Even for elementary school students, the public-school administrators used a tracking system that assigned children to classrooms according to prior performance and a judgment about academic aptitude. Since I was entering from outside the system, the administrators initially placed me in a mid-tier classroom with students deemed of average achievement and ability. However, I was soon reassigned to the most advanced class, where I still stood out as a high achiever.[2]

In Catholic school, my academic success never led to conflict with other students. In public school, however, it was one of several reasons (along with parochial-school manners and freshly pressed shirts and trousers) I stood out. As a result, I wasn't just the new kid in a school where most everyone else had been together since kindergarten; I was also quickly marked as a target for bullying.

I did my best to ignore the bullies throughout fifth grade, but things got worse the following year until I put aside "turn the other cheek" idealism in favor of standing my ground and defending myself during an after-school attack. The first time I fought back, my attacker and onlookers threatened me with more trouble in the days and weeks ahead. But most of the bullying subsided. The cycle repeated itself at the start of junior high school, when a troublemaker chose me as his target in the school cafeteria; I again stood my ground, and that turned out to be the last major school-related incident.[3]

Personal Interests and the Wider World

During my early years in public school, I accepted that I didn't quite fit in with many of my classmates, and so long as I wasn't being bullied, it really didn't bother me. I rode my bicycle in the Waltham Highlands and across the city to Grandma Angie's house, explored Prospect Hill with my brother Frank, skated on a local pond in winter, and even played pickup baseball with whoever happened to be at the local playground (although it seemed everyone spent far too much time disputing plays and arguing over the status of "invisible men" on base). I also enjoyed attending the Waltham Recreation Department's summer day camp, swimming at the city's public pool, and learning to sail a Sunfish dinghy on Cape Cod (where my parents shared cottage rental expenses with members of Madeline's family). In addition, I participated in Cub Scouts and Boy Scouts, Little League baseball, hockey skills workshops, and city-sponsored youth football. I wasn't an exceptional athlete, but around age twelve I completed a mile swim organized by the Boy Scouts and a few months later managed to set my football team's record for most tackles in a season.

Meanwhile, my father did his best to interest his sons in industrial arts, applied sciences, gardening, and raising animals—drawing heavily on his own skills, craftsmanship, and curiosity. After transforming our house's basement into livable space (and encouraging us to observe and assist), Charlie created a work area where he kept stacks of *Popular Mechanics* and introduced us to magnetism and electromagnetics, Morse code, model rockets, woodworking, and photography.[4] He also constructed a pair of backyard hutches in which we raised rabbits, and leased a patch of land in the city's community gardens, enticing us to tend it by involving us in what was planted.[5]

Years later, Charlie explained that the basement projects, many of his home improvements, and even the rabbit hutches were meant to teach us how to work with tools (so we could do our own home repairs and improvements in the future), provide us with a hands-on introduction to the natural world, and foster our interest in science and "how things work." The only college-educated people my dad interacted with on a regular basis were Polaroid engineers, and through those home projects he made a conscious effort to spark our interest in engineering. In the case of Frank, it worked; after high school, Frank studied electrical engineering at Syracuse University and continues to work as an engineer in the Boston area. My dad also had some success with John, my much younger brother; he did undergraduate and graduate studies in environmental sciences before turning to a technology-oriented career involving hospital management systems. But I marched to a different drummer.

Unlike my dad and brothers, I never had much interest in "building stuff" or "taking things apart and putting them back together." I preferred reading books—and writing.[6] To keep up with my appetite for reading, mom arranged for her sons to visit the Waltham Public Library at least once a week. She also allowed me to purchase several titles whenever a Scholastic Book Club flyer was distributed at school.[7] In addition, Madeline kept me supplied with plenty of pencils, pens, and writing paper; and when I was about nine years old, I was introduced to a manual typewriter that had been collecting dust in a closet. Inspired by children's magazines such as *Highlights* and *Boy's Life*, I used the typewriter to create a 4-page newspaper called "Kids' Fun News," boldly selling copies to my neighbors for ten cents apiece.[8]

Looking back years later, I realize that my dad and I were both driven by a common urge to be creative; it just expressed itself in different ways. Today, just like Charlie—who died in 2021—each of my brothers has a home workshop, where they build and fix all sorts of appliances and devices (phonograph turntables, drones, and radio-controlled sailboats, for example). And I have a home office, surrounded by hundreds of books, where I retreat to craft sentences and paragraphs. I think my dad also eventually recognized that beneath what appeared to be our very different personal interests was in fact a shared commitment to creativity and pride of workmanship, but when I was young those surface differences sometimes frustrated him and became a source of friction between us.

In addition to not sharing my dad's enthusiasm for working with my hands, I also diverged from his main interests regarding the wider world. Dad was fascinated by nature, especially birds and plants, and by the Apollo missions that sought to meet President Kennedy's goal of landing a man on the moon by the end of the 1960s. I was drawn to more terrestrial human challenges, including poverty, civil rights, and international conflicts. After all, I first developed an awareness of my place in the world during the era of President Lyndon Johnson's War on Poverty and Great Society initiatives, the US civil rights movement, the war in Vietnam, and the assassinations of the Rev. Dr. Martin Luther King Jr. and Senator Robert Kennedy. In addition, my representative in the US Congress from 1971 through 1981 was the Rev. Robert Drinan, a Jesuit priest and outspoken critic of the Vietnam War, who for me embodied the melding of Christian commitment and public service.[9]

At first, national and international news came into my home mainly by television in the form of "The CBS Evening News" with anchor Walter Cronkite; later, it also came by way of *The Boston Globe*. In the 1960s, my family—along with most of the viewing public—tuned in nightly for the evening television news broadcast.[10] Then, in 1970 I began delivering *The Boston Globe* to homes in my neighborhood, which led to reading the paper daily.[11] Like many young people with a paper route, I started by reading the comics and sports sections; but I was soon reading it all—especially national and international news, editorials, and the arts and entertainment section.[12] The newspaper seemed to bring the world to my door: reading the paper on the front steps of my boyhood home, I felt that each issue offered a personal tutorial on current issues.[13]

From the nightly news and daily paper, I became interested in the nation's social problems and the attempts of policymakers and other public leaders to address them. Seeking to better understand policymaking inspired me to learn about US politics and political history. Over time, I also became interested in political theory and—when price inflation became more serious—even economics (at least the sort of economics offered by John Kenneth Galbraith and others like him who wrote for the public). Looking back, I see I was trying to find directions for public policy that resonated with my understanding of the world and the social-justice and public-service aims I picked up from my religious education. In many ways, I'm still pursuing that same goal today. But the decade or so between the early 1970s and early 1980s is when that interest began to take shape.

Music—and a Warning

Beyond coping with bullying, I have few memories of sixth grade except for weekly trumpet lessons. Several memories of junior high school also involve making music, but I also recall an early and close-to-home warning about the reality of socioeconomic prejudice.

I began to learn the trumpet in fifth grade. The Waltham Public Schools music program offered free band instrument lessons in grades five and six, and my parents took a chance and bought me a trumpet.[14] It turns out that my Ambassador trumpet, manufactured in 1970 by F.E. Olds and Son, was perhaps the best student horn ever produced—a high-quality instrument made by American craftsmen on the eve of industry consolidation and business pressures that would soon force most instrument makers to dramatically cut corners and drive many out of business (including Olds, which was shuttered by 1979).[15] But at the time I didn't appreciate any of that; in fact, although I felt it was a privilege to learn a musical instrument, I wasn't a very motivated trumpeter until junior high school (which spanned grades seven through nine).

The first incident that changed my view toward playing music occurred during an afternoon band rehearsal about midway through seventh grade. Because of my grade and last name, I was sitting in the last of the trumpeters' chairs when the school band director—frustrated with the sound of the entire brass section—assigned us a musical scale to learn by the next week. I may have been unenthusiastic about the horn, but it was a school assignment, so I approached it with the same intensity I brought to any other school obligation. A week later, the director asked each trumpeter to play the scale. Most of the students couldn't make it beyond the first couple of notes—many didn't even try. When it was my turn, I played the scale up and down as assigned, and as I finished the director pointed toward the first trumpet chair and ordered the other players to move down so I could take the lead chair.

The new responsibility that came with that move to first trumpet—and the attention it brought from several girls in the band (including some in ninth grade)—made me take music much more seriously. I practiced more frequently, listened more often to the two collections of classical-music albums that my parents bought to encourage music appreciation, and explored the FM radio, where I found a variety of musical styles with the turn of a dial.[16] I also attended local youth dances, usually at the invitation of band members a grade or two ahead of me. I was too shy and inhibited to dance much, but I did like the cover bands and generally felt comfortable around my female classmates, provided we weren't on the dance floor.

The other crucial incident affecting my relationship with the trumpet—and music in general—came a bit later in seventh grade. As preparation for a New England jazz competition, the Waltham High School Jazz Ensemble performed for an assembly in the gymnasium of my school. The ensemble treated us to an entire set of contemporary, big-band jazz—mostly hard swinging, but full of dynamic contrasts, and laced with bits of Latin, soul, and rock and roll. What struck me most were the trumpeters, lined up in the back row (the only ones standing) playing horns that seemed to soar over the top of the sonic mix—like surfers on the crest of a musical wave.

I still remember sitting in the wooden bleachers and thinking aloud: "Now I get it. *That's* what you do with a trumpet!" Soon thereafter, I was practicing even more, listening regularly to jazz radio shows, and buying albums by the jazz-rock group Chicago, which featured a three-piece horn section.[17] Then a neighbor with a drum set organized a rock band and I was asked to join; we practiced in his basement and eventually played a few gigs at local youth dances.[18]

Once I opened the door to making music, I didn't stop with trumpet. During eighth grade, the keyboard player in my neighborhood band, a newcomer to Waltham who studied piano from a young age, suggested that I learn piano to better understand music theory. That newcomer, Paul Harriman, was from a family of musicians and with their assistance I purchased a used upright piano with money from my paper route and began lessons with a local piano teacher. I was much older than most of the teacher's students, but that didn't trouble me. I never aimed to become a world-class pianist, and my teacher provided a solid introduction that indeed helped me better understand music.

Throughout junior high school I continued to excel in my academic subjects—including Italian, the foreign language I studied from seventh grade through eleventh grade. But Waltham had three junior high schools at the time, and mine was not considered the home of academic highflyers. I attended Central Junior High School, a massive, four-story brick building—located in the center of town—that served as the city's senior high school from 1902 until 1969. Most students from Waltham's more affluent and more highly educated families attended the modern and better equipped, John F. Kennedy Junior High School, located near the city's newer and leafier northside neighborhoods.[19]

Returning from meeting the teachers at Central Junior High, my mom reported that one teacher admitted I was an outstanding student; yet that teacher also added a warning, "Of course, he'll never be able to compete with students from Kennedy Junior." And it seemed the bulk of those working in the school system accepted that stratified outlook. In fact, around that same time I attended a citywide event at Kennedy Junior High and that school's principal began the program by welcoming "the heathen" from Waltham's two other junior high schools.[20]

High School

I attended Waltham High School from September 1975 through graduation in June 1978. At that time, it was the second-largest high school in Massachusetts, enrolling about 3,000 students across its three grades (tenth through twelfth).[21] During those years, I had four main interests: music, academics, student government, and sports. I also worked summer jobs, which included loading boxes in the shipping department of a brake factory, and helping technicians build and test new products at a small Waltham-based engineering firm that designed communications equipment. I was fortunate to have the job at the engineering firm; it spared me from manning a punch press for an entire summer at Polaroid. I did that work for a single day—and that was long enough.[22]

Musician

My high-school experience received a jump start in spring 1975 (ninth grade) thanks to my reputation as a serious trumpet player. Under the direction of Thomas Ferrante, the Jazz Ensemble at Waltham High School (the group that I heard in my junior high gymnasium a couple of years earlier and inspired me to pursue the trumpet in earnest) was known as a powerhouse within the New England community of jazz educators.[23] But Ferrante was looking ahead to the 1975–1976 season of jazz competitions and needed to bolster his trumpet section. After reaching out to music teachers in each of the city's junior high schools, he invited me and Joe Orlando, a ninth grader at Kennedy Junior High, to participate in weekly after-school rehearsals with the band that spring. Although I had been listening to a lot of jazz, I hadn't studied it formally, so those spring sessions were a crash course in reading jazz charts and playing with a jazz feel.

In large part because of the jazz ensemble opportunity, music was a major preoccupation of mine in high school.[24] In addition to playing in that group—judged the top high-school jazz ensemble in New England at a competition when I was in eleventh grade—I participated in the school Wind Ensemble, Marching Band, and Brass Ensemble. I also performed with the Massachusetts Northeast District and All-State Wind Ensembles, at church services, and in pit orchestras for musicals at Waltham High School, the Dana Hall School (a private school for girls in Wellesley), and Brandeis University (which needed a trumpeter on short notice for performances of *The Pirates of Penzance*).[25] I was even hired to perform "Taps" at a Charles River bridge dedication that memorialized a local public official.

With the help of partial-tuition scholarships, I attended the Summer Youth Music School at the University of New Hampshire in 1976 and 1977.[26] Two other students from Waltham also attended the program in 1976—drummer Doug Nally and saxophonist Bobby Ricketts. Both went on to study at Berklee College of Music and achieve success as accomplished professional musicians.[27] Attending summer music school inspired me to ask Ferrante to teach a course in music theory, and I was among the handful of students enrolled in that course during my senior year. But, unlike Doug and Bobby, I wasn't willing to commit all my energy to a career in music. I thought public service, not music, was my calling, so I pursued music with a bit less intensity in the last year or two of high school, allowing more time for my academic coursework.

Student

Math and sciences were at the center of my high school course load, and they were rigorous, college-level "Honors" (similar to "Advanced Placement") classes. Although my goal was always to pursue the social sciences in college, I found physics especially fascinating—partly because it showed me the practical relevance of calculus, an academic subject I found particularly challenging. Night after night, I'd grind through the calculus textbook's end-of-chapter questions and compare answers with my classmate Lois Griff, and the next day we'd meet with our teacher to review the problems we couldn't solve on our own.

My three most memorable teachers were Julia Kerr (biology), Ira Steinberg (English), and Michael Macy (social studies). Mrs. Kerr, one of the school's few African American teachers, was my overall favorite: she always expected excellence, while also putting students at ease. Mr. Steinberg was a bodybuilder who liked to put up a stern front; he taught the mechanics of essay writing, perhaps the most enduring lesson of my entire education. Mr. Macy was a bearded, recent graduate of Harvard who encouraged me to look at US public policy with a critical eye and introduced me to politically progressive news publications such as *In These Times*.[28]

School Representative

I participated in schoolwide student government as a class representative from the start of junior high school through grade 12, but I also represented Waltham High School in the statewide Massachusetts Student Advisory Council (SAC). While schoolwide student government addressed matters ranging from cafeteria menu options to the creation of a paper-and-plastic recycling program, SAC embodied a pioneering effort to involve students in making educational decisions at the state level. Established by the Massachusetts State Legislature in 1971, SAC was organized as follows: every high school in the state elected a delegate to one of eleven regional SACs, and representatives from those regional councils made up the statewide SAC.[29] Three elected student officers led the statewide group—a chairperson, who served as a voting member of the Massachusetts Board of Education, as well as a moderator and associate moderator, who collaborated to lead the state SAC meetings, chair statewide taskforces, and set meeting schedules and agendas. I was elected to the regional SAC in tenth grade and the state SAC in eleventh grade; then I served as statewide associate moderator in twelfth grade.[30]

In the mid-1970s, many of the issues addressed at monthly SAC meetings involved implementing state and federal antidiscrimination laws that applied to educational institutions. Over the past several decades, those laws (such as Title IX at the national level) enabled significant progress toward greater educational equality, especially for women. But the legislation was still rather new when I was in high school and there was much to be done in the areas of regulatory development and compliance.[31] State laws and regulations affecting student rights and school records also received attention from SAC during my years of service.

Serving on the Massachusetts SAC offered an extraordinary high school experience. Participating in such a large student-run organization (representing 400,000 secondary school students) and contributing to public-policy formation and administration offered a glimpse into much more than education policy.[32] It also served as a hands-on course in policymaking and democratic governance; offered me the chance to develop leadership, management, and communication skills; and introduced me to students from across the state, many of whom became my friends throughout high school. In addition, the experience taught self-reliance and resourcefulness because participation in SAC required travel and absences from school a few times per month; that meant not only making my own travel arrangements (using public transportation) but also learning course material on my own and arranging after-school sessions with my teachers.

Athlete

By the time I entered high school, I wasn't beefy enough for the football team, so I became a member of the track and cross-country teams and played pick-up ice hockey on Sunday mornings at a rink near my home. In the late-1960s and early 1970s, I followed the Boston Red Sox and Bruins, but in high school I was less interested in keeping up with professional sports and focused on just staying active.[33] The track and cross-country teams helped keep me in shape, and hockey was both a great workout and no-pressure pre-dawn fun.[34]

The Big Decision

According to my mom, I was so eager to attend kindergarten that I waited by the door at age three and cried when the school bus passed without stopping. I don't remember that, but I recall that as a high-school senior I was eager to leave home and attend college.[35] The main question was where would I go?

Since my parents knew nothing about colleges and the application process, I was fortunate to receive guidance from Bob Loventhal, a young attorney who lived in Waltham and coached my youth football team while attending Brandeis University and Boston College Law School.[36] Bob knew I was interested in public policy and aspired to eventually attend law school. He introduced me to liberal arts colleges and their academic programs, and I leaned, not surprisingly, toward the possibility of majoring in political science. Then he gave me a thick guidebook to the nation's best colleges and universities, and explained how to choose several "reach," "target," and "safety" schools. He even arranged for me to visit Amherst College and Williams College.

When looking at colleges, I had an exceptional academic record and extensive involvement in extracurricular activities. Throughout elementary and secondary schools, my grades were always a solid A or even A+, and my high-school class rank was "within the top five students" (some of us apparently held the same grade point average) in a graduating class of nearly 1,000 students.[37] However, I was slow to become aware of the Scholastic Aptitude Test (SAT) and didn't have access to an SAT preparation course. Fortunately, I took Loventhal's advice and purchased SAT study guides at the end of my junior year, making time for summer self-study. As a result, my scores on standardized tests were high enough to avoid them being a barrier to admission at even the most selective colleges and universities.

With Loventhal's help, I eventually settled on applying to about nine schools—including Yale, Cornell, Colgate, and Bowdoin. In my senior year, I was required to meet at least once with an assigned school guidance counselor, but when we met and I shared the list of where I intended to apply to college, the counselor became bad-tempered: "Who the hell do you think you are? Who do you think your parents are? And what kind of family do you think you come from? Someone from your family should apply to two schools: MassBay [Massachusetts Bay Community College] and maybe the University of Massachusetts. That's it!" He was partially correct; that was "it" for the two of us: I applied to the schools on my own list and never met with him again.[38]

The guidance counselor was certainly right that the schools on my list would be a financial stretch for my family, but there were scholarships, loans, opportunities for part-time college employment, and summer jobs. Besides, my parents and Bob Loventhal never discouraged me from "shooting for the moon."[39] I ultimately received a "waiting list" decision from Yale, turned down a major tuition scholarship from Colgate, and accepted admission to Cornell, where, during a campus visit in late 1977, I changed my application from the College of Arts and Sciences to the School of Industrial and Labor Relations (Cornell ILR).

I chose to attend Cornell ILR because I was impressed by the social-science focus of its curriculum and because labor-relations issues were regularly in the news owing to plant closings, widespread attention to wage negotiations in a time of high inflation, and even a national coal strike that highlighted the role of federal labor mediators (the seriousness of that strike eventually led President Jimmy Carter to invoke the national emergency provisions of US labor law). Early twentieth-century economist Robert Hoxie argued long ago that studying labor relations offers a glimpse into "practically every social pie that is baking"; that was certainly my impression in the mid-1970s.[40] I also admired Cornell's beautiful campus and the surrounding Finger Lakes region. The "big decision" about college was really a rather easy choice.

Reflections

Reflecting on childhood through high school graduation, I'm struck by not only how my early Catholic education shaped my values and aspirations, but also the extent to which much of the Waltham school system accepted, reinforced, and even perpetuated a social hierarchy according to the income, occupational status, and educational achievement of students' parents. In Catholic school, I was led to think I was living in a meritocracy, or at least a society that aspired to that end.[41] But many people working in the public school system apparently saw things differently. It turns out there's some truth to both perspectives, and the tension between them is something I've confronted time and again over the years.

Because my parents and early teachers encouraged and celebrated academic achievement, I came to believe I could go far in the academic and professional worlds by having a strong work ethic, personal initiative, and an earnest willingness to develop my talents and abilities. That belief inspired me to work hard and motivated me to dream big. To be sure, I wasn't naïve enough to think my opportunities were equal to those of children from the Kennedy clan or others born into extreme wealth, but I did allow myself to envision a career beyond the factory gate—in a service-oriented field such as law, public policy, or dispute resolution. After several years in Catholic school, I hadn't convinced myself that family background was irrelevant, only that it wasn't the sole determinant of one's destiny and that hard work would pay off.

The public school system apparently had a different objective than Catholic schools. Rather than inspire achievement, much of that system seems to have been aimed at reproducing the status quo—by means of social ranking within and across schools. The most affluent neighborhoods had the best schools and the most resources. Children were sorted early into distinct achievement tracks and rarely able to advance once sorted, especially since each track placed its own set of academic expectations on students and served to lock them into place. Teachers, principals, and academic advisers tended to internalize the existing social hierarchy and behave in ways that preserved it, such as by seeking to discourage and block students whose aspirations seemed to overstep conventional socioeconomic boundaries.[42]

Meanwhile, there were several reasons I never accepted the local assumptions regarding "my place." It wasn't just that a drive to succeed was nurtured by my parents and private-school teachers during my formative years, and that I often proved wrong those who prejudged me in public school. I also had the opportunity to regularly work alongside, socialize with, and even compete against top students from other schools in Massachusetts and New England through my student-government and musical endeavors; and those experiences taught that I could hold my own just fine.[43] Because I had both an extensive peer group beyond Waltham (where as early as fifth grade I didn't fit in) and the encouragement and mentorship of Bob Loventhal, whose own view of the world was shaped by growing up in a highly educated family on Long Island, my aspirations were never shaped by my hometown.

On August 2, 1978, the rock band Boston released its second album, "Don't Look Back." A few weeks later, on the eve of my drive to central New York to begin studying at Cornell, a preordered copy of that record arrived in the mail. It was the last item I packed for the journey. The next morning, I left Waltham—and didn't look back.[44]

PART TWO

ITHACA

4 SEEKING PRACTICAL SOLUTIONS IN AN AGE OF LIMITS

In late August 1978, a few days before my 18th birthday, I arrived at Cornell University and settled in for new student orientation, marching band camp, and the start of my first semester as a college student. I entered the university with a work ethic grounded in my parents' immigrant roots, a "can do" attitude that reflected the national spirit of the Kennedy era through the Apollo moon landings, and a progressive idealism inspired not only by my religious upbringing but also by President Lyndon Johnson's vision of a Great Society and Robert Kennedy's presidential campaign centering on economic justice, racial equality, and social improvement.

America and the world in the 1960s through the mid-1970s were far from perfect. That was evident in many areas, including civil rights, women's rights, and US foreign policy, as well as in the executive branch wrongdoings that led to impeachment proceedings against President Richard Nixon. But I accepted the belief of Dr. King that the arc of the moral universe "bends toward justice," as well as his insistence that achieving such justice—indeed, all human progress—requires "the persistent work of dedicated individuals."[1] I saw the nation's social problems as a call to action, not a source of discouragement. In fact, making a living by helping to find and implement practical solutions to such problems, especially challenges affecting working men and women such as those who raised me, was my own idea of the American Dream.

A Shift in the National Mood

Contrary to my own upbeat outlook, it was clear by the end of my freshman year (mid-1979) that the national mood had gravitated in a pessimistic direction. Part of that pessimism reflected the headline economic reports on inflation and unemployment. Between 1955 and 1969, consumer prices rose at a modest average annual rate of 2.1 percent; but then the Arab oil embargo of 1973–1974 (which resulted in major gasoline shortages across the country) and other factors caused consumer prices to rise at an average annual rate of 7.1 percent between 1970 and 1979.[2] The jobless rate also showed a worrisome upward trend: the average annual rate of unemployment jumped from 4.9 percent between 1955 and 1969 to 6.2 percent between 1970 and 1979.[3] With rates of inflation and unemployment each exceeding 7 percent several times in the 1970s, it was understandable that much of the previous decade's optimism had eroded.[4]

At the same time another economic trend, a growing wave of factory shutdowns, indicated the start of a serious long-term problem: the unraveling of the social contract between business and labor. In the early postwar era, workers sometimes experienced layoffs during periods of economic slack, but those spells of joblessness tended to be brief and accompanied by a return to the same company not long thereafter. Then a noticeable change began toward the end of the 1960s and into the 1970s: a growing number of American manufacturing plants closed their operations permanently, often as part of a relocation outside the United States. Writing on the trend as it emerged, a trio of economists wrote:

> Between 1969 and 1976, at least 15 million jobs were destroyed in the United States as a result of plant closings and shutdowns, an average of 2.1 million jobs each year. And the loss of each job is magnified by the negative effect on family and community—an effect rarely mentioned in corporate analyses of capital movement.[5]

The trio digging into that new business development—Barry Bluestone, Bennett Harrison, and Lawrence Baker—admitted that plant closings hit workers and communities especially hard in the Northeast and Midwest, but they also refuted the argument that closings were merely a regional phenomenon. Instead, their research pointed to a nationwide problem:

> The rate at which manufacturing plants have been closing is actually *higher* in the South than anywhere else; from 1969–1976, the odds that a plant which employed more than 100 workers in 1969 would be shut by 1976 were better than one in three in the South.[6]

Some Americans found it easy to dismiss the human impact of that era's plant closings because the effects were often concentrated in "working class" communities and most of the jobless had neither college degrees nor political clout. But the end of career-long employment for those blue-collar workers was merely an early stage in a more comprehensive undoing of the social contract.

Crisis of Confidence

When President Jimmy Carter took office in 1977, he aimed to reduce unemployment by boosting the pace of economic expansion.[7] Then international oil supplies were cut back in the wake of the revolution in Iran, resulting in another round of gasoline shortages and a spike in energy prices. That spike sent inflation soaring, which caused the Federal Reserve to counter by raising interest rates sharply, undoing the administration's progress in the fight against joblessness.

On July 15, 1979, Carter addressed the nation and described not merely an energy and economic crisis, but also a deeper "crisis of confidence" that eroded the nation's unity of purpose and threatened to destroy America's social and political fabric.[8] Carter intended his remarks to be a rallying cry that would cause people to recommit to each other and to the national purpose. Instead, however, a strong critical reaction to his address—which journalists dubbed the "Malaise Speech"—merely served to highlight just how much the nation's confidence had diminished since the early 1960s.[9]

A close look at Carter's speech and his term as president suggest that much of the erosion in American confidence during that era can be traced to a sense of lost control. In the first two decades after the Second World War, the United States appeared to have considerable control over domestic and international affairs. In addition, policymakers believed the nation could have both "guns" (military goods to fight communism abroad) and "butter" (consumer goods to foster prosperity and fight poverty at home); and energy supplies seemed limitless. But by the end of the Carter presidency, it was clear the nation was losing ground on several fronts, including not just influence in international affairs (as in the case of Iran), but also in areas such as world trade, international finance, and energy security.[10]

On issue after issue, the nation's policy maneuverability seemed severely constrained. For example, America's near-term possibilities appeared limited by the inability of conventional economic policies to address the mix of high unemployment and inflation known as "stagflation." And our longer-term possibilities were narrowed by mounting political and economic challenges from abroad, a shrinking manufacturing base, finite oil supplies, the growing recognition of environmental constraints, and the power of well-financed special interests. In short, the United States found itself in what one observer called the Age of Limits.[11]

On the Lookout for New Approaches

I accepted much of the reality of the Age of Limits but refused to surrender my aims, especially my emerging commitment to advancing the interests of working families. I also refused to support politicians who offered scapegoats and simplistic fixes such as tax cuts favoring the rich, public benefits cuts for the poor, and a broad-based rollback of government regulations. I similarly refused to ally myself with academics who insisted on radical change rather than reform. Instead, as the postwar prosperity of the era of managerial capitalism began to unravel, I remained on the lookout for creative solutions grounded in innovative thinking—new approaches for the new era. At Cornell, my undergraduate courses fueled that interest. Over time, they also pointed me toward a graduate program in which I could further explore the national problems I found most pressing.

5 STUDYING WORK

My parents seldom talked about the American Dream, but when they did the focus was on having a job to support one's family, combined with the hope that each new generation would lead a somewhat better life through hard work and overall US economic progress. It was a modest but widely held version of that dream, and my university enrollment—as a first-generation college student—seemed to validate their vision.

In my parents' conception of the American Dream, a university degree was important entirely for its practical usefulness. From their vantage point, workers with such a degree earned better pay, had more opportunities for occupational advancement, and enjoyed greater job security than workers with only a high-school diploma. In fact, even with those practical benefits the culture in which Madeline and Charlie were raised—and even I was raised but ignored—tended to look disparagingly on higher education. For example, relatives on both sides of my family (including, on rare occasions, even my parents) mocked "college boys" for having "book smarts, but no common sense." It was also a constant refrain among my dad's coworkers in the Polaroid machine shop; and many of my schoolmates and their families (especially those I encountered during my early public-school years) held a similarly derisive view of the college bound. Of course, many college grads didn't help the matter by looking down on those who never attended college.

My parents' strictly pragmatic view of higher education was evident during my search for the right college. For them, "liberal arts" meant "no job skills" and evoked images of taxi-driving English majors. Studying in a professional or technical field such as accounting or engineering seemed a much safer bet. Although they left the decision to me, Madeline and Charlie were relieved that I chose to study labor relations at Cornell, a field they considered career relevant and thus fit with their conception of what it took to successfully pursue the American Dream. My own dream was a bit more ambitious than theirs because I hoped to mix public service with "paying the bills and putting food on the table," but we all agreed on the latter—and that studying at Cornell seemed the right place for me to begin.

All Aspects of Work

The New York State School of Industrial and Labor Relations at Cornell University (known as both Cornell ILR and the ILR School) is the product of a partnership between that university and the State of New York. The state legislature authorized its creation in 1944, in anticipation of labor strikes at the end of the Second World War. According to the authorizing legislation, the school aims to "improve industrial and labor conditions in the state through the provision of instruction, the conduct of research, and the dissemination of information in all aspects of industrial, labor, and public relations affecting employers and employees."[1] In short, the school was founded with an intended focus on promoting harmonious labor-management relations and improving labor conditions, but the scope of inquiry has always encompassed all aspects of the world of work.[2]

Since 1945, Cornell ILR has offered an undergraduate program as well as programs for graduate students. Founding members of the Cornell ILR faculty were chosen for applied expertise as well as scholarship. As a result, the school's earliest professors brought to the classroom insight from experience in unions, management, government, and dispute resolution (such as arbitration)—and many of the faculty members who taught my courses decades later also had a mix of practical and academic experience.[3] A short time after the school enrolled its first students on campus in the small city of Ithaca, it also established a Division of Extension and Public Service, with faculty in Buffalo, New York City, and other cities across the state, offering workplace-oriented courses and assistance to business, labor, and communities. Over the decades, the school's teaching, research, and service have benefited greatly from the interaction of faculty members in Ithaca with those in the Extension cities.

Cornell's undergraduate program in industrial and labor relations (ILR)—an interdisciplinary area of study also known as "labor relations," "industrial relations," and more recently as "work and employment relations"—was the first of its kind in the United States. When I attended, the school enrolled about 100 new undergraduates each year (a very small college within a large university, a combination I found particularly attractive) and was the only college in the country offering a four-year program leading exclusively to a Bachelor of Science degree in the field. That remains true today.[4] Throughout the school's history, the undergraduate curriculum has reflected not only the breadth of the labor relations field, but also its interdisciplinary nature and grounding in the social sciences.

"I Love Reading"—Not Labor Economics

The curriculum I followed at Cornell consisted of an almost equal number of required and elective courses. Many required courses covered foundational subjects, including psychology, sociology, history, economics, and statistics. Other mandatory courses covered ILR-specific subjects, including labor-relations history, labor law (often taught by law school faculty), labor economics, collective bargaining, personnel management, and public policies aimed to promote economic security (such as social security, workers' compensation, and unemployment insurance). The courses involved lots of reading. In fact, students throughout the school's history have joked that ILR really stands for "I Love Reading."[5]

During a winter break in the middle of my second year at Cornell, I reviewed the decision to choose Cornell ILR and concluded the school and I were a good fit. Labor law, taught "law-school style" (Socratic method), had been a challenge but gave me confidence to think a legal career continued to be a viable option. Dispute resolution (mediation or arbitration) was also an option; in fact, through Cornell's "Neutral in Residence" program, I met Jim Foss, a federal mediator based in Boston, who arranged for me to observe one of his union-management mediation sessions during a semester break.[6] The ILR field also seemed to offer plenty of avenues for a policy-oriented career. In fact, there was only one area of study within the college that disappointed me: labor economics.

My dissatisfaction with labor economics was rooted in uneasiness about the underlying economic theory. As a first-year undergraduate, I was fine with macroeconomics, which focuses on the national economy and policy debates about how to best use monetary and fiscal policies (taxes and government spending) to manage national output, inflation, and the country's overall employment level. I even accepted microeconomics, the study of specific industries, sectors, and markets, at least as pure theory. But the labor economics course I took in my sophomore year applied microeconomic theory—which textbooks refer to as "price theory," "choice theory," or "neoclassical theory"—to conclude that labor unions, minimum wages, and a wide range of government regulations and labor-market policies were little more than interferences in what would otherwise be a smoothly operating market.[7]

Applied to the labor market, choice theory boils down to three assertions: (1) individuals make labor-market choices to maximize their personal or household well-being; (2) businesses make employment decisions with an eye to maximizing profits; and (3) impersonal market pressures coordinate employee and employer interests to determine, with socially optimal results, the number of workers hired, wage rates, and other terms and conditions of employment. From that perspective, adding unions, government regulations, or labor-market policies merely creates institutional barriers that interfere with a self-adjusting system of wages and prices. For me, the theory seemed out of touch with reality, especially the reality of unequal bargaining power between workers and firms. Choice theory didn't feel right; it didn't meet the smell test.

Since I ultimately pursued a PhD in economics, it's ironic that my labor economics course left me so dissatisfied as I approached the halfway point in my undergraduate studies. In fact, I was studying labor economics when the ILR School assigned me a faculty adviser. His name was Walter Galenson, a professor I hadn't yet encountered at Cornell. Looking up his name, I learned that he was a member of the school's department of labor economics and, on that basis, asked for another adviser. The school administrative office was happy to make the change; Professor Galenson, they explained, would be away from campus for most of the academic year anyway, and I was assigned an adviser specializing in labor history.[8] After two years at Cornell ILR, I had come to embrace the school's attention to all aspects of work, and to accept with a smile the curriculum's heavy reading load; I just didn't buy the theory underlying labor economics. I had no idea that a career-shaping turn toward economics was just around the corner.

Human Resource Economics

In my third year at Cornell, I happened upon a different approach to labor economics. That approach, called "human resource economics," resonated with me because it was problem focused and policy oriented. It also helped bring clarity to my concerns about "choice theory."

Human resource economics finds inspiration in the emphasis that Adam Smith (the pioneering eighteenth-century political economist) placed on the "skill, dexterity, and judgment" of workers when accounting for the wealth of nations.[9] The approach emerged in the United States after the Second World War, when labor economists conducted national and international studies that showed a strong connection between the development of a nation's human resources and its economic growth. Over time, economists with a focus on human resources further demonstrated that policy initiatives such as education and training can help stabilize the economy in the face of business-cycle downturns and even benefit individuals and groups facing competitive disadvantages in the labor market. As a result, much of the work of these economists aimed to help public officials devise and administer constructive policies such as job training programs, apprenticeships, and public service employment.[10]

In fall 1980, I took two courses in human resource economics and public policy. One course, taught by economist Vernon Briggs, surveyed this area of research, focusing on public employment and training programs in the United States since the 1960s, but also giving attention to human resource policies in other countries. Briggs explored how policymakers could use those policies to reduce both unemployment and inflation, such as by designing targeted jobs programs to eliminate labor-market shortages. He also examined the relevance of employment and training programs to the labor-market challenges faced by several groups of workers, including women, minorities, older workers, youths, and rural workers. The other course, taught by sociologist Susan Mueller, examined the history and debates surrounding public-sector job creation in the United States and Europe.[11]

From those courses, I discovered that human resource economics rests largely on an academic tradition called "institutional economics." Institutionalism emerged in the United States at the start of the twentieth century, in the work of economists including Thorstein Veblen and John R. Commons. It was created as an alternative to the sort of theory I encountered in my labor economics course.[12] Instead of presuming a narrow reliance on wages and prices to coordinate economic activity, institutional economics recognizes that economic coordination depends on a broad network of public and private *institutions*—each with its own web of rules and conventions.[13] In fact, economists in this tradition have long stressed that the wide-ranging institutional features of employment relationships produce not one labor market but many segmented markets, with varying conditions, barriers to entry, and opportunities for advancement.

Learning about institutionalism helped me understand the intuitive discomfort I felt toward labor economic theory. Modern price theory began at the end of the nineteenth century with the work of British economist Alfred Marshall, who admitted that his "neoclassical" theory has practical limitations that make it "only an introduction" to real-world economic studies.[14] For example, the theory largely overlooks or minimizes the significance of imperfect information, uncertainty about the future (which leads to expectations that are always subject to change), incessant economic-system evolution, power imbalances, and the inevitable role that culture and government play in shaping socioeconomic institutions.[15] Unlike economists building on Marshall's theory, institutional economists stress that those limitations point toward rejecting neoclassical theory, and its fantasy of a self-adjusting economic system, in favor of an institutionally and historically grounded economics and a focus on finding pragmatic solutions to real-world problems. That made sense to me—and caused me to give the economics discipline a second look.[16]

Diving In

After my two courses in human resource economics, I suppressed my opposition to neoclassical theory and devoted the bulk of my remaining electives to economics courses. The way I saw it, focusing on economics was unavoidable: I was interested in the problem of unemployment and other important issues facing workers, and in an era characterized by stagflation and the spread of large-scale plant shutdowns, the most pressing problems were unmistakably economic. So, I dove in—to learn as much as possible about economics from all angles and search for sensible policy solutions.

Over the next few semesters, I found courses that fit my interests in several university departments. Within the ILR School, I took a trio of policy-oriented courses in the department of personnel and human resource management: on planning local employment and training programs, the social tensions of labor market reform, and immigration policy.[17] I also took courses in the department of labor economics on professional and college-trained labor markets, labor in developing economies, and—in a seminar taught by Ken Mayhew, a visiting professor from Oxford University—the problems of unemployment and inflation.[18] Outside the ILR School, I took a course in the College of Arts and Sciences on current economic issues, taught by Alfred Kahn, who served in the Carter administration and focused his course on deregulating industries and fighting inflation, policy areas in which he played a leading role. I also took a summer course on community economic development in the department of city and regional planning, part of the College of Architecture, Art, and Planning.[19]

Despite the common Cornell refrain that "ILR" stands for "I Love Reading," my experience suggests it also means "I Love wRiting."[20] My electric Smith-Corona saw heavy duty thanks to a steady stream of short reaction papers (crafted in response to course readings or lectures) and longer research papers. My first research paper, written for a first-semester labor history course, explored the development of longshore unionism in the United States and its response to the emergence of containerized shipping. One of my final papers, written for Mayhew's course, examined theories of inflation and their implications for making economic policy. Here are some other paper topics, all from courses involving the development and use of the nation's human resources:

- An analysis of the usefulness of New Deal work-relief programs, which identified several advantages of public jobs programs over the alternatives of providing direct income assistance to the unemployed or giving employment subsidies to employers;
- An assessment of War on Poverty job-training programs, which highlighted the effectiveness of those programs, but also concluded that periods of high unemployment require direct job creation by the public sector;
- A survey and appraisal of public policies designed to improve women's wages and employment opportunities, which called attention to the success of several initiatives, including one that provided employment outreach and placement services for minority women in the 1970s; and

- An argument for a stronger national commitment to achieving and sustaining full employment, which emphasized the considerable social and economic losses resulting from joblessness, unused skills, and undeveloped talents.[21]

Reflections

Cornell introduced me to human resource economics as a serious and useful alternative to the choice theory of neoclassical economists. But in my undergraduate days, neoclassicals dominated the economics profession—and, alas, it remains so today. The early 1980s was also a period in which it became increasingly unpopular to call for government to take an active role in economic problem-solving. During my junior and senior years as a Cornell undergraduate, I was on my way to becoming not simply an economist but, in fact, an economic maverick.

6 CORNELL THROUGH A WIDER LENS

On August 12, 1980, Senator Edward Kennedy—who represented my home state of Massachusetts since I was two years old—brought his quixotic presidential campaign to a close. Addressing supporters at the Democratic National Convention, Kennedy said, "There were hard hours on our journey, and we often sailed against the wind. But we always kept our rudder true, and … stayed the course."[1] A few months later, Ronald Reagan was elected president and, for those who shared Kennedy's vision of worker-oriented policies in pursuit of broadly shared prosperity and social justice, the headwinds were to remain strong for at least a dozen years.

The Reagan era began as I started to focus on economics and public policy at Cornell. Looking beyond coursework and reviewing my Cornell experience through a wider lens reveals not only a course charted against the trends of the moment, but also efforts to keep a toe in musical waters, earn and save money, and decide what to do after graduating. Throughout it all, I tried to keep the rudder true, yet, deep down, I also felt some anxiety about where I was heading.

Headwinds

My undergraduate courses and research suggested that practical policies could indeed be found to address the economic problems affecting the nation and its workers. To be sure, there were new limits that emerged in the 1970s (such as the ineffectiveness of conventional policy approaches in the face of stagflation, as mentioned in Chapter 4), and rising competition from foreign manufacturers undermined the postwar accord between corporations and labor unions. Still, I thought the historical experience of the United States and other advanced industrial democracies provided plenty of evidence that creative and innovative approaches could be found to protect workers while meeting our challenges.

It was also clear the future I envisioned wouldn't be realized overnight. I recognized that my general outlook and policy preferences were at odds with the dominant currents in academic and political circles. I understood I was navigating against the wind.

I was most obviously out of step with the trend in economics toward neoclassical theory, which I considered a major obstacle to more sensible public policies. During the first half of the twentieth century, institutional economists held a prominent place in many of the nation's top university economics departments; they contributed key ideas that shaped the New Deal and helped policymakers contend with the Great Depression. Some institutionalists even influenced the War on Poverty. However, the notion of a self-adjusting economic system made a comeback after the Second World War and neoclassical theorists pushed to the margins economists most sympathetic to an active role for government, not just institutionalists but also followers of John Maynard Keynes who saw public policy as essential to promoting full employment. Labor was among the last of the economics fields to fall under the spell of price theory, but by the time I studied at Cornell, neoclassical price theory was dominant even in the ILR School's labor economics department. In fact, Briggs, my human resource economics professor, wasn't appointed to the department of labor economics when joining the Cornell ILR faculty in 1978; instead, he shared a department with non-economists specializing in personnel management.

Another trend was the anti-union sentiment of many classmates. While Cornell certainly had a few pro-union student activists during my undergraduate years, a surprisingly large number of ILR students believed unions had outlived their usefulness. I even found that view among students from blue-collar backgrounds.

My perspective on unions was different. Although my dad worked for a non-union company (Polaroid), I understood that his wages and benefits depended partly on the collective-bargaining success of unionized workers in other manufacturing firms, and I believed in the continuing relevance of organized labor—even as I understood that business, government, and labor had to adapt to new conditions in a changing world. When Cornell's service and maintenance workers clashed with the university administration over forming a union in late 1981, I supported the workers in an essay for the university's newspaper, *The Cornell Daily Sun*. In contrast, most of my classmates expressed little interest in the matter, except for their concern about a possible disruption of campus services.

The views of my classmates were understandable; they reflected public opinion and the dominant political views of the time. For example, in August 1981, over 12,000 members of the Professional Air Traffic Controllers Organization (PATCO) walked off the job when negotiations with the Federal Aviation Administration broke down. Their action wasn't unprecedented for federal workers or even air traffic controllers, but President Reagan, still in his first year in office, responded by demanding union members return to work and firing those who didn't comply.[2] That action underscored a marked turning point in US labor relations, away from the notion of a social contract between management and labor and toward aggressive anti-unionism.[3]

The election of Reagan in 1980 was itself a sign that I wasn't in sync with the dominant thinking on public policy. Instead of calling for the major institutions of society to find new, constructive adaptations, Reagan appointed people to the National Labor Relations Board and US Department of Labor who weakened worker protections and shifted the balance of labor-management power squarely in favor of employers.[4] Meanwhile, the federal government was Reagan's scapegoat: "Government is the problem," he said in his first inaugural address, and promptly cut taxes mainly for the wealthy, reduced social spending (but greatly increased defense spending), and slashed government regulations on corporations.[5] The Reagan tax cuts were presented as part of a heavily promoted "supply side" economics, which was, in fact, simplistic and unsound.[6] At the same time, education and training programs that would have boosted the supply of the nation's qualified workers were among the first budget items slashed.

Reagan's assault on job training and public-service employment programs was an attack on policies I knew were valuable because of my coursework in human resource economics.[7] In 1981, the jobless rate was high and rising (peaking at a post–Great Depression record of 10.8 percent in late 1982), but when the Reagan administration came in, the safety-net employment programs went out.[8] In fact, during the winter break before my spring semester in 1981, I interned in Boston with the Massachusetts Department of Manpower Development, which administered the state's federally funded job training programs. I had hoped to learn how to use such programs to help the unemployed; but with that department facing federal spending reductions, I instead helped the agency's personnel office prepare to cut its own workforce.[9]

Despite being out of step with both the thinking of conventional economists and the politics and policies of the Reagan era, I was never attracted to the group of academics who argued that reform of the capitalist system is futile.[10] I had no time for those who thought organized labor was misguided for rejecting radical social change and choosing instead to advance workers' interests through collective bargaining and economic reform, including policies that aimed to strengthen social security and provide universal health insurance. And I completely rejected the idea that solving our socioeconomic problems requires tearing down the economic and political systems in the hope that something better might follow.[11] After all, my Cornell courses provided enough exposure to the study of comparative economic systems for me to know that capitalism comes in many varieties, which meant there was plenty of room for reform.[12]

Finding myself swimming against the stream in economics and politics didn't discourage me. Much of the economics profession might have been headed in what I considered the wrong direction, but there were still several practical economists who provided me with optimism and even inspiration: not just my professors Briggs and Mayhew, but also John Kenneth Galbraith and John Dunlop at Harvard University, Lester Thurow and Michael Piore at the Massachusetts Institute of Technology (MIT); and Ray Marshall, who served as President Carter's Labor Secretary and taught at The University of Texas at Austin.[13] I also fully expected that the political tide would eventually turn, and that I'd be well prepared to make a constructive contribution to public policy when it did. Besides, I was used to ignoring the crowd, following an inner compass, and finding my own way.

Making Music—and Money

The heavy reading load and many writing assignments of my Cornell academic program left little time for extracurricular activities.[14] But I devoted countless hours to making music in the years leading up to college, so I brought my trumpet along to Cornell and decided that participating in university bands would provide a refreshing, periodic break from my studies. I also needed to find ways to reduce the financial burden of college expenses on my family; in addition to working during summer breaks, that meant taking on a part-time campus job, exploring the possibility of military service, and even graduating early.

The first Cornell band I joined was its "Big Red" Band (BRB), a marching band that performed at university football games and other campus events. I hadn't taken marching band seriously in high school (I took part only because it was required of students participating in the school's other bands), but I gave the BRB a try not only because it fulfilled the university's physical education requirement, but also because marching bands in the Ivy League had a reputation for not taking things too seriously and it seemed a great way to meet people beyond my dormitory. The BRB experience was even better than I expected, thanks to a friendly and fun group of students from a variety of academic fields. And it led eventually to a band of a different sort: at the band camp that coincided with the university's student orientation period, I met flutist Linda Burns, to whom I've been married since 1986.

Since the marching band met only in the fall, I joined the university's Wind Ensemble at the start of the spring semester and found myself assigned to the first trumpet section, probably in large part because the BRB kept my playing from getting rusty. Although both groups were affiliated with the university's music department, the Wind Ensemble was a more serious and demanding organization. I participated in that group for two years, earning academic credit that counted toward my degree as an elective. I also successfully auditioned for the Cornell Symphonic Band and took part in its recording and premiere of a work by Samuel Pellman, a Cornellian who earned his doctorate as a student of the world-renowned composer Karel Husa and later had an illustrious career as a creator of electro-acoustic music.[15]

To help cover my university expenses, I worked on weekends as a short-order cook at Cornell's Pancake House, painted houses during school breaks, and held summer jobs in the stockroom of Torque Systems, a Waltham-based subsidiary of EG&G, a major national defense contractor. Torque Systems manufactured electronic motors for the medical, automotive, and aerospace industries, using a factory constructed in the 1850s to house the Waltham Watch Company, the world's first (and for a century the largest) enterprise to mass produce watches. The factory floor in the 1970s looked much as it did in the 1870s, only the workers of my era assembled motors at their benches, not watches.

Although the state-sponsored ILR School charged lower tuition than Cornell's privately endowed colleges (such as the College of Arts and Sciences and the College of Engineering), it was still quite expensive for my family. Campus employment and summer jobs helped, as did the student loans that took years to pay off after graduation, but my brother was only two years behind me and would also soon need my parents' financial assistance. Since various branches of the military offered tuition assistance and students assumed no service obligation until their junior year, I walked into the campus office of the Army Reserve Officers' Training Corps (Army ROTC) at the start of my first semester and enrolled in the program, which involved mainly courses in leadership and management, in the hope of receiving a scholarship in the spring.

At the time, my aim was to attend law school after college, which meant hoping to fulfill my service obligation as a military lawyer. However, ROTC scholarship funds didn't materialize until partway through my second year, a short time after the program's instructors learned that I explored opportunities offered by another service branch. Then, at the start of my third year, my dad, a Marine veteran who volunteered while still in high school, discouraged me from making a service commitment before law school. He appreciated that I wanted to reduce the burden of college expenses on the family but also understood there was no guarantee I'd get a law school deferment. He didn't oppose military service; he just wanted me to put school first.[16]

Still, my parents (especially my mother) were clearly uneasy about the cost of supporting sons who were in college instead of working for a living.[17] Around the same time that I was contemplating an ROTC commitment, I recall asking my parents about taking part in the Cornell "Semester in Washington" program, which involved a combination of coursework and an unpaid public-policy internship. "A semester of unpaid work? Absolutely not," said my mom. Despite my strong interest in public policy, that idea was a nonstarter.[18] In the end, I dropped all thoughts of a semester in the nation's capital, took my dad's advice on ROTC, and came up with another penny-pinching plan: to save much of the cost of an entire semester, I proposed to graduate early—in December 1981, instead of May 1982. It worked.

To graduate early, I took three Cornell courses in summer 1981. The first was a three-week seminar on community development, offered as part of the city and regional planning department's Progressive Planning Summer Program. The others were six-week ILR courses on organizational leadership and dispute resolution. I rented an inexpensive room in a nearly empty fraternity house during the three-week session and worked as a residence-hall adviser for summer students throughout the longer session. During the rest of the summer, I painted houses.

Graduate School? What's That?

Over that summer, I also considered what I would do after completing my undergraduate program. A graduate degree in industrial relations didn't seem to make much sense; Cornell was the preeminent program in the field, and I had taken all the core courses offered by such schools as well as most of the electives of interest to me.[19] In fact, many of my ILR electives were graduate-level courses, including my two summer courses.[20]

I thought seriously about law school (which was the initial plan when I arrived in Ithaca), as well as graduate programs at public policy schools, but decided I wanted to deepen my expertise in economics and human resource policy. After much exploration (almost entirely on my own), I narrowed the options down to two doctoral programs in economics: one at Boston University and the other at The University of Texas at Austin.[21] In fall 1981, I applied to both universities and each economics department admitted me to begin coursework in January 1982.[22]

I liked Boston University (BU) because its economics department had some excellent policy-oriented labor economists, including Peter Doeringer and Paul Osterman, and it offered labor and human resource policy as one of the department's primary areas of concentration. In fact, the department housed the university's Institute on Employment Policy, created in the mid-1970s to conduct research and teaching aimed at strengthening human resource policies locally and nationally.[23] In addition, the labor economists at BU were part of a network of labor researchers in the Boston area and had close ties to colleagues at Harvard and MIT who were doing pathbreaking work.[24]

However, I decided instead on the University of Texas (UT). The main reason was the chance to study with former Labor Secretary Ray Marshall, who returned to Austin after President Carter's unsuccessful reelection bid and held appointments in both the economics department and the Lyndon B. Johnson School of Public Affairs (LBJ School). Marshall (who today is in his late-90s) was a policy-focused labor economist and arbitrator with an institutionalist orientation and a strong commitment to full employment and human resource development policies. He wrote extensively on policies aimed at combatting labor-market discrimination and advancing economic opportunities for low-wage workers, and he founded the university's Center for the Study of Human Resources in 1970, now called the Ray Marshall Center, which aims to find "creative solutions to poverty" through applied research and policy analysis.[25] In addition, Marshall was known as a leading progressive voice on economic policy and a close associate of liberal politicians including Senator Edward Kennedy and former Vice President Walter Mondale, who was expected to mount a presidential bid in 1984.

The University of Texas was attractive for other reasons as well. For example, its graduate program in economics offered courses in institutional economics and other alternatives to the neoclassical perspective. Students in the UT program were required to take at least a couple of courses in alternative perspectives, a rarity among graduate economics programs, and the department included perhaps the largest contingent of institutionalist professors anywhere.[26]

There was also the opportunity to take courses in the LBJ School, one of the country's top policy schools, and to live in a different part of the country. In addition to Marshall, the LBJ School faculty included former US Representative Barbara Jordan, whom I admired greatly, and several former public administrators and policy advisers who held key positions in the Johnson administration. That group included Wilbur Cohen, who studied in Wisconsin under labor economist John R. Commons, went to Washington to help create the social security system, and ended his service as President Johnson's Secretary of Health, Education, and Welfare.[27] Meanwhile, the state of Texas was booming along with the rest of the Sun Belt, and Austin was gaining a reputation as a dynamic city—an emerging hub of not only technological innovation and economic expansion, but also live music of all sorts. It seemed sensible to use my time as a graduate student to simultaneously experience life outside the Northeast "Rust Belt."[28]

There was even one more reason I decided to study at UT: the tuition was remarkably inexpensive, even for out-of-state students.[29] That was important because neither BU nor UT offered me financial assistance in the form of a graduate teaching or research position for the spring semester (at both universities, such assistance was allocated to coincide with the start of the academic year). But I still needed to convince my parents to go along with the idea.

My proposal to pursue graduate work in economics didn't go over well with my parents. "Graduate school? What's that? We already sent you to college!" shouted my mother. If I had proposed law school, perhaps she would have understood a bit better; but at that moment I realized she had no idea what I was talking about. She knew nothing about bachelor's, master's, and doctoral degrees. As she saw it, she sent me to college, which not only imposed a financial burden on the family but also required a huge leap of faith since she was most accustomed to young adults leaving home as soon as possible and working for a living; now she just wanted me to find a full-time job. For my dad, meanwhile, this was worse than raising an English major who drove a taxi; it looked like he raised exactly what his factory coworkers had mockingly warned him about: a perpetual student—someone who'd always mooch off his parents and *never* make a living!

In making my case, I explained that my goal was to get a PhD and become a professor at a school of industrial relations or public policy, which would allow me to do all the things my professors did, including testify before Congress on important policy matters, work as a labor arbitrator, and perhaps even serve in the federal government as an executive-branch appointee and policy adviser. I also pointed out that the Texas program was the least expensive of the programs that interested me, that financial assistance might be available in the fall, and that UT allowed me to work directly toward a PhD, enabling me to save time and money by bypassing work on a master's thesis. And I promised to find and take on as much part-time work as I could manage. In the end, my parents relented—largely, I think, because I was graduating from Cornell a semester early, which showed I was both frugal and driven. That made it easier for them to approve my proposal to give Texas a try.

Reflections

At the age of seventeen, I arrived on the Cornell University campus with optimism and ambition. I certainly had determination to excel academically and professionally, and to prepare myself as best I could for a career aimed at improving economic security and well-being for workers and their families. I was eager to learn, willing to work hard, and sought to go as far as possible in the pursuit of my conception of the American Dream.

Was I being unreasonable? Was I recklessly shooting for the moon, destined to eventually come crashing back to earth as my high school guidance counselor probably expected and several members of my family feared?[30] Looking back on my three and a half years at Cornell, I don't think I was motivated by unreasonable expectations. The foundations of our economic system were beginning to change in ways that would affect the career trajectory of countless members of my generation; in fact, I had a front-row seat to that transformation in several of my courses. But there's no way the personal consequences of that change could have been anticipated and avoided in those early years. All in all, I'd say I had healthy optimism, a constructive drive, and modest, not blind, ambition.

My academic performance at Cornell was certainly no cause for concern; I did well in my courses, including those listed at the graduate level. Even more important to me than my respectable grade-point average was the positive feedback I received on my research papers, which consistently received very high marks. Researching and writing papers was certainly lots of work, but I enjoyed the process and for me working on a paper usually seemed the best way to learn.

In fact, I enjoyed the entire Cornell experience. The campus was attractive; the gorges and hillsides were beautiful in every season; the libraries were excellent; the courses were interesting; and the professors were leaders in their field. In addition, the university's wide range of majors produced a student body with diverse interests and backgrounds, which enhanced the vibrancy of the campus community.

Yet life at Cornell also highlighted ways in which our entire society was not just diverse but also stratified. Some people drew a bright distinction between students enrolled in the state-sponsored colleges and those in the endowed colleges, often even suggesting the university's Ivy League designation only really applied to the endowed portion.[31] Meanwhile, it seemed many Cornellians, even in the endowed colleges, harbored feelings of inferiority, envy, and perhaps even resentment toward students at universities such as Harvard, Yale, and Princeton.[32] And many students thought nothing of taking semester-long unpaid internships or studying abroad, whereas others had parents like mine who ruled those out as unaffordable indulgences.

Learning about my classmates' summer activities often revealed the divide beneath the surface of our common Cornell experience. For some, every summer was filled with impressive résumé-building experiences or cultural adventures. Meanwhile, I worked in a factory stockroom and painted houses, and others worked in landscaping, construction, and neighborhood restaurants. Perhaps the first time I observed this divide—clearly and unexpectedly—was when a classmate told me she "did some painting" over the summer: I quickly discovered that her "painting" and mine were worlds apart.

It was, of course, impossible to observe that sort of socioeconomic divide and not feel a bit apprehensive, even with my solid academic record and modest ambitions. For me at Cornell, there were no career-building mentors, trust funds, or other financial safety nets; there were no country-club buddies of my dad to count on if I needed a professional favor.[33] I was earning a university degree, but in the 1980s that meant merely what social commentator Barbara Ehrenreich described as moving from the "working class" to a college-educated "middle class" that's still always anxious and financially insecure. As Ehrenreich wrote in 1989, unlike the truly wealthy, those in the middle have little more than their knowledge and skill to get them through even the hardest of times. And that means the middle class is always afraid of a downward economic slide: "There is the fear, always, of falling."[34] Ehrenreich's description of that middle class would have resonated with me at Cornell, just as it did when her book appeared the year after I received my PhD.

There was also an underlying worry that maybe I didn't really belong where I was heading. At Cornell and for many years thereafter, I was haunted by the words of my hometown friend Paul Harriman's uncle who heard about my interest in a policy-oriented career and responded: "They won't give you a chance. If you're lucky, maybe they'll use you for a time. But in the end, they'll chew you up and spit you out." Paul tried to dismiss the matter, "Charles is smart; he won't let that happen." Deep down, though, I wasn't so certain.[35]

All I knew for sure was that I wasn't going down without a fight. And opportunities weren't going to come my way if I didn't try. After all, there were really no alternatives. Ehrenreich's middle class might have been anxious, but the "working class" from which I came was no less insecure—especially in the era of manufacturing decline. There were no guarantees of success for me, but the country needed worker-oriented policies. Besides, I had manned a punch press at Polaroid in the summer before starting college (for just one day, but that was plenty) and was going to do everything I could to avoid doing that for a living.[36]

Although I enjoyed Cornell, leaving central New York to start graduate work in Austin wasn't difficult. In January 1982, I was eager to begin my life's next chapter. The toughest part was leaving Linda Burns. Since the fall of my first semester, we were constant study companions, encouraging and supporting each other through the seemingly endless work. In fact, she generously proofread all my undergraduate papers, starting with the first-semester report on longshore workers. We also jogged, ice skated, and played racquetball together.

I knew it would be a big change to connect with Linda only through long-distance phone calls, but she was considering a yearlong dietetic (nutrition) position at a hospital in Dallas, which would begin that summer. That possibility made the separation easier. Throughout my youth, I was often told, "It's not *what* you know but *who* you know that counts in life." I suppose that's true; meeting Linda at Cornell was ultimately much more important than what I learned there as a student.

PART THREE

AUSTIN

7 THE MAKING OF A MAVERICK ECONOMIST

I arrived at Austin's Robert Mueller Municipal Airport on the evening of January 3, 1982, and took a shuttle bus to the Holiday Inn near the University of Texas campus. I came with two suitcases, one of which included my Smith-Corona typewriter.[1] After settling into my room, I unpacked the economics department's graduate program brochure and the university course catalogue; then I sketched an academic plan on a hotel notepad.

My plan had several parts, beginning with taking some catch-up courses because I hadn't majored in economics as an undergraduate. Then I had to complete each of the following: (1) the doctoral program's core theory courses, followed by comprehensive theory exams; (2) advanced courses in three economics fields of my choice, followed by comprehensive field exams; (3) courses in quantitative methods; and (4) a PhD thesis (dissertation). I also needed three courses outside the department, in areas that could be considered "supporting work." Working late into the evening, I explored the course catalogue and selected the specific courses I wanted and the order in which I intended to take them.[2]

Getting Settled

After a night at the Holiday Inn, I took a taxi to the university and moved into the graduate housing section of the Jester Center dormitory, one of the largest residence halls in the country. For me, the dorm location was perfect: across the street from both the Perry-Castañeda Library (the main library in the University of Texas system) and the Business and Economics Building, where most economics courses were taught. Jester Center also sat on the side of campus nearest the Texas State Capitol. In the days that followed, I explored both the university and the Capitol between registering for courses and shopping for books and supplies.

Because I entered in the middle of the academic year, I was initially assigned a temporary dorm room—a large study hall converted into a suite. I shared the space with a diverse quartet of other new graduate students, from San Antonio,

Mexico City, India, and even Boston. Dan Martin, from Boston's Dorchester neighborhood, was a graduate of Catholic University who came to Austin to study business administration.[3] We each found it amusing to be rooming with another "Yankee" from the Boston area, but it made for instant camaraderie, and we enjoyed sharing observations about moving to the Southwest.

I eventually settled into a suite with three other students: Robert Crookshank, a politically conservative law student whose family lived near Houston; Jim Koga, a physics PhD student who grew up in California and did undergraduate work at MIT; and Varuna Thotawatte, an engineering major from Sri Lanka. We all got along well, so at the end of the spring semester we moved together to an off-campus two-bedroom apartment on the university bus line, eventually replacing the graduating Thotawatte with Bob Hoover, an economics graduate student from North Carolina.[4] We were serious students, but often took breaks to watch Star Trek, check out a Tex-Mex or BBQ restaurant, and explore the Hill Country. In addition, Jim taught me tennis with the help of Jane Manchester, a Cornell classmate who moved to Austin in mid-1982; they were patient teachers, and it became our favorite way to get exercise in the evening when the Texas heat became somewhat bearable.[5]

Catching Up—and Meeting Ray Marshall

I devoted my first semester in Austin, and a large part of summer 1982, to courses that helped me catch up with other new economics graduate students. By the end of that summer, I completed three mathematics courses and two economic theory courses that I hadn't taken as an undergraduate. In fact, during my first semester in Austin I took only one graduate-level course: Ray Marshall's LBJ School seminar, "Labor and International Economic Policy," which counted toward my graduate degree as supporting work.

Marshall's course met in a classroom within Sid Richardson Hall, adjacent to the Lyndon Baines Johnson Presidential Library, and included about a dozen students. It convened once a week for three hours, usually with only a short break at the midpoint. Although listed as a seminar, Marshall organized it as a lecture course—and I feverishly took notes to catch his every word.

I thought Marshall's course was fabulous. The first few weeks offered an introduction to theories of industrial relations and a comparative survey of labor-management relations in industrial democracies. The next few weeks focused on the post-Second World War evolution of the American economy and its impact on industrial relations. The final weeks of the course assessed current national and international economic policies, their implications for workers and overall national economic well-being, and a range of policy alternatives. Marshall's approach to labor economics was exactly the blend of industrial relations and economics I hoped to find, and his critique of the Reagan administration agenda on labor and economic policy (presented against the backdrop of what was then the most severe recession since the Great Depression) offered a refreshingly different (pro-worker) perspective from that offered by most economists.

Looking back, I was extraordinarily bold and naïve. I had never met Professor Marshall, or even corresponded with him, before appearing in his classroom in January 1982. In fact, I didn't interact with him very much during the semester (mainly because of the lecture format) and waited until the end of the term to really introduce myself, thinking it was best to first do well in his course. It's possible that even then Marshall didn't realize I graduated early from Cornell and moved to Austin at the start of that year with the aim of taking his courses and having him supervise my doctoral work, although perhaps Cornell's Vernon Briggs mentioned it to him (Marshall and Briggs had been colleagues in Austin and collaborated on updates of a labor economics textbook after Briggs moved to Ithaca).

At the end of that first semester, I returned to Massachusetts energized by Marshall's seminar and took summer courses at Brandeis University in differential and integral calculus.[6] Brandeis was only a short distance from my family's home in Waltham, and even closer to two apartment houses (a duplex and fourplex) that my parents purchased as rental properties—at interest rates of 13.0 and 17.5 percent—in 1980 and 1981.[7] I divided my summer break between painting those houses and studying calculus to prepare for the mathematically oriented economics courses I would begin in the fall.

Completing the Core and Riding the Greyhound to Dallas

During the 1982–1983 academic year, I tackled the core theory courses in my degree plan. I met those requirements with two courses in macroeconomics and one in each of the following: microeconomics, institutional economics, and "economic methodology," which examined the scientific and philosophical foundations of economic theory. I rounded out my schedule that year with a labor arbitration course offered by the Graduate School of Business (my second "supporting work" course) and a required "Math for Economists" course.

As expected, the theory courses in macroeconomics and microeconomics consisted mainly of using mathematical models to generate conclusions predetermined by initial assumptions. However, I was fortunate to take the microeconomics course with economist and lawyer Herbert Liebhafsky, who drew on his legal training to insist that we consider not only the mechanics of economic models, but also the real-world appropriateness of their assumptions.[8] Liebhafsky also taught the methodology course, in which he encouraged a relentless critical look at the preconceptions held by each school of economic thought; Liebhafsky's course greatly affected the way I look at economics.

What I learned in my institutional economics course also stuck with me. It was taught by the lanky, modest, and soft-spoken Wendell Gordon, who served as the main torchbearer of institutionalism during my time in Texas. Gordon earned his PhD from New York University at the age of 23 and joined the economics faculty in Austin shortly before the Second World War. His teaching in the 1980s bore the influence of a long association with Clarence Ayres, a legendary figure in the Austin economics department and a leading contributor to institutional economics from the 1920s through the 1960s. Gordon's course, which centered on the dynamic interplay of institutions and human knowledge, offered an unparalleled glimpse into Ayresian institutionalism.

Yet Gordon, who was on the verge of retirement when I worked my way through the economics department's courses, was not an Ayres clone. Ayres's institutionalism could be dogmatic and is often interpreted as suggesting the existence of eternal truths. In contrast, Gordon's institutionalism, consistent with his innate modesty, focused instead on the need for societies to regularly reassess the ends and means of public policies and economic institutions.[9]

Gordon might have been modest, but he also wasn't afraid to take a stand and defend his convictions. For example, at the start of the Second World War, he traveled to Dallas with two departmental colleagues in the hope of defending federal 40-hour workweek rules at a business-sponsored rally against government workplace regulations. Not given a chance to speak at the event, Gordon and the other economists shared their viewpoint with a newspaper reporter. Their outspokenness cost them their jobs, so Gordon joined the military, where distinguished service paved the way for his return to teaching in Austin after the war.[10]

Forty years after Gordon and his colleagues made their trek to Dallas, I too traveled there from Austin—on a Greyhound bus. In fact, I made the trip many weekends throughout the academic year. That's because my best friend and Cornell study partner, Linda Burns, began a one-year dietetic internship at the Presbyterian Hospital in north Dallas during summer 1982, after completing her undergraduate work at Cornell a few months earlier.

The bus rides were easy for me. I attended classes and studied in Austin from Monday through midday Friday. After my final class of the week, I walked from campus to the downtown Greyhound station and rode a bus to Dallas, arriving just in time for Linda to pick me up at the station after work. And on Sunday evenings I traveled back to Austin, caught a taxi to my apartment, and began another week of studying. I read textbooks on the bus and always brought a backpack filled with course material, but those weekend visits helped sustain me through the year.

In addition to traveling north to Dallas, I made one trip south to San Antonio in spring 1983.[11] My arbitration professor, Isadore ("Beber") Helburn, was selected to decide a case at what was then called Kelly Air Force Base and allowed me to come along to observe the hearing. That's when I learned about his graduate work in industrial relations at the University of Wisconsin, which is where that academic field emerged from the work of John R. Commons. That meant we shared a common educational background and orientation. In fact, I often felt that Helburn and I had more in common with each other than he had with most of his business school colleagues and I had with most of my economics professors and classmates.[12]

Studying Throughout the Summer—and a Remarkable Coincidence

In 1983, I studied throughout the summer. I began by returning to Cornell's Progressive Planning Summer Program for a three-week course on national industrial policy and a two-day workshop on how to reindustrialize American communities.[13] Then, after a short visit with my family in Massachusetts, I returned to Austin for a one-on-one tutorial with William ("Sandy") Darity on postwar developments in macroeconomics.[14] I also prepared for my department's comprehensive theory exams, which were given at the start of the fall semester.

I considered the Cornell course and workshop important and timely. In the early 1980s, industrial policies and community reindustrialization strategies were of great interest to progressives looking beyond the ups and downs of the business cycle and seeking to grapple with the plant closings and job losses that many described as a process of deindustrialization.[15] In fact, it wasn't just progressives who worried about factory shutdowns and their adverse consequences for workers, communities, industrial competitiveness, and national economic well-being. For example, the editors at *Business Week* devoted an entire special issue to "The Reindustrialization of America" in 1980. During that same year, professors Robert Hayes and William Abernathy of Harvard Business School produced a widely discussed article, "Managing Our Way to Economic Decline," which blamed the nation's competitiveness woes on the short-term, financial focus of corporate managers.[16]

At the end of my Cornell industrial policy course (which counted toward my PhD as the last of my "supporting work" courses), I submitted a 56-page industrial policy proposal.[17] Conceived as part of a coordinated economic policy agenda, my proposal called for a national industrial bank, worker and community adjustment mechanisms, and ongoing policy guidance grounded in research on environmental and resource constraints. All those policies remain worth implementing today.

During my return to Ithaca, I stopped by the ILR School in the hope of seeing some of my former professors. Instead, I visited with two Cornell professors I hadn't met previously. The first was Walter Galenson, the economist assigned as my ILR academic adviser some years earlier (but who was away from the university at the time). In Austin, I read some of Galenson's research and learned about a remarkable coincidence: Galenson served as Ray Marshall's dissertation adviser in the 1950s at the University of California. I didn't expect to see Professor Galenson in Ithaca, but it was a pleasure to find him in his office and willing to chat.

I also met Larry Mishel, a labor economist who pursued doctoral work at the University of Wisconsin and was just beginning his career. When I told him about my interests, he shared with me that several of his fellow Wisconsin graduate students met informally in Madison to read institutional economics because the department didn't teach it. After a few years at Cornell, Mishel became an economist with the labor movement, and in 1987 he became research director at the Economic Policy Institute (a think tank cofounded by Ray Marshall and other pro-labor scholars), where he eventually served as president and currently works as a distinguished fellow. Mishel and I have remained in contact over the years, and in the 1990s he participated in a policy-oriented conference panel I organized on worker insecurity.

Arriving back in Austin, I enrolled in Professor Darity's course, which counted as advanced coursework in macroeconomics, one of my three areas of specialization. It had to be taken that summer because Darity was leaving Texas to begin a position at the University of North Carolina in the fall. Darity's course was unique for giving attention to a wide range of theories that emerged in the post-Second World War era, not just the dominant theories of the economic mainstream, so I didn't want to miss my opportunity to learn from him.[18]

After I worked my way through Darity's reading list, we discussed that material and the macroeconomic topics that interested me most, including business cycles and full employment. Then he assigned me books by American "post-Keynesians" Sidney Weintraub, Paul Davidson, and Hyman ("Hy") Minsky, suggesting that I take my time with the new material and send him a paper assessing or building on that research.[19] A short time later, Darity moved to Chapel Hill and I turned my attention to the comprehensive theory exams, passing them at the start of the fall semester.

Finishing Coursework and Preparing for the Dissertation

For the next two academic years (fall 1983 through spring 1985), I concentrated on completing my coursework and preparing for my dissertation, which included taking two comprehensive field exams and forming a dissertation committee. Two courses were in econometrics (the use of statistical techniques to analyze economic data): a theory-oriented version of the subject offered by the economics department, and a more applied course offered by the LBJ School. The other courses were in my areas of specialization: labor economics, public economics, and macroeconomics.

Ray Marshall taught both of my labor economics courses.[20] One was a seminar on labor and national economic policy, which complemented the LBJ School course I took with Marshall in 1982.[21] My research paper for the course, which ran 165 pages, explored what the United States could learn from Japan on the development and use of human resources.[22] The paper impressed Marshall, which gave me the confidence to ask him about supervising my dissertation.[23]

The other labor course involved a tutorial on theories of wages and employment, which aimed to prepare me for the department's comprehensive examination in the labor field. For that course, I read and annotated eight books and more than two dozen articles and book chapters. I also sketched an outline of the history of wage theories, giving attention to both mainstream theories and alternative perspectives. The annotations alone ran nearly 100 pages. Shortly after completing that course, I passed the labor field exam.

Public economics encompasses all aspects of government in the economy but mostly analyzes public spending and taxation. In Austin, Randolph Lyon taught the spending-oriented course and Randall Mariger taught the taxation course. Both professors approached economics in a mainstream fashion, but they also had a keen interest in public policy—in fact, each of them left Texas in the mid-1980s for federal government work in Washington. Conventional public economics, a field sometimes called "public finance," has significant limitations; in fact, most of its models use assumptions that severely restrict their practical relevance. But my aim was to understand that literature and its theories, and I accomplished that, and passed the last of my comprehensive exams, thanks to the Lyon-Mariger course sequence.

Macroeconomics was my other area of specialization.[24] One course in this field, listed in the course catalogue as "Dynamic Macroeconomics," involved constructing models that struck me as little more than intellectual exercises. The other was Darity's course, which I completed by submitting a 100-page paper evaluating the business-cycle theory and policy prescriptions of Hy Minsky, one of the post-Keynesians on the book list Sandy created for me before moving to Chapel Hill.

Darity offered extensive comments on my paper because he took my work seriously and wanted to help deepen my thinking about Minsky. In fact, Sandy invited me to leave Texas in mid-1985 and complete my PhD under his supervision in North Carolina. But by then my courses were finished and Professor Marshall had agreed to chair my dissertation committee, so it made sense to stay in Austin.[25]

In addition to Marshall, my dissertation committee included Beber Helburn from the business school, Vernon Briggs from Cornell, and two senior members of the economics department with whom I hadn't taken courses: Stephen McDonald (a monetary economist) and Forest Hill (an economic historian). Finding two economists from within the department took the most work because so many of the faculty were retiring or leaving for jobs elsewhere—and most of the new hires were a different breed, who seemed much more interested in mathematics than real-world economic problems. McDonald and Hill were excellent committee members, but the truth is they came to mind only when I saw they were each as bored as I was during a department seminar that used economic theory to study having children as a "utility-maximizing" decision.[26]

Wendell Gordon retired just before I began my dissertation, but he still played a vital role in helping me complete my degree. That's because Gordon donated funds that created the university's doctoral research fellowship in institutional economics, and, in summer 1985, I was its first recipient. Prior to receiving the Gordon fellowship, I worked as both a research assistant for a professor in the LBJ School and an economics instructor for two tutoring services, but the Gordon fellowship allowed me to focus on the dissertation.[27]

Writing and Defending the Dissertation

I began working on my PhD dissertation in July 1985. The project changed shape a few times before it was completed and defended in July 1988. My first idea was an overly ambitious effort to reshape economic theory. The second aimed to focus more directly on policy-oriented case studies of institutional reform. That idea centered on "consensus-building" economic forums: regional or industry-focused groups that enable representatives of business, labor, and government to engage in collaborative problem-solving. But studying those institutions wasn't considered "economics" by many of the department's younger economists.[28] My third idea, which offered a scaled-back mix of theory and policy, proved to be the proverbial charm.

I successfully defended the dissertation on July 11, 1988.[29] I called it *Beyond Neoclassical Thought: Economics from the Perspective of Institutionalists and Post-Keynesians*.[30] The committee members complimented me on the quality of the research and on how well the dissertation was written. Two committee members even wrote separate notes to let me know it was the best dissertation they'd reviewed during their careers.

Beyond Neoclassical Thought makes a confident and optimistic case for institutional economics as a vital tool for US economic problem-solving. The dissertation begins by arguing that key preconceptions and various shortcomings of conventional (neoclassical) economics limited its usefulness for understanding and addressing some of the most important economic difficulties of the 1980s, including persistently high unemployment, widespread plant closings, erosion of the nation's industrial base, and wrenching community economic dislocation. Then institutional economics is offered as a constructive, problem-oriented alternative, partly because it is grounded in an understanding of economic history and real-world institutions, but also because it has a long record of shedding light on business cycles and even longer-term economic transitions (involving major changes in economic structures, strategies, and practices). In fact, the foundations of institutionalism are shown to have enough breadth and sturdiness to support a synthesis of institutionalism, industrial-relations theory, and much post-Keynesianism.

When the discussion in *Beyond Neoclassical Thought* turns to public policy, considerable attention is given to combining overall (macro) economic policies with selective industrial and labor-market policies. The goal of that combination is to achieve and sustain a full-employment economy characterized by family-supporting jobs, meaningful work, and abundant opportunities for people to develop and use their talents. Special attention is given to institutionalism's emphasis on the role of consensus-building forums in shaping economic decisions and public policies—and to the successes and failures of community-wide labor-management committees in Buffalo, New York, and Beaumont, Texas.[31] Those communities were examined to highlight the real-world strengths and limitations of such committees as tools for community development, and to consider the possible usefulness of similar forums in shaping national economic policy.

The dissertation succeeded at integrating the strands of my academic background into a coherent framework for economic analysis, resulting in a foundation I've relied upon throughout my career. And it turns out that my economic framework also dovetails with the perspective of the Catholic Church on capitalism, the dignity of work, economic justice, and social reform. In fact, I later learned that Charles K. Wilber, a University of Notre Dame economist whose research influenced my effort to synthesize post-Keynesianism and institutionalism, served as a key adviser to the US bishops who prepared a pastoral letter on Catholic social teaching and the American economy in the mid-1980s. No wonder that framework felt right; although I completed the dissertation almost two decades after leaving Catholic school, it was infused with the same ethics and social philosophy that I absorbed in those early days and have carried with me ever since.[32]

8 TEXAS PEOPLE AND POLITICS

Throughout my Austin residency, I spent time outside the classroom with a small circle of friends that centered on my roommates and a few classmates.[1] Some of those classmates were from Venezuela and they often invited me to play softball with their families.[2] I also had friends from the LBJ School, but most of its students were in Austin for only two years, after which many moved to Washington, DC.

In summer 1984, John Quinn joined the circle. I met John through the university's Catholic Center. He moved to Austin to pursue a PhD in Classics, having just graduated from the University of Notre Dame, and we agreed to share a two-bedroom apartment, which provided more quiet space than my earlier four-person arrangements.[3] John was also amenable to me adopting a kitten, an orange tabby we named Pepys.

Faculty Candidates

Between studying economics, tutoring students, and attempting to keep up with current events at the national level, I didn't find much time for campus or local events.[4] But I did attend several presentations by candidates vying for faculty positions in the economics department, including institutionalist William ("Bill") Dugger, who earned his PhD in Austin and was teaching at DePaul University. Dugger, interviewing to replace the just-retired Wendell Gordon, had an outstanding record as an institutionalist scholar and would become recognized as a leading institutionalist in the 1990s, during which I had the opportunity to collaborate with him on a few book projects.

Alas, it seemed no institutionalist was quite good enough for the Texas economics department and Gordon was not replaced with a like-minded economist. However, around that same time the LBJ School hired non-mainstream economist James ("Jamie") K. Galbraith, son of institutionalist John Kenneth Galbraith. At the suggestion of Sandy Darity, who taught briefly with Jamie at the University of Maryland, Jamie and I met soon after he arrived in Austin (to discuss post-Keynesian economic theory) and we've stayed in touch ever since.[5]

Political Candidates

In addition to presentations by economics job candidates, I attended a few Austin events related to politics and current affairs.[6] For example, I took part in an LBJ Library reception organized by Lady Bird Johnson for Democratic presidential adviser Clark Clifford; enjoyed an evening of humor and social commentary featuring Austin natives John Henry Faulk (who successfully fought "Red Scare" blacklisting) and Cactus Pryor; watched Jesse Jackson deliver a presidential campaign speech; and heard lectures by John Kenneth Galbraith (speaking on the fiftieth anniversary of the New Deal), political consultant Patrick Caddell, and writer Michael Harrington (author of *The Other America*). In Spring 1984, I also sat in on a technology-policy event featuring Ray Marshall, presidential contender Walter Mondale, Ann Richards (Texas State Treasurer), and Bobby Inman (CEO of the Austin-based Microelectronics and Computer Consortium).[7]

At the end of the technology symposium, a friend studying at the LBJ School brought me to the stage and introduced me to Richards, for whom he'd been a campaign volunteer. Ann recognized him immediately and greeted us warmly, "Why don't you boys grab a jacket and tie and meet us in a couple of hours at the Quorum? We're havin' a little reception for Fritz [Mondale]." We accepted the invitation, arriving just in time to share an elevator ride with a television news crew.

Approaching the entrance to the exclusive Quorum Club, a woman at a reception table welcomed us, adding, "And you'll be making a donation today . . ."—to which I responded, "Um, we're with Ann Richards," and we walked on into the room. Inside, everyone had a chance to meet the presidential candidate (with microphones and news cameras in our faces) and watch Senator Lloyd Bentsen announce his support for Mondale for the first time in the race, just a few days before the Texas caucuses. The next morning, the *Austin American-Statesman* reported: "Bentsen appeared in Austin at a $500-a-head fund-raising cocktail party for Mondale at the Quorum, where a number of state leaders were gathered."[8]

That was the only time I met Mondale. Despite making several inquiries, I didn't succeed at finding work with his campaign. However, I was pressed into service by the security detail at a Mondale-Ferraro rally on the grounds of the Texas State Capitol on August 1, 1984. I attended on my own, expecting to be just another spectator, but arrived so early that the Secret Service gave me a lapel pin (which indicated I wasn't a security threat) and event organizers assigned me to help with crowd control along the rope line surrounding the stage. After President Reagan's landslide reelection, I felt bad for Mondale and wrote him a note thanking him for his courageous campaign. His reply made no attempt to hide disappointment but also expressed confidence that "the values and purposes we espoused are essential to the healthy future of our nation." In the closing, he wrote: "With warmest personal regards. Sincerely, Fritz."[9]

My other brush with politics in Austin was when I nearly worked with James Carville and Paul Begala on their first campaign, the unsuccessful 1984 run by Lloyd Doggett for an open seat in the US Senate.[10] Hearing through my LBJ School friends that the campaign of Texas State Senator Doggett (an Austin native and graduate of the University of Texas) was looking for volunteers, I intended to attend a volunteers' meeting and recruited Bob Hoover, my economics classmate, to join me. However, at the last minute I decided to stay home to work on a course assignment. I never did visit the campaign office, but Bob worked on the campaign and I reviewed and edited drafts of position papers he shared with me—along with stories about the colorful pair running the campaign. Several years later, Carville and Begala became campaign superstars when they managed Bill Clinton's presidential bid.

9 EARLY ACCOMPLISHMENTS, BUT LIMITED OPTIONS

Earning a PhD in economics provided the credentials and knowledge I needed to take on the arguments behind public policies I considered harmful to the interests of working people. It enabled me to advocate not only for better economic theories, but also for more constructive policies and institutional reforms to improve workers' well-being and the overall economy. And I stayed focused on that goal throughout the Reagan years, even when demonization of government activism and labor unions evolved in the mid-1980s from the prevailing fashion to a long-term trend. In fact, I interpreted that shift as meaning my graduate work had become even more important.

Even now, I remain convinced I was on the right track even though it was against the stream. In fact, there's now ample evidence and widespread recognition that the economic polarization and worker insecurity that concerned me back then have become among the defining issues of the past several decades—even if the nation remains divided over what to do about them. But when I completed my degree in 1988, academia wasn't much more interested in what I had to offer than was the political world, despite my demonstrated ability to identify important topics and publish academic articles, which is usually considered a hallmark of academic achievement.

Professional Accomplishments

Between receiving the Wendell Gordon Doctoral Research Fellowship and successfully defending my dissertation, I published three academic articles in the *Journal of Economic Issues* (*JEI*), produced by the Association for Evolutionary Economics (AFEE), an organization of economists who tend to hold an institutionalist viewpoint.[1]

The first article, published in early 1987, offers a critique of conventional economics.[2] I wrote the manuscript by drawing on material from the draft of a dissertation chapter and sent it to the *JEI* in mid-1986. I was surprised when the editor enthusiastically accepted the paper without sending it to referees, which rarely happens in the world of academic journals.

The second article, published in mid-1987, presents the case study of a countywide labor-management committee based in Buffalo, New York, which pursued innovative, collaborative solutions in response to huge job losses in Western New York. The article originated as a paper for an AFEE conference held in December 1986—my first paper delivered at a professional conference.[3] The paper received a positive response during the follow-up discussion; the program organizer even rose from the audience to emphasize that it highlighted constructive initiatives meriting the attention of academics and policymakers. In addition, Alfred Eichner, a prominent institutionalist and post-Keynesian, later tracked me down to encourage my work.[4]

The third article, based on a conference paper delivered the following year, appeared in the *JEI* in mid-1988. It draws attention to the compatibility of the business-cycle perspectives of Hy Minsky and his University of Chicago professor, Henry Simons, dispelling the myth that their views were sharply at odds.[5] In the 1970s, mainstream economists developed a new approach to business cycles and argued it was grounded in the economics of Simons. Advocates of that approach, called "new classical economics," opposed policy efforts to stabilize the economy in the face of business downturns, arguing that unemployment is ultimately a personal choice stemming from a person's unwillingness to accept a low-wage job.[6] But I used a mix of widely available publications and rare documents (including memos by Simons located with help from the famous conservative economist Milton Friedman) to show that the new classical approach represented a major departure from over half a century of work on business cycles by a broad range of economists including Simons, Keynes, and Minsky. My article called for using that earlier research to construct a sound and practical alternative to the new classical view of cycles.

Other early professional accomplishments included organizing a pair of sessions for the country's largest recurring economics conference, the Allied Social Science Associations annual meeting, which took place in late 1987.[7] One session, sponsored by the Industrial Relations Research Association, featured a panel of experienced academics offering career advice for doctoral students interested in industrial relations.[8] The other session, sponsored by AFEE, focused on the economic ideas of Minsky (who at the time was a professor at Washington University in St. Louis).

The AFEE session featured several papers on Minsky's ideas (including one by me) as well as Minsky as the discussant. The conference room was packed; there were even people straining to listen from the hall. That's because the stock market had recently experienced its largest single-day drop in history (on October 19,

1987) and economists wanted to hear what Minsky, perhaps the world's leading expert on financial crises, had to say about that event and its aftermath.[9] It was an impressive turnout, and organizing a session that generated such wide interest was certainly an accomplishment for a graduate student.

Limited Job Options

My job search, however, was not nearly as successful. Most of the academic job market operates on a schedule resembling the college admissions process. Job seekers apply in the fall for advertised faculty positions. Then there are preliminary interviews at professional conferences, campus visits for finalists, job offers for top candidates, and appointments that begin with the new academic year. But when I started searching in fall 1987, there weren't many positions matching my qualifications and research interests—even though my research and graduate training spanned the disciplines of industrial relations, public policy, and economics.

I was striking out in the job market of all three disciplines. Industrial-relations programs weren't looking for someone to focus on stakeholder engagement; most of them at that time aimed mainly to shore up teaching and research on the management of workers in non-union settings. Policy schools also didn't have positions that aligned with my expertise.[10] And fewer economics departments than I expected were looking for someone capable of introducing students to a range of approaches to economic analysis; there were usually several colleges and universities looking to bring such economists on board in a tenure-track capacity each year, but not in the 1987–1988 recruitment year.[11]

In the end, I received few interviews and only two offers—both for non-tenure-track jobs. One was at University of Massachusetts Boston, and the other was at the liberal-arts Hobart and William Smith Colleges (HWS) in Geneva, New York.[12] I accepted the HWS offer partly because a pair of institutional economists at the colleges strongly encouraged me to join them, emphasizing that I could teach the types of courses I wanted and that the department was slated to add a tenure-track slot in the same teaching areas within the next few years (although I would still need to apply for the new slot). Another consideration was that Linda and I had recently married and she was working an hour's drive from Geneva, in the quaint village of Bath where she directed a two-county federal nutrition program.[13] Taking the HWS position meant Linda could keep her job while I commuted to campus. I was wary about accepting a non-tenure-track appointment but I didn't have other offers. And my parents, who couldn't imagine turning down a job, argued it was a good way to get my "foot in the door." Alas, I soon learned that was *not* the case.[14]

10 A CITY AND NATION TRANSFORMED

I defended my dissertation in Texas less than two months before starting my first semester on the faculty of Hobart and William Smith Colleges. The Austin I left behind after my defense in 1988 was startlingly different from the city I found when first arriving at the beginning of 1982. Gone was the quaint community with a small-town—and somewhat counterculture—feel, and in its place was a sprawling, high-tech magnet and burgeoning financial center.[1] In all directions, bulldozers and construction cranes, often called the state bird, pursued a seemingly nonstop expansion of single-family housing developments, condominiums, commercial space, and gleaming office towers that increasingly obstructed views of the Texas State Capitol. A rising star even when measured against other Sun Belt cities, Austin blossomed into one of the nation's most vibrant communities during the 1980s. In fact, many Austinites placed their city at the heart of what they called the "Third Coast."

But the upside of the economic expansion occurring in Austin and other Sun Belt cities was only part of the story of America in that decade. While many in Austin benefited from a regional transformation fueled by the rise of a global, information economy and the migration of jobs to the South and West within the United States, certainly not everyone prospered. Throughout the city, residents of affordable apartments were displaced by the rise of luxury condominiums, as I experienced firsthand in 1984. And in rural communities, not just in the South but across the nation, hundreds of thousands of farms went bankrupt in that decade because of high interest rates, while agricultural workers suffered from competition with temporary migrants and undocumented workers.

Meanwhile, the new manufacturing and service jobs of the Sun Belt often paid considerably less than the jobs lost across the Frost Belt where pink slips frequently affected more than a thousand employees at a time. And the economic pain felt by workers who had long considered themselves middle class wasn't limited to residents of the Northeast. My own research found that even communities in the South, especially those with a high concentration of unionized jobs (such as Beaumont, Texas), struggled in the 1980s in the face of global economic developments, technological changes, investor demands for higher profits, and business efforts to achieve union-free workplaces.

Not even workers in America's non-union companies were immune from the adverse effects of technological change and globalization. My father experienced those effects firsthand at Polaroid. That company's gamble on the invention of instant home movies failed, arriving too late to compete with the growing popularity of videotape-based systems. At the same time, Polaroid's share of the consumer photography market declined steadily with the arrival of one-hour film-processing centers and single-use cameras. As the business faltered, the company fired thousands of US workers and relied increasingly on lower-paid workers located elsewhere.

For longtime Polaroid employees, it was gut wrenching. I recall my dad telling me that his coworkers trained Polaroid factory workers from Ireland and that equipment was then stripped from Polaroid plants in Massachusetts and reinstalled overseas where workers earned less. My father didn't lose his machine shop job in the 1980s (that happened in the 1990s), but many Polaroid production workers found themselves out of work in that decade, part of an overall (net) loss of 1.6 million US manufacturing jobs (a decline of over 8 percent) between 1979 and 1989.[2] And the factory shutdowns and offshoring contributed to wage stagnation because that precarious environment dampened the upward movement of wages for those still employed.

A major strength of my graduate program was it allowed me to look closely at the evolution of the American economy in the postwar era—and to think long and hard about policy alternatives. As the postwar social contract eroded and workers across the industrial heartland lost family-supporting jobs, most conventional economists either denied there was a serious problem or argued the solution was to reduce constraints on business decision-making.[3] My institutionalist professors ensured that I understood the standard economic arguments, but also enabled me to explore a different perspective, one grounded in history and the study of the economy's various socioeconomic institutions.[4]

Corporate Restructuring and the Great U-Turn

In the year I completed my graduate work, Bennett Harrison and Barry Bluestone published a book that presented a persuasive argument compatible with my institutionalist viewpoint: *The Great U-Turn: Corporate Restructuring and the Polarization of America*.[5] According to Harrison and Bluestone, America's period of postwar prosperity (which I call the managerial era) broke down in the 1970s because companies responded to heightened international competition by pursuing "corporate restructuring."[6] As companies restructured work and production, career ladders vanished, factories were shuttered, and unions faced intense pressure to make concessions that reversed past advances. At the same time, boardroom attention shifted from productive investment to less risky avenues promising short-term financial gains, such as licensing technology to foreign competitors, selling manufacturing divisions, and buying financial services firms.

That restructuring yielded a "great U-turn" for workers: in the direction of employment instability and financial insecurity. "After improving steadily for a generation, average wages have fallen, family incomes have stagnated, and wages, incomes, and wealth have become increasingly polarized," wrote Harrison and Bluestone in 1988.[7] They also observed that the situation only worsened as public policies focused increasingly on deregulating businesses and fighting inflation with high interest rates. With no new era of sustained and widespread prosperity on the horizon, Harrison and Bluestone concluded it was time for a new policy direction.[8]

Recognizing and Addressing the New Poverty

Social critic and pro-worker activist Michael Harrington also helped me make sense of what was happening in the 1980s. In *The New American Poverty*, published in 1984, Harrington argued that a new type of poverty emerged as our economy evolved in the 1970s and 1980s.[9] That new poverty affected people who found themselves out of work, and often without a pension, after devoting years and even decades of their lives to jobs in auto, steel, and other manufacturing industries.[10]

After many years of working in positions enabling a middle-class lifestyle, those displaced workers often couldn't find another job, while others accepted new work at much lower rates of pay. Entire communities suffered, home values plummeted, and families trying to move away faced the added economic challenge of selling their home in a depressed market. Even worse, Harrington warned that the new poverty was likely to spread: "The same [economic and technological] trends that are now attacking the blue-collar workers in the smokestack industries may well affect white-collar workers, college graduates, and even middle-level managers."[11] And that's exactly what happened.

In addition to shining light on the new poverty, Harrington spelled out what policy steps were needed to address the old and new poverties. Like institutional economists, Harrington understood that government always structures markets and channels economic behavior. In fact, he argued that even the Reagan administration had an industrial policy: it shifted tax breaks and government support toward large corporations and the rich (and away from the poor, workers, and the middle class) in the belief that such a shift would revitalize the private sector and enable it to succeed in the new global economy.[12] Harrington envisioned economic and industrial policies rooted in a different strategic objective: revitalizing the economy from the middle out.[13]

Harrington put full employment at the center of his policy agenda.[14] From his perspective, creating a full employment economy isn't just the best way to eliminate poverty; it's also the best way for the nation to achieve economic prosperity and social well-being. To get there, Harrington called for a combination of aggressive macroeconomic policies, community-driven adjustment strategies (to anticipate and address plant closings and business relocations), and public investments to create jobs for the unemployed and revitalize troubled regions and industries.[15] In other words, instead of energizing the economy by "unleashing" private enterprise, Harrington's pragmatic vision called for direct and constructive action by government, the coordination of public and private action, and community engagement in public-policy development.[16]

More Insecurity Ahead

Harrington recognized that moving public policy in the direction he had in mind would not be easy, but he also saw an opportunity in the growing sense of insecurity he observed around the country. With insecurity spreading, Harrington thought the key to progressive reform was to stress the common problems faced by American families across different social classes. He argued that as existing trends continued it would soon be possible "to talk about a majority movement in the United States to confront these issues."[17]

I was convinced Harrington was correct that Reagan era policies contributed to rising economic insecurity, but I also worried that a widening of the problem might spawn a right-wing populist firestorm rather than the democratic, progressive movement Harrington and I wanted.[18] Yet that made me even more committed to my work, and once my dissertation was successfully defended I turned eagerly to teaching and writing about our economy in my new academic position. What I hadn't counted on was that academia and the labor market were going to teach me a few lessons as well.

PART FOUR

COLLEGES OF THE SENECA

11 REAL-WORLD ECONOMICS

The second half of 1988 began with an air of optimism. Early that summer, I successfully defended my doctoral dissertation and started a faculty appointment at Hobart and William Smith Colleges (HWS), overlooking Seneca Lake in Geneva, New York. That combination signaled my readiness to teach and write about the real-world economy. I was eager to explore economics with students and pursue research that could help policymakers foster broadly shared prosperity.

By mid-December, it seemed I was making good progress. I completed my first courses as an economics professor, receiving favorable reviews from students and praise from colleagues for well-organized courses and a commitment to teaching excellence. I also completed a paper to present at the annual year-end meeting of the nation's economists,[1] and, in a nod to departmental service, agreed to join other HWS economists at the conference to interview applicants for a faculty position in statistics and other quantitative methods.[2]

However, a brief incident I observed prior to an interview soured everything and ended the year on an ominous note. During a break in the appointment schedule, a colleague retrieved applicant files from the event's Job Placement Center and skimmed them in the interview room. After he dismissively placed one file to the side, another colleague asked about that applicant. Looking up only momentarily from the files, the professor replied, "He has a PhD, but no tenure-track job; must be something wrong with him."

My heart sank. No wonder my own applications that fall resulted in very few interviews; I was in a similar position. Departments wanted doctoral students who were about to graduate. Since I had my degree and lacked a tenure-stream post, it apparently suggested that I couldn't be very good. With a simple toss of the hand and a few words, my interview partner revealed how academics tend to perceive people in my situation.[3]

The irony was extraordinary. I came to HWS to teach about economics in the real world, but the academic job market was teaching me.[4] And it seemed I should have known better because the labor field was my specialty. I understood—perhaps better than most economists—that there were "primary" and "secondary" labor markets and that while the *primary* markets offered workers job security, good pay, solid benefits, and opportunities for advancement, the *secondary* markets tended to offer much less.[5] I also knew that workers rarely moved from a secondary market to a primary market, and that secondary markets were notorious for their high rate of job turnover. By taking a non-tenure-track job, I didn't manage to "get my foot in the door"; instead, I fell awkwardly into academia's secondary market, from which there was no easy escape.

There seemed only three ways out, and none was a sure thing. One involved HWS converting my appointment into a tenure-eligible position, most likely through the colleges' creation of a new tenure-track slot in my teaching areas. (This possibility was stressed to me when I was recruited by HWS in early 1988, but the conversion wasn't guaranteed.) Another meant accumulating a record impressive enough for me to beat the odds and find a tenure-eligible post elsewhere. The third called for landing a stable policy-related job in the public sector or at a think tank.

I preferred to stay at HWS because it had very good students, an economics curriculum that made room for alternatives to conventional economics, and a location that met the needs of my family.[6] But it was out of my hands, except for doing all I could to shine in each of the areas that faculty members are judged—teaching, research, and professional service—which seemed necessary for getting out of my predicament by *any* of the paths I envisioned. In fact, there seemed little else I could do, except perhaps also find time for policy-oriented political work in the hope that it would prove useful when searching for policy jobs.

For six years, I worked obsessively on teaching, scholarship, service, and job search. Even time with my family was sacrificed far too often in pursuit of a permanent position. I accomplished quite a bit, even squeezing in time for policy-related political engagement in 1992, but it didn't make a difference. When my contract ran out after the maximum-allowable six years, I ultimately accepted a one-year fellowship at a public-policy think tank located nearly a four-hour drive from my home.

Teaching

I taught *many* courses during my half-dozen years at HWS, not just six courses a year (taught over a trio of 10-week terms) but sixteen entirely different courses over the period of my appointment, amounting to roughly one new course per term.[7] Those courses covered all my graduate fields of specialization: labor economics (including industrial relations), macroeconomics, and public economics. But my primary teaching area was what HWS called "political economy," which probed the foundations of economics (drawing on my graduate work in economic methodology) and examined the full range of schools of economic thought. My courses in that area included an introduction to political economy (required of all economics majors), electives on specific types of economics such as institutional and post-Keynesian economics, and seminars on current issues, which meant moving away from textbooks to construct my own reading lists.[8]

I worked hard to create informative and engaging courses, not only when fashioning course outlines, but also when preparing classroom sessions. Students appreciated that I encouraged critical thinking over rote learning and presented a range of views for them to assess on the way to developing their own conclusions. They also welcomed that I emphasized discussion-based classes and aimed to keep lecturing to a minimum.[9]

It was clear to my students that I was interested in the material I was teaching—and in their academic success. My courses were rigorous, but students consistently reported that they were motivated by my enthusiasm and supportiveness.[10] Students also appreciated that I kept my courses in touch with the real world and important national economic challenges.

A seminar on the debate over US deindustrialization was especially well-received because of its timeliness.[11] It was offered against the backdrop of rising insecurity not only for blue-collar workers, but also for mid-level managers and other white-collar workers. Between 1979 and 1989, more than 1.5 million managers and professionals lost their jobs because of plant closings and permanent layoffs, with more than half of the losses coming between 1985 and 1989, a period of strong economic expansion. Administrative-support workers fared similarly, losing roughly 1.2 million jobs over the same period.[12]

The deindustrialization course also came at a time of much public discussion about whether the transfer of high-value manufacturing to locations overseas threatened not only American economic well-being but also national security.[13] The leading mainstream economists of the time argued it didn't matter whether US-based companies made computer chips or potato chips,[14] but many students hearing about downsizing and the erosion of high-paying jobs in technology-driven sectors (not only from the nightly news but also from family members and friends) weren't so sure.[15]

In addition to teaching my own courses, I also taught two multidisciplinary courses with colleagues from other departments. One, called "The Me Generation," provided a historical look at contemporary American society and values. The other, called "Capitalism and Socialism Revisited," assessed the world's major economic systems after the fall of the Berlin Wall and breakup of the Soviet Union. I teamed with three other professors to jointly develop and deliver each of those senior-year capstone courses; the aim was to illustrate how investigations across academic disciplines are vital to understanding reality.[16]

I taught a variety of HWS courses to demonstrate my versatility and ability to respond to the needs of the department and its students. I was also trying to identify areas in the curriculum (beyond labor and political economy) that had been neglected and that I could claim as my own. That's how I began teaching a course in public economics, which was in the course catalogue but hadn't been taught for years. I turned it into a successful seminar (taught in 1991 and again in 1993) that explored the role of government in the economy, theories of public finance, and ongoing debates over federal spending and deficits. A similarly neglected course in the HWS catalogue examined US economic history.

From teaching my deindustrialization seminar and the two multidisciplinary courses, I recognized that much of what I taught fit within the realm of economic history. HWS had an American economic history course on the books, but nobody could recall the last time it was taught. As an institutionalist, my perspective has always been grounded in history and institutional reality, yet I didn't formally study economic history as a graduate student.[17] So I wrote to Peter McClelland, a world-renowned professor of American economic history at Cornell, and asked to attend his graduate courses on the subject. McClelland responded that he stopped teaching those courses because economics PhD students at the nation's top universities were "no longer interested" in history; but he appreciated my interest, sent me his course syllabi, and encouraged me to work through them on my own.[18] That's exactly what I did, and that exploration led to my revival (in 1992) of the HWS course in economic history.[19]

Research

Consistent with my PhD dissertation and much of my teaching, my research at HWS used insight from institutional and post-Keynesian economics to explore problems affecting workers and the overall economy. One of my first research contributions from that period provides an overview of institutional economics for an academic encyclopedia of the social sciences.[20] In addition to outlining institutionalism's history and essential elements, the article identifies three important topics of institutionalist research during the period 1970–1990: stagflation, business cycles, and the ongoing evolution of national and international economic systems. Another of my early publications, an academic article deriving from part of my dissertation, explores the significance and continuing relevance of research by John R. Commons, whose institutionalism provided a foundation for much of the New Deal and the War on Poverty.[21]

Other publications written while at HWS include a pair of additional journal articles and a trio of book chapters.[22] The articles highlight institutionalist and post-Keynesian contributions to understanding and counteracting business cycles. The chapters, all of which appear in research volumes, explore the following:

- The constructive role of government in the economy;
- The postwar evolution of the US economy and the inability of conventional economists to appreciate that evolution and its consequences; and

- The ability of institutionalism to contribute to an emerging feminist economics and a complementary public policy agenda, including, for example, work restructuring to accommodate paid family leave.[23]

My work on those articles and chapters was encouraged by a small, but dedicated community of institutionalist researchers.[24] Summer conferences, which accompanied two of those book projects, further contributed to the research environment that helped produce my early publications.[25]

I also organized my own collaborative research project before leaving HWS. My inspiration was a book called *The Trend of Economics*, edited in the 1920s by Rexford Tugwell, a Columbia University professor who later became a key member of Franklin D. Roosevelt's "Brains Trust."[26] Tugwell's book explored the possibility of reshaping economic theory to make economics more relevant to society's major problems: *The Trend* was a "manifesto" of professors (mainly institutionalists) critical of conventional economics and open to jointly offering something new.[27]

In a nod to that earlier volume, I named my book *Political Economy for the 21st Century: Contemporary Views on the Trend of Economics*.[28] Written by a mix of emerging scholars and well-known economists including Lester Thurow (who served as dean of the MIT Sloan School), Alice Amsden, and Barry Bluestone, the book rethinks economics from the ground up—from methodology and microeconomics to macroeconomics and the global economy. I selected the topics and wrote the book's introduction; Robert Heilbroner, one of the most distinguished economists of the postwar era, composed the concluding chapter; and Hyman Minsky contributed the foreword.

Published at the start of 1996, *Political Economy for the 21st Century* received a strong pre-release endorsement from John Kenneth Galbraith and was reviewed favorably not only in academic journals, but also in a nationally syndicated newspaper column. In fact, the authors of that column—called the "Instant Economist"—put *Political Economy for the 21st Century* at the top of their list of the year's best economics books, above works by prominent authors including Paul Krugman. They wrote: "For a synopsis of where the economics profession currently stands and where people who are critical of it think it ought to be headed, this book cannot be beat."[29]

Service

Because I hoped my position at HWS would eventually get converted to a tenure-eligible appointment, I followed the advice of the economics faculty and regularly participated in various types of service to the department and its students. That service included writing countless letters of recommendation for students, accepting a full share of the department's student advisees, reviewing baccalaureate essays and honors projects, arranging course offerings as a member of the department's course scheduling committee, and organizing a public event at the end of each term to showcase research by economics majors. I even served on three teams that conducted preliminary interviews for economics faculty positions (two positions in the field of quantitative methods and one in environmental economics)[30]—and, still more ironically, on a tenure-review committee.[31]

I also engaged in other forms of academic and professional service. I organized campus visits and lectures by prominent economists as well as by Hobart alumni Ben Wattenberg (a national political commentator) and Edward ("Ned") Regan (who served as New York State Comptroller).[32] I presented lectures at HWS faculty luncheons and as a guest speaker at Wells College and Cornell University. And I found a variety of ways to contribute to my profession, including refereeing academic manuscripts, composing over a half-dozen book reviews for economics journals, and participating regularly in economics conferences not only as a paper presenter, but also as a panel discussant and session chair.[33]

Political Engagement

In the run-up to the national elections in 1992, I tried to participate in two political campaigns. My first attempt went nowhere but resulted in receiving a Christmas card for several years from the White House. The second attempt kept me active for months.

Beginning in late 1991, immediately after New York Governor Mario Cuomo declined to enter the presidential race, I tried several times to volunteer with Bill Clinton's presidential campaign. My inquiries never got anywhere and were always met with: "What organization do you represent?" or "What union are you with?" In frustration, I wrote a letter to Clinton in Little Rock and expressed my disappointment.

Several weeks later, I received a call from his campaign office and was asked to hold the line. A few moments later, Clinton was on the phone and apologized for my difficulty in attempting to volunteer. It was a remarkable gesture, but his call didn't provide a solution—and I was too surprised by the call to ask. Although I never did participate in the Clinton campaign, I received Christmas cards from Bill and Hillary in the White House throughout his first term.

Several months later, an attempt to become politically active a bit closer to home yielded different results. In summer 1992, I wrote a letter to the Democratic candidate for US Congress in the district that included Geneva. The letter led to an extraordinary four months of constant political engagement. Soon after a short visit with the candidate at HWS, I became issues director for his campaign to represent a district that included 100 cities and towns and stretched 140 miles from the suburbs of Buffalo to the outskirts of Syracuse.

In the state of New York, decennial battles over congressional redistricting usually drag into the summer, and 1992 was no exception. When the dust settled and new maps were approved in early July, Geneva was in the state's newly formed 27th District. The Republican candidate to represent that district was incumbent Representative Bill Paxon, a 38-year-old anti-tax protégé of former Representative Jack Kemp.[34] The Democratic contender was Doug Call, a 52-year-old attorney, Air Force veteran, and former three-time county sheriff from a farming community in the heart of the district.

In my letter to Call, I offered to assist with input on regional and national issues involving workers and the economy.[35] He responded with an enthusiastic phone call, and we met a short time later. The meeting went so well that I was invited to the Call campaign office to participate in his team's regular strategy sessions. After just a couple of meetings, it was clear I was going to coordinate all the campaign's issues, not just advise on the economy.

The Call campaign relied heavily on volunteers, most of whom had limited political experience. Professional Democratic campaign managers and consultants—including the staff of the Democratic Congressional Campaign Committee—didn't think Call had a chance, so they kept their distance from the 27th District race. The professionals understood Doug's team lacked both the time and money necessary to run a solid campaign. After all, Call didn't enter the fray until the district maps were settled,[36] while Paxon—in Congress since 1989—had been relentlessly expanding his campaign war chest since his previous race in 1990.[37]

I understood I was joining a long-shot campaign, but I also believed in the cause and appreciated the opportunity to cut my teeth in politics by playing a large role in a federal race. In the first few weeks, my work involved conducting opposition research, drafting campaign speeches and flyers, and leading a team that crafted position papers.[38] Then the focus shifted to fielding media inquiries, composing press releases, and preparing the candidate for appearances and debates. Before the campaign ended, I also organized events, joined Doug in endorsement meetings with newspaper editorial boards, and substituted for him when scheduling conflicts arose, including appearances as his surrogate at candidate forums.[39]

If newspaper endorsements decided the election, Call would have won by a landslide. Across the district, Doug received praise from editorial boards for his record as "a creative problem-solver" with "fresh ideas" and a "moderate philosophy."[40] In contrast, Paxon was criticized for his "rigid right-wing ideology" and "a voting record of bleak negativism"—including opposition to family leave legislation, stricter environmental protections, and even to increased funding for breast cancer research.[41]

The vote count was a different story. Paxon won 63 percent of the vote. Paxon also spent nearly $800,000, while Call raised and spent well under $100,000.[42] Much of Paxon's campaign spending came in the form of a media blitz during the last few days of the race, which accused Call of supporting all sorts of wild tax increases. The Paxon ads weren't a complete surprise. In fact, it's the reason I warned Doug in our first meeting (and throughout the campaign) to avoid endorsing any proposals that could be seen as involving a tax hike. It turns out that most of the taxes mentioned in those ads were based on the Paxon campaign's interpretation of public comments Doug made in the *mid-1980s*, while the other taxes were funding ideas floated by the American Association of Retired Persons (AARP) to pay for a health care plan Paxon said Doug endorsed at an AARP event. (Doug insisted that he only agreed to review the plan.)[43]

Exploitation Off the Tenure Track

My HWS position was never eligible for tenure. Instead, it was structured as a two-year contract that could be renewed twice, conditional upon satisfactory performance reviews in years two and four.[44] The department's staffing plan in 1988 called for adding a tenure-eligible position in my areas of specialization within a few years, which would have given me a chance to move into that slot. But there were no guarantees. Adding a new position would trigger a national search; I'd still need to apply and hope to be selected for the job. The colleges promised only to provide me with the same comprehensive, third-year performance review that it conducted for all tenure-track faculty, which meant if a tenure-eligible post became available and HWS selected me to fill it, then I could move smoothly toward a tenure review in my sixth year.

In the end, HWS didn't create the new tenure-track slot, and I served the full six years the colleges allowed. The professional and economic uncertainty accompanying my HWS position, and the ultimate inability to secure a tenurable post there, was enormously stressful and unpleasant.[45] Nevertheless, as a young economist I accomplished a lot—especially considering that I was also constantly searching for a permanent job. All three of my performance reviews (years two, three, and four) provided solid evidence of teaching excellence. And even with my commitment to teaching a wide range of courses, I still managed to publish regularly and keep an active agenda of scholarly research.[46] In fact, the performance reviews found my work to be "of very high quality" in all areas—teaching, scholarship, and service.[47]

There's no question that I gave up much family time in my pursuit of economic security during those half-dozen years, but Linda remained extremely supportive and we continued to build a family life as best we could.[48] For example, in the fall of my second year, Linda gave birth to our daughter, Katie, and decided not to return immediately to the workforce.[49] In my third year, the family relocated from Bath to Geneva, where we purchased a modest house not far from campus; we also adopted an adorable puppy from an animal shelter in Ithaca.[50] And in the summer before my fifth year, just as I joined the Call congressional campaign, Linda began a full-time position with the New York State Department of Health.[51]

The colleges' decision not to add a new tenure-track position came, ironically, about a month after my third-year performance review received unanimous approval from the economics department.[52] At the same time, the administration allowed the department to fill an existing tenure-eligible position in my teaching fields. That existing position became available because the department's other labor economist had just been denied tenure, and on the surface that seemed to offer one last chance for me to remain at HWS.[53] But the final nail in the coffin was that the administration allowed the position to be filled on the condition that the appointment increased faculty diversity.

The news came as a gut punch. I had a terrific performance record at the colleges, and the right expertise for the new opening, but it didn't matter. The administration's notion of greater faculty diversity did not extend to first-generation college graduates, and I was excluded from consideration for the position.[54]

A few months later, I crossed paths with an HWS administrator while walking with my daughter on campus. I expressed concern that both my career and family were hurt by my inability to interview for the open position, especially since the fields listed in the HWS job advertisement matched my main areas of teaching and research.[55] The administrator listened to what I had to say, and then replied, "Charlie Whalen: White boys have networks. Get yourself into a network."[56]

I knew I wasn't alone in my employment struggles; but that didn't make the situation any less troubling. While I was being passed over at HWS and becoming increasingly anxious about finding a job elsewhere, an article published by the American Association of University Professors (AAUP) reported that as much as one-third of all college instruction was delivered by faculty not on the tenure track, including more than 10 percent of full-time faculty. The article, "Exploitation or Equity Off the Tenure Track?" also summarized the AAUP's position, which certainly made sense to me: "There should be only two kinds of positions, probationary and continuous."[57] The administrators at HWS might not have intended their arrangement as exploitation, but by the end it surely felt like exploitation to me.[58]

And, alas, it turned out that my next job also came with a short-term contract.

12 THE SIX-YEAR SEARCH—INCLUDING A HUGE NEAR MISS

It's often said that searching for a job is itself a job. I certainly spent countless hours looking for work while at HWS. And my six-year search (1988–1994) was especially challenging because throughout that period I felt the need to shine at the colleges: It seemed that outstanding performance was the only way I might convince either HWS to retain me or another institution to hire me. It was also a difficult time because Linda and I wanted a community to call home, a place where we could settle down and raise a family. It wasn't easy for Linda to host students at the house for dinner, or help me organize a public event on campus, and then see me work on job applications into the wee hours; but that was our life.[1]

Beating the Bushes

Just as I did when completing my graduate work, I searched for jobs in the fields of economics and industrial relations as well as in related disciplines such as public policy.[2] It wasn't hard to get acquainted with the institutionalists, post-Keynesians, and industrial-relations professors; their academic communities were small and I participated actively in the relevant professional associations even in graduate school. But there were also few job openings each year in those fields—and dissertation advisers had their own doctoral students to assist.

Through my scholarly work, I managed to earn the admiration and support of several established scholars. In those days before email, I often received letters from professors who met me at conferences and wrote that they considered me among the most promising institutionalists of my generation. However, many of the letters also reported with regret that those professors didn't have a way to help in an era with few positions, strong resistance to non-mainstream economics,[3] and rising institutional pressure to hire women and minorities.[4] Still, some professors tried to help, not only by writing formal letters of recommendation, but sometimes also by phoning colleagues to spread the word about my work and availability.[5]

My own dissertation adviser, Ray Marshall, was always willing to help with a glowing letter of reference, yet it seems he also couldn't help much within academia.[6] Nevertheless, Marshall did forward my name to Sheldon Friedman, research director of the United Auto Workers (UAW), who called me in late 1989 to report that his union wanted to hire someone to calculate the costs of collective bargaining proposals. I appreciated the offer, but it didn't seem like the right job for me, especially while there was still the chance of a permanent post at HWS. Had the call been from the AFL-CIO in Washington, DC, to contribute to the activities and publications of its Committee on the Evolution of Work (which published reports on the changing nature of work and employment relations) it would have been a perfect fit with my background and interests. But the UAW position in Detroit was quite different.

We're Going to Washington!—Oh, Never Mind

A more intriguing call came from Professor Marshall's secretary shortly after Bill Clinton won the 1992 presidential election. "Send me your résumé, right away," said Cheryl McVay. "I'm getting together a package for Little Rock. We're going to Washington!" It turns out that Marshall was a key Clinton campaign adviser and the president-elect planned to appoint him to serve again as Secretary of Labor. I knew that some of Marshall's doctoral students in the 1970s held policy positions at the Labor Department during his first appointment, so I immediately sent my résumé to his secretary. Then there was nothing but silence. I learned later that Senator Lloyd Bentsen surprised Clinton by asking to serve as Treasury Secretary (a position originally earmarked for Robert Rubin) and accommodating Bentsen triggered a reshuffling of the planned top-level appointments, which left Marshall in Austin.[7]

Over the course of my time at the colleges, I managed to receive about one on-campus job interview per year on the US academic job market. Most of the interviews were at institutions comparable to HWS, and in each case I was chosen from hundreds of applicants to interview as one of three or four finalists. However, none led to a solid offer.[8] Faculty hiring often brought to the surface intradepartmental squabbles, and my non-mainstream approach always had both supporters and staunch opponents. In fact, in one case the factions were so deadlocked that the institution made no appointment.

When my HWS appointment expired, I accepted a one-year fellowship as a resident scholar at the Jerome Levy Economics Institute of Bard College, a nonpartisan public-policy think tank in New York's Hudson Valley. Although Bard College was about a four-hour drive from my home, I was familiar with the Levy

Institute and its people, having attended a few of its weekend conferences (which featured some of the nation's leading economists and policymakers) as well as a summer workshop organized by Hyman Minsky, who took up residence there as a Distinguished Scholar in 1990. Minsky became a mentor of mine in the late 1980s (following the hugely successful conference session I organized on his work at an annual meeting of US economists) and encouraged me to apply for a Levy Institute fellowship at the start of his residency.[9] I applied during the final year of my HWS contract, and joined Minsky and his colleagues at the institute in August 1994.[10]

13 PERSEVERANCE AND ACCOMPLISHMENTS ARE NOT ENOUGH

When I began teaching at HWS, I was cheerful, optimistic, and looked so young that clerks at the circulation desk of the campus library often stamped my borrowed books with the student lending period instead of the much longer period for faculty members. By the end of my contract, I still looked quite young and tried to remain upbeat, but it was hard to deny the HWS experience was dispiriting.[1] Still, I'd been discounted and dismissed before, and I refused to be ground down by callous people and tough circumstances.[2]

I learned long before arriving at HWS that it's often possible to eventually prevail over detractors through determination and perseverance. That even proved true on occasion at HWS. For example, when Robert Heilbroner, one of the nation's most prominent economists, came to visit the colleges, an economics professor told the organizer of the visit that I wasn't worthy of a meeting with Heilbroner (which I can't imagine happening had I been in a tenurable position). But it turns out that Heilbroner, a longtime supporter of institutional economics, met me a short time later under other circumstances and became a friend and mentor; he even contributed the key concluding chapter to my 1996 book. In fact, when Heilbroner saw me at a luncheon organized to recognize him with a distinguished career award in early 1994, he insisted that I join him at the head table.[3]

But the HWS experience also taught that persistence—indeed, even a record of accomplishment—is not enough to overcome all obstacles. Starting out as a non-tenure-track faculty member relegated me to the secondary labor market, which offered no easy way out. In fact, after six years the way out seemed more elusive than ever. Looking back after all these years, the irony remains astounding: I went into economics to fight for greater economic security for working families such as the one that raised me, but from the very start of my career I was mired in a constant uphill battle for economic security for my own young family.

While I struggled, I met several professors from top-ranked universities who told me they never experienced the stress of a job search because their doctoral advisers arranged their job interviews and paved the way for their appointments. Those may have been exceptional cases (although it was something I heard quite a few times), yet they underscore a reality that's true even outside top-tier institutions: work ethic, training, and early career achievement are not enough to enable a young person to avoid my situation. It also requires professional development guidance and strong job-market advocates, especially when positions are scarce.[4] Maybe the blue-collar workers and family members of my youth had it right all along: "It's not *what* you know (or even what you do); it's *who* you know that counts."[5]

Sponsored Mobility and Path Dependence

To some extent, then, the HWS administrator who advised me to "get into a network," had the right idea. She was admitting that the academic world was no different than the corporate world that my fellow Texas alumnus Bill Dugger described in his book *Corporate Hegemony*. According to Dugger, people don't get jobs and advance based on talent; that notion, which he describes as "contest mobility," is a myth. Instead, the career game is driven by "sponsored mobility." As Dugger writes, when an attractive position becomes available in the corporate world, "the hopefuls draw on their networks to 'put in the fix' in their favor."[6]

Looked at from Dugger's perspective, I was an academic "hopeful" without any solid employment networks or weighty career mentors—at best, my networks and mentors could assist with my scholarship, not my career. Minsky probably had some influence on my selection as a Levy Institute fellow, but even that influence wasn't enough to get the institute to offer me a career-building position. Dugger seemed to be writing precisely about my insurmountable job-market challenges when he pointed out that people from well-connected backgrounds learn early that the world is driven by sponsored mobility, while "hopefuls from less-enriching backgrounds usually have to learn this lesson the hard way."[7] But it's even worse than that: When you've learned the lesson, there's still not much that can be done; those of us not born into well-connected networks can do very little to make our way in.

Economists have a term that further explains why it's nearly impossible to climb out of the labor market of dead-end jobs once you've landed there. The concept of "path dependence" stresses that the economic opportunities and outcomes of today and tomorrow depend heavily on previous events. Applied to the job market, it means that working in the insecure, secondary labor market casts a long shadow: current and future job opportunities and career paths will always be constrained by that experience.[8] The career ladder of tomorrow is forever shaped by what happened in the past.

Here's just one example of how my HWS experience cast a long shadow. In early 2000, I interviewed at a university in Rochester for an endowed faculty position with an emphasis on public policy research. At the time, I was employed at Cornell University, where I worked with regional policymakers, and had been away from HWS for nearly six years. I also had an extensive record of national policy research from my time at the Levy Institute (including congressional testimony) and served as a Fulbright Scholar in China. Nevertheless, the chair of the selection committee told me during my campus visit that a university colleague who had previously taught at HWS expressed disapproval upon learning I was a finalist for the position: "Why on earth would you hire him? He was just a temp with us at HWS. He couldn't even get a tenure-track job." It didn't come as a surprise to learn the position was offered to someone else.

"You Already Have Students"

As I look back, some satisfaction comes from knowing I was ahead of the crowd with much of my teaching and research. That was true of my attention to rising worker insecurity and economic polarization, emphasis on the economic and national security threats associated with erosion of the US industrial base, and attempts to highlight the value of strategic trade and industrial policies (as well as a constructive role for government overall). Also ahead of the crowd were my explorations of economic history (which has become a hot subject in academia over the past couple of decades), the intersection of institutionalist and post-Keynesian traditions, and even the feminist possibilities of work restructuring to accommodate the introduction of paid family leave policies.[9] I think this track record validates my unconventional approach to economics; what's allowed me to be ahead of the curve so often is that my economics has always been rooted in the practical research of institutionalists and in investigations of real-world work and employment relations.

I also take pride in the positive feedback I received on my teaching from HWS faculty and students. For example, in my third-year performance review an economics professor wrote that my courses showed "tremendous breadth of knowledge and preparation, and care in guiding students through the material covered." Another professor wrote that my courses were "well-structured, rigorous, and interesting."[10] In addition, the teaching portfolio I compiled at the end of my contract shows that students (in anonymous end-of-term course evaluations) consistently complimented me for presenting informative material, encouraging student participation, and inspiring academic success.[11] Even more rewarding are the comments in letters I received from students over the years: Many wrote to report that I prepared them well for graduate school—and some even included a news article or recommended a book that related to my courses.[12]

I can even take satisfaction from knowing that my students stood up for me. As my final semester at HWS neared its end, forty economics majors wrote to the top administrators of the colleges and asked them to find a way to keep me on the faculty. After receiving no reply, the students published their letter in the colleges' newspaper. In part, they wrote: "Professor Whalen has provided a positive influence towards the institution, the students, and the community surrounding the campus…. It is indeed sad to learn that the institution has no room for a professor who is genuinely liked and appreciated by the whole community."[13]

A week later, the campus paper published a response in which I thanked all my students. I wrote: "I hope my courses have not merely provided valuable information but also encouraged independent and critical thinking. I will miss teaching but will miss equally the opportunity to learn from my students each week. Our work has truly involved mutual exploration."[14] I also wrote that leaving the campus community was difficult for my family, observing that our ties to HWS over the preceding six years "always extended beyond the classroom." In addition, I shared the response of my young daughter to news that I was interviewing for a faculty post elsewhere, "But daddy, you already have students!" That was painful to hear in 1994, and it remains painful to recall today.

As my career derailed and the family struggled to move forward, Linda's support kept everything together. I've always had tenacity, but she's always been extraordinarily sensible—and strong. Hers is a quiet strength, perhaps best characterized as "unwavering resilience, boundless empathy, abundant kindness, and persistent optimism."[15] Unfortunately, all of that would be tested further as things became more difficult over the next few years.

PART FIVE

HUDSON VALLEY

14 BUDGET SIDESHOWS AND THE SILENT DEPRESSION

In August 1994, I moved from Hobart and William Smith Colleges (HWS) to Blithewood Mansion on the campus of Bard College. Located in Annandale-on-Hudson, 90 miles north of New York City, Blithewood has been home to the Levy Economics Institute since 1987, the year after it was founded with financial support from Bard trustee Leon Levy. A pioneer in the creation and management of mutual funds and hedge funds, Levy founded the institute to honor his father, Jerome Levy, an economist and business executive who emphasized the role of profits in influencing the direction of the economy.

Blithewood provided an ideal workplace. Situated at the western edge of Bard's campus, on a bluff overlooking the Hudson River, it's a beautifully restored turn-of-the-century Georgian-style manor. Outside, it features an Italianate walled garden at the bluff's edge, and the Catskill Mountains in the background. Inside, the first floor contains conference rooms, including one used in the early 1990s to film several segments of William F. Buckley's public affairs television show *Firing Line*, and the second floor includes a suite of offices and a library. Throughout the 1990s, the institute's lectures, workshops, and conferences featured leading academics and practitioners in the fields of economics and public policy, including Lawrence Summers, Janet Yellen, and Senator William Proxmire. During my stay at Levy, the second floor housed Hyman Minsky and other researchers, about half of whom held a 12-month fellowship (usually while on sabbatical from their home academic institution). My office was adjacent to the one used by Minsky.

I came to the Levy Institute to explore sensible directions for US tax and spending policies at a time when much attention in Washington centered on the persistence of federal budget deficits and the increasing national debt. Leaders in both major political parties considered deficits a mounting problem and Ross

Perot made containing deficit spending a centerpiece of his third-party run for president in 1992.[1] Against that backdrop, I planned to explore two policy ideas: biennial (two-year) federal budgeting and federal capital budgeting.

In many respects, my position was a dream job. I had no teaching responsibilities, just a research agenda devoted to analyzing the US economy and offering constructive public policy suggestions—and the institute offered a stimulating intellectual environment in which to carry it out. The research was also self-directed, which, as is always the case with academic work, meant an opportunity to pursue new directions as conditions changed.

As it turned out, conditions did change dramatically in November 1994, when the Republican Party took control of the House of Representatives. The first item in the Republicans' "Contract with America" was a proposed balanced budget amendment to the US Constitution. That amendment would have severely constrained the ability of the US government to respond to economic downturns. It would have also eliminated any chance of capital budgeting. With the support of the institute, I shifted my attention to the balanced budget amendment following the election, which kept me busy for most of the rest of the fellowship year and led the institute director, Dimitri Papadimitriou, to approve my reappointment for another year beginning in August 1995.

In my second year at the institute, I returned to my original research topics as well as to an examination of rising worker insecurity in the United States, a subject that served as the starting point for my doctoral dissertation and received attention in several of my HWS courses. Working on the budget amendment and those other topics at the institute and shortly thereafter, I produced over a dozen publications, including Levy Institute reports, newspaper op-eds, essays for public affairs magazines, and even testimony for congressional hearings. There were also academic articles, including an analysis coauthored with Minsky on the evolution of the US economy after the Second World War, a process of transformation leading to what Minsky described as "money manager capitalism."

Toward the end of my second year, Papadimitriou offered another one-year extension of my contract, but the temporary arrangement couldn't be sustained. Blithewood might have been an ideal workplace, and the work was particularly well suited to my interests and abilities, but without the predictability and health and retirement benefits of a continuous position, it wasn't sensible for my wife and daughter to move to the Hudson Valley.[2] By late spring 1996, my resident scholar arrangement, which involved living in a basement apartment in Rhinebeck during the week and driving four hours each way between the institute and Geneva on weekends, had already gone on for too long. When the institute wasn't willing to replace my annual stipend with an ongoing appointment at the end of that second year, it was clear I'd reached the end of the line.

Balanced Budget Amendment

Throughout the post-Second World War era, believers in the need for federal "fiscal discipline" have often called for a constitutional amendment to balance the budget of the US government on an annual basis. Under such an amendment, the amount of each year's federal spending could not exceed that year's tax revenues, meaning the end of budget deficits and the gradual elimination of federal debt. Interest in a balanced budget requirement intensified as the nation's deficits and public debt increased markedly in the 1970s and 1980s.[3] Serious but unsuccessful votes to secure congressional approval for such an amendment occurred in 1986, 1990, and 1992.

In the run-up to the 1994 midterm elections, Republicans in the House of Representatives placed the balanced budget amendment at the top of their list of priorities as they campaigned to wrest control of the House from Democrats. According to the GOP's Contract with America, that amendment would be the first item introduced and among the first voted on during the new congressional session in January 1995. By the end of election night on November 8, 1994, it was clear the Republicans had retaken the House—and the Senate.

The morning after the midterms, I expressed interest in preparing a case against the budget amendment and said I'd have a report in December that could be distributed when legislators convened in January.[4] The leadership of the Levy Institute had no objection. In fact, S Jay Levy, chairman of the institute's Board of Governors, argued it was the only policy issue he could imagine on which the Levy Institute deserved to take an official position.

By mid-December, I completed a report that was initially circulated internally at the Levy Institute. At the start of January, that report was published and distributed widely in the institute's Working Papers series.[5] A short summary of my argument ran as a letter to the editor in *The New York Times* on December 22, 1994—and another ran as an op-ed essay in *USA Today* on January 13, 1995.[6] At the same time, I circulated a letter of opposition to the budget amendment among economists and policy experts, inviting them to add their names to my call for Congress to reject the proposal.[7]

My case against the balanced budget amendment had three parts. I debunked the widely held misconception that the amendment would merely require Congress to "live under the same budget restraints as families and businesses." I also argued that the amendment would be both an economic and political toxin, not the tonic its proponents claimed.

In countering the notion that a balanced-budget rule would force the federal government to behave like households and corporations, I observed that nearly all households borrow for long-term investments. If households operated under the same constraints as the proposed constitutional amendment, they would need to pay cash for cars, homes, and higher education. If companies acted within those constraints, they couldn't borrow when investing in equipment or constructing a new plant. Even states and localities have capital budgets that allow borrowing for major public investments, which the amendment would rule out for the US government.

The key economic danger of a balanced budget amendment is it would severely limit the ability of the federal government to prevent mild economic downturns from developing into severe recessions. In fact, a balanced budget amendment would require the government to increase taxes or cut its spending to accommodate the upsurge in government outlays that normally occurs in an economic slump (such as payment of unemployment benefits to laid-off workers). Such fiscal belt-tightening would only deepen the downturn, just as following the balanced-budget principle added to the severity of the Great Depression. That economic crisis didn't begin to stabilize until the federal government ran deficits to finance the New Deal.[8] If any sort of balanced budget made sense, it would be—as Minsky often stressed—a balance achieved over the course of the entire business cycle, not on an annual basis.[9]

The chief political danger of such an amendment is it would lead to greater citizen frustration with federal policymaking, further eroding confidence in our political institutions. That's because such an amendment is merely a statement of intention; it doesn't produce the political will or legislative pathway necessary to make balanced budgets a reality. Both the experience of state governments and federal budgeting under the Gramm-Rudman Balanced Budget Act of 1985 showed that binding budget constraints often lead to spending evasions and other unsound practices, including deferred maintenance of infrastructure and public facilities, increased use of government mandates (imposed on the private sector or on other levels of government), and budget gimmickry such as selling government assets and then leasing them back.

On January 10, 1995, I submitted a written statement on the balanced budget amendment to the staff responsible for hearings by the Subcommittee on the Constitution of the House Judiciary Committee.[10] Along with that statement, I delivered not only a copy of my Levy Institute report, but also the letter of opposition to the amendment that I circulated within the academic community. The letter had 220 signatories, including five Nobel winners in economics, several former presidents of the American Economic Association and the American Political Science Association, and former US Representative Barbara Jordan.

Two weeks later, the House of Representatives passed the budget amendment proposal, but in early March the amendment failed in the Senate by a single vote.[11] However, Senate Majority Leader Bob Dole stated his intention to bring the matter before the Senate again prior to the 1996 elections, so I prepared an updated version of my report after the March vote. A short time later, the Levy Institute published it as a Public Policy Brief titled "Assessing the Constitutional Route to Federal Budget Balance."[12] I also kept abreast of the subject throughout the year and wrote essays on related federal budget issues for several newspapers and magazines, including *Los Angeles Times*, *Time*, and *Challenge*, a bimonthly popular among economic policy analysts.[13]

My work on the budget amendment quickly attracted the attention of news talk radio producers and progressive groups. I appeared as a guest on several radio shows with large audiences (including stations in New York City, Phoenix, and Dallas); composed a pair of articles on deficits and sensible budget directions for the progressive *Social Policy* magazine; and delivered a presentation on budget policy at the annual meeting of a national association of social workers.[14] That work continued to receive attention into 1996, when one of my articles spelling out a case against the balanced budget amendment was reprinted twice: in a college-level textbook of readings in American government, and a guide to national issues for high-school students and teachers.

Biennial and Capital Budgeting

I began my second year at the Levy Institute (1995–1996) by returning to research on biennial budgeting and capital budgeting. Each of those proposed innovations offered an opportunity to improve the effectiveness of federal policies.

Efficiency-oriented legislators and conservatives tended to favor biennial budgeting, while liberals and progressives most often supported capital budgeting. Proponents of "good government" measures liked the biennial budgeting proposal because it would set federal appropriations just once every two years, reserving the second year of each congressional term for greater attention to agency implementation and congressional oversight of existing policies (which could later lead to legislative tweaks or even entirely new policies). Progressive leaders favored capital budgeting because it would distinguish between public investments and government operating expenses, opening the door to the possibility of a different budgetary treatment for each, which, in turn, might better enable legislators to make vital investments.

Biennial Budgeting

In the mid-1990s, two-year budgeting received support from several major government leaders. Among them were Leon Panetta, Alice Rivlin, and Pete Domenici.[15] Two-year budgeting was also proposed in 1993 by the National Performance Review, a panel created by President Bill Clinton and led by Vice

President Al Gore with the aim of making the federal government "work better, cost less, and get results Americans care about."[16]

In 1995, I resumed research on biennial budgeting by exploring the theory and history of the budget period. I found that annual budgeting is a customary practice, with roots in agricultural cycles, not a procedure based on fiscal theory. I also learned that although the federal government has always used annual budgeting, states began trending toward two-year legislative sessions and budget cycles in the mid-nineteenth century (to rein in state legislatures), and that by 1940 only four states had annual sessions and budgets. Since then, the pendulum has changed direction a couple of times: toward annual budgeting after the Second World War (in response to demands for greater government action on many issues) and back in the biennial direction in the 1980s (as states sought to focus more attention on program reviews and long-range policy goals). In the mid-1990s, twenty states made use of biennial budget and appropriations cycles, thirteen of which had annual legislative sessions.

In addition to examining trends on the budget period, I reviewed the history of federal biennial-budgeting proposals and the arguments of supporters and opponents. But how could those arguments be evaluated? Since states provide natural "laboratories of democracy," I decided to look to the states for lessons. It was my good fortune to learn that the New Jersey budget office had just completed and released the findings of a survey of budget officers in the twenty states with two-year budgets.[17]

Combining the historical record, arguments for and against two-year budgets, and my assessment of those arguments based on results from the survey of state budget officers, I produced a working paper for the Levy Institute in late 1995 and an academic article released months later in *Policy Studies Review*.[18] My research concluded that federal biennial budgeting would likely have two main effects: (1) it would enable legislators to focus more attention on oversight of government programs (leading to increased program effectiveness) and to better consider the long-term consequences of fiscal decisions; and (2) it would promote economic stability by reducing policy uncertainty. Between 1997 and 2000, federal lawmakers called on me to use that institute research as a foundation for testimony before three congressional committees (two Senate committees and a House committee).[19]

Capital Budgeting

At the start of 1996, the focus of my institute work shifted from biennial budgeting to capital budgeting. In the 1980s, economists often focused on two types of deficits, the federal budget deficit and national trade deficit. But in the early 1990s, a shortfall of investment by the public sector, especially infrastructure investment, was widely considered America's "third deficit."[20]

According to research by economist David Aschauer (published in 1990), the amount of public investment in the United States in the 1980s was just one-fourth that of the investments in the 1950s and 1960s. Aschauer also found that the investment slowdown significantly weakened US productivity growth and other measures of economic performance.[21] Capital budgeting, which draws a distinction between public investment and other public spending in the budget framework, offered one way to highlight the investment shortfall and make it easier to bolster the nation's commitment to its long-term future. Although President Clinton didn't explicitly call for capital budgeting, his 1992 campaign stressed the need for an investment-oriented agenda for the federal government.

During my fellowship period, the leadership of the Levy Institute expressed interest in using my research as the starting point for creating and analyzing an in-house framework for the nation's federal capital budget. The data needed to construct such a budget was available in a federal document published annually by the Office of Management and Budget (under the dry-as-dust title *Analytical Perspectives*), but the first step was to determine what should be defined as a capital expenditure in that type of budget. I was sympathetic to the argument that capital budgeting should avoid favoring investments in tangibles such as roads and bridges over valuable intangibles such as education, job training, and research and development (after all, human resource policies were what first attracted me to economics). However, the institute's leaders and I agreed it would be best to begin by defining a capital budget narrowly and using it as a stepping-stone toward a more comprehensive budget for federal investment.

My research on capital budgeting led to a paper I submitted to the institute in April 1996, which proposed a narrow definition of public capital expenditures. The paper, "Paving the Way for a Sensible Discussion of Federal Capital Budgeting," drew on policymaking efforts within states and other nations to address not only the matter of tangibles versus intangibles, but also in-the-weeds details such as whether capital budgets should include only assets that require very large expenditures, have a long duration of expected usefulness, and fall under direct control of the federal government (since federal funds often pay for state and local projects).[22] Ned Regan, a Levy Institute Distinguished Fellow and former Comptroller of New York State, reviewed the paper and approved of its focus on the definition and scope of such expenditures: "You're starting the discussion with exactly the right topic," he wrote.[23]

Silent Depression

In my second year at the Levy Institute, I also returned to the subject of rising economic insecurity among American workers, an issue that inspired me to become an economist and received attention in both my research and teaching prior to coming to Bard. In large part, I resumed work on that subject in response to both a presentation at the Levy Institute by Wynne Godley, a UK economist who spent part of each year at Blithewood as a Distinguished Scholar, and discussions with Minsky about the changing US economy. But I also resumed research on worker insecurity out of frustration with the budget sideshows that passed for policy deliberations in the nation's capital. In addition to the calls for a balanced budget amendment, those sideshows included not only a budget stalemate that led to two government shutdowns in late 1995 (the latter of which lasted three weeks and continued into early 1996), but also GOP demands for a "dynamic scoring" of the effects of tax cuts on federal revenue—a derivative of Reagan-era "supply side" economics that former Congressional Budget Office director Rivlin called "nonsense" and "a license to bust the budget."[24]

At a Levy Institute workshop in 1995, Godley looked beyond the expanding economy and downward-creeping jobless rate and presented striking details on the stagnation of average wages in the United States between the 1970s and the 1990s.[25] His findings were not new: the Economic Policy Institute (EPI) highlighted the same trend in annual reports on *The State of Working America*; and institutionalist Wallace Peterson described the trend as "a quarter-century of wage squeeze and middle-class decline," placing it at the heart of his 1994 book, *Silent Depression*.[26] Inspired by Godley's presentation and those related publications, I wrote a paper I titled "The Anxious Society: Middle-Class Insecurity and the Crisis of the American Dream," published in October 1995 as part of the bimonthly Levy Institute *Report*.[27]

The "Anxious Society" essay struck a chord with many readers: newspaper reporters cited the paper and various organizations invited me to write and speak on the subject.[28] I composed related articles for a variety of publications including the *Durell Journal of Money and Banking*, *The Humanist*, *Nebraska Report* (published bimonthly by Nebraskans for Peace), and *Bard Journal of Social Sciences*.[29] I also took the train from Annandale to New York City to make presentations at events sponsored by groups including the Broadway Democrats and the National Jobs for All Coalition.[30]

Discussions with Minsky at the Levy Institute also contributed to my return to the subject of economic insecurity. In fact, Minsky's work at the time provided a framework for understanding the problem. Although he was best known for explaining financial crises, Minsky's research in the 1990s focused on the postwar transition of the US economy from what he termed *managerial* capitalism, dominated by leaders of the country's largest corporations, to *money manager* capitalism, dominated by institutional investors who demand that corporations focus relentlessly on short-term profits and stock-market values. Using Minsky's framework, it was possible to show that emergence of money manager capitalism was accompanied not only by growing financial instability, but also by corporate downsizing, offshoring of production, rising worker insecurity, and widening economic inequality.[31] In other words, Minsky offered an approach that explained Peterson's "silent depression" as part of the rise of a new, finance-driven form of capitalism and the accompanying erosion of the US industrial base.

During my time at the Levy Institute, I organized several sessions at professional conferences. Two examined rising economic insecurity and featured presentations by prominent economists including Lester Thurow, Larry Mishel (then research director at EPI), and Heidi Hartmann (founder of the Institute for Women's Policy Research). Another commemorated the 50th anniversary of the Employment Act of 1946, which made the federal government responsible for minimizing unemployment. Hy Minsky and James Tobin, a Nobel winner in economics, were among those agreeing to participate in the Employment Act session.[32] Then Minsky surprised me by suggesting that we collaborate on a paper for the session.

My collaboration with Minsky led to "Economic Insecurity and the Institutional Prerequisites for Successful Capitalism," published as the lead article in the *Journal of Post Keynesian Economics* in late 1996.[33] It was among the first academic articles to discuss Minsky's notion of money manager capitalism, and neatly interwove his perspective with my dozen or so years of research on deindustrialization and economic insecurity.[34]

The Age of Anxiety

In September 1996, I integrated Minsky's insight about the managed-money economy into an article I wrote as the lead essay for a news magazine feature on "What's Killing the American Dream?" The other contributors were Labor Secretary Robert Reich, Senator Edward Kennedy (D-Massachusetts), and Senator Paul Coverdell (R-Georgia). My article for that feature, "The Age of Anxiety," endures as a snapshot of challenges to the American Dream in the mid-1990s.[35]

The article spotlights several alarming trends and findings involving the US labor market. Drawing on government data and research from several sources, I report on trends involving jobs, wages and benefits, and the distribution of income. The trends include:

- *Relentless downsizing:* America's largest 100 companies cut employment by 22 percent (on net) between 1978 and 1995.[36]
- *Increasing job loss among professional and managerial workers:* In the early 1990s, professional and managerial job cuts accounted for about one in every four layoffs, roughly double their share in the early 1980s.[37]

- *Costly unemployment:* Wages for workers who lost their jobs in the early 1990s dropped an average of 23 percent when they regained full-time employment.[38]
- *Explosive growth in nonstandard work arrangements:* Research covering the period 1970–1990 found that temporary jobs increased 210 percent; part-time employment by workers seeking full-time jobs rose 121 percent; and overall US employment grew by less than 54 percent.[39]
- *Wage stagnation:* After adjusting for inflation, average hourly wages in 1995 were *lower* than in 1965. Although many households responded to the wage trend by working more hours (including moonlighting) and sending more family members to work, real median family income still fell more than five percent between 1989 and 1994.[40]
- *Erosion of worker benefits:* Consistent with reports on employer cutbacks to healthcare, retirement, paid leave, and other benefits, the rate of annual growth in total compensation (wages plus benefits) trended downward throughout the 1980s and into the mid-1990s.[41]
- *Rising income inequality:* In the early postwar era, the inflation-adjusted income for most American families rose about 2.5 percent each year, but income became more unequally distributed after 1973. Families in the bottom 40 percent of the income distribution saw their income fall; families in the next 40 percent saw their income stagnate; and families in the top 20 percent of the distribution saw meaningful gains. The gap between ordinary workers and corporate chief executives (CEOs) grew especially wide: In the mid-1970s, CEOs received forty-one times the pay of the average worker; by the mid-1990s, the multiple increased to 225.[42]

The article then links growing worker insecurity to the undoing of managerial capitalism and the rise of an economy driven by institutional investors. Throughout the postwar era, steady growth in the share of corporate stocks, bonds, and other financial assets held by managed-money funds (including pension funds, mutual funds, bank trust funds, and private equity funds) gave fund managers control over the bulk of those assets by the early 1990s.[43] Because the single-minded focus of those managers encouraged corporate executives to concentrate on the short term, corporations diverted their attention from long-term investments (including investments in workers) and instead pursued practices including downsizing, outsourcing, mergers, acquisitions, corporate breakups, leveraged buyouts, and stock buybacks—whatever promised to offer the biggest and quickest boost to managed-money portfolios.

Arguing that money manager capitalism and its consequences for the American Dream are unsustainable, I close the article by offering several public policy lessons we could learn from our global competitors. They include using public investments to fashion a forward-looking industrial strategy and reforming the tax system to reward corporations for upgrading workers' skills. The policy agenda I crafted overlapped considerably with those outlined in the articles by Reich and Kennedy.[44]

Writing with Minsky and contributing work that sat comfortably alongside essays by Reich, Kennedy, and Coverdell created the impression that my career was taking off in 1996. Instead, in the absence of a continuing position at the institute or a conventional faculty post elsewhere, that career was on the verge of hurtling back to earth.

15 END OF THE LINE

From the start, Linda and I knew the Levy Institute position would be a challenge for the family. But we made the sacrifice, even when the position was extended for a second year, because I had no other job prospects after my HWS contract ended. While there was never a promise that something permanent would materialize at Levy, emergence of an ongoing institute appointment would not have been unprecedented, and it didn't hurt to have Minsky in my corner. However, at the end of two years the situation was no different than in 1994; I again couldn't parlay my record of accomplishment into an appointment as a professor or policy researcher at Bard or elsewhere.

With no other options on the table in mid-1996 (despite submitting countless job applications and letters of inquiry), I took a position as a workplace educator with the Division of Extension and Public Service at Cornell ILR (ILR Extension). Located in Buffalo, not Ithaca, that extension faculty position was a two-hour drive from my home and geared toward someone with a master's degree, not a doctorate—while I already had eight years of post-PhD experience. Despite all the sacrifices, relentless effort, and accomplishments, my academic career seemed in a shambles; the moonshot project of my childhood seemed to have ended with a hard landing.

"Academic Administrators Are Sheep"

One might have thought my career was beginning to take off in the wake of those productive two years at the Levy Institute. After all, I had a growing list of publications and often fielded calls from news reporters on the federal budget and other economic matters.[1] Instead, in many ways it was the end of the line, and it would take a few years of continued struggling to get things somewhat back on track.

I intended to do more work with Minsky, but those plans were dashed when Hy was diagnosed with pancreatic cancer in early 1996, shortly after receiving the Veblen-Commons Award from AFEE in recognition of his decades of work related to institutional economics. Despite aggressive treatment, he survived only until mid-autumn. I assisted him in converting his AFEE award address into a journal article, and we jointly worked on the Employment Act paper; but that was the end of our collaboration and the loss of a dear friend and brilliant colleague.

My career prospects also nosedived. I hoped for an ongoing position at the Levy Institute, rather than another one-year extension of a fellowship that came with a decent salary but no benefits and would have meant a continuation of the workweek separation from my family. A steady position at the institute would have allowed Linda to relocate to a state job in Albany or the Hudson Valley, and Minsky hinted that he was lobbying for just such an arrangement for me at Blithewood. But the Levy Institute was willing to offer only another twelve months.

The institute director also told me that if I stayed at Levy I couldn't continue to write about economic insecurity. According to institute research associates and staff, one or more members of the institute Board of Governors complained that rising worker insecurity was an imaginary problem—after all, working families "have a television in every room of their house."[2] Rising worker insecurity was far from imaginary, and the number of televisions per household was a ridiculous yardstick.

There was certainly nothing imaginary about the well-documented stagnation of US wages, erosion of retirement and healthcare benefits, and the trend toward part-time jobs and non-permanent work arrangements (such as project-based employment or full-time work done under a short-term contract)—as I knew all too well from personal experience as well as my research. At issue was also the loss of family-supporting jobs, especially in the manufacturing sector, owing in large part to plant closings, downsizing, offshoring, and outsourcing.[3] That too hit close to home: In 1995, my dad lost his job to downsizing at Polaroid following thirty years of service to the company. As shown in my research on economic insecurity, workers losing jobs in the 1990s often never found another job (especially older workers), and those who did tended to take a pay cut of more than 20 percent relative to the income provided by the job they lost. Meanwhile, economic projections, which ultimately proved correct, suggested that many affected workers would never see a return to their past income levels.[4]

To make matters worse, the head of a public-policy think tank with experience as an academic administrator gave me a bleak assessment of my fruitless search for a position. "Academic administrators are sheep," he told me. "No one wants you because nobody else wants you. If someone wants you, then everyone else will want you. Until then, no one will hire you," he explained.[5] He also implied that the same logic applies in the policy world, which I had already learned was rarely open to outsiders. Over time, I've observed that other employers are often no different, even in organizations well beyond academic and policy circles.

In the end, I applied for and accepted a position in the Extension Division of Cornell ILR, despite the position not requiring a PhD or including a research dimension. Because academia is exceedingly hierarchical, taking an "extension" position was a considerable step off the conventional ladder for someone with my education and experience.[6] At HWS, I was a professor, but could not be tenured. At Cornell, I was to be neither. And since the job was based in Buffalo, it was two hours from my home in Geneva and three hours from the Cornell campus in Ithaca.

Bruce Kaufman, a prominent labor economist I met while still in graduate school, was the first person to hear the news, and he emailed back to say I was making a big mistake. But economists should understand better than others that the key question is always: What are the alternatives? And, since I wasn't going to remain in the Hudson Valley without my family, I had none.

While the Cornell post was far from ideal and involved the risk of further eroding my professional standing and career prospects, it did have some attractive features. Since it was clear that partisan wrangling meant little constructive action on worker issues was going to come from the federal government in Washington, I thought perhaps I could make a difference by engaging with business and labor to address practical problems within workplaces and communities. And as a labor economist who put little stock in standard economic theory and instead found inspiration in on-the-ground research pioneered by John R. Commons, I knew the Cornell job provided a chance for me to learn more about economic reality by working directly with employers, employees and union leaders, and local public officials—including some I met in Western New York during my dissertation research and on the campaign trail with Doug Call.

Reflections

My residency at the Levy Institute was tremendously productive, providing opportunities to write about important public issues not only in a scholarly manner but also in a way that's accessible to a general audience. In many ways, the location, colleagues, and research opportunities were unbeatable.[7] The policy ideas I generated during that period were constructive, the analyses were fresh, and the attention to economic insecurity was way ahead of the crowd, especially among economists.[8]

But the Levy Institute experience was also tremendously hard on my family. We tried to make the best of it, spending quiet weekends at home in Geneva or together in the Hudson Valley, where we visited Franklin D. Roosevelt's home and explored the region's small towns. Nevertheless, sustaining the workweek separation for two years placed a dreadful burden on Linda—and deprived young Katie of the two-parent home environment we'd envisioned for her.[9]

As a family, we persisted in the hope that the sacrifices and effort would pay off in the form of a lucky break just around the bend. But the break never came. The opportunity to work as a professor or policy-oriented researcher in the service of working families and the nation remained just out of my reach. Meanwhile, I faced the constant struggle to defend a modest notion of the American Dream for my own family.

A few years after I left the institute, one of my former Levy colleagues noted in an email that, in the face of many difficulties, I always seemed to land on my feet. Perhaps that's been true, but it's a long way from the gradual upward trajectory for which I'd hoped—and, as was certainly the case in 1996, the landings have seldom been soft.

BOOK II

FROM THE FACTORY FLOOR TO THE NATION'S CAPITAL

PART SIX

BUFFALO AND GUANGZHOU

16 SAVING GOOD JOBS AND CREATING NEW ONES IN THE FACE OF GLOBALIZATION

At the start of August 1996, I began working in the Western Regional (Buffalo) Office of Cornell ILR Extension, trading in my regular eastbound travels on the New York State Thruway from Geneva to the Hudson Valley for westbound commutes to New York's "Queen City" on the shores of Lake Erie.[1] In the early twentieth century, Buffalo was among the busiest inland ports in the nation, and the Western New York region served as a major center for producing steel, manufacturing automobiles, and storing and milling grain. But the opening of the St. Lawrence Seaway in 1959 enabled most shipping to bypass Buffalo, and the 1970s brought the start of a seismic shift in the nation's economic geography, which eroded nearly all the region's major industries. Buffalo lost tens of thousands of good paying jobs in the 1970s and the economic decline continued into the 1990s. Arriving in the city on my first day of work, I exited the highway and was greeted by a sign painted on the side of a building: "Will the Last One Out of Buffalo Please Turn Out the Lights?"

The ILR School's Buffalo office oversaw development and delivery of all labor-relations "extension and public service" programs west of Rochester.[2] Those programs included courses and forums open to the public as well as customized training and technical assistance designed to meet the needs of specific organizations; and they all aimed to promote business success, worker prosperity, and community vitality by fostering cooperative labor-management relations. Buffalo was the site of the first regional office established after the state legislature created the ILR School toward the end of the Second World War. In fact, I arrived in Buffalo just as the office began preparations to celebrate its fiftieth year in the city.

Cornell ILR Extension hired me as a "senior extension associate" with the ILR School's Institute for Industry Studies (IIS), one of several units based in the Buffalo office. That institute provided industry-focused research and education to help enterprises and workers cope with rapid industrial change in a dynamic and competitive economy. Most of its programs were commissioned jointly by companies and unions, and when I arrived its two major clients were a national partnership between the United Auto Workers (UAW) and Ford Motor Company, and a local partnership between the United Steelworkers and Outokumpu American Brass (OAB). During my first two years at Cornell, I worked with both partnerships and searched for additional clients.

Toward the end of those two years, I also taught an evening college-level course—"Labor and the American Economy" (spring 1998)—as part of Cornell's Buffalo Labor Studies Program, another unit of ILR in Buffalo. With a two-hour commute each way, long working hours, evening courses, and frequent nighttime events, my position wasn't much of an improvement over the Levy Institute job for me as a husband and dad.[3] I knew in my second year that the ILR Extension post wasn't right for the long term, so I again picked up the pace of my endless search for a conventional academic position. I also applied to teach in China as a Fulbright Scholar.

Workforce Education at Ford

Automotive Industry Studies (AIS), an education program designed by Cornell for the UAW and Ford, was the most ambitious of the IIS programs. Created in 1991, it was modeled after a program developed for employees at General Motors by labor, management, and academics from several universities in the 1980s. The AIS program aimed to deliver a five-day curriculum to the entire Ford workforce (hourly and salaried) in the United States, in groups of about 100 people, over the course of roughly a decade. A team of instructors presented the program, and I taught a segment of the course about a dozen times, at various sites including the UAW–Ford National Programs Center in Detroit, the UAW Education Center in northern Michigan, a Ford engine plant in Ohio, and hotel conference centers in St. Louis and Los Angeles.

The AIS course, for which all participants earned 1.5 college credits, presented a broad historically grounded perspective on challenges facing the auto industry; its goal was to enable the Ford workforce to address those challenges cooperatively and innovatively. The program began by examining auto industry trends in the context of changing global markets and evolving technologies, and it then used that examination as a backdrop for exploring not only union-management relations, but also workplace concerns. AIS provided a common language and delivered much information, most of it reproduced in a large reference document called the *AIS Course Manual*. But instructors also respected the individual expertise and collective wisdom of the participants by relying on a discussion-based format and making extensive use of innovative, interactive classroom methods.[4] In addition, the course taught strategic planning concepts and approaches that participants could use not only at work but also in their personal lives.

My contribution to the AIS program focused on the economic and political context within which the company and union operated, with attention not only to national and global developments, but also to trends in US employment and the quality of life. In addition to teaching that stage-setting course segment, I was responsible for annual updates of the relevant course material. Because that portion of the course was chock-full of information, my colleagues and I made a special effort to use the latest approaches to displaying data in an engaging manner.

Industry Education in Western New York

Just as I arrived in Western New York, representatives of OAB and United Steelworkers Local 593 asked ILR Extension to develop a copper and brass industry program that would serve as the third in a series of joint education programs for the company's factory in Buffalo. I was sent to the factory and helped management and labor fashion a forward-looking strategic planning course called "2001: A Vision in Progress."[5] The program, open to all of the more than 800 workers at the plant, reached 640 participants in small classes (about 25 participants per session) over a period of two months in early 1997. Unlike the auto industry program, each session of the brass program ran for just one day (about eight hours) and was presented at the factory during all three shifts, which meant sessions sometimes began around midnight and continued until sunrise.

Buffalo was a leading producer of copper and brass in the United States throughout the twentieth century, and the education programs of ILR Extension played an integral part of the industry's story in Western New York in the 1990s. The city's brass factory opened in 1906 as Buffalo Copper and Brass Rolling Mill and saw many changes to its name and ownership over the decades. But the plant also had a long history of labor-management strife and faced the threat of being shuttered in the early 1990s when owned by Outokumpu, a metal and mining corporation based in Finland. That's when Cornell's IIS entered the picture.

Plant managers and union leaders responded to the plant-closing threat by committing to boost the factory's performance through joint decision-making, worker education and training, and employee involvement on the factory floor. The IIS contributed to that effort by designing and delivering (in small-group sessions) a three-day education program in 1991, followed by a two-day program in 1995. The first focused on the evolution and future of the US copper and brass industry, and the second concentrated on business decision-making, company and industry finances, work teams, and approaches to continuous improvement. The strategic planning program my IIS colleagues and I developed in 1996 represented a continuation of the OAB-Steelworkers commitment to collaboration through worker education.[6]

With vital input from managers and union leaders at OAB, the Cornell team offered strategic planning as a way for organizations and individuals to respond to, prepare for, and even initiate, workplace change. The "Vision in Progress" program explored how to craft and refashion plans by assessing goals in the context of opportunities, threats, and available resources. The program served as a way for participants to directly contribute to ongoing planning by the company and union, but also—like the UAW-Ford program—provided tools that employees could use to construct individual action plans in pursuit of personal goals and ambitions.

More, More, More

While Cornell hired me for the important work of organizing and teaching courses that promoted constructive labor relations, another attractive feature of the job was the opportunity to learn from workers and managers, which included the possibility of writing about what I learned. Through years of studying and teaching about the ongoing transformation of industrial relations in the United States, I understood not only the importance of companies treating their employees as a source of competitive advantage, but also the value of employee involvement in creating high-performance workplaces.[7] Working at ILR Extension gave me a chance to observe and further the reality of labor-management collaboration on the eve of the new millennium. At the same time, I made no secret of also wanting to advance the labor relations literature, for both academics and practitioners, by contributing to the long tradition of participant observers (including many from ILR Extension) writing about what they learned.[8]

What I initially proposed to Cornell was the opportunity to devote a couple of days each month to academic writing related to my ILR work. At IIS, I worked with people in companies and unions who tried hard to save good jobs and even create new ones in the face of globalization, and I knew research on such efforts was vital to keeping academics, practitioners, and policymakers in touch with the ever-evolving state of employment relations. The director of the Buffalo office was supportive of the idea in principle, but the reality was that my work assignments always took up much more than a full week.

The day-to-day workload only intensified with mounting pressure on ILR Extension offices to generate income that would finance the division's operations. Although ILR Extension began at the end of the Second World War to provide a public service, state appropriations were scaled back repeatedly starting in the 1970s, as government finances were strained by a mix of economic weakness, pressures to restrain state taxes, and growing demands for public services. It's often reported that when asked what labor wants, union leader Samuel Gompers responded, "More, more, more!"[9] In the 1990s, many units within Cornell ILR Extension depended increasingly on the fees they charged for educational services, which meant what ILR Extension administrators wanted was more, more, more fee-based programs—and that edged out time for Extension faculty research, no matter how attractive the notion of such research sounded in principle.[10]

At the same time, it was important for ILR Extension faculty to engage in community education and outreach by organizing public events, participating in public forums and regional professional associations, and keeping in contact with union leaders, employers, and public officials.[11] Those activities took me to dozens of union halls, government offices, and factories including the iconic Nabisco Triscuit production facilities in Niagara Falls and a sinister-looking American Axle plant in Buffalo (built for General Motors in 1923), where I dodged sparks from welding machines to get to the factory's meeting room. But too many of our outreach activities felt like thinly veiled marketing pitches and my education and experience were a poor match for the work of crafting promotional material and making "cold calls" to companies and unions to sell IIS services.[12] Meanwhile, I was learning daily from workers and managers not only about their experience with innovative labor-relations approaches, but also about shop-floor conditions, changes, and challenges—yet I had no time during the workweek to write about what I learned or carefully assess IIS work.[13]

On my own time, I did manage to write a few short conference papers and prepare congressional testimony based on my previous Levy Institute research.[14] One paper drew on my IIS work to highlight the need for companies to view workers as valuable assets; it was later condensed into a short essay for a newsletter of the National Labor Management Association.[15] Two other papers, both of which were published not long after their delivery, extended my earlier research on economic insecurity and were prepared, by invitation, for annual meetings of economists and industrial-relations scholars in 1997 and 1998, respectively.[16]

The Ongoing Job Search—with a Novel Twist

Although I had been warned toward the end of my stay at the Levy Institute that I'd never find a conventional academic appointment, I continued to search each year while at Cornell. After all, I was still being invited to conferences and publishing academic articles, and I received excellent teaching evaluations from my Cornell IIS programs as well as my evening Labor and the American Economy course, my first semester-length course with adult learners.[17] I even had a few job-market nibbles between early 1997 and mid-1998. In one case, a small college recognized how my Cornell work related to the field of business strategy, but narrowed its search to business school graduates; and an economics department at another college reached a deadlock that left its position unfilled (and caused members of the hiring committee to contact other departments and programs on campus, including American Studies and Women's Studies, in search of a way to hire me).

By my second year in Buffalo, I could see from the emphasis on selling training programs to a rapidly shrinking group of unionized firms that my position at ILR Extension was not a good fit for the long term. But the continuing nature of the job meant that for the first time in my career I could teach abroad as a Fulbright professor and still return to a position at home after that international assignment. As a result, I added a bit of variety to the job search by applying to teach in China for the 1998–1999 academic year, which led to an appointment at Zhongshan University in Guangzhou (not far from Hong Kong) and a 12-month leave of absence from Cornell.[18] In August 1998, my family flew from upstate New York to Beijing for a brief orientation and then on to South China, where we moved into a university-provided apartment that would be our home for nearly a year.

17 "THE FUTURE WILL BE CHINESE"

In 2009, British journalist Martin Jacques wrote in *The Guardian* that "the future will be Chinese," and that, by mid-century, residents of Western nations "will find ourselves in an increasingly unfamiliar world" in which China will be the dominant influence.[1] But residents of Western New York already sensed that emerging influence in the 1990s. That's because production from the region's companies—such as toymaker Fisher-Price, which became a subsidiary of Mattel in 1993—was increasingly outsourced to China throughout that decade.[2]

Of course, China had a far more ambitious goal than becoming the toy making center of the world. It had a long-term strategy that involved boosting its human and technical capabilities enough to dominate the "brainpower" industries of the twenty-first century.[3] In the second half of the 1990s, with the twentieth century rapidly winding down, the leadership of China made no secret of its belief that China's millennium was fast approaching.

As an economist deeply concerned about the future of American workers, I was interested in getting a firsthand look at the nation that not only had become a magnet for so many jobs but also aspired to surpass US economic dominance in the global economy. That's a major reason I went to China to teach as a Fulbright scholar during the 1998–1999 academic year, accompanied by Linda and Katie. But I also wanted Katie, who turned nine years old a couple of months after we arrived, to understand China not as an abstraction or images in a book, but as a real place—populated by people she would get to know and perhaps stay in touch with for decades. Even today, we continue to refer to that yearlong experience as our China Adventure.

Zhongshan University

I was fortunate to receive a Fulbright appointment to teach as a visiting professor at Zhongshan University—one of China's top research universities—located in Guangzhou, the capital of Guangdong province.[4] In many countries, Fulbright professors apply to teach or conduct research at a specific university. However, the case of China was different: US academics interested in China applied to the Fulbright Scholar Program (administered by the US-based Council for International Exchange of Scholars) and then China's Ministry of Education matched applicants with interested host institutions and offered the appointments, subject to approval by the United States Information Agency.[5] Zhongshan University (also called Sun Yat-sen University) was considered one of the best assignments available in China and I later learned that US officials lobbied behind the scenes to connect me to that university because I was among the program's youngest scholars and they viewed my appointment as a long-term investment.[6]

Zhongshan University's location in South China was certainly attractive for an economist. While Beijing has long been China's political center and Shanghai emerged as its financial center, the area along the Pearl River between Guangzhou and Hong Kong became a major center of trade and industry in the wake of national economic reforms that began in the late 1970s. In fact, a train ride from Guangzhou to Hong Kong passes through both Dongguan and Shenzhen. When I taught in China, Dongguan bustled as China's leading export and manufacturing base, home to countless factories churning out clothing, footwear, and toys for companies including Fisher-Price; and Shenzhen grew explosively as the country's first "special economic zone," established in 1979 to become a center of trade and advanced technology by attracting foreign direct investment.

"Welcome to China"

Arriving in the Guangzhou airport after a Fulbright orientation in Beijing, my family met Liang Weijian, an undergraduate entering his final year at Lingnan College, a school of economics and management at Zhongshan University.[7] Weijian, who at the time was experimenting with English names and eventually settled on "William" (a name he continues to use today), was sent by the college to accompany us to campus and help us settle into our apartment. I was assigned to teach at Lingnan—a lecture-oriented course in US economic history for third-year undergraduates, and a seminar on selected topics in "Western" economics for graduate students—and soon learned that the entire university campus was originally the site of Lingnan University.[8] Established in 1888, Lingnan was founded by American Presbyterian missionaries from Pennsylvania and New York, who initially called it Canton Christian College; it existed until 1952, when the Communist Party took control of campus and Lingnan faculty and staff relocated to Hong Kong. In the late 1980s, Lingnan College was reestablished within the now state-run university, part of China's effort to forge closer ties with the West and pursue an "opening up" of its economy.[9]

On the way to campus, William and our van driver decided the fastest route meant entering the university through its North Gate, located along the shore of the Pearl River. By the time our year in China ended, the North Gate area was well paved, beautifully landscaped, and surrounded by sparkling new high-rise apartments. Yet on the day we arrived the road was a largely unpaved obstacle course with large heaves, deep muddy ruts, and chickens running in all directions; and the surrounding structures consisted of tin and tarp shacks with open sewage pits. Linda didn't need to say a word for me to know she wondered where on earth we agreed to live.[10]

Once inside the university, however, we found a campus that looked remarkably like an American university, albeit with distinctive Chinese decorative elements and rooflines. There were even tree-lined quadrangles, swimming pools, basketball courts, and a baseball field.[11] We also quickly learned that our ample and air-conditioned two-bedroom apartment[12] (part of a four-story housing complex for foreign teachers, complete with a cafeteria and public restaurant) was only a short distance from the university's *South* Gate, which opened to a busy, modern commercial district and featured a McDonald's restaurant just across the street.[13] We didn't eat much fast food in the states, but McDonald's came in handy during the week or so it took us to get situated in our new residence.

Part of settling into Guangzhou meant swapping short-term visas for extended-stay visas. Having carefully read the visa regulations, my family came prepared with medical records, results of recent blood tests, and even full-size films from our chest X-rays. But the provincial authorities wanted us to submit to their blood tests, which our healthcare providers and the Fulbright team advised us to avoid at all costs (for fear of possible needle contamination); so, we refused.

Before long, I was meeting with the university's top Foreign Affairs officer The official listened patiently to my explanation of how we thoroughly followed the published visa rules, then sat back in his chair and said, "Welcome to China. This is your first lesson: In China, authority trumps the law." In the end, I promised (OK, it was a threat but presented as politely and cordially as possible) to leave China when my short-term visa expired in a few weeks unless the longer visas could be secured without blood tests. It worked: our new visas arrived a couple of weeks later. I'm glad the visas arrived; I enjoyed teaching at Lingnan College, where some of my students were among the best I've ever taught. Nevertheless, the experience did teach me an important lesson about a nation run by party rule versus the "rule of law" to which I'd been accustomed.[14]

The visa situation also prepared me to expect the unexpected, especially when matters could be interpreted as touching on the authority of the state. Still, I was blindsided early in my first semester when I was expelled from a campus lecture in which the speaker was to discuss the government's recent shutdown of the Guangdong International Trust and Investment Corporation (GITIC), a development already widely covered by the international press. Even after learning I was a visiting professor, the event moderator insisted foreigners shouldn't be allowed because the topic involved "state secrets."[15] That lecture was the first in a yearlong series on economics topics, and it apparently also didn't matter to the moderator that the second speaker in the series was me!

An even more eye-opening situation occurred some months later, in the aftermath of the NATO bombing of the Chinese embassy in Belgrade. What my family observed in the days following that bombing made it abundantly clear that China was not the open society it appeared to be during more tranquil times.

News of the NATO bombing on May 7, 1999, reached China just as my family was returning to Guangzhou from a visit to Xian, the location of Emperor Qin Shi Huang's extraordinary army of long-buried terra-cotta warriors.[16] In the cab from the airport, we knew there was trouble when martial music and stern talk of "Zhongguo" (China) and "Meiguo" (the United States) replaced the usual Cantonese pop music on the taxi's radio. Although we continued to access English-language news from the internet in our apartment (our use was monitored but not blocked), the Hong Kong television signal with ABC's World News Tonight was jammed for a couple of weeks.[17]

Meanwhile, State Department officials in the US Embassy and consulates, including the one in Guangzhou, couldn't provide much information or assistance because they were attacked for days by protestors. Most of the protesters were university students, bused in from their campuses (including Zhongshan University) via rides organized by student leaders, party members known on campus (and in each classroom) as "class monitors." It's clear the Chinese government wasn't merely encouraging the anti-American sentiment; in fact, it was orchestrating the public outrage and hostile response to the tragedy.[18]

Yin and Yang

Traditional Chinese philosophy emphasizes that all aspects of the world involve a dynamic resulting from the constant push and pull—"yin and yang"—of contrasting forces. Consistent with that outlook, *dynamism* and *contrasts* represented perhaps the most fundamental features of the Chinese society that Linda, Katie, and I observed in the late 1990s.

My family's year in China coincided with an ongoing and frenetically paced national economic expansion and modernization. That expansion combined the most advanced technologies and heavy equipment with rudimentary sledgehammers and bamboo scaffolding, resulting in astonishing changes to the landscape of cities and rural areas alike. Our China year also marked the 10th anniversary of the Tiananmen Square protests and massacre, as well as the first anniversary of Britain's withdrawal from Hong Kong. Under the policy of "one country, two systems," Hong Kong became the only place in China where people could legally gather to remember the Tiananmen incident.[19]

Meanwhile, my students were steeped in socialist theory, but also highly skeptical of government regulation, even when the goal was to contain financial crises such as those then affecting countries throughout East and Southeast Asia. Many of the students also took to heart Deng Xiaoping's statement that "to get rich is glorious," aspiring to become fund managers at asset-management firms in Shenzhen, Shanghai, Hong Kong, or perhaps even New York.[20]

My family experienced a startling illustration of China's contrasts when running into one of my students a few days after the Chinese embassy bombing. "I just returned from protesting and throwing paintballs at the US Consulate," he told us. "It was so exhilarating to express my feelings! Want to play badminton?" His words certainly caught us off guard at the time, but in retrospect that moment captured much of China in a nutshell: Yin and yang, thoughts and ideas always pushing and pulling, but also coexisting side-by-side.[21]

Of course, we all contain yin-yang dualities. But perhaps sometimes it takes immersing oneself in another culture to better appreciate them or see things in a new light. For example, although I always viewed myself as both an educator and a student while working in the United States, my time in China really drove home that dualism: Despite regularly being addressed as "professor," I even more fully that year embraced the opportunity to learn from each experience, especially by noticing and reflecting on the many similarities and differences between life in China and America.

In China, even a train ride from Guangzhou to Hong Kong proved educational. It provided regular glimpses of isolated, gated factories in which young women (almost always women from my railcar observations) were often marched from their tight living quarters and dining rooms to production lines, where they worked very long hours, in often hazardous conditions, usually for at least six days a week.[22] The extensive pollution of air and waterways was also obvious; in fact, a seemingly ever-present ominous haze reminded me of the dystopian science-fiction film *Blade Runner*.[23] Each train ride offered snapshots of what it truly means for people and a planet to be caught up in a global "race to the bottom" on labor and environmental conditions.

As my Fulbright appointment approached its end, I hoped what I learned would affect my teaching and writing: helping me not only advance the interests of workers in the United States, but also deepen Americans' understanding of labor conditions in developing nations—and perhaps even contribute in some way to improving the well-being of workers in South China and elsewhere.

Parting Thoughts

The preceding barely does justice as an account of an American family living for a year in China. For example, a more thorough account would cover Katie's experiences as a clothing model for a China-based line of children's apparel, dance soloist in a university-sponsored telethon,[24] and blonde-haired youngster roller skating across campus with her Chinese friends.[25] It would discuss Linda's experiences at the local outdoor food market, where vendors spoke only Cantonese and didn't use Western scales and measures, as well as her time spent homeschooling Katie and volunteering on campus as an English teacher. It would also consider my family's participation in touch rugby events and Dragon Boat races.

A deeper dive into my own experiences would discuss the friendship I developed with the dean of the School of Labor and Human Resources at Renmin University in Beijing;[26] the guest lectures I arranged for my students (featuring accomplished professionals in business and finance); the afternoon Chinese language lessons I received from middle-school students while waiting for Katie outside the local primary school;[27] my dalliance with television acting;[28] and the short trip I took back to the states to participate in an economics conference at the invitation of the Levy Institute.[29] But all those events and encounters need to be discussed in detail at another time and place.[30]

Meanwhile, my family remains in touch with Liang Weijian, who saw us off when we left Guangzhou, just as he greeted us when we first arrived.[31] William eventually earned a PhD in statistics from New York University, and I had the honor of participating in his wedding in New York some years later. (He married a Zhongshan University classmate who also came to the United States for graduate school.) Today, he's a principal portfolio manager and director of multi-asset research at PGIM Quantitative Solutions, a business unit within the global asset management arm of Prudential Financial, Inc. Hy Minsky would be amused: the era of money manager capitalism indeed!

18 UNION ENGAGEMENT IN REGIONAL DEVELOPMENT

When I returned to Buffalo from China in summer 1999, the US economy was as robust as it had been in decades.[1] The nation's real output grew at an impressive annual rate of nearly 5 percent, and a record-setting economic expansion that began in 1991 showed no sign of letting up. The jobless rate was under 4.5 percent, lower than at any time since 1970. The inflation rate was a meager 2 percent, the result of a long downward trend since the double-digit price increases of the late 1970s and early 1980s. Even the federal budget seemed under control, as the US government was about to close the fiscal year with its third consecutive budget surplus, after not recording a surplus in any year since 1969.

Yet not all workers and communities benefited equally from the expansion. A large segment of the country continued to be hurt by increased globalization and the ongoing erosion of US manufacturing that began in the 1970s. Many residents of Buffalo and the surrounding areas were concerned that their communities were among those left behind.[2]

To better attract capital investment to the region, business and labor leaders knew they needed to try something new. For the business and banking community in early 1999, that meant partnering with several county industrial development agencies to form the Buffalo Niagara Enterprise (BNE), a private organization designed to coordinate support for business attraction, expansion, and entrepreneurship in Western New York (WNY). The path forward for labor was a bit less obvious. For years, unions engaged in labor-management cooperation within workplaces and at the enterprise level.[3] They even tried working with the business community in a regional labor-management committee, but that committee lost its long time executive director around 1990 and was largely inactive thereafter.[4]

What the labor leaders hadn't tried was an all-union organization devoted to regional development. And that's what they resolved to fashion in mid-1999, seeking assistance from ILR Extension in Buffalo just as I prepared to head home from China. Asked to participate in facilitating the leaders' early meetings devoted to that effort, I agreed with enthusiasm.

I remained in Buffalo for only about a year after returning from China, and most of my Cornell work during that year involved helping the area's union leaders with efforts to advance regional development in WNY.

Regional Initiatives

I returned to work at ILR Extension in early August 1999, only about a week after union leaders publicly announced their creation of the WNY AFL-CIO Economic Development Group (EDG). The group selected a chairman (Kevin Donovan, area director of the UAW) and other officers, secured a full-time coordinator (Phil Wilcox, an electrical workers' union member), and crafted a mission statement.[5] But the EDG still needed to engage in strategic planning and identify its first initiatives. Working with Lou Jean Fleron, director of ILR Extension in the Western Region, and Richard Lipsitz, head of the Buffalo Labor Studies Program,[6] I helped facilitate the EDG's early planning and strategy sessions, which resulted in a focus on three types of initiatives: promoting and advancing cooperative labor relations and high-performance workplace practices; ensuring a reliable and affordable supply of electrical power for the region; and promoting workforce development and neighborhood revitalization.

Labor Relations

In collaboration with ILR Extension, labor's EDG approached the business community's BNE with two ideas to promote and advance constructive labor relations in the region. The first was to establish a network of business and labor practitioners that could field business inquiries about the WNY workforce, engage in regional marketing efforts, and act as an "early warning" mechanism to identify and address workplace-related problems that might lead to job losses. The second idea was to jointly ask ILR Extension to conduct a study of the region's labor force, workplace practices, and employment relations, which the EDG anticipated would demonstrate that WNY is a "world-class region" in terms of workforce quality, productivity, and adoption of innovative labor-management initiatives.[7] Cornell's Fleron began referring to these ideas as the "Champions Network" and the "Champions at Work study," and the names stuck.

By early 2000, the ILR Extension faculty in Buffalo helped the EDG identify and recruit over fifty labor and business leaders for the Champions Network. But not even a roster of practitioners was enough for the network to get off the ground. Union leaders suggest that's because the network was conceived as a joint business-labor project and the BNE never really embraced it.

In contrast, the BNE welcomed the idea of a Cornell regional employment study, which received front-page attention in *The Wall Street Journal* upon its completion in September 2000. The study's positive findings impressed local leaders and the business community; it even exceeded the expectations of the EDG chairman.[8]

Once the EDG and BNE jointly invited ILR Extension to engage in a study of the region, I was appointed to lead the project, assisted by the rest of the ILR faculty and staff in Buffalo.[9] The first order of business involved fundraising to support the work (including my research time): With the help of Brian Higgins and other WNY members of the New York State Assembly, the research team received a grant from a fund controlled by the Assembly speaker. Then I organized the project into two main parts: interview-based case studies of labor relations in the region, and survey-based investigations of WNY workplace practices. ILR Extension faculty in Buffalo conducted interviews that yielded fifteen case studies, and Cornell's Computer Assisted Survey Team in Ithaca conducted the surveys. Comparing the results to national data demonstrated not only that the region had a highly productive workforce, but also that its companies and unions were pioneers in forging cooperative labor relations and building high-performance workplaces.[10]

Regional Power

The EDG took on the issue of regional power at the urging of Wilcox, a member of the International Brotherhood of Electrical Workers. From the earliest EDG meetings, Wilcox explained that the Niagara Power Project (NPP), which operates hydropower facilities on the Niagara River near world-famous Niagara Falls, needed renewal of its federal license by August 2007; he also stressed that allocation of NPP electricity affected tens of thousands of jobs in the region.[11] Although the renewal date seemed far off to some, Wilcox emphasized that the relicensing process is cumbersome and that uncertainty about long-term allocation of the plant's inexpensive power was already causing some WNY businesses to put expansion plans on hold.

Wilcox proposed that the EDG spearhead a consensus-building alternative to the traditional approach to relicensing. That alternative centers on community involvement early in the process, unlike the more common approach that gives area stakeholders a voice late in the proceedings and often gets bogged down in lengthy legal challenges. Wilcox convinced the EDG that the approach aligned well with the labor leaders' expertise in collective bargaining and that the relicensing project gave the labor group a chance to demonstrate its ability to advance the interests of the whole community.

The idea worked. Within a year (mid-2000), the EDG shepherded into existence the WNY Relicensing Consensus Committee, co-chaired by the EDG's Donovan and Samuel Ferraro, a Niagara County public official. The work of that committee produced vital relicensing agreements and enabled NPP to file its application for a 50-year license renewal in August 2005, two years before license expiration.[12] Both the relicensing agreements, which determine power allocation and the community impact of plant operations, and the EDG's leadership in the process received high praise across the region.

The relicensing project was a team effort, but Wilcox's work was crucial. His vision and persistence enabled the initiative to take shape. In late 1999 and early 2000, my responsibilities included accompanying Wilcox to several meetings in which he pitched the idea to public officials. In the earliest days, I even found myself tagging along as he called on area legislators without an appointment, and there were times when it was hard to imagine the project would succeed. Today, though, the NPP relicensing effort represents one of the EDG's most significant accomplishments.

Workforce Development

The EDG aimed for what the labor movement often calls a "high road" economic development alternative to the "low road" strategy characterized by plant closings, workforce downsizing, erosion of wages and benefits, and aggressive anti-unionism. But the group also wanted to ensure that the high road leads to broadly shared prosperity, which requires paths to family-supporting jobs for women and minorities often excluded from such work. To help provide those paths, the EDG devoted much effort to making career-relevant education and training widely accessible, as well as to linking workforce development projects to initiatives that strengthen neighborhoods.

As a first step, members of the EDG met with community college administrators, owners of construction companies, community activists, and local religious leaders. Those discussions led to formation of a workforce development committee that convened regularly in the basement of a downtown Baptist church. I often attended those meetings to represent ILR Extension and signal the university's willingness to help.

Over time, the basement meetings led to a construction education program that the EDG fashioned to dovetail with a major renovation of Buffalo's public schools. The EDG's Buffalo Niagara Jobs Initiative began delivering that program in mid-2005, teaching skills that offered a pathway to union apprenticeships as well as to work as a private contractor. In the following year, three homes were refurbished as part of an offshoot program aimed at neighborhood stabilization.

A separate initiative brought together workers, managers, administrators, and educators associated with a range of health professions. It led to establishment of a charter high school, the Health Sciences Charter School, which opened in 2010 and serves some of the area's most economically disadvantaged students. The school stands as a testament to the power of a shared vision and community-wide collaboration.[13]

From the Queen City to the Big Apple

My final academic year with ILR Extension (1999–2000) was a very good one. Working with the EDG and directing the Champions at Work research project were highlights of my ILR employment. But that community and regional work was only temporary. As the end of 1999 approached, I knew that the Champions research project would end in about six months and that the EDG would require much less assistance as the group found its footing. That led me to intensify efforts to find another position and leave Cornell on a high note. I was determined to avoid a return to making cold calls and selling joint training programs.[14] That was the wrong job for me, and it was nearly futile for anyone in the face of such severe union decline.[15]

I was also increasingly concerned about the gap between being part of ILR Extension as opposed to a member of the faculty in Ithaca.[16] I returned from China with valuable ties to Chinese corporations, government agencies, and academic institutions, especially through my relationship with the dean of the labor relations school at Renmin University.[17] But the Cornell ILR administration in Ithaca at that time seemed to have little interest in taking advantage of such ties, especially with an extension associate, not an ILR professor, taking the lead.[18]

My job search in late 1999 and early 2000 explored a variety of possibilities. At one point, I was in serious contention for an endowed faculty appointment at a university in Rochester, but it didn't yield an offer (as discussed in Chapter 13). In the aftermath of that disappointment, I even contacted organizations that didn't have advertised job openings but seemed a good fit for me, such as the AFL-CIO's Working for America Institute, which partnered with unions, employers, and community organizations across the country to pursue efforts like those of the EDG. Still no luck.

Then in spring 2000 I read a position announcement that *BusinessWeek* posted in search of an associate economics editor.[19] I applied, and the editors flew me to New York City for an interview at the magazine's offices in the McGraw-Hill Building, part of Rockefeller Center. By the end of an afternoon meeting with several editors, it was clear I'd be offered the job. A months-long search down many avenues came to an end that day on the Avenue of the Americas.[20]

PART SEVEN

NEW YORK CITY

19 VIEWING THE ECONOMY FROM THE 43RD FLOOR

Working at *Business Week* was an opportunity I couldn't pass up. While there was usually little time to write at Cornell, here was a chance not just to write full-time, but to do so at a premier business publication. While the position was based in midtown Manhattan, the magazine employed reporters worldwide to assist with stories and enjoyed a reputation so solid that almost anyone would take a call from its writers.[1] Looking at the economy from the magazine's offices on the 43rd floor of a high rise in Rockefeller Center would certainly offer a different perspective from the one I had when dodging sparks and heavy machinery on factory floors in Buffalo. But that was part of the attraction—the opportunity to view the economic system from a different angle.

Business Week was also attractive because it placed a high value on economists and economic journalism. The magazine, which began publishing just weeks before the 1929 stock market crash that triggered the Great Depression, pioneered writing about economic issues from its earliest days. From 1954 to 1969, the economics coverage was led by Leonard Silk, who took courses from some of the world's leading institutional economists as an undergraduate at the University of Wisconsin and then earned a PhD in economics at Duke University. Silk eventually became a columnist with *The New York Times*, but not before bringing Bill Wolman on board at *Business Week* in 1960 (shortly after Wolman completed his PhD in economics at Stanford University). When I arrived at the magazine, Wolman served as its chief economist and Michael ("Mike") Mandel, who earned an economics PhD from Harvard University in 1985, was the economics editor.[2]

Of course, jumping into the world of journalism came with much uncertainty about how the job would work out. I was hired largely because of my broad familiarity with the economy (most economists are highly specialized and inclined to downplay real-world institutional details) and on the strength of a steady flow of newspaper op-eds and magazine articles written during my appointment at the Levy Institute. Nevertheless, *Business Week* represented a major-league employer in the world of print journalism, and I completely bypassed the minors. That's why Linda and I concluded the family would, once again, continue to remain in Geneva while I commuted weekly—catching flights from Rochester and renting a small, one-bedroom walk-up for what Linda and I considered a one-year "trial run."[3]

I stayed at *BusinessWeek* for about a year and a half.[4] When the trial period ended, it was difficult to decide to leave. The trial arrangement was clearly unsustainable for the family in the long run, but at least the travel logistics were workable—except at the very end, when terrorists destroyed the city's twin towers in an attack that shook the nation. Until then, an early Monday flight on JetBlue meant I could make it to the office for the magazine's start-of-the-week editorial meeting and then fly home Friday evening to spend the weekend in central New York. I could even keep my return trips flexible thanks to the availability of affordable last-minute flights. In fact, if I worked late on a Friday, I had the option of booking a Saturday morning flight home or simply walking through Times Square to the Port Authority Bus Terminal and taking a midnight bus (destined for Toronto) that arrived in Geneva, about a 20-minute walk from my house, in time to share Saturday morning breakfast with the family.

"Writing Is Not Fun—It's Hard Work!"

My first article for *BusinessWeek*—"Is the Fed Fighting a Phantom Menace?"—appeared toward the end of May 2000, just a few weeks after I joined the magazine.[5] It provided an analysis constructed around the trademarks of a *BusinessWeek* story: it responded to a recent news event by offering a point of view grounded in the latest economic research and supported by fresh quotes from leading experts. The story concluded by emphasizing that a recent interest-rate increase by the Federal Reserve (Fed), on top of other increases earlier that year, risked squelching a healthy economy over the fear of inflation. It turns out that rates stayed high until year's end, contributing to the bursting of the technology-driven "dot-com bubble" and to the recession that followed in early 2001.

In addition to stories offering economic analysis, I also wrote more pointed commentaries (starting in June 2000, with another essay on Fed policy).[6] In fact, the heart of my job was to deliver analysis and commentary. The word "editor" in my job title was partly an honorific that reflected the publication's respect for those covering the economy. In other departments across the magazine, the label for those similarly providing analysis and commentary was "writer."

Yet there was also an expectation that everyone writing for the magazine should be willing and able to edit the work of their colleagues. As I became more experienced, I was increasingly called on to edit, especially in my second year when a young research assistant began crafting his own stories. I also substituted regularly for Gene Koretz, who edited a feature called "Economic Trends." Each week, that page presented three or four brief stories highlighting new economic research.[7]

My day-to-day work involved close coordination with Mandel, who not only headed the economics unit but also served as the magazine's leading analyst of the technology-driven "New Economy," and with Peter Coy, whose title (associate economics editor) was the same as mine. Peter graduated from Cornell a few years ahead of me; he majored in history and edited *The Cornell Daily Sun*, and worked for a decade with the Associated Press before joining *BusinessWeek* in the late 1980s. Mike and Peter are extraordinary writers, and they were patient mentors, always generous with their time.

Mike, Peter, and I reported to Seymour Zucker, a senior editor who earned his economics PhD at The New School for Social Research. Zucker provided the first edit on everything coming out of the departments of economics and finance. During my job interview, I made the mistake of saying that I enjoyed writing. Zucker looked at me sternly over the top of his glasses and said slowly, "Writing is not fun—it's hard work!"

Zucker edited your work while you sat beside him and followed along. Every editing session was a one-on-one master class in writing. He often pointed to a sentence and asked, "What does this mean?" After I gave my answer, his usual reply was: "Write that!"

One-Year Assessment

In May 2001, Mandel requested that I visit the magazine's in-house library and review his first year of articles from the late 1980s. A few days later, he asked what I found. I wasn't exactly sure how to answer, so I hesitated. "That's OK; I know what you found," Mike volunteered. "I published much less in my first year than you did. I'd say you're doing great."

Covering Lots of Ground

I indeed published steadily throughout the year, often week after week (although many stories took longer than a week to research and write). I covered a lot of ground and addressed major economic issues. For example, in addition to challenging the Fed over its tight monetary policy, I proposed alternatives to unsound and inequitable tax-cut proposals offered by President George W. Bush.[8] On the subject of tax cuts, I may have even had some influence on federal policymakers, who made tax rebates a key part of an economic stimulus package in mid-2001: Until I contacted key leaders on both sides of the political aisle and wrote about the potential of using broadly distributed tax rebates to shore up the faltering economy, neither party gave the rebate idea much notice.[9]

In addition to addressing monetary and fiscal policy, I wrote on the economic impact of consumer confidence, energy industry profits, high-technology investments, productivity growth, the North American Free Trade Agreement,[10] and even the public construction of stadiums for professional sports teams.[11] I also composed the lead article for annual features including the magazine's industry outlook and corporate forecast, contributed to a team-written cover story about the recession of 2001, and wrote three stories on major developments in economic theory.[12] I even reviewed a pair of books,[13] won an in-house prize for a short article on how economists used data to argue that professional sumo matches were often fixed, and branched beyond economics with a travel article on China for a lifestyle supplement to the magazine's international edition.[14]

The one area I rarely covered at *BusinessWeek*, despite my experience and interest, was the intersection of work, employment relations, and the economy. That's because Aaron Bernstein was the workplace writer. However, I did write one article on the value of labor engagement in business decisions, based on a two-day return visit to Buffalo. That article centered on union leader Charles ("Charlie") Humphreys, who drove me around the region—stopping mostly at the site of factories now long gone—and used his own family story to trace the industrial rise, decline, and potential rebirth of Western New York.[15]

My article looked favorably on the region, but it took an approach that Buffalo business leaders hadn't expected. When the business community heard a *BusinessWeek* writer was coming to WNY, they hoped for an article written from a corporate-relocation angle. But any chance of that ended when I attended a business-sponsored event at which thumb-sized "Little People" figures were distributed bearing tags that read: "There's nothing little about our productivity. Ask Fisher-Price." Flipping over a character with a hard hat, I saw the inscription: "Made in China." That's when I resolved to call Charlie and tell a story centering on real people.

Rewards, Challenges, and Mounting Risks

Zucker was right that writing is hard work, but it was also rewarding. I put in extremely long hours, often not leaving the office until 10 p.m. or later—in fact, my late nights were so frequent that I became a familiar face to nightclub doormen along the route to my apartment. Still, the constant writing in the company of great writers and editors provided unparalleled on-the-job training, and I was catching on. It was also gratifying to walk through airports and see people reading my articles.

The first year had been particularly rough. To be sure, the family spent enjoyable weekends at home and occasionally in New York, where we climbed the Statue of

Liberty, attended a Broadway revival of "Annie Get Your Gun," took in a legendary Red Sox-Yankees matchup, and watched Katie whiz around the city on a Razor scooter.[16] But *BusinessWeek*'s industry outlook feature required work over the year-end holidays, and another major assignment meant I missed a long-planned beach vacation with Linda and Katie.

The pace eased a bit after my performance review. And perhaps the load would have lightened a bit more over time.[17] But there were also significant drawbacks to moving the family downstate and trying to make a long-term career at the magazine. For example, I watched as my colleagues endured long commutes to cope with the high cost of living in the region, and I knew Linda had concerns about transferring to the metropolitan regional office of the state's Department of Health. I loved writing, but the toll on my family didn't seem worth it.

There were also mounting risks. In 2001, *BusinessWeek*'s advertising revenue fell precipitously as the dot-com boom imploded, which meant story space contracted. Good articles were increasingly held or dropped entirely. Then the magazine announced it would soon use "stacked ranking" in performance reviews, an approach that pits workers against each other and usually forces the dismissal of a predetermined portion of the workforce each year. Stacked ranking always struck me as an ill-conceived management tool, and it seemed absurd in the case of a world-class magazine, but the mention of its introduction only underlined my biggest nagging concern about moving the family to New York: If I lost my post at *BusinessWeek*, where would I find a comparable job in the tri-state area? The family could get by on one salary in Geneva, but that would be much more difficult downstate.[18]

"Nobody Leaves a *BusinessWeek* Job Voluntarily"

Throughout my employment at *BusinessWeek*, I continued to scan academic job listings, often applying for intriguing positions in business schools and other programs outside the field of economics. I also aggressively explored policy-oriented employment possibilities outside academia and even tried to find a point of entry into the field of dispute resolution (mediation and arbitration) that had long been one of my interests. But the searching again yielded only nibbles.[19] Approaching summer's end in 2001, with Katie preparing to enter seventh grade, I decided to move back to Geneva with or without a job.

The moment of decision came one evening after listening to one of Katie's softball games from my office over Linda's cell phone, as I'd done several times that summer. Linda was at the ballpark, her parents (who lived not far from Geneva) were also there, but I was, once again, a few hundred miles away composing yet another article about the economy. A short time later, I gave my notice to leave in mid-September. A senior editor asked about my post-*BusinessWeek* plans, and, still lacking a polished answer, I said the first thing that came to mind, "I'm not sure yet, but maybe next spring I'll coach my daughter's softball team."

When word of my decision to leave spread across the 43rd floor, most people were astonished. The consensus view was: "Nobody leaves a *BusinessWeek* job voluntarily." And on top of that, I had no new position lined up.

In the end, I found two employment opportunities to keep me busy almost as soon as I left *BusinessWeek*: I became editor of a practitioner-oriented labor relations journal called *Perspectives on Work*, published by the Industrial Relations Research Association, the nation's primary organization for scholars and practitioners in the field of employment and labor relations. I also led a civic engagement project on the future of retirement for the Interactivity Foundation, a fledgling nonprofit based in Parkersburg, West Virginia.

In the first days after announcing my departure from *BusinessWeek*, I must admit there were times I nearly attempted to rescind the resignation and stay on board. Then terrorists took down the World Trade Center's iconic twin towers in Lower Manhattan. That put an end to my ambivalence about heading home.

My move turned out to be the correct decision, and not merely because the attacks of September 11 offered a stark reminder of the fragility of life and the importance of family time. Within a year following publication of my final *BusinessWeek* article (in late November 2001), the magazine experienced two rounds of job downsizing, one of which occurred about a month before Christmas, and my replacement lost her position. By the end of 2009, the financially struggling publication was sold to Bloomberg and many more jobs were lost. When the magazine began publishing in early 2010 as *Bloomberg BusinessWeek*, Peter Coy was the only remaining member of the economics team.[20]

20 "THIS IS TERRORISM"

Tuesday, September 11, 2001, began beautifully. The New York City sky never looked more gorgeous: a deep, cloudless blue that pilots call "severe clear." The temperature also seemed perfect—mid-60s at sunrise, with high 70s forecast for the afternoon. On the walk from my apartment on East 55th Street to my midtown office at *Business Week*, I considered taking the subway to the World Trade Center (WTC) to attend morning sessions at a conference of the National Association of Business Economists. But I decided to first stop by the office to check my email and discuss a story with a colleague.

I reached the office in Rockefeller Center just after 8:45 a.m. When I entered the magazine's 43rd floor reception area, two writers were staring at the television. CNN showed a live image of 1 WTC, the North Tower. Black smoke billowed from a gash about three-quarters up the massive, 110 story structure. "A plane just hit the building," said one writer.

After staring at the screen for a few minutes, it occurred to us that we didn't need to watch television. From the windows of the magazine's south-facing offices, just outside the reception room, we had a clear view of the towers. A half-dozen writers and editors soon gathered, everyone staring toward Lower Manhattan, wondering how the pilot could have made such a tragic miscalculation. Flames were starting to spread, and flickering lights—perhaps fire alarm signals—could be seen on many of the floors.

A jet suddenly entered our vision on the right. It was flying south along the Hudson River, at an altitude that seemed troublingly low. "Get that plane out of there; it shouldn't be flying so close to the accident," an editor scolded. Just before the jet slipped past the towers on the side farthest from us, one writer observed that its colors were those of United Airlines (UAL).

Relieved that the plane had passed, we turned our attention back to the fire. It seemed unlikely that anyone above the crash site could escape. I kept thinking: What a horrible accident.

No Accident

Suddenly, the UAL jet was back—it had turned and was accelerating as it came into view. It slammed into the middle of 2 WTC, the South Tower, sending a red fireball into the sky and a shower of building fragments to the ground. "This is terrorism. It's terrorism," exclaimed Peter Coy, my economics colleague.

I watched for another thirty seconds or so, surrounded by what was then well over a dozen writers and editors staring mostly in silence through a set of long windows facing the burning towers. Then I realized where I was—in a landmark complex that serves as the media hub of the nation. If there were two planes, why not three or four? It occurred to me that "Rock Center" could be included on a larger list of New York targets. Perhaps I was exaggerating the risk, but at that moment nobody knew the source or extent of what was happening, and I wanted to get down to street level.[1] I turned quickly from the window, bumping into a coworker and spilling some of his coffee as I headed for the elevators.

Once I reached the street, I jogged a couple of blocks to St. Patrick's Cathedral, on Fifth Avenue. It seemed the only appropriate destination—a place of solitude, located a safe distance from the area's tallest buildings. Before entering the church, however, I called my wife from a pay phone. She had just arrived in her upstate New York office and knew nothing about the two planes. "Please contact Kate's school and get word to her that I'm OK," I said hurriedly. Only days earlier, I mentioned the business economists' conference and its location to Katie while at home in Geneva; I wanted to be sure she wasn't worried about me.[2]

When I entered the cathedral, there were only a few people inside, most sitting in silent contemplation. I offered a short prayer for those in the towers and tried unsuccessfully to stop replaying the crash in my mind. It hadn't yet occurred to me that the planes were loaded with passengers. However, I did recall reading a news headline that scrolled along the side of the Fox News building about a month earlier: intelligence reports indicated that terrorists were seeking to use planes as weapons.

Too uneasy to sit in the church for long, I walked outside. Sirens wailed from every direction, traffic appeared gridlocked, and sidewalks filled with workers evacuated from their offices. Having nowhere to go, I sat on the cathedral steps.

In Manhattan, people seldom talk to strangers. In fact, they usually avoid eye contact. Not this day. Everyone congregated in small groups on the sidewalk—workers, students, tourists, and shoppers. Some filled each other in on the latest mix of news and rumor, including reports of bombs in Grand Central Station; most just shared their shock and disbelief.

A woman sitting near me tried frantically to reach someone on her cell phone. A policewoman spoke with her briefly but then the officer was called away by a burst of instructions blaring through a hand-held radio. The woman with the cell phone began sobbing. I asked if there was some way I could help. "My brother works in one of the World Trade towers. There's no answer at his office, and I can't reach him on his cell phone," she replied.

"It's Going to Come Down"

Fifth Avenue offers an unobstructed view in the direction of the WTC, so most people were watching the burning towers. At one point, I looked up and noticed the outside wall of the South Tower begin to buckle near the plane's point of impact "Oh God, it's going to come down," gasped several onlookers. Then it did—each floor collapsing onto the one below. In an instant, a huge cloud of dust and debris replaced the tower's spot in the city skyline.

The North Tower followed soon after, its rooftop antenna remaining upright all the way to the ground. As the building collapsed, a man cried out, "Do you realize how many people just died?" Not yet aware of the poor evacuation advice and difficulties that many WTC workers encountered while trying to exit the building, I silently hoped that at least the floors below the crash sites were empty when the towers fell. Meanwhile, the scope of the attacks began to hit home as word spread about a plane that crashed into the Pentagon.

The woman who couldn't reach her brother asked me to walk with her to her daughter's school a few blocks away. There were still a few cars and trucks on the roads, but most streets were quickly being taken over by emergency vehicles and pedestrians. An air compressor released a loud blast nearby—everyone on the block tried to duck for cover.

Soon after we reached the midtown schoolyard, jets could be heard overhead The woman thanked me for accompanying her, I wished her well, and she walked briskly toward the crowded school entrance. As the military planes circled, I learned that Manhattan was now closed to traffic at all bridges and tunnels. On every street, hotels erected barricades, and shops closed.

I found a deli that was still open and bought hot oatmeal and fruit, items located on a counter near the entrance. Since I was leaving the magazine, I had little food left in my apartment refrigerator and with so many people in the city and so few establishments doing business, I thought this might be my last meal for the day. On a display rack near the cash register, the twin towers beckoned from sun-faded postcards.

I ate the oatmeal while sitting on a wall outside my office building. Across the street, ground-floor televisions outside the Fox News studios carried continuous coverage of the day's events, including reports of a plane headed toward the US Capitol. A car at the corner of 48th Street and 6th Avenue—about a dozen yards from where I sat—struck a bicycle-riding courier, but there was no medical care available. Some bystanders worried aloud that the courier might die. On the sidewalk, just a few feet from where I sat stunned, a businessman began having a heart attack. A few people knelt on the concrete to help; one administered CPR and another ran to get a defibrillator.

Meanwhile, a steady stream of people walked northward, away from the towers. Police had closed much of Lower Manhattan and were sending everyone uptown. Some people coughed from exposure to the thick dust. Others wore masks, which I later recognized on television as those issued to workers in the towers following the 1993 WTC bombing.

Asbestos and Locked Doors

Turning back toward my office entrance, I noticed a police car covered with about six inches of soot and fine, grey particles. Much of the material was probably pulverized concrete, but some of it looked like asbestos, and I shook at the thought. With a dust-cloud still hovering over part of the city, it occurred to me that a staggering number of people were exposed to the particles—and that the day's disaster might continue to take lives for decades. (I later learned that indeed the towers were among the last buildings in the nation to be treated with asbestos.)

At the entrance to the McGraw-Hill Building, the location of *BusinessWeek* offices, security workers would admit only writers, editors, and other "essential" personnel. On the 43rd floor, a small contingent of dedicated and brave editors reworked the magazine to meet its Wednesday night publishing deadline. Mandel and Coy asked me to do some "on-the-street" reporting to add a human element to our stories and dictated a list of questions. I was apprehensive about approaching people during such a tragedy; but with the unsettling sound of fighter jets in the air I was glad to get out of the building.

I walked to a nearby blood bank, where the wait to donate was more than four hours. Most people, quite understandably, had nothing to say to me; they were stunned beyond words by what was at that point widely known to be a series of airline hijackings. Others echoed the sentiments of city resident Ned Somers: "It's so awful it takes your breath away. It's almost unimaginable. It feels like a science-fiction movie."

I saw a young couple with hair that seemed to have been turned grey by the dust. The man wore a bloodstained T-shirt. "How close were you to the buildings," I asked—assuming they were standing nearby when the towers collapsed. "We were on the 83rd floor of Tower 1 [the North Tower]," said the woman. "We got out just before the building collapsed." She was exhausted and angry, "Some of the stairway doors were locked. It took us a while just to find a door that would open."

Two men stood nearby, talking on their cell phones. They also had grey particles in their hair—and the same material caked on their shoes. Both wore T-shirts wrapped as bandanas around their necks. Adam Mayblum put down his phone and described the entire ordeal for me.

"I'm Sure They're All Dead"

Mayblum worked at the May Davis Group, an investment firm on the 87th floor of the North Tower. He was at his desk when the first plane hit, sending him about 10 feet across the room. From his window, he could see paper flying, "like a ticker tape parade," he said.

As fire and smoke spread through the office, Mayblum and his coworkers headed for the stairs. About three floors down, however, they realized that one coworker wasn't with them. "Two of us ran back upstairs to get him, at which time the entire floor was filled with smoke. We couldn't find him." Mayblum continued:

> We stopped a couple of times on the way down to tell some firemen the conditions—I'm sure they're all dead. At the 53rd floor, there was a heavyset man who couldn't move any more. We couldn't carry him because pipes had burst and the floor was wet. We said we would send help. All the way down we kept telling SWAT teams and firemen that there was a guy up on 53 and that we thought we lost a friend on 87. The rescue workers went up there; they didn't come down.

When Mayblum reached the third floor, the other tower collapsed. His building went dark, and for the first time he feared he wouldn't make it to the ground. The stairwell was blocked and it took three tries for Mayblum and his coworkers to find an exit that led out of the building. Rescue workers hurried him away from the tower, while people were falling to the pavement from overhead. He ran for blocks to escape the expanding cloud created when his tower fell. "I still don't believe what happened," he said.[3]

City Under Siege

After talking to Mayblum, I rushed back to my office, typed his account along with the remarks of other people I interviewed (all of which I taped with a cassette recorder), and emailed everything to Coy. A few minutes later, Peter bounded out of his office, calling "Charles! This is amazing! How'd you get this?" I wasn't sure Mayblum's account had a place in the magazine, but Peter was certain there was a way to publish it and forwarded my reporting to editors in the front office. Editors combined excerpts from my interview with other reporting by my colleague Diane Brady, and the story was released hours later in the September 12th edition of *BusinessWeek Online*.[4]

As evening approached, streets and sidewalks across Lower Manhattan became deserted except for firefighters, journalists, police, and soldiers. At 5:20 p.m., a new dust cloud appeared as the 50 stories of WTC Building 7 were reduced to rubble in an instant, apparently weakened by the fall of the nearby towers. I saw it on a television in the office pantry as I walked by, thinking at first that it was a replay from earlier in the day.

By 9:00 p.m., the only people in midtown's usually overcrowded Times Square were police equipped with shotguns and riot gear. An armored personnel carrier lumbered its way through an intersection and down Seventh Avenue toward the WTC. The day had indeed started beautifully, but in a dozen hours the New Economy seemed a distant memory and New York had been transformed into what the headline writer working on my coauthored story aptly described as a "city under siege."[5]

PART EIGHT

BACK TO THE FINGER LAKES

21 PICKING UP THE PIECES

During summer 2001, I looked forward to making a fresh start and reconnecting with my family by moving back to the Finger Lakes region. Instead, it was a somber homecoming in the wake of the terrorist attacks of September 11. I was happy to be with the family—and it was a pleasure to drive Katie to and from school—but the pall of that national tragedy made it difficult to enthusiastically pick up the pieces of my career and start a new chapter. Fortunately, my garage and several rooms of the house were overdue for painting, so I managed to make constructive use of a rather subdued autumn.

In October, I also began editing *Perspectives on Work* (*PoW*), a journal of the Industrial Relations Research Association (IRRA). Created in 1997, *PoW* complemented a long-running IRRA research series for academics by delivering articles oriented toward practitioners; it even described itself as a "magazine." When I became its editor, the journal was published each summer and winter, and I eventually expanded the coverage by adding spring and fall online editions.

Around the same time, I began discussions with Julius ("Jay") Stern, a West Virginia businessman who had been trying to build an operating foundation—a "think and do" tank—for several decades.[1] Stern, then in his late eighties, envisioned his Interactivity Foundation (IF) fostering civic engagement on vital public issues, and he said what it lacked was a leader with my experience: achievement in the academic and public-policy worlds, a successful record of working with diverse groups of people as a collaborator and facilitator, and the demonstrated ability to write about contemporary issues judiciously and for a wide audience. At the end of 2001, he appointed me an IF "fellow" after a meeting in which he described his intention for my role to evolve from developing the foundation's civic-engagement process in collaboration with other newly hired fellows, to using that process to lead my own IF project, and then to taking on organization leadership, including overseeing broad dissemination and widespread public discussion of the findings from IF investigations. It was enticing; and although the position required regular trips to West Virginia, much of the work was to be done from my Geneva home.

In the end, it didn't work out as presented to me, but I led a thought-provoking IF project on the future of retirement in the United States, and employment at the foundation came with enough flexibility for me to edit *PoW* and fulfill a promise to teach a course in spring 2002 at Wells College. When my work at IF ended in mid-2004, I even volunteered with the presidential campaign of John Kerry. Recharged and professionally reengaged because of the IRRA editing, the IF civic-engagement project, and the chance to reconnect with college students, not even the disappointment of Kerry's election defeat slowed me down. Instead, I threw myself into several research projects, including work that led to four books.

Jobless Recoveries, Reengineering, and Emergence of the Gig Economy

My transition back to work after leaving New York City went rather smoothly, all things considered. After all, the US economy remained in recession through November 2001 and the unemployment rate in that month, 5.7 percent, was the highest in six years. In fact, the jobless rate continued to trend upward to a peak of 6.3 percent in mid-2003, mirroring the unusual pattern of rising unemployment that followed the end of the 1990–1991 recession. Because of the relatively slow employment growth after those recessions, economists dubbed both expansionary periods "jobless recoveries."[2] Across the economy, it was becoming increasingly difficult for workers to distinguish recovery from recession.

Workers weren't sharing in the recovery for a reason: An accelerated pace of corporate restructuring fueled the rebound in business profits.[3] At the start of the new millennium, one consequence of that restructuring was the spread of job offshoring from factory employment to the service sector and increasingly into scientific and technical fields. But that's not all: Corporate downsizing and business "reengineering" (often just a sexier name for restructuring) were increasingly accompanied by employment in the form of short-term, freelance, and project-based work—as I warned years earlier in my Levy Institute research.[4] Steady work was becoming harder to find across the economy as companies, often pressured by institutional investors, offered their own workers less and less security and profited from relying more and more on global supply chains, outsourcing, and independent contractors.[5]

In short, in the wake of my departure from *Business Week*, insecure employment was becoming the new normal across the economy. In the 1990s, writers, editors, and graphic designers—doing painstaking work on tight deadlines for modest wages—were among the first to find themselves in the financially insecure "gig economy," a term deriving from the "gigs" that supported the itinerant lives of jazz musicians. However, such gig work began to spread rapidly in the first decade of the new millennium, and it has only accelerated more recently (and is now often coordinated by internet-based platforms and mobile apps).[6]

Precarity and the Reluctant Participant-Observer

There was little joy in watching my research validated by an increasingly precarious world of work. It wasn't good for the economy and American society, nor was it good for my own employment security. In the first half-dozen years following my departure from *BusinessWeek*, my own career was still caught up in some of the same disturbing trends that were at the center of my research.

But I was also lucky. Linda's civil service job was among the most secure sort of work to be found anywhere. Our mortgage payments and health insurance premiums were affordable. And I no longer missed Katie's school events and music recitals. I even coached her softball team.

22 PERSPECTIVES ON WORK

The cover of the first issue of *Perspectives on Work* (*PoW*) laid out its ambitious mission by asking: "What are the critical issues confronting people at work today and what will they be tomorrow?" *PoW* began as a joint project of the Industrial Relations Research Association (IRRA) and centers of employment relations research at MIT and the University of Pennsylvania. It commemorated the 50th anniversary of IRRA, a group created to advance academic and practitioner understanding in the world of work.

PoW aimed for a practitioner focus while still holding the interest of the organization's professors and their students. Never a big-budget operation, it produced only two, 50-page editions per year.[1] But its style was very much like that of *BusinessWeek*: the writing was crisp and accessible to a wide readership; the articles offered informative discussions of pressing current issues; and the authors didn't shy away from presenting a point of view. It also paralleled *BusinessWeek* in offering a variety of perspectives. In fact, while each issue of *PoW* addressed several themes, it also sought to offer different perspectives on the same topic, an aim that reflected IRRA's diverse membership from the spheres of business, labor, government, dispute resolution, and academia.

In the first few years, employees at MIT's Sloan School of Management shouldered much of the editorial burden of producing *PoW*. By early 2001, however, the responsibility fell on Hoyt Wheeler, a professor at the University of South Carolina, assisted by IRRA's small staff, housed in the Labor and Industrial Relations School at the University of Illinois. Wheeler did a wonderful job of keeping the publication on the cutting edge of employment issues, but he announced his intention to retire from academic life just as I prepared to leave *BusinessWeek*. I contacted IRRA in response to an advertisement seeking Wheeler's replacement and expressed an interest in the journal; Wheeler announced my appointment to *PoW* readers in his final issue, released in December 2001.

Seven Years of *Perspectives*

PoW didn't pay well—$6,000 dollars a year plus expenses—but it was part-time work I could do from my home office, and editing an entire publication (regardless of whether one wanted to call it a "journal" or a "magazine") seemed a good project to take on for at least a couple of years. I had been active in IRRA since graduate school in the mid-1980s, so I knew the organization and was a familiar face to many of its members. They were getting an editor with professional writing and editing experience, and I was getting a chance to keep on top of the latest developments in employment relations and engage with the world's best labor-management professionals.

It sometimes felt like editing *PoW* was a one-person operation.[2] I chose the topics, lined up most of the authors, edited the articles, selected the artwork and cover layout, and even decided the text ("pull quotes") to highlight in each story. I also organized and led *PoW's* editorial advisory board, which met each year at IRRA's annual meeting and kept in regular contact between meetings by email and phone. But the advisory board members made vital contributions not only by writing articles but also by proposing *PoW* features (clusters of articles on selected topics).[3] They did a terrific job of keeping me informed about what was happening across a broad, interdisciplinary, and ever-changing field.

I edited *PoW* for over seven years. In 2004, shortly before the IRRA changed its name to the Labor and Employment Relations Association (LERA), I added semiannual online issues.[4] At about that same time, *PoW* became a refereed journal, which meant each draft was reviewed by experts before publication, a change I made because professors faced increasing pressure to contribute only to refereed publications. It meant extra work for me, but it also provided a valuable quality check on each article.

I only stepped away from *PoW* in 2009 after continuing to edit it for a year while also working a full-time academic position with administrative and teaching duties. By the time I completed my editorship, the journal presented features on the changing nature of work in a wide range of industries including aerospace, healthcare, financial services, and even casino gambling. There were also regular "policy forums" examining free-trade agreements, striker replacement rules, union organizing, low-wage employment, retiree health benefits, overtime regulations, immigration, and social security reform. A partial list of other topics covered during my term as editor includes:

- The new world of work after September 11;[5]
- The internet-driven workplace;
- Multinationals and human resource management;
- New directions in dispute resolution;
- Religion and work;
- Retirement and pensions;

- Labor standards and business ethics in the global economy;
- Women and unions (with contributors including Linda Chavez-Thompson, executive vice president of the AFL-CIO);
- Forging and sustaining labor-management partnerships;
- Privatization of government work (including military services);
- Bullying and violence in the workplace;
- Facilitating organizational change (with articles highlighting novel approaches and innovative cases);
- Job offshoring; and
- International workers' rights.[6]

In the Company of Practitioners

Because I was investigating important employment-related issues, I found editing *PoW* as invigorating as writing for *BusinessWeek*. It might not have done much to "put food on the table," but I otherwise considered it immensely rewarding to become so well informed about the world of work and share what I learned with others. I found it especially gratifying to know that professors used the "magazine" to bring current and emerging issues into their economics, business, and labor courses.

One of the unexpected pleasures of my *PoW* work was getting to know the practitioners who participated in LERA. It was a diverse group, including union and management attorneys, human resources managers, corporate labor-relations directors, union leaders, arbitrators, and mediators. While I had long considered myself an outsider among the association's academics, the organization's practitioners, especially those serving on the association's board of directors, were always warm, welcoming, and appreciative of my work.

During my *PoW* editorship, I attended LERA board meetings as a nonvoting member, and when my work with the publication came to an end, I served an additional three-year term as a voting member owing to a nomination from LERA practitioners. A few years later, when I was a government economist at the Congressional Budget Office, another nomination from practitioners led to my receipt of LERA's Outstanding Practitioner Award in 2014. The opportunity to spend time in the company of those professionals, learning about their careers and gaining insight about employment relations from their experiences, was a highlight of my work for the association.

23 THE FUTURE OF RETIREMENT

Jay Stern was an extremely private person whose frustration with American public policy in the 1970s led to a very public ambition. That ambition prompted his creation of the Interactivity Foundation (IF) in 1987 and led to my employment as an IF fellow shortly after leaving *BusinessWeek* in 2001. I worked for the foundation through the end of June 2004.

As a young man destined to take over his father's retail, banking, and investment businesses, Stern studied business and engineering administration at MIT, although pursuing philosophy (as the first step toward an academic career) would have been much more to his liking. Until the late 1970s, he continued along the path of the dutiful son: graduating from MIT in 1935; working in his family's retail clothing business until serving in the Second World War; returning home to West Virginia after the war and marrying a woman he met during his military service; working for his father at the Wood County Bank; and rising to become the bank's president and board chairman following his father's death. But dissatisfaction with US monetary and banking policies that produced double-digit interest rates in the 1970s and early 1980s caused him to resign his positions with the bank and donate his majority stake in it to the US government (which he considered a $585,000 contribution to deficit reduction). Stern viewed his actions as a protest over financial policies he described, in one of countless unpublished memos and journal entries, as "economically, socially, and politically wrong."[1]

Leaving the bank allowed Stern to focus on managing the investments of an energy holding company inherited from his father, as well as to pursue what by then had become his true passion: transforming a grant-making nonprofit foundation geared to Ohio Valley community development, which he created in 1965, into an operating foundation aimed at improving public policy formation in the United States and perhaps beyond.[2] At the same time, his frustration with the country's financial policies provided a basis for thinking about how to refocus the foundation. Stern believed the deeply flawed US financial system was only one expression of a larger problem with the way our society practices democracy: the failure to make room for thoughtful explorations of public issues through processes that include not only the voices of experts, but also ordinary citizens who often best understand the day-to-day effects of government policies. He was convinced that finding a way to broaden the discourse on policy alternatives and their likely consequences would improve policymaking—and strengthen our democratic way of life. Stern's IF was created to find such a way.[3]

It's no surprise I found Stern's aim attractive. His vision for IF rested on an element at the core of institutional economics, which is that stakeholder engagement provides an essential basis for constructively addressing social issues and shaping sound public policy.[4] The aim of IF also corresponded with the IRRA goal of advancing knowledge and public policies by bringing together academics and practitioners to discuss current and emerging issues. In fact, the public-policy forums featured in IRRA's *PoW* resembled an early idea of Stern's, who once suggested to a magazine editor that the publication should address issues of current concern by presenting a statement of facts as well as responses from individuals with differing viewpoints.[5]

The Discussion Process

The first nine months or so of my IF work involved sketching out the organization's discussion process through monthly meetings in Parkersburg, West Virginia, with Stern, about eight other fellows, and Jack Byrd, Stern's close adviser who taught systems engineering at West Virginia University. The IF discussion process (IFDP) that came out of those meetings is designed to supplement the existing processes that shape public policy in a democratic society.[6] The process starts when the foundation identifies an "area of concern," a social issue that appears on the policymaking horizon as a matter of increasing significance but, at least ideally, has not yet become a crisis demanding great urgency. If the foundation believes it can contribute to public discussion and understanding of that emerging topic, then an IF fellow recruits panelists to explore the policy area using the discussion process.

During its initial project stages, the IFDP involves convening two panels, each with approximately six people, for a series of monthly meetings. In those meetings, panelists explore the various meanings and dimensions of the area of concern, identify and flesh out possible policy approaches, and consider the likely consequences of each. One panel includes a varied group of citizens interested in exploring the area of concern; the other panel consists of people with some professional experience relevant to that issue.[7] Panelists are recruited with an eye to diversity of background and experience, but a key requirement is that everyone must be willing to explore the topic from a variety of viewpoints.[8]

A major reason for beginning a project with two panels is that IF doesn't want explorations dominated by "experts." The foundation emphasizes that all citizens have valuable insight to contribute to its explorations, and using two panels early in the process can widen the range of perspectives generated by the project. The foundation also stresses the value of having panelists meet in a "sanctuary" setting, which means the facilitator and panelists work in a supportive environment where panelists can speak freely. Panelists must be confident that their input will be appreciated and that the final project report will reflect the work of the group as a whole, without disclosing the personal views of individuals.

After some months, the two panels are combined and complete the project as a single panel. After several meetings, that panel draws on its own discussions (informed by the earlier two-panel meetings) to fashion a final project report. The report contains an overview of the issues examined, a presentation of several alternative policy directions, and a description of foreseeable consequences for each alternative. The aim is to produce a document capable of laying the groundwork for a rich public discussion and eventually for reasoned policy action.[9]

The Retirement Security Project

By autumn 2002, four fellows remained—and I was the first to identify a project topic acceptable to the foundation and recruit project panelists. I was the only economist in the group,[10] and Stern hinted that he would like an IF project on the financial system.[11] But I thought the subject was a bit too challenging to tackle as a first project, even assuming the scope of investigation would narrow somewhat before panel recruitment began.[12] Instead, because my early visits to Parkersburg coincided with release of the final report of President George W. Bush's Commission to Strengthen Social Security, I suggested a project on the future of retirement in the United States. Receiving the foundation's approval, I saw the project as an exciting opportunity to demonstrate the strengths of the IF civic-engagement model relative to the expert-driven approach of a presidential commission.

By identifying the uncertain future of retirement security in the United States as a rapidly emerging area of concern, the retirement project fit neatly into the IF discussion framework. The project's broad scope encompassed the future of the Social Security program as the baby boom generation approached retirement age (which was the focus of the Bush commission).[13] But it also enabled panelists to reflect on other retirement-related matters, including the erosion of employer-provided retiree health benefits and the dramatic shift from defined-benefit to defined-contribution retirement plans, which transfer the risk of unfavorable investments from employers to workers.[14] Even the meaning and value of retirement were on the table for discussion.[15]

Adopting an "expanding network" approach to panelist recruitment, my adaptation of a technique used by anthropologist Joel Savishinsky in an award-winning book on retirement, I selected fourteen panelists from a pool of forty interested candidates living in or near Rochester, New York.[16] Using the IFDP, panelists met monthly for just over a year at a conference center in Rochester, first for several meetings as two panels of seven people and later as a joint panel of twelve, not long after two panelists (one from each panel) withdrew because of mounting personal obligations.[17] The panel began work in November 2002 and issued its final report to IF in January 2004, a product of seven men and five women, whose ages ranged from 27 to 73 at the start of the project (average age of 53).

The diversity of the panel exceeded my expectations. Panelists came from a mix of urban, suburban, and rural communities in a three-county area; and it was not a provincial group because fewer than half were lifelong residents of the region (one panelist spent her youth in the Caribbean). Panelists were never asked their political affiliation and were all very good at thoughtfully considering retirement issues from a range of perspectives, but everyone agreed it was safe to say the group's political leanings ranged beyond Democrat and Republican to incorporate social-democratic (such as the Green Party) and libertarian perspectives.

The panel's occupational mix was extraordinary. For example, panelists included a graduate student in social work, a town supervisor and cattle farmer, a retired employee-benefits manager, a professor specializing in elder care, a minister who previously served as the chief executive of nonprofit healthcare and mental health organizations, a retired nurse, a union leader whose members lost most of their retirement funds in the era's wave of corporate takeovers and accounting scandals, a semi-retired CEO of a high-tech company, and a retired IBM engineer who volunteered with local community-service and social-justice organizations. Most panelists were chosen for the multiple perspectives they could contribute to the project. For example, an actuary with extensive experience in the design and administration of retirement benefits also brought a detailed knowledge of Social Security reform proposals and keen insight garnered from observing two sets of grandparents who experienced retirement in very different ways.

The panel's final report began with an exploration of the meanings of retirement and dimensions of retirement security. The report suggested that retirement most often involves a change in a person's relationship to paid work, but it also stressed that retirement does not necessarily mean a complete departure from the paid workforce. Instead, retirement primarily involves a "state of mind" and a change in how one perceives their own identity. The report also emphasized that individual perceptions tend to evolve over the course of retirement.

The report further explored retirement's complex meanings by identifying the many favorable and unfavorable views people have toward retirement, as well as the numerous reasons for retiring or not retiring. Dimensions of retirement security were similarly recognized as complex and varied. That section of the report touched on numerous aspects of physical, emotional, and material well-being, including finances, healthcare, personal freedom, control, privacy, information security, adaptability, and social relations.

Then the report shifted to a presentation and discussion of alternative policy possibilities and their likely consequences. The panel focused on four broad and contrasting (but not necessarily mutually exclusive) policy directions, which the group summarized as follows: (1) government *regulation and enforcement* are necessary for retirement security (this approach emphasizes laws protecting workers' rights and assets); (2) the public sector must ensure citizens can *access the tools* needed to achieve retirement security (such as financial education and retirement planning); (3) seniors need a publicly provided *safety net* (to protect those who would otherwise be in financial distress); and (4) retirement security must be recognized as a *shared responsibility* of individuals, employers, and government (achieved through private savings, workplace retirement benefits, and social security). The report identified both positive and negative consequences that could reasonably be expected to arise from pursuing each policy direction, and it ended with an invitation for reader comments and further discussion, as well as with the hope that the report would spur a national dialogue on this vitally important area of concern.[18]

Shelved

By nearly all measures, the retirement security project succeeded impressively. The participants were thoughtful, engaged, and deeply interested in their work. The process achieved IF's goals of providing a "sanctuary" setting for open discussion, serious reflection, and meaningful interaction. In fact, during a reflective discussion following completion of the project one panelist observed, "It's been a safe place, where it's OK to share dissenting opinions."

Most impressive is the panelists' joint report. Even today, their analysis of retirement, public policy, and consequences strikes me as an extraordinarily rich document that exemplifies the power of interactive engagement and collaborative exploration. Every section demonstrates that cooperative work produces powerful synergies, leading to ideas and a final product that could only come from combined effort.

The report also fares well when compared to the expert-driven presidential commission on strengthening Social Security. The commission's recommendations centered on a controversial proposal to redirect a portion of payroll taxes into personal retirement accounts, worsening the financial condition of Social Security trust funds and exposing workers' retirement contributions to the swings and uncertainties of financial markets.[19] The report of the IF panel allowed plenty of room for retirement accounts, promoting household saving, and fostering personal responsibility for retirement planning, but it also shed light on the broader individual and social considerations surrounding retirement. From the perspective of the IF panelists, the presidential commission represented a missed opportunity to initiate a meaningful dialogue on retirement security in the new century, leaving a gap they hoped the IF project report would help fill.[20]

However, the panel's report never spurred the nation's much-needed dialogue on retirement in America. After I submitted the final report, the foundation invited me to engage in an additional year of convening small-group discussions based on the panel's report, tweaking the report along the way. Nevertheless, the foundation wasn't ready to publish it. Having watched the panel form into a community that took pride in its work on the project, the foundation's decision on the project report came as a disappointment.[21]

It was difficult to break the news of IF's decision to my panelists. They were crestfallen. "Let us talk to Mr. Stern," said several panelists. An arbitrator on the panel drafted a letter to Stern, circulated it among the panelists for comments and suggestions, and sent it to Parkersburg. It expressed their gratitude for the chance to participate in the project, stressed the quality of the final product, and praised my facilitation. It also asked Stern to reconsider the foundation's decision to shelve the report, closing by inviting him to meet with them in Rochester or via telephone. According to the arbitrator, the letter received no reply.

In the end, I agreed to stay at IF for a short period (through June 2004), conducting a small-group discussion using the IF panel report and then writing a supplementary report that incorporated my findings from that discussion. Like the retirement panel, that small group was politically, occupationally, and demographically diverse, and included, for example, a real estate appraiser, nurse, social services worker, and retired farm manager. I wasn't surprised that the small group found the report valuable, both as a stand-alone document and means of spurring thoughtful discussion. But I was pleasantly astonished when I ran into one of those participants nearly two decades later and found her eager to tell me that she still finds the IF report thought provoking and that she returned to it—and her notes from the small-group discussion session—on several occasions before and after her own decision to retire.

In my final meeting with Stern in Parkersburg, I thanked Jay for the opportunity to pursue the retirement project. Then I returned home to Geneva, where I applied for unemployment benefits for the first and luckily only time. In the month my work at IF ended, another of the foundation's projects was wrapping up its panel meetings, and other projects by my cohort of fellows were ongoing. The earliest date that I find IF project reports available on the foundation's website is March 2006.[22]

After Stern's death in June 2009, at the age of 95, the foundation became more active in public engagement. In fact, a member of my cohort of IF fellows used the Rochester panel's retirement report as the basis for new panel discussions in

December 2009, resulting in an IF report published in March 2010 called "How Will We All Retire?"[23] The 2010 publication barely skims through valuable insight generated by the Rochester panel's yearlong exploration of retirement meanings and dimensions, but it also appears to serve as a useful discussion guide—a handy and concise tool for facilitating a discussion of retirement and alternative policy directions.

Reflections

"History doesn't repeat itself, but it often rhymes," Mark Twain is said to have quipped. And my experience at IF did seem eerily reminiscent of that at Hobart and William Smith Colleges. Neither the foundation nor the colleges promised a job with a future and opportunities for advancement, but both dangled bait during recruitment—and then seemed to pull the rug out from under me despite solid achievements and even strong performance relative to others.

Of course, I was not alone. Just as the IF retirement panel prepared its final report, Barbara Ehrenreich set out to explore how white-collar workers fare in the aftermath of corporate downsizing. Her grim findings were published in *Bait and Switch: The (Futile) Pursuit of the American Dream.*[24] It reports on the countless American workers who "did everything right" (worked hard, earned higher degrees, met or exceeded workplace benchmarks, etc.) and still found themselves unemployed for long periods and unable to get their careers back on track, often forced to take a "survival" job paying low wages, offering no healthcare or retirement benefits, and making no use of their education or skills.[25]

Ehrenreich's book argues that the experience of those white-collar workers calls into question an essential pillar of the American Dream, which is that hard work and accomplishment will be rewarded.[26] Instead, her investigation found that employment success has become increasingly disconnected from experience and accomplishment, and that "creativity, innovation, and critical thinking ... are exactly the capabilities that can sink a career." According to the workers she met during a year of research, much of it spent posing as an unemployed job seeker, the key requirement (but not a guarantee) for surviving in the contemporary workforce is "go along to get along" and view your boss as "your most important customer," which suggested to Ehrenreich that flattery might be an employee's most essential work product.[27]

The glimpses that Ehrenreich offers of accomplished workers and their families affected by unemployment are often heartbreaking and remind us that downward mobility tends to produce more than tremendous financial precarity. It also "carries a sense of failure, rejection, and shame."[28] Even recognizing that you're caught up in sweeping economic trends doesn't immunize a worker from those feelings—or from self-doubt and the tendency to ask, over and over, what might I have done differently?[29] I know that from personal experience.

Still, I was fortunate. To be sure, I wanted a secure and upward career path and was disheartened by instead enduring a bumpy ride from the start. It began with six years of employment without any prospect of tenure, followed by two years of contingent work (annual contracts) at the Levy Institute. Next came nearly three years of "underemployment" in an ILR Extension position with uncertain long-term prospects, followed by roughly a year and a half in a terrific position (*BusinessWeek*) with considerable mounting risks.[30] Then I was jobless after working the better part of three years at an unknown foundation with a limited track record.[31] But my family lived frugally, so we weathered it all thanks to Linda's supportiveness and her steady civil service work. Even as I recognized that I was living out my own case study on the increasingly futile pursuit of the American Dream, I remained passionate and undeterred.

What kept me going is what motivated me from the start: the aim of helping to advance the interests of workers in their pursuit of a widely held and modest version of the American Dream, which I continue to see as essential to achieving broadly shared prosperity and societal well-being. That version doesn't involve being wealthy; it aims only for steady work and economic security during one's career, a secure retirement with dignity, and the chance for the next generation to achieve just a bit more through education, training, and hard work.[32] But that American Dream, despite its humble aims, had become increasingly out of reach—even for workers with advanced degrees, diligence, and ambition.

Thwarted in their pursuit of that goal—and caught instead in a current of global trends tugging in the direction of downward mobility—working people rarely have the time and opportunity to speak up for themselves, especially in ways that can go toe-to-toe with armies of so-called experts. And those working people include retirees like my late father, whose employer unilaterally terminated its long-promised "health-insurance-for-life" benefit that he and thousands of coworkers earned by providing thirty or more years of loyal employment.[33] Working people deserve someone to fight for them.

The health insurance termination letter arrived in my parents' mailbox on October 13, 2001, effective immediately. Around the same time, the company's employee pensions were also wiped out, leaving only what was protected by the federal government. That's why I remained determined to contribute constructively to economic and policy discussions on behalf of working families—and tried to find ways for workers to have a meaningful voice through forums like those used at ILR Extension and IF.[34] Meanwhile, my own employment insecurity only illustrated the widening scope of the economic problem and the increasing importance of what I aimed to achieve.

24 RECHARGED AND REENGAGED

In the six-year period between autumn 2001 and the start of 2008, my primary employment was at the Interactivity Foundation (IF), where my position ended in June 2004. But I certainly kept busy during the entire period, which coincided with my daughter Katie's years in junior and senior high school, as well as her first semester in college at the Webb Institute in Glen Cove, New York. After traveling east, west, and south for work between 1994 and 2001, I was fortunate to be back home with Linda and Katie (as well as Patches, the basset-beagle mix we adopted as a puppy in 1992) during those important years.[1] It also helped me recharge and provided the stability I needed to reengage as a professor, political campaign worker, and economic researcher and writer.[2]

Katie

Katie has her mom's steel-trap memory—and broad smile. Thanks to my dad's genes, she also has Linda's blonde hair and blue eyes. Katie may have also inherited my dad's height: she always measured at the top of the youth growth charts. Meanwhile, Katie's independence of mind reflects both her mom and dad.

Katie has always been an outstanding student, whose activities outside the classroom also benefited from a willingness to work hard and ability to learn quickly.[3] Those activities included softball, ice skating, dancing, playing violin, cooking, and swimming, where she excelled at the butterfly stroke and long-distance events. American history and filmmaking also ranked at the top of her interests in junior and senior high school, and she intrepidly pursued them by teaching herself whatever new skills were needed to accomplish her goals. For example, a nineteenth-century living-history museum in the Rochester area piqued her interest in that era's fashions. Katie borrowed books from a Cornell library, learned about the clothing of the period, taught herself to sew (with assistance from Linda), and made dresses and other apparel with historical accuracy. Later, she wore, displayed, and discussed that clothing as the docent at the museum's dressmaker shop.

A particularly memorable incident captures Katie's independence, ingenuity, determination, and indomitable spirit. One sunny afternoon, she picked dandelions from the lawn and asked me to buy walnuts at the supermarket. I thought the dandelions were for a flower arrangement and the walnuts were for brownies, but Katie had grander ambitions. After a few hours in the basement, she emerged with yards of fabric dyed soft yellow from the flowers and golden brown from the nut shells. Of all the volunteers at the living-history museum, Katie may have been the youngest (beginning at age 16); she was also the only docent dressed entirely in period-appropriate attire, right down to the fabric, cuts, stitches, and dyes.

Of course, I should have known what was coming when years earlier, barely able to climb onto a stool at the local library, Katie insisted on checking out all the books available on Paul Revere and his famous "midnight ride." While she spun around on the stool, I read each title listed on the library computer screen. "Fiction or nonfiction?" she would ask, and unless I answered, "Nonfiction," her reply was a curt, "Next." Soon, her newfound knowledge was indelibly etched into her memory, and heaven help any teacher whose history lesson on the start of the Revolutionary War relied too heavily on Henry Longfellow's poem.

My six years at home with Katie didn't make up for the earlier years away while trying to chart a stable and secure career, or the endless hours devoted to academic work and pursuit of a permanent teaching position while at Hobart and William Smith (HWS). Still, we had fun completing melodic phrases while listening to classical music on the car radio during school commutes, performing together in the pit orchestra for a church Easter pageant,[4] and taking a break from visiting colleges to attend the Commonwealth Shakespeare Company's staging of "The Taming of the Shrew" on Boston Common. Also, I was poolside when she competed in statewide swimming competitions; and I didn't have to fly into town to watch her deliver the valedictory address at her high school graduation or help her move downstate and into a dormitory at Webb Institute, where I found myself sitting next to its president, Admiral Robert Olsen, who personally interviewed every Webb applicant and told me Katie was the best applicant he interviewed over the years.[5]

Looking back, I recall that if the Levy Institute hadn't offered me a research post when my contract expired at HWS, my plan was to stop searching for an academic job and write a book about the experience of being *Katie's Dad*. When the Levy position became available, I thought taking it would be in the best interest of my family in the long run. But today I'm not sure that was true. Jumping off the career path wouldn't have been easy, but remaining in Geneva as "Katie's dad" would have been the best job on earth. At the end of the day, that designation continues to mean more to me than any title I've held during my career.

Wells College

In mid-2001, when I began to seriously consider leaving *BusinessWeek* and returning to the Finger Lakes, I contacted a former HWS colleague, Muin Uddin, an economics professor at Wells College, and expressed interest in a visiting faculty appointment at Wells. Teaching as a visiting professor, even on a full-time basis, rarely pays well, but I hadn't taught in a conventional campus setting within the United States since 1994, so I thought it would be good to reengage with students.[5] Wells, a small liberal-arts women's college overlooking Cayuga Lake, seemed a good choice because class sizes were small and the campus was just under an hour's drive from my home in Geneva. Uddin, whom I liked personally and respected professionally, was eager to help me join the Wells faculty and paved the way for me to teach a couple of courses as early as spring 2002.

I eventually agreed to teach just one course at Wells College that semester because of the opportunities that also arose at IF and *Perspectives on Work*. Since the Wells administration was especially interested in my experience as an editor at *BusinessWeek*, I used a "special topics" seminar designation to create and deliver a course we called "Economic Journalism." About ten students enrolled in the writing-intensive course, including a few who wrote regularly for the college's weekly newspaper, *The Onyx*. The course offered an introduction to writing for a variety of journalistic formats, ranging from op-eds to magazine features, organized around a mix of brief lectures, class discussions of exemplary writing and the latest news stories, workbook-based homework, and weekly writing assignments. There were also regular exchanges of papers among students, which provided editing experience as well as valuable peer feedback.

The course even included a campus visit by Mara Der Hovanesian, a finance journalist with whom I worked at *BusinessWeek*. Der Hovanesian's visit allowed my students to interact with one of the country's top business journalists, and I knew she would inspire them. Mara met with my students in a small group setting, delivered a public seminar in which she talked about the craft of writing, and shared an engaging dinner with faculty and students.[7]

My course and the Der Hovanesian visit were well received, and Wells asked me to return for another course the following year, an offer I needed to decline because of my IF retirement project. However, in spring 2004, I agreed to return as faculty adviser to *The Onyx*, which took the form of a weekly seminar with that paper's writers and editors. I enjoyed working with the students, faculty, and administrators at Wells, but the college had a long history of financial difficulties, which only became worse in the new millennium.[8] In 2005, the college became coed, and when that didn't solve its problems the 156-year-old institution shuttered after commencement in May 2024.

The Kerry-Edwards Presidential Campaign

On July 30, 2004, the morning after Senator John Kerry accepted the Democratic Party's presidential nomination, I emailed my dissertation adviser Ray Marshall at the University of Texas and expressed interest in working with the campaign. Marshall responded that he would arrange for me to be added to the campaign's Workforce Development Policy Team, and I was soon participating in regular conference calls with members of the campaign staff, Marshall, and other economists and policy experts.

After about a month, the policy team's work was winding down and the campaign focused on efforts to get out the vote. On one of our last policy calls, a member of the campaign staff invited us to work on voter turnout activities in the swing state of our choice. The work was to be unpaid, but the campaign arranged housing with Kerry-Edwards supporters; travel reimbursement was also mentioned. I agreed to work from early October through election day in Claremont, New Hampshire, staying at the home of area residents and asking only that the campaign reimburse mileage and tolls roundtrip between Geneva and Claremont.

On my first morning in Claremont, I arrived at the campaign office as its door was being unlocked by the area's chief field organizer, Lauren Mattison, a graduate student in mechanical engineering at University of Massachusetts Amherst. After brief introductions, she gave me my first assignment: "Go make some coffee." Being neither a coffee drinker nor a coffee maker, I didn't know where to begin, and thought, "This could be a very long month." But election day came quickly and I fully enjoyed working with Lauren and the other volunteers, including Tom Glick and Minda Kauffman, who were also in Claremont for the month, and Debra Manfredi, who worked the phones in the closing days, just as she did on Kerry campaigns since his first foray into politics in Lowell, Massachusetts, in 1972. Much of my work focused on organizing volunteers to maximize voter turnout, but I even learned to make coffee.

I also became friends with Ray Gagnon, Claremont's mayor. On at least two occasions, Gagnon took me along when he conducted political business at the campaign's state headquarters in Manchester. I joined him on the first trip to glimpse the statewide Kerry-Edwards operations center; Ray used the drive time to share stories about campaigning for Bill Clinton, who credited New Hampshire with saving his presidential bid and appointed Gagnon as a federal marshal in a gesture of gratitude. Another trip was timed so we could attend Senator Kerry's speech at a rally in the final days of the campaign. Ray also introduced me to someone in Manchester who he thought could arrange my travel reimbursement. I never did get reimbursed, but Gagnon treated me to lunch—and plenty of political stories—at the Merrimack Restaurant, one of the city's celebrated presidential campaign stops.

Research—Lots of It

Leaving *BusinessWeek* caused my annual income to plummet, but it didn't slow my writing about the economy and economics. I resumed researching and writing almost as soon as I returned to Geneva, combining that work with a return to active participation in economics and industrial relations conferences as a paper presenter and session organizer.[9] Over the next six years I published more than two dozen articles, mostly in academic journals, but also in venues reaching a wider audience, including an op-ed for *The Washington Post* to mark 25 years since President Reagan fired striking air traffic controllers and emboldened private-sector employers to pursue their own hard line against unions.[10] I also began four books, and even made time for over a dozen book reviews.

Business Cycles and Worker Engagement

One of my first post-*BusinessWeek* publications combined Hy Minsky's emphasis on the US economy's tendency toward cycles of prosperity and recession with evidence that the nation's built-in economic stabilizers—progressive taxes, the minimum wage, unemployment benefits, and other income supports—had been allowed to erode for more than two decades. That meant the country risked more severe recessions and slower economic recoveries, a view consistent with the historical record even today. The idea to write about that trend toward greater instability and the need to shore up the economy's stabilizers came from a discussion with Jeffrey Wenger, a policy-oriented economist I met through IRRA, and we cowrote the piece quickly. With that article, published in 2002 and highlighted in a *New York Times* essay by columnist Jeff Madrick, I quickly reverted to being cited by journalists rather than working among them.[11]

Other articles drew on my experience in Buffalo (combined with additional legwork to bring myself up to date on regional developments) to explore worker engagement in business and community decisions. One article, coauthored with Art Wheaton, a former colleague from Cornell ILR Extension, uses cases from our work with companies and unions to explore how employee involvement contributes to effective business decision-making.[12] It also describes how workforce education programs focusing on industry challenges, like the programs I helped shape on the auto and brass industries, enable organizational change by providing a starting point for worker involvement. Another article looks at how union-driven community organizations, such as the Economic Development Group (EDG) in Western New York, can bring about socially responsible business development.[13] I even revisited the EDG in two more articles a few years later: one presents the EDG as a case study of labor-community engagement, which historians often call "social unionism"; and the other, which won the year's best-paper award from *Advances in Industrial and Labor Relations* in 2011, highlights the enduring value of addressing economic problems through broad-based stakeholder engagement and consensus building.[14]

Offshoring and Retirement

Another pair of articles addressed the growing trend toward job offshoring, which was then becoming an increasing threat to the livelihoods of service workers and "white-collar" scientific and technical workers. It was impossible for me to ignore offshoring. When I worked in Buffalo, customer service "call centers" were touted as a source of new jobs to offset losses in manufacturing; but just a few years later more than a thousand of those jobs were lost in Western New York as call centers moved rapidly overseas.[15] Closer to my Geneva home, Carrier Corporation—an air conditioning pioneer and major employer whose name had been on the domed arena of Syracuse University since the stadium opened in 1980—closed operations in central New York. It relocated 1,200 jobs from Syracuse to the Sunbelt and Asia in 2004, adding insult to injury by making the closing effective on the Fourth of July.[16] Offshoring also affected one of my brothers, who learned painfully that not even the jobs of engineers are safe, when his work was relocated from Massachusetts to India.

Offshoring was certainly in the news, but the coverage was often superficial.[17] In early 2004, a *Time* cover story quoted President George W. Bush's chief economic adviser, Gregory Mankiw, who said offshoring is "a good thing" for the US economy.[18] The story also made no effort to suggest how government might help the jobless workers left behind. After serving in the White House, Mankiw could return to a secure university position, yet the evidence showed not only that at least one out of ten American jobs were under threat from offshoring (and perhaps as many as one in three), but also that reemployment prospects, especially at comparable wages, tended to be quite dim.[19]

My offshoring articles, published in 2005, debunked the suggestion that offshoring has been unambiguously good for America; they also identified ways government could play a more constructive role.[20] In both articles, I stressed it was impossible for American workers to compete based on wage rates when computer programmers could be hired in the Philippines for $1.50 an hour and factory workers in China often earned 64 cents an hour. I also emphasized the huge costs that offshoring inflicts on US workers and their communities. Then, turning to public policy, I combined practical policy recommendations (such as expanded training, income, and healthcare assistance for affected workers) with a vision of a different direction for US competitiveness—one in which government fosters industrial innovation and rewards companies for treating human resources as a source of competitive advantage, rather than costs to be minimized.

In addition to writing on the worker insecurity that accompanies offshoring, I also wrote about the financial precarity of retirement insecurity. In the wake of the Interactivity Foundation's decision not to publish the Rochester retirement panel's report, I wrote an op-ed and two articles on retirement from my own perspective but based on what I learned from the panel over the course of its project.[21] The op-ed, which appeared in Rochester's daily newspaper, stressed the need for the country to broaden discussion of retirement beyond the narrow focus of President Bush's commission (on personal retirement accounts). An article for a policy-oriented journal compared the findings of the president's commission with my interpretation of the IF panel's deeper insights. And an essay for an economics journal expressed my view that broad-based civic engagement offers a solid foundation for meaningful public discussions and policy development.

Money Manager Capitalism, Worker Insecurity, and the Reconstruction of Economics

Much of my return to academic writing after leaving *BusinessWeek* focused on the ongoing evolution of the US economy and the need for a reconstruction of economics to better understand that evolution. At the heart of that research and writing was an effort to update and flesh out my work with Minsky on the rise of money manager capitalism and the accompanying worsening of worker insecurity. Because that sort of work required a firmer grounding in history and institutional reality than conventional economics provided, I also gave attention to advancing the alternative of post-Keynesian institutionalism (PKI), a synthesis I first pursued in Austin.

My effort to advance PKI and apply it to the US economy drew on material from the American economic history course I taught in China. It also built on an article I wrote at *BusinessWeek* on economist Joseph Schumpeter, whose writings from the 1940s on the dynamic nature of the US economy were popular with economists during the internet-driven boom of the 1990s and early 2000s. All that material came together in an academic article I wrote on weekends while at *BusinessWeek*, highlighting Schumpeter's influence on Minsky's historical approach and using that approach to trace the US economy from its earliest days to the managed-money era.[22] An economics journal published that work as its lead article in December 2001, certainly a good way to mark my return to academic research.[23] That research stream soon led to more publications, including: an article stressing the public sector's role in laying a technological foundation for the boom of the late 1990s and early 2000s; a book chapter tracking the spread of US economic insecurity up to the eve of the global financial crisis in 2007 (including attention to public policies that accelerated the development of managed money); and an award-winning article on the perennial need for government to serve as a creative and stabilizing force in economic life.[24]

Four Books and Early Work on the Global Financial Crisis

In the wake of my departure from IF, I began editing four books; I also unexpectedly found myself providing one of the earliest analyses of the global financial crisis of 2007–2009. The first book, which I started shortly after leaving IF, aimed to synthesize my work on managed-money capitalism and worker insecurity, but was soon pushed aside by other projects. I returned to it at the start of the COVID-19 pandemic, resulting in *Reforming Capitalism for the Common Good*, a collection of twenty-six essays spanning more than three decades.[25] Reviewing the book, published in 2022, economist Jacob Powell concludes:

> It was inspiring to see a large collection from one successful academic bound in a single collection, allowing me the opportunity to reflect on what my own research agenda is while thinking about how to achieve the success embedded in this volume. It is clear an alternative human-centered approach [to economics] is needed, and Whalen offers us one through this collection.[26]

Two other books from the post-IF period focus on labor relations and human resource economics.[27] *New Directions in the Study of Work and Employment*, a product of my involvement with *Perspectives on Work*, brought together some of the world's finest scholars of industrial relations to explore how to revitalize that field as both an area of academic research and a realm of real-world labor-management engagement. *Human Resource Economics and Public Policy* assembled colleagues and students of Vernon Briggs, my Cornell professor, in celebration of his retirement in 2007. The *New Directions* project began in 2006, and the book was published in 2008; *Human Resource Economics* began shortly after Briggs retired and was released in 2010.

The fourth book began in 2006 as an exploration of post-Keynesian institutionalism at the annual meeting of AFEE. When the global financial crisis hit a year later, the contributors (including one of my Lingnan students, who came to the states to pursue a PhD) redirected their analyses to investigate that crisis, resulting in *Financial Instability and Economic Security After the Great Recession*. While explaining the post-Keynesian institutionalist approach and applying it to offer American and international perspectives on theory and policy, the book offers an early assessment of the financial crisis and the deep recession it triggered. When the book was published in 2011, Charles K. Wilber, a key originator of PKI, wrote, "Charles Whalen has been the torchbearer for post-Keynesian institutionalism for many years. The fruit of his thought and time is reaped in the publication of this valuable work; ... a first-rate book."[28]

In mid-2007, a contributor to the *Financial Instability* book invited me to lecture at his university; the result was one of the first analyses of the financial turbulence that quickly became a global financial crisis. The invitation came from Fadhel Kaboub, a professor of economics at Drew University, who asked me to deliver a lecture to his students in mid-September on the ongoing relevance of the economics of Minsky. After using Minsky's approach to financial crises to explain the turbulence that was then considered merely a "credit crunch," I wrote a paper based on my talk and sent it to the Levy Institute, which published it as a Public Policy Brief in October 2007.[29]

Drawing on Minsky's "financial instability hypothesis," I explained the credit crunch as a product of our economy's tendency toward increasing fragility over a period of prosperity, which occurs largely because borrowers and lenders gradually take on greater risk and because financial sector innovation tends to evade regulatory constraints. While my policy brief was in production, I realized that although I highlighted Minsky's groundbreaking attention to the dangers of financial "securitization" (the bundling and selling of shares of assets such as mortgages), I missed the chance to show how securitization and its role in the mounting crisis related to Hy's work on the emergence of money manager capitalism. But the crisis only deepened in the following months, which gave me a chance to revisit the topic in January 2008 for *Challenge* magazine and again in March 2008 for an Italian economics journal, each time with more attention to the new managed-money era.[30]

The Endless Job Search—and Glimmers of Hope

Throughout my six years of working mostly from home in Geneva, I continued to look for an academic or policy job. The prospects weren't always bright, but that seemed to change in late 2004 and early 2005, shortly after my departure from IF. During that job-market cycle, nibbles from a half-dozen search committees led to on-campus interviews at two locations in the Midwest: a liberal-arts college and a university with a doctoral program that attracted many institutionalists and post-Keynesians.

I liked the faculty and students I met at the college, and they apparently liked me as well. On the afternoon I gave a public presentation and met with students, a student leader told the professor in charge of the faculty search, "You've gotta hire this guy!" But when the college's offer came, the university search was still ongoing and I took a risk by passing on the offer in the hope of a chance to work with PhD students in a department focused on reshaping economics.

The university eventually chose to go with a much less experienced applicant (a PhD candidate), so I continued my at-home research and writing. I also looked on the bright side: staying in the Finger Lakes region enabled Katie to graduate from Geneva High School in 2007, and allowed Linda to continue working for New York State, where she already had more than a dozen years of service. We had even recently paid off our mortgage.

Meanwhile, across town on the campus of Hobart and William Smith Colleges, a student in the "Political Economy" course I taught during my 1988–1994 appointment had returned to Geneva with a PhD and was now teaching that same course. She wrote to me sometime after beginning to teach at the colleges, thanking me for preparing her so well and expressing gratitude for having my course syllabus to use as a guide.[31] The news was bittersweet given that I was sitting at home unemployed just a short distance away. The bitter side became even more pronounced when she decided to leave in 2006, accepting a position in England to be a bit closer to her family overseas.

In the wake of my former student's departure, the chairman of the economics department at HWS surprised me by dropping by my home and asking whether I'd fill the department's teaching gap for the coming year. There was no mention of the fact that in 1994 I was told the institution couldn't retain me because allowing a seventh year of service would require granting me tenure, but I said I'd think about the offer. A short time later, I emailed the department chair and said I'd be happy to return to HWS if the appointment came with tenure since my record at the colleges as well as my subsequent experience were clearly worthy of it. That quickly brought the matter to a close.

The year 2007 brought two new developments, each of which offered a glimmer of hope in its own way. At the start of the fall semester, thanks to Professor David Lipsky (whom I knew mainly through LERA), the Cornell ILR faculty in Ithaca appointed me as a visiting fellow, which was an unpaid position but enabled full access to the Cornell University libraries and allowed me to participate in regular ILR faculty seminars. That fall also brought a position announcement from Utica College, which sought an "executive director of business and economics," a faculty appointment roughly equivalent to what many colleges and universities call an associate dean. The difference was that at Utica the business and economics disciplines did not have separate department chairs for fields such as accounting, management, and economics. Instead, the executive director, who reported to the dean of the School of Business and Justice Studies, oversaw all those programs.

Utica College, just under a two-hour drive from my home, wanted someone to begin at the start of 2008, which was fine with me, so I applied. That led to an interview in Syracuse over lunch with the dean and an accounting professor, during which they stressed that the reason for urgently filling the position was because the business programs were pursuing accreditation by the Association to Advance Collegiate Schools of Business (known as both AACSB International and AACSB); in fact, the application for accreditation candidacy was behind schedule and a key responsibility of the executive director would be to get that effort back on track. Then I met the college president and provost, who extended me an offer that included a light teaching load, appointment as a full professor, and a tenure review in my second year. I accepted the offer and began working in Utica at the start of 2008.[32]

PART NINE

MOHAWK VALLEY

25 UTICA COLLEGE

Syracuse University created Utica College in 1946 to meet the needs of military veterans after the Second World War.[1] It was named Utica College of Syracuse University until shortly before my position began in 2008, and undergraduates at the newly independent Utica College continued to receive Syracuse University degrees until 2011, through a partnership agreement with the university. When I arrived in Utica to lead the department of business and economics, that unit included over a half-dozen degree programs (including onsite undergraduate programs in several fields and online graduate programs in business administration and accounting), a dozen full-time faculty, and nearly two-dozen adjunct instructors. The unit enrolled about 300 undergraduate majors and 150 graduate students.

To compete with other college business programs in upstate New York, Utica College sought accreditation by AACSB International (AACSB). The college needed to meet a deadline extension in 2008 to keep the pursuit alive: an accreditation plan needed to be submitted and approved for the college to enter a stage called accreditation candidacy. Leading the accreditation initiative was my primary administrative responsibility, but managing the unit also came with many other duties, including organizing a public speakers' series that was to have occurred the previous year.

The accreditation standards for AACSB were explicit and well-known to the dean of the School of Business and Justice Studies, who regularly attended AACSB-sponsored conferences and met often with the mentor assigned to Utica College by the accrediting body. The college's provost and president also seemed to understand the accrediting standards and their implications, and I certainly did my best to be sure the administration was fully aware of what was required. After all, the administrators above me were the institution's decision-makers, and accreditation required major financial commitments that only they could make—mainly commitments to hire more tenure-track faculty with doctorates as well as to reduce teaching loads (to enable increased faculty research and professional engagement).

When I first met the president and provost during the position recruitment process, they both stressed the importance of AACSB accreditation. The president, Todd Hutton, even explained it was part of his plan to create a separate School of Business for just the business and economics programs, a plan he said included me becoming its dean. It sure sounded as though securing the college's vital accreditation would lead to the deanship, but similar sorts of enticing bait had been dangled before me in Geneva and Parkersburg, so I nodded politely and silently resolved not to get sucked in for a third time. Besides, since Hutton hadn't agreed to appoint me with tenure, I still had tenure to pursue in addition to accreditation.

Executive Director

My job title at Utica College may have been "executive director," but there was often nobody to direct. For example, directors of programs seeking AACSB accreditation often delegated the accreditation work to a member of their organization's faculty or staff; but at Utica, if the work was going to get done, the bulk of it would have to be done by me. After all, the department's faculty members were already teaching a heavy load of courses—at least four a semester—and pursuit of AACSB accreditation meant they each needed to increase their scholarship and related forms of professional engagement. The college's administrative assistants were also stretched thin, with just two covering the School of Business and Justice Studies, although both Sue Cox and Jo Ann Hayward were exceptional professionals and helped in all sorts of ways.

I worked steadily on the AACSB accreditation plan throughout my first semester at Utica and into the summer, submitting the plan and supporting material in August 2008, ahead of its deadline. In January 2009, the plan was accepted, admitting Utica College as a candidate for accreditation. Much still needed to be done to achieve the accreditation, but at least the roadmap was there. In October 2009, the department submitted an update to AACSB focusing on the faculty's accreditation-related activities, and the college's AACSB mentor (Linda Garceau of East Tennessee State University) wrote that we were "making good progress."[2]

The department also delivered a successful speakers' series for the Utica community, finding ways to use each event to interact with other college departments as well as with businesses and civic groups across the Mohawk Valley. Speakers included: Aaron Feuerstein, owner of a textile mill in Massachusetts who received national attention for retaining his workforce after a fire in December 1995, and who later battled with lenders to keep his company's production in the United States;[3] Bruce Marks, a community organizer, housing activist, and mortgage broker, who founded Neighborhood Assistance Corporation of America and fought to provide low- and moderate-income households with affordable fixed-rate mortgages in an era of widespread predatory lending;[4] David Cay Johnston, a former *New York Times* journalist and winner of the Pulitzer Prize for writing on business issues; Tia Denenberg, a pioneer in workplace violence prevention; and John Zogby, an internationally known pollster based in Utica. The department even presented a public event with eight faculty members addressing the mounting financial crisis—in February 2008, perhaps the first public examination of the crisis by a group of professors on any campus in the nation.

Pursuit of Tenure

From a family perspective, the job at Utica College didn't offer much improvement over my earlier positions. After devoting most of my first summer to the AACSB accreditation plan, I spent a good part of my second summer preparing a tenure portfolio for submission to Utica College in fall 2009.

A large portion of my tenure submission addressed teaching, which included a fall semester course called "Government and Economic Life" and a year-long sequence of courses called "Economic Research Proposal" and "Economic Research Methods." The government and the economy course examined an array of perspectives on the role of government, applying them to analyze current issues including the relative merits of two very different approaches to economic success: the Wal-Mart cost-cutting model, which even now continues to represent the dominant approach in many industries, and the market-expanding alternative of an "innovation nation," championed by entrepreneur John Kao.[5] The research proposal and methods courses were required of all economics majors and culminated with a substantial research paper by each student, comparable to a "senior thesis."[6] All three courses were well-received by students as well as by faculty observers, and I was pleased to find that students were willing to put in the effort that made each course a rewarding experience for everyone.[7]

In addition to teaching, my tenure portfolio addressed "service" and "professional accomplishment." It wasn't always easy to distinguish service activities from my work as a program director, but some participation fell neatly into the service category, such as taking part in the college's Honorary Degree Committee. I also served my profession as a member of editorial boards for three academic journals, co-chair of a labor economists' study group affiliated with LERA, and editor of *Perspectives on Work* through March 2009. All that activity was covered in the tenure application, as was a discussion of professional accomplishments, including publication of new and forthcoming books and articles based on research conducted prior to working in Utica, as well as a description of new streams of research related to the global financial crisis and accompanying Great Recession.

Reviewers of my tenure application didn't have to worry about me finding opportunities to make professional contributions by speaking and writing about the economic crisis. As in the case of the stock-market drop in 1987, the financial turmoil that hit in 2007 generated sizeable interest in the economics of Minsky among academics and policymakers. Since I was a main proponent of his approach, I had plenty of invitations for research-related professional engagement over the next few years, including some from the Levy Institute.

26 "WE'RE ALL MINSKYITES NOW"

Hyman Minsky anticipated the global financial crisis of 2007–2009 as early as the mid-1980s. That's when he first sounded the alarm over economic risks linked to the growing securitization of home mortgages and other financial assets. A close observer of financial markets, Minsky explained that the securitization process took often risky financial assets, bundled them in a way that magically transformed them into highly rated financial products, and sold them to investors worldwide. It led him to conclude that securitization, a key feature of the new era he described as money manager capitalism, illustrated a fundamental flaw in financial-sector deregulation: it allowed the spread of increasing risks across the global economy while also reducing the power and authority of central banks and government regulators to respond to a crisis.[1]

At the heart of the trouble in 2007 was securitization of "subprime" mortgages: loans that enticed borrowers with checkered financial histories by offering short-term teaser rates and later left them on the hook for huge monthly payments when interest rates on the loans skyrocketed. Conventional economists dismissed Minsky's securitization concerns. Instead, they argued that securitization—in fact, the entire financial sector—was a model of sound risk management based on rationality and economic efficiency. The financial crisis caught mainstream economists flat-footed because they denied it was even possible.[2]

In summer 2007, financial market turmoil was so unnerving that *The Wall Street Journal* featured a cover story on Minsky, noting that his ideas had suddenly come into fashion even though Hy died more than a decade earlier.[3] A year later, financial markets were in such a dire condition that the US Treasury Department proposed a plan to acquire up to $700 billion worth of mortgage-backed securities to prevent widespread bank failures; and Federal Reserve Chairman Ben Bernanke reportedly told congressional leaders that if they didn't soon pass an emergency stabilization package "we may not have an economy."[4] The emergency package became law in early October 2008, and the following month *The Nation* published an article with the headline, "We're All Minskyites Now."[5]

Rethinking Economics and Public Policy for the Real World

In the wake of the global financial crisis, some prominent economists acknowledged that Minsky's ideas deserved more attention. Lawrence Summers of Harvard University admitted that economics had "forgotten a fair amount" about real-world financial markets since the days of Minsky.[6] Paul Krugman (recipient of the economics Nobel Memorial Prize in 2008) tried to revisit Keynes and Minsky to recapture what was forgotten, but came away with little insight from his effort to "reread" Minsky.[7] Janet Yellen, then head of the Federal Reserve Bank of San Francisco, had more success. In a speech at a conference sponsored by the Levy Economics Institute in April 2009, Yellen stressed the enduring relevance of Minsky's theory of financial crises (the "financial instability hypothesis") as well as his emphasis on the need for ongoing supervision and attentive regulation of the financial system to prevent such crises.[8]

The financial crisis and economists' rediscovery of Minsky brought several invitations to write and speak over the next few years. Consistent with the global nature of the economic problem, early invitations came in the form of requests for book chapters from England and Australia: one seeking an analysis of the financial crisis and the other requiring an examination of the global recession it triggered.[9] I was also invited to make presentations at an international economics conference at Buffalo State College, faculty workshops at the University at Buffalo Law School and Cornell ILR in Ithaca, summer programs for graduate students at the Levy Institute, and a conference on global financial fragility in Tianjin, China. An important theme in most of those presentations was that a deeper understanding of the global crisis requires moving beyond Minsky's instability hypothesis to a synthesis of that approach with his attention to key features of the investor-driven, managed-money era. I also addressed the need for both economic recovery and reform, stressing the importance of restructuring home loans to prevent foreclosures as well as replacing the leaders of bailed-out financial institutions.

Each of my presentations on the crisis led eventually to a journal article or other publication, including remarks delivered at the Levy Institute in summer 2010, published in its *Policy Notes* series as "Economic Policy for the Real World."[10] That presentation highlighted the link between the financial crisis and the ongoing problem of worker insecurity. Meanwhile, my crisis-era appearances at the institute found such receptive audiences that they resulted in invitations to write additional papers, including the lead article for an issue of a European journal in which I offered post-Keynesian institutionalism as the starting point for economics after the Great Recession.[11]

A Constructive Alternative with Insight When It Mattered Most

Most economists retreated to their standard models soon after the financial crisis receded. Many policymakers retreated as well, moving away from the goal of devising a new financial architecture characterized by prudent regulation and reverting to attacking government for stifling private enterprise. "We're all Minskyites" turned out to be short-lived, but the global financial crisis showed that when it mattered most the economic mainstream had nothing to say—and post-Keynesian institutionalism, grounded in the work of a cavalcade of unconventional thinkers including Commons, Keynes, Schumpeter, and Minsky, proved its worth.

27 MOMENT OF TRUTH

In early 2010, I learned that Utica College acted favorably on my application for tenure. But the real moment of truth involved what the college's president would do on the commitments needed for AACSB accreditation. The AACSB matter didn't end well. Yet I somehow again managed to land on my feet.

Writing on the Wall

In January 2010, the head of AACSB's initial accreditation committee requested an updated progress report from Utica College.[1] The letter identified two key concerns: the department needed more full-time professors with doctorates (or at least a clear hiring timeline), and the college needed to demonstrate a commitment to providing the financial resources necessary to secure faculty sufficiency and other accreditation standards. The update was requested by the end of the semester.

A short time later, the college asked me to attend the annual meeting of an alternative accrediting body—along with Herb Rau, a Utica College professor of management—and report back on whether that group was a viable alternative to AACSB. The request was disconcerting because it was my understanding that the college had already done considerable homework on the various accrediting bodies and concluded that AACSB accreditation was essential for competing with peer institutions. Still, my colleague and I agreed to travel to Newport, Rhode Island, and attend the meeting of the International Accreditation Council for Business Education (IACBE) in March 2010.

In Newport, Rau and I attended all the plenary sessions and split up to participate in separate breakouts. We also quizzed as many of the 120 attendees as we could during meals and breaks. Then we delivered a memo to the Utica College dean and provost. Our bottom line: Since the bulk of our competitors in the state of New York were AACSB accredited, and since the college sought to expand its market reach nationally and even internationally (where AACSB is the best-known accreditor), AACSB seemed vital, and IACBE didn't seem to offer a meaningful alternative.[2]

The next month, I attended the annual meeting of AACSB in Anaheim, California. It wasn't my first AACSB meeting, but this time I carried a list of questions the college wanted me to ask its members; the list focused on how and why they chose AACSB accreditation. Reporting back, I explained that representatives from colleges and universities in the Northeast most often said that AACSB accreditation was essential for them to compete for faculty and students in their region.[3] In fact, Utica College experienced the challenges of competing for faculty, especially in the field of accounting. As for attracting students, I noted that the coach of Utica College's track team contacted me shortly after I returned from California to report that he just lost yet another prospective student athlete to an institution with AACSB accreditation.

Game Over

A few weeks later, on May 12, 2010, President Hutton met with the business and economics faculty for a meeting in which he was to announce whether the college would make the necessary commitments and proceed with AACSB accreditation. Instead, the meeting centered on criticizing the unit for making what the president described as little progress toward strengthening its programs. At the end of the brief meeting, someone asked directly about AACSB: would the college continue to pursue its accreditation? Hutton's reply: "Of course, we have to do that."[4]

In fact, the department made much progress in the two and a half years since I arrived on campus. In my first year, we revived a stalled AACSB effort and secured accreditation candidacy. Then, even without major financial and hiring commitments from the college, we managed to recruit a diverse and talented team of additional full-time professors in economics, management, marketing, and accounting—all with doctorates. At the same time, another faculty member, who enrolled in a doctoral program to help the department meet AACSB standards, completed his PhD coursework and began his dissertation, while still teaching in the department. We also made considerable progress on reducing the department's reliance on adjunct faculty, building a community supportive of increased scholarly activity and professional engagement, and increasing the profile of the department across campus and the greater Utica community.

There was even more—a lot more—that we achieved and attempted. But it didn't matter. The president's meeting left me convinced the best way forward was to leave my administrative post. On June 7, 2010, I wrote to the provost and resigned my position as executive director of business and economics.[5] With that letter, I included a six-page list of accomplishments and activities by the department under my leadership. The letter closed by describing my plan to remain at the college as a full-time professor and teach a load of three courses each fall and spring, a six-course load consistent with our pursuit of AACSB accreditation.

Unexpected Opportunities

I wasn't surprised when the Business and Justice Studies dean soon reported that my course load would have to be eight courses per year (four courses per semester), not the six-course load that aligned with the AACSB effort. Over time, I had increasingly suspected the college wasn't truly willing to implement the changes that accreditation required, and my mention of a six course load in the June 7th letter was a final test of that willingness.

The college's insistence that I teach eight courses each year put me in a difficult spot. From the start of my career, I avoided applying for any faculty position with a load of more than six courses per year, which is what I had at Hobart and William Smith Colleges (HWS) under a trimester system. To me, six courses needed to be the upper bound if a faculty member was to be effective as a researcher as well as a teacher.[6] I accepted the job at Utica believing that its administration was committed to a plan that would reduce teaching loads from eight to six courses per year.

Then an unexpected opportunity emerged. An economist at the Congressional Budget Office (CBO) contacted me about a letter of inquiry I sent months earlier in response to a job advertisement. The CBO was looking for an economist who covered the national economy (macroeconomics), but the ideal candidate was someone who also had extensive experience writing for people who aren't economists. After all, the agency works for members of Congress and, through them, for the public. From its earliest days in the mid-1970s, CBO sought to make its research and reports accessible to non-economists, but Douglas ("Doug") Elmendorf, the agency's director since early 2009, thought the global financial crisis and accompanying severe recession demanded even more attention to the goal of producing widely understandable documents. After a brief phone conversation, arrangements were made for me to visit the agency in Washington, DC, a short distance from the US Capitol.

During my visit to Washington, I learned from Elmendorf that my position would be in the agency's macroeconomic analysis division, and that the search for an economist/writer was an experiment he hoped would lead to similar positions in other CBO departments. I also learned that my unusual background contained a good mix of the academic and writing-related elements he thought the job required. Meanwhile, I was familiar with Elmendorf's work and admired his nonpartisan spirit as well as his openness to Keynesian economics in a profession that had largely moved in a different direction.[7] On June 22, I received Doug's job offer.

A few days later, a second unexpected opportunity came my way. This time, it came in the form of a call from the Levy Institute asking whether I was available to return to the institute and write an economics-focused biography of Minsky. The Levy Institute offer had the advantage of involving work that I could often do from home in Geneva, although there was still much to be done at the institute where Minsky's personal papers are stored. It was also self-directed work on a topic that interested me, and a body of work I knew quite well. But the downside of the offer was the position would end once the book was finished; in other words, it was more gig work.

In contrast, CBO's offer involved an ongoing position in an agency with a history of often career-long employment. With the nation still recovering from the global financial crisis, it also offered a chance to contribute to policymaking on the country's most pressing economic issues. In addition, it was easy to reach Washington by plane, and Katie was in college so working away from home would be less of a concern than when she was young.

Because accepting the CBO job meant walking away from tenure, I might have stayed at Utica had the college shown some flexibility with the teaching load. In fact, under different circumstances a short unpaid leave to work on the Minsky book might have even been possible. But the college still hadn't budged on my teaching duties by mid-July, and my experience there suggested it was never going to be a comfortable place to work. At that point, I submitted my resignation from the faculty and accepted a principal analyst post at CBO. Utica College never did commit to AACSB accreditation and its accompanying reduced teaching load.

PART TEN

WASHINGTON, DC

28 IN THE SHADOW OF THE CAPITOL

In September 2010, I joined the Macroeconomic Analysis Division (MAD) of the Congressional Budget Office (CBO), a group of nearly two dozen economists in an agency of 250 people.[1] The division included an Economic Projections Unit and a Fiscal Policy Studies Unit, and I was allowed to choose the unit to which I was officially assigned, since, as the head of MAD explained, it didn't really matter because I would work on projects in both areas. I selected the fiscal policy unit because I had experience analyzing fiscal policies (taxes and government spending) but no forecasting experience.

But I understood the projections and could write about them, so during my stay at the agency I composed semiannual reports describing the agency's 10-year "economic outlook" as well as annual reports with CBO's estimates of the likely economic effects of the president's budget proposals.[2] I also contributed to analyzing the economy, clarifying policy alternatives and consequences, and ensuring the transparency of CBO's work. I even brought to Washington my habits of pursuing independent research and engaging in professional service. And, in a refreshing change from Utica, my contributions and initiative were welcomed and appreciated at CBO.

Ensuring Transparency, Analyzing the Economy, and Clarifying Alternatives

Since CBO serves the members of Congress, the agency strives to keep its methods transparent. To that end, MAD often publishes reports outlining the methods used to conduct analyses and make projections; it also highlights the major sources of uncertainty that could affect its forecasts and findings. For example, I wrote reports explaining how CBO analyzes fiscal policies, projects national income, and addresses the uncertainties affecting near-term and long-term projections.[3]

Working on those documents, I often thought of a career recommendation my dad made when I was in high school: that I should become a technical writer because I could explain complex matters to laypeople. I always dismissed such writing as glorified production-line work, and I felt that way about my role in some CBO reports (as I often did when editing the Economic Trends column at *BusinessWeek*). But I also saw working on them as a means of quickly gaining a thorough understanding of CBO's work, which I considered vital to playing a larger, analysis-oriented role at the agency over time.[4]

My two biggest opportunities to play a larger role occurred in 2012 and 2013, and both involved analyzing the economy by collaborating with economists from the projections unit. The first opportunity, a partnership with macroeconomist Mark Lasky, led to a major CBO report on why the US economy recovered much more slowly in the three years following the Great Recession of 2007–2009 than after other postwar recessions.[5] The report, published in late 2012, traces about two-thirds of that sluggishness to long-term trends slowing the growth of the economy's productive capacity, including slower growth not only in the population of working-age people, but also in business investment.[6] The remaining one-third of the economy's sluggishness was attributed to the more immediate shortfall in demand for goods and services, owing to slower growth in consumer spending, residential investment, and purchases by government (federal, state, and local). In short, much of the slow recovery reflected a long-term trend, but idiosyncrasies of the latest business cycle also played a role—including the slower growth in government spending, which may have surprised many readers.[7]

The second collaboration, with labor economist David Brauer, led to a related report on the weak recovery of the labor market.[8] While the work with Lasky focused on slow growth in economic output, the work with Brauer focused on a shortfall of 6 million jobs at the end of 2013, compared with where employment would have been if the unemployment rate returned to its pre-recession level and the rate of labor force participation rebounded from its cyclical weakness. The labor market report, published in early 2014, explains that the higher unemployment rate and lower participation rate, which results partly from jobless workers becoming discouraged, accounted equally for the jobs shortfall.[9]

That report highlights the danger of economic conditions that keep people out of work for an extended period. During the Great Recession and its aftermath, labor-market weakness caused by the downturn—that is, "cyclical" weakness—often became a more intractable "structural" problem owing to the stigma and erosion of skills accompanying long-term unemployment. Meanwhile, extension of unemployment benefits, often viewed as a major cause of labor market sluggishness by conservatives (who argue benefits extensions discourage the jobless from finding new work), was found to have little effect on the unemployment rate.

In addition to conducting economic analyses, macroeconomists at CBO often assist the agency director in preparing congressional testimony on economic policy alternatives and their likely consequences. During my first fifteen months at CBO, I joined several of my MAD colleagues in working with Doug Elmendorf on presentations for three hearings, two for the Senate Budget Committee and one for the Joint Select Committee on Deficit Reduction. In fact, one of Doug's statements to the Budget Committee was the first project to which I was assigned. On each of those occasions, I admired Elmendorf's assessment of the nation's policy challenges, including his attention to the large number of unemployed workers and other signs of continued weakness in the economy, and his effort to remind members of Congress that the most important policy matter goes well beyond the size of the federal deficit or debt: "The most fundamental question is what role the government should play in the United States economy and society."[10]

Working with Economists and Editors

To improve the clarity and accessibility of CBO's macroeconomic reports, I worked with each of MAD's economic analysts. That often involved reviewing drafts of their reports—providing comments, suggestions, and even first-round edits. In just my first year, I offered substantial input on over a dozen of my colleagues' reports, while still writing several of my own. In 2012, I was also asked to mentor a colleague, who had recently joined the agency, by working jointly with him on two CBO working papers. That side-by-side approach worked so well that I soon began to collaborate with a coauthor on each of the agency's semiannual economic outlook reports, working with the same economist twice and then taking on a different coauthor the following year. That close collaboration sometimes reminded me of working alongside editors and writers at *BusinessWeek* (except within MAD I was usually suggesting the edits); and every report was a reminder of the value of "learning by doing."

While CBO's economists might have learned a bit about writing from me, I certainly learned from CBO's editors.[11] I worked with the entire team of CBO editors, and all of them were terrific. We worked together on countless MAD reports, usually with me as a go-between, crafting solutions that would meet the needs and concerns of not only the analysts and editors but also the agency's front office. Deadlines were often tight, and weekend work wasn't unusual, but collaborating with the editors was a highlight of my job. Working with CBO editors made me a better writer at least as much as working with MAD analysts made me a better economist.

Independent Research and Service

Prior to working at CBO, I always found ways to engage in independent research as well as in service to my workplace and profession. That continued during my years in Washington. Several of my publications were already in the pipeline when I arrived at CBO, but additional journal articles came from work done on my own time while employed by the agency. I also wrote book reviews for economics journals, evaluated research proposals for publishers, organized policy-oriented sessions for professional conferences, arranged guest presentations at CBO, and represented the agency at student-centered events.

Two articles prepared on my own time drew on a work project with a colleague that explained how the agency assesses the economic effects of changes in federal spending and taxes. One article examines the role of the "fiscal multiplier" in making those assessments.[12] In other words, it describes how economists estimate the extent to which each dollar change in the federal budget gets multiplied as that change ripples across the economy from the person or organization initially affected to other businesses, government agencies, and consumers. It's a technical matter, but different estimates of the multiplier are often at the heart of debates that determine federal spending and taxes, so there was great value in publishing an article in a respected mainstream economics journal on the models and assumptions that analysts use. The other article reviews an even more technical matter (but also important to policy debates) centering on how workers are likely to respond to changes in tax policies.[13] Both articles, which appear as coauthored works in a nod to the original CBO project, are still cited regularly by economists and policy analysts.

Other independently prepared articles attempted to advance the economic tradition of post-Keynesian institutionalism (PKI), which offers a perspective I find most useful for understanding the economy. PKI stresses that the steady shift toward shareholder-driven, money manager capitalism has fueled decades of rising economic insecurity among working families; and former President Bill Clinton offered the same assessment in September 2011. According to Clinton, "The American Dream has been under assault for the last 30–35 years," mainly because corporations focus on the interests of shareholders and downplay the importance of employees, the public, and the constructive role of government.[14] Clinton's remarks encouraged me to find a way to contribute further to PKI while still engaging in the much more measured work done at CBO. The solution came in the form of an invitation to write a paper marking the retirement of Robert Brazelton, an economist associated with PKI. In the next few years, I composed a trio of articles each highlighting the research of a significant contributor to PKI.[15]

In my previous jobs, one way I served my workplace community was by arranging guest lectures; my stay at CBO was no exception. The first lecture, delivered in early 2011, was by Mike Mandel, who served as economics editor when I was at *BusinessWeek* and later became chief economist at the Progressive Policy Institute. I ran into Mike on a Metro subway car in Washington and invited him to speak about his work on rethinking the measurement of key economic variables (including gross domestic product and productivity growth) in what he called the new "global supply-chain" economy. Another lecture brought economist and venture capitalist William Janeway to CBO in mid-2013 to discuss "Doing Capitalism in the Innovation Economy." Janeway admired Hy Minsky, and we first met at the Levy Economics Institute in the 1990s; I invited him to CBO after hearing him speak at a Ford Foundation event on finance and sustainable prosperity in late 2012.

CBO also presented opportunities for new types of professional service. In 2013, for example, I accepted an invitation to speak on behalf of my CBO colleagues at a forum on the range of career paths available to economists, which took place in Tampa at the annual meeting of the Southern Economic Association. A tenured university professor on the panel discussed the job market in economics and concluded, "The sorting works," by which she meant the market successfully matches people to the "right" jobs. I let the remark go without comment; it was, after all, what you'd expect a successful academic economist to say. After the career forum, I visited with economics majors at the nearby University of South Florida as an ambassador for CBO, which often hires college graduates as interns. A year later, I represented the agency as a judge at the national finals of the Policy Solutions Challenge USA, a competition for teams of college students from the nation's public policy schools.

Respect and Recognition

Working at CBO was rewarding because many citizens and most economists and public policy professionals respected the agency's estimates and analyses. During my CBO employment, I recall several times when the quality of our work received praise from outside economists and recognition from members of Congress.[16] The agency also showed appreciation for the collective work and individual accomplishments of its staff—with notes of thanks, celebratory gatherings, and sometimes even a bonus after a solid performance review.

I worked under two CBO directors, Doug Elmendorf and Keith Hall, and both sought to maintain the collegial organizational culture established in the mid-1970s under the agency's first director, Alice Rivlin. But I interacted more with Doug, perhaps because there was so much macroeconomics to be addressed in the aftermath of the Great Recession and because he hired me to help MAD devote more attention to its writing. I often saw Doug recognize analysts' work by inviting them to accompany him to hearings on Capitol Hill, and he was so pleased with my fiscal multipliers article that he insisted the agency publish the accepted manuscript as a CBO working paper.[17]

In April 2013, I received the CBO Director's Award. It's the agency's highest honor recognizing the work of a CBO employee. But for me perhaps an even greater honor was Doug stopping by my office on his last day as director (at the end of March 2015) and thanking me for my contributions to the agency.

29 THE OTHER DC

Shortly before starting work at CBO, I rented a small, second-floor studio apartment on Capitol Hill, about a 25-minute walk from my office and close to a Metro rail station with easy access to the airport. The apartment's main windows faced Marion Park, green space two blocks long and one block wide, and my walking route to the office crossed through two other neighborhood parks, where I was often greeted by gabby mockingbirds. Sometimes I'd catch a flight home for the weekend, but usually Linda would instead fly to Washington from upstate New York so we could explore the DC area together.

After about two years of working at CBO, I began looking to buy a row house on Capitol Hill because interest rates were extremely low and house prices were still weak following the financial crisis. At the end of an alley cul-de-sac, a narrow two-bedroom house—12-feet wide, with just 672 square feet of living space—became available in December 2012, and Linda and I placed an offer without in-person viewing (except by our real estate agent) because I had just returned to central New York for the holidays. The offer (which included an inspection contingency) was accepted, and we moved into Gessford Court on February 13, 2013.

Brick-paved Gessford Court is tucked away between 11th and 12th Streets in DC's Southeast quadrant, about a 25-minute walk from the US Capitol and 35 minutes from CBO's offices in the Ford House Office Building. Developer Charles Gessford built the alley's mews in 1892 as rental housing for unskilled and semi-skilled African Americans and immigrants.[1] Gessford's business was wiped out by the financial crisis and depression of 1893, and he died early the next year. After the Second World War, Adam Clayton Powell Jr. resided on the street while representing the Harlem neighborhood of New York City in Congress for a quarter century.

I stumbled upon the alley a few months before the property came on the market. While house hunting one weekend, I happened to walk by Gessford Court during the residents' semiannual block party. Children were riding bicycles (cars aren't permitted to park in the alley), adults were dishing out food, and people of all ages were dancing to a jazz band that played in the shade of a tall redwood tree (yes, a redwood in DC!). The musicians were part of the 21 Gessford Court jazz combo, the house band for a monthly party and jam session at that address.

The accidental discovery of that secluded and neighborly cul-de-sac gave me a glimpse into another DC, a community with families (and many jazz musicians), not politicians, at its center. When I moved to Washington, I hoped it might fulfill some of my aspirations to contribute to making sensible public policies. I never expected it would reignite musical interests I set aside decades earlier, but that's exactly what happened.

Back-Alley Comeback

Shortly after moving into Gessford Court, I stopped by David Weiner's house party and found the host behind the drum kit. Weiner, who opens his home on the 21st of each month in the tradition of the Harlem rent parties of the 1920s, explained that the house band plays an opening set and then the jam session runs until around midnight. I quickly learned that during the event Weiner's musicians and guests tend to fill his home (two row houses combined into a single residence), with many neighbors arriving—usually with wine or a dish to pass—just to listen and socialize.

After a few months of scoping out the scene, I brought my trumpet from Geneva to Washington, along with a mute to avoid disturbing the neighbors, and began practicing regularly. Except for a brief period when Katie and I played music while she was in high school, I hadn't picked up the horn since college. And even in high school I rarely improvised, so there was much to learn. But the musicians at Weiner's parties were encouraging, especially guitarist and band co-leader Mark Johnson, who saw I had a passion for jazz and appreciated my commitment to making a musical comeback.

Over the next year, I made steady progress with the playing but remained a shy novice with the improvising. Still, Weiner and Johnson invited me to Sunday evening practice sessions with their band and even added me to the group for gigs ranging from posh fundraisers to outdoor neighborhood festivals. Vocalists from the Gessford sessions also invited me to Sunday afternoon jam sessions across town at Dalhak, an Eritrean restaurant on the southern edge of the city's nightlife-heavy Adams Morgan neighborhood.

At Dalhak, I was inspired even more thanks to the DC area's many highly talented jazz musicians, including several members of military bands based in the region. I soon became a regular listener at the city's jazz clubs and slowly gained the courage to play at some of the weekly jams, including one that ran each Friday night from 11 p.m. until at least 2 a.m.[2] Linda often came along when she was in Washington, finding it remarkable that we were in our 50s and getting home at 3 a.m., when we never stayed out nearly so late when we were younger.

Soon I was playing regularly with several bands, as well as gigging with small groups at one-time events. For example, a trumpeter I met at Dalhak recruited me to both a big band and jazz combo sponsored by DC's Different Drummers, a lesbian, gay, bisexual, and transgender music organization open to all musicians. Another trumpeter invited me to play on an ongoing basis with his Jazz Orchestra (a modern big band) as well as his Free-Jazz Consort (which used no written music). In addition, a member of the 21 Gessford band included me on a couple of gigs with his own jazz-fusion group; and a keyboardist added me to his band for a Mardi Gras–themed nonprofit event. A colleague at CBO even connected me with a jazz combo of economists, with whom I played a concert at the annual meeting of the American Economic Association in January 2014.

Dial 251 for Jazz

At a jam session in summer 2014, I was asked whether I had a band or could organize one to perform at a "Wine and Roses Jazz Festival" scheduled for a Saturday afternoon in early September. The "festival" turned out to be a wine tasting event at Old Line Fine Wine and Bistro, a supermarket-size liquor store with its own restaurant and event space in Beltsville, Maryland. Still, it featured five bands, each playing a 45-minute set, and the organizer paid $50 per musician, which was just enough to attract the guys I had in mind, all of whom worked day jobs. Although I didn't have a band, I had been obsessively collecting musicians' business cards and contact information at jams and performances, so I knew I could cobble something together.

Performing as the "Old Line All-Stars," my band included guitarist Johnson (from the Gessford band), saxophonist Bryan McEntire (a newcomer to Washington, whom I met at Dalhak), vocalist Steve Washington (a professional singer and familiar face at many local jams), and the rhythm section (keyboards, bass, and drums) of the house band from Tuesday night jam sessions at Takoma Station, a jazz and blues club on the border of DC and Takoma Park, Maryland. Everyone enjoyed our set, which we didn't rehearse but mapped out on paper and discussed in detail about a half-hour before taking the stage. We opened, appropriately enough, with "Days of Wine and Roses" and a pair of other instrumentals (with trumpet, sax, and guitar trading melody lines), then Steve's charisma energized the crowd with a mix of jazz and soul, including "Fly Me to the Moon," "Moondance," and "Stand by Me."

About a month later, the manager at Takoma Station asked whether I had a jazz band that could play between 7 and 9 p.m. on a Friday night in mid-November (2014), as the warm-up act for an R&B group. He said, "Two hours, maybe five guys, for $100 plus tips—and we need the band's name." The words "two (hours)...

five (guys)… one (hundred dollars)" reminded me that Dial Records used its "200" series for postwar recordings of Charlie Parker, Dizzy Gillespie, and other Modern Jazz artists; and when I confirmed the gig—for my "Old Line" instrumentalists, but with a different drummer and keyboardist—I told him to call us "Dial 251 for Jazz."[3] We couldn't afford to also hire a vocalist (even the sextet was really too large for what the gig paid), but Johnson liked to sing as well as play guitar so we could still perform vocal numbers in addition to instrumentals.[4]

Since we were a warm-up band, Takoma Station didn't begin to get crowded until late in our second set. But we had spread the word among friends and colleagues, attracting a friendly and appreciative audience for both sets, and the manager invited us to play regularly as an opening act. We continued to perform monthly for a year, including a show in June 2015, presented and advertised as part of the DC Jazz Festival. Playing regular gigs at Takoma Station into fall 2015 allowed the band to gel and gave us a chance to try out new material in public with little pressure.

The first show the band headlined took place in January 2015, at the Corner Store Arts Center, a 70-seat venue not far from my Gessford Court home on Capitol Hill. Vocalists Steve Washington and Kathleen Reilly (who often sang at Gessford jams) joined us for the event, which took place before a sold-out crowd. The success of that event helped us land another gig a few months later, at the nearby Mr. Henry's Restaurant, where Roberta Flack performed weekly in the late 1960s.[5]

Our first shows at Mr. Henry's—on Pennsylvania Avenue SE, six blocks from the US Capitol—were booked shortly after I popped into the restaurant one evening on my way home from work and talked with the manager about my band. The timing was perfect: the restaurant's jazz lounge had just reopened after being closed for years, and the manager was looking to book live music on a regular basis. We began playing in April 2015, with three-hour weekend performances (8:00 to 11:00 p.m.) about twice a month. Shows on the first Friday of each month featured our band, sometimes with Steve Washington singing during the second and third sets, while shows on the third Saturday featured the band with a female singer, part of the restaurant's "Ladies of Jazz" series. We even performed there on New Year's Eve at the end of 2015.

The ongoing Friday shows enabled the band to develop a solid repertoire, while the Saturday shows increased our versatility and capacity to make on-the-spot changes. During a year of Saturday shows, the band showcased Reilly and several other excellent local singers, including Anita King, Karen Gray, and Renee Tannenbaum. Keyboardist Matt Leonhardt, who began his career playing with a Marine band in Hawaii and joined Dial 251 in the early months of our Takoma Station engagement, served as music director for the shows with guest vocalists.[6] The ability to draw on Matt's experience was vital to the success of our "Ladies of Jazz" gigs.

Over time, Dial 251 settled into a monthly first Friday residence at Mr. Henry's, which lasted until COVID-19 put live music on hiatus in Washington and beyond. By the time we landed the Mr. Henry's gig, the band members had outgrown driving through rush-hour traffic with equipment for 7 p.m. gigs at Takoma Station. Instead, we rehearsed one Saturday afternoon a month, initially in my narrow row house (with advance warning for my neighbors), but later in a church basement. We also shifted gradually from performing with guest vocalists to focusing on our own sound and finding gigs that either paid more or increased our exposure in the region.

The burden of searching for gigs fell on me (along with creating set lists and managing the band's music library), but I was eager to find them—and quickly got good at it.[7] In fact, astonished at how I managed to land one gig after another, the spouse of one of my bandmates nicknamed me "The Impresario." By the time the pandemic hit, Dial 251 had performed at numerous events and venues, including the DC Art All Night festival, the US Botanic Garden, National Cherry Blossom Festival, and DC Downtown Holiday Market. Our swankiest event series was the Awards Gala Dinner of the World Vaccine Congress, held annually in a DC hotel ballroom, and our favorite venue was Twins Jazz, one of the area's few remaining jazz "listening rooms."[8] Between 2016 and 2019, the band played a weekend of four shows at Twins semiannually, and a review in *The Washington Post* described the first of our performances as "ambitious and rewarding," adding that "Dial 251 is a crisp, cohesive unit with gifted soloists and a lot to say."[9]

At the end of 2016, Mark Johnson retired and moved to California. I was grateful for the opportunity to learn by playing alongside him in Dial 251, but Johnson's departure also allowed the band to advance by clarifying its identity and streamlining its collective voice. Without a guitarist (in Mark's case, one who also dabbled as a singer-songwriter), we took on the shape and sound of a classic "hard bop" quintet: trumpet and tenor sax on the front line; piano, bass, and drums in the rhythm section; and sets full of straight-ahead jazz "with a shot of R&B."[10]

The melodic, harmonic, and rhythmic roles were now clearly defined. There was nothing superfluous, no place to hide. When the band began in 2015, I was musically shy; by the time the quintet version of Dial 251 arrived, the shyness was gone. I had come a long way since the start of the band and was looking forward to growing further with the streamlined lineup.

30 THE PERSONAL AND THE POLITICAL

Rediscovering a passion for playing music came at just the right time for me in Washington. Shortly after I received the CBO Director's Award in 2013, my work for the agency began to lose its allure because research opportunities began to narrow despite my track record and increased experience. I managed to stay there until early February 2017, but I probably would have left sooner if I hadn't become a part of the city's jazz community.

Upon leaving CBO, I became a research fellow in the Baldy Center for Law and Social Policy at the University at Buffalo, which sponsored a law and economics workshop I attended in 2010. I also retained musical ties to Washington. I even briefly pursued a plan to get back to the city and Capitol Hill on a full-time basis, though if it had worked there would've been little time for jazz. The decision to leave DC was personal; the decision to attempt a return was political.

Leaving CBO

The turning point at CBO came in summer 2014, a year after publication of my report on how CBO analyzes and projects income. I had been waiting months for an assistant analyst's technical assistance, which I needed to revise a paper initiated as a follow-up to the income report; but there was no sign the help was coming. The paper was on the important matter of an unusual 12-year decline in the share of national income received by workers, and the *Monthly Labor Review*, a major labor economics journal, expressed interest in publishing it. I just needed technical assistance to get results from the agency's macroeconomic model and then make a few revisions. In late July, when we reached the first anniversary of the initial report, I started to feel the help would never come. (It never did.) In mid-2013 and again in early 2014, I also undertook research laying a foundation for possible CBO work on how income inequality affects economic growth (the unsurprising answer is that inequality weakens economic growth, but my research pulled together the relevant analyses) but that too went nowhere.[1]

Around the same time, there was much speculation that the agency's managing editor was planning to retire, and many CBO editors encouraged me to apply for the job, which eventually became available in 2016. I was gratified by the compliment but didn't want to surrender my identity as an economist for the work of full-time editing. I was trying to bolster the economic research side of my CBO work, not bury it.

Nevertheless, I did apply, in mid-2015, for the position of CBO's associate director for legislative affairs. I understood from the retiring incumbent, Sandy Davis, that the position involves serving as the chief liaison between the agency and members of Congress. I also learned that Davis previously served as an analyst at CBO, so there was a precedent for moving from my position as a principal analyst to the legislative affairs job. Although I didn't get the job, the successful applicant had also been a CBO analyst in addition to more recently working as special assistant to the CBO director, which made her a fine choice.

With my labor share paper in limbo for lack of technical assistance, and no new project to take the place of my two major "slow recovery" collaborations, I was feeling that my work had become limited to writing new versions of the same reports year after year, so I again began looking for a new job. I reached out to the International Labour Organization, several think tanks, and the labor movement. In the process, I learned that Ron Blackwell, chief economist at the AFL-CIO, planned to retire. I knew Blackwell from my involvement with LERA and for a time it looked like I would be hired as his deputy and then move up when he retired. We even discussed the parts of his job that would be mine from the start, including international labor initiatives. But circumstances required Blackwell to retire earlier than he originally intended, and the federation never made me an offer.

Although I applied mostly to organizations in Washington, I also had several discussions with the executive director of the Institute for New Economic Thinking (INET) in New York. Devoted to a constructive reshaping of economics, and cofounded by Minsky's friend William Janeway, INET looked like a good fit for me; and for a time—in fact, on two occasions—the possibility of working there looked quite promising. But, again, an offer never materialized.

Then, in mid-2016, my immediate supervisor at CBO, the chief of the macroeconomics division's Fiscal Policy Studies Unit, accepted a job at the nonpartisan Tax Policy Center. I applied for his position because I had administrative and managerial experience from working at Utica College, as well as project management experience from my days at Cornell ILR, the Interactivity Foundation, and even *Perspectives on Work*. I also had a thorough understanding of the unit's work and an ability to explain it to economists and nonspecialists. In addition, there was my solid record at CBO of collaborative problem-solving, taking initiative to coordinate work within and across divisions, and ensuring that projects were on schedule and moving forward. Perhaps most important of all, unit chiefs were responsible for reviewing and offering constructive comments on first drafts of analysts' reports, which I had been doing within the Macroeconomic Analysis Division (MAD) from the moment I arrived at the agency.

Another colleague, who came to the agency with two decades less professional experience and whom I had been asked to mentor on his arrival to CBO, was ultimately given the unit chief position. It didn't seem right for the first review of my reports to be conducted by a person the agency arranged for me to mentor, so I asked to report instead to the chief of the Economic Projections Unit. After all, as I explained to the economist leading MAD at the time, my work straddled both units and I was allowed when hired to select the unit of my choice because the division leader who hired me said it didn't make any difference to the agency. In fact, although I produced important work for the fiscal policy unit (including the multipliers article that was done on my own initiative and impressed former director Elmendorf), slightly more than half of my published work fell into the projections unit realm rather than the fiscal policy realm.

The leader of MAD, the third person to head the division since I began at the agency, said he'd discuss my request for a unit change with the CBO director. But then I heard nothing. I had to ask a few times before I received an answer, which, in the end, was simply, "No. We can't make the change." Given how I'd been feeling about the position for two years, I went home and composed my resignation letter. Ironically (at this point in my career, it was obvious there are always ironies), I stayed on at the agency until early February 2017, mainly to complete my work as coauthor of an annual projections unit report.

The CBO that I left in 2017 felt and looked quite different from the agency into which I was hired. During my years of service, the policy momentum in Washington shifted steadily toward Republicans: the GOP took control of the House in 2013, the Senate in 2015, and the White House in 2017. Back in vogue were tax cuts, federal spending cuts, deregulation of business and finance, and calls for the "dynamic scoring" of fiscal policy, which too often boils down to the discredited argument that tax cuts pay for themselves by increasing economic growth.

The agency remained assiduously nonpartisan following the change of directors in early 2015. And despite being hand-selected by Republicans, our new director made it clear that "tax cuts do not pay for themselves."[2] Still, the mood on Capitol Hill and in the halls of CBO had changed. In the words of one manager, the agency seemed increasingly relegated to the role of an umpire who must "throw down the flag" on unsound ideas.

The macroeconomics division, once a model of CBO employment stability, also experienced tremendous turnover during my agency service. By my count, only five of the twenty analysts who were there when I was hired remained when I departed. In addition, several analysts hired after me chose to leave even before

I did. On the day of my departure, only one economist in the fiscal policy unit remained of those who worked in the unit when I was hired, and he and the newly appointed fiscal policy unit chief both left CBO within several months of my departure.[3] The division's management also experienced considerable turnover: During my years of service, there were three fiscal policy unit chiefs in addition to the three heads of MAD; the division even saw the departure of its longtime deputy. Through all the changes, the agency and division continued to do excellent work; but for me it was time to leave.

What about the Row House—and the Band?

After I decided to leave CBO, Linda (pleased to have me coming home) and I faced two big questions: What to do about the DC row house, and what about Dial 251? After considering the possibilities of listing the house for short stays on Airbnb or making it available for rent on a longer-term basis, we decided to sell. Hiring a property manager would have lightened the burden of making the unit available for rent, but my parents' apartment rentals seemed to generate an endless stream of headaches and time-consuming problems; their experience soured us on the idea of getting into the rental business. My preference for selling was probably also influenced by being attacked on a Metro train by several youths toward the end of 2016 (it happened in the evening just after rush hour, on a subway car at the station nearest the US Capitol); I didn't appear to be seriously injured, but it did leave me with a concussion from a punch to the head. The house was listed for sale in early January 2017 and sold in mid-February.

What to do about Dial 251 was an easier decision. Linda knew the band had become an important part of my life and made great musical progress in a few short years. It was a serious, high-quality combo, so she gave me the green light to keep the quintet together. After all, the band had a great reputation around town. Among the region's musicians, we were known for "killer setlists," featuring tunes that went well beyond the usual jazz standards, as well as for tight arrangements that were obviously a product of many hours onstage and in the rehearsal room. In addition, first-time audiences were impressed by the band's signature "dual horns" sound (trumpet and tenor), while regular listeners appreciated our commitment to keeping our repertoire fresh and varied.

After I stopped working at CBO, I returned to Washington at least once a month to gig with the band, usually driving to DC by car, but occasionally catching a flight from Syracuse. I became a familiar face to the staff at the Capitol Hill Hotel and booked well in advance for the lowest rates. I also scheduled band rehearsals so I could combine a rehearsal and performance in the same trip; we often gathered at a DC rehearsal studio on Saturday mornings following our Friday night shows at Mr. Henry's.

The band continued to perform until the start of the pandemic lockdown, which took effect shortly after our first Friday gig in March 2020. When the pandemic hit, we had several regular commitments: in addition to our monthly residence at Mr. Henry's, there were the ongoing spring and fall weekend engagements at Twins Jazz, and annual performances at the US Botanic Garden and the World Vaccine Congress.[4] Other gigs also came our way frequently in the post-CBO period, including an outdoor concert as part of a music festival in Silver Spring, Maryland (July 2018) and a feature performance at the Hill Center event space on Capitol Hill (June 2019). At the time of the COVID-19 lockdown, the band included keyboardist Matt Leonhardt, who joined the group in early 2015; drummer Greg Reaves, who I met at Takoma jams and invited to play with the group in late 2015; bassist Phil Ravita, a professional performer and music educator who I met at my first Dalhak jam session in 2013 and who became part of the band in 2018; and saxophonist Lionel Lyles, another local professional who replaced Bryan McEntire (who had been with me since the initial "Old Line" event of September 2014) in early 2020.[5]

Hitting the Campaign Trail

In the months leading up to my departure from CBO, I arranged an unpaid position as a research fellow in the Baldy Center for Law and Social Policy, part of the School of Law at the University at Buffalo, a flagship campus of the State University of New York. As if on cue, the research director at the Levy Institute asked me to return to work at Blithewood—this time on a full-time, ongoing basis. That led to over a year of email exchanges, during which I continued to express interest in returning, but the job offer never came.

My interaction with professors associated with the Baldy Center began when I accepted an invitation to participate in a summer workshop there in May 2010. The law professors who organized the event were looking for a broader approach to law and economics than that provided by conventional economics, so my attempts to reconstruct economics resonated with them. My participation in the workshop led to several enduring academic relationships as well as my collaboration on a paper with Kenneth Casebeer, a professor at the University of Miami School of Law, resulting in a coauthored law review article that proposed a new approach to the foundations of law and economics.[6]

The Baldy Center workshop in 2010 also brought me back in touch with Tim Canova, a law professor I met in the mid-1990s when he directed the National Jobs for All Coalition and I worked at the Levy Institute. Canova, who began his career as a legislative assistant for Senator Paul Tsongas, specializes in issues at the intersection of law and economic policy, so our common policy interests kept us in contact during my years at CBO. That included the period in 2016 when he attempted to unseat US Representative Debbie Wasserman Schultz in the Florida Democratic Party primary, during which he received the endorsement of Senator Bernie Sanders and considerable assistance from Sanders's supporters.

In late spring 2017, I thought of Canova's willingness to step into the political arena as I watched several inexperienced candidates, all first-time political aspirants, enter the Democratic Party's primary race in my upstate New York district. They were vying to face off in November 2018 against incumbent Republican Tom Reed, whose votes sided with President Donald Trump 96.7 percent of the time.[7] At first there were only men (two women from Ithaca would enter the race later in the summer), residents from very different communities in a district shaped like an elongated high-top sneaker (encompassing all or part of 11 counties in the Finger Lakes, Southern Tier, and Western New York). The four initial candidates included a retired Air Force officer and lawyer from the southeastern end of the district, a young attorney from a city in the southwestern corner of the district, a longtime teacher from a town near the center of the district and close to the Pennsylvania border, and the owner of a specialty shop for runners in Ithaca, on the eastern edge of the district and about 40 miles north of the Pennsylvania state line.

Looking at the field in early summer, I began to think about jumping into the race as well. Yes, I'd also be a first-time candidate, but at least I had congressional campaign experience in a large swath of WNY during the 1990s. I also knew the district; Geneva had been the center of my family's home life since 1990, but I had also lived in Ithaca as a university student and in Bath (located at the center of the district) during the late 1980s. In addition, I worked with labor leaders from Chautauqua County at the western end of the district during my employment with ILR Extension in Buffalo.

I soon sketched out a vision of what I believed was a winning message—one grounded in my longstanding policy goals as well as lessons learned over the course of my career. New York's 23rd Congressional District included a few Democratic strongholds, especially the university town of Ithaca, but the overall district solidly favored Republicans and many of them were extremely conservative. However, it wasn't a wealthy district, and the policies of the GOP didn't advance the interests of the bulk of the region's residents. That meant a Democratic victory appeared possible by a candidate focusing on practical issues of concern to working families—good jobs, family-supporting incomes, retirement security, affordable healthcare, safe communities, a clean environment, and educational opportunity.

The Republicans controlled the House, Senate, and White House, so they had a policy record and a clear agenda of "you're on your own" extremism. It seemed to me that the key to ousting Reed was to highlight the harm to district residents from the existing policy course, offer pragmatic down-to-earth alternatives, and stress that what unites everyone across the 200-mile-long district is much greater than what divides us. There was, I believed, plenty of common ground for constructive action—and ample opportunity to improve the lives of people in the district.

Even Congressman Reed seemed to know that solving practical problems was valued by residents in the district. He often talked about the need for bipartisan action, and in 2017 he became co-chair of the House Problem Solvers Caucus, an outgrowth of work by the nonpartisan group No Labels. But it also appeared Reed was too beholden to his party and its big donors to craft innovative solutions and make the gutsy votes needed to be a genuine problem solver on the most important issues facing his constituents. An example was his support for repealing the Affordable Care Act, which would have reduced health insurance coverage and increased medical expenses for families across the district and the nation.

Meanwhile, the Democrats seeking to face Reed in November 2018 seemed headed for defeat by making rookie errors. For example, they eagerly endorsed the Medicare for All single-payer proposal championed by Bernie Sanders, which I immediately recognized as political kryptonite in a general election.[8] At least one candidate also frequently offered starkly different positions on issues when speaking before different audiences, even after it became clear that Reed's team was recording all public events to accumulate raw material for attack ads.

Linda knew I had the creativity and drive to run a serious race, and she recognized that throwing my hat into the ring reflected my career-long commitment to standing up for working families. That's why she was willing to support my entry into the fray. We both knew it was a long shot, but Linda also argued it was better to try than have regrets later. With her backing, I contacted several major political consulting firms in mid-July for ideas on how to initiate a campaign built around the watchwords "Bold and Practical."

Jon Vogel, a founding partner of MVAR Media, was most helpful. Vogel was a former executive director of the Democratic Congressional Campaign Committee and his advice began with fundraising and timing: "Contact everyone you know personally—friends, family, neighbors, professional contacts, former classmates." I think he said to contact at least 150 people (but in retrospect 1500 wouldn't have been outrageous). "Tell them you're exploring a run and that you'd like them to pledge a donation. Then contact the party chairs in your district's counties and let them know you're interested in running and what you have for financial commitments," he advised. Vogel also explained some campaign nuts and bolts, such as that I could raise funds during an exploratory period before officially becoming a candidate and registering with the Federal Election Commission (FEC), and he put me in contact with fundraising consultants and specialists in FEC compliance.

Thanks to Vogel's help, things quickly began to take shape. I immediately drafted a fundraising email and began three solid weeks of emailing and dialing for pledges. Toward the end of August, I contacted the county chairpersons across the district, inviting assistance and announcing more than 100 pledges, at an average of $200 each (amounts ranged from about $100 to over $1,000). In the weeks that followed, I met individually with the county chairs and began attending political events across the district.

I also set out to hire experienced people to deliver essential campaign services. For example, I met a few times with a political adviser to Representative Louise Slaughter, and he drew up a consulting agreement for a relationship that would officially begin on October 1, 2017, the day I would announce my candidacy and file as a candidate with the FEC. At the heart of the agreement was his promise to develop and execute a fundraising plan to yield at least $125,000 by the end of the year. I also hired Slaughter's compliance officer to serve as secretary to my campaign committee, "Charles Whalen for Congress," and contracted for a campaign website by the web designer who crafted the site of a candidate who faced Reed in an earlier election cycle.

But the campaign ran into serious trouble from the very start. First, the operation hit a major pothole when my campaign consultant withdrew on the eve of the campaign's kickoff, apologizing for being overcommitted and leaving me scrambling to handle fundraising on my own with whatever donor lists I could dig up. Then, later that same month, the "#MeToo" movement against sexual assault went viral, and many party activists turned their attention to a woman from Ithaca who had overseen Cornell's information technology policy. Even Democrats supportive of my campaign pulled me aside and whispered that it seemed this year's candidate just had to be a woman.

I consistently received compliments for my command of the issues as well as for offering thoughtful policy views; and there were several other positive developments. Drawing on personal contacts, including those from my work with the Kerry-Edwards campaign in 2004, I received free campaign advice on an ongoing basis from some excellent political consultants. One of my former bandmates volunteered his professional experience with political ads, even drafting a few I could produce and run inexpensively on Facebook. A student from William Smith College proved a reliable assistant at campaign events. And a retired history professor from Hobart and William Smith Colleges wrote me a check for a sizeable contribution after an event, adding: "I don't think you realize just how good a candidate you are." I suppose that meant I came across as both capable and modest, which seemed high praise given the rough treatment I experienced from many at HWS over the years.

But none of that was enough. I needed a network of volunteers, like the one that joined forces with me during Doug Call's congressional run, not only to help with campaign work but also to hold coffee socials and other fundraising events. I also needed endorsements, and in February 2018 when the "Pugnaciously Progressive" Working Families Party devoted the entirety of my brief meeting with them to telling me to get out of the race because they were going to support a woman. I knew I was in the right place at the wrong time. Their choice: a candidate who regularly touted support for repealing (not tweaking, but eliminating) New York State's SAFE Act, a firearms law with provisions that include a life sentence for killing police officers and other first responders. So much for Pugnaciously Progressive.

That same month, Linda's mom suffered a stroke and the recovery proved difficult. (She ultimately passed away July 4, 2018, just three days before Katie's wedding.) With Linda at her mother's hospital bedside each day, it didn't seem right to continue traversing the state in a race with dim prospects. At the end of the month, I suspended my campaign, ending it officially in mid-April with one final FEC filing.[9]

In the November election, Reed defeated his opponent, who appeared on the ballot for both the Democratic Party and the Working Families Party, 54 percent to 46 percent. Reed's opponent contended that she suffered from having to face a crowded primary field before the general election, and the party paved the way for her to run unopposed in the 2020 primary. She lost the 2020 general election 58 percent to 41 percent. On May 10, 2022, Reed resigned from Congress amid charges of sexual misconduct. In August 2022, Reed's former campaign manager won a special election to serve the remainder of his term, and in November 2022, the district's voters elected Nick Langworthy, chair of the New York State Republican Committee; in both races, Democrats fielded the retired Air Force officer whose initial run was during the 2018 primaries.

Gun Violence and Campaign Aftermath

As with so many aspects of my career, it seemed new ironic twists came around every turn in the campaign. On the issue of gun violence, those twists extended even into the campaign aftermath.

In the days leading up to my official entry into the race in October 2017, the beta version of my website offered just one line on the right to bear arms: "I respect the Second Amendment to the Constitution." In nearly all corners of the district, hunting has long been a way of life and many residents took pride in National Rifle Association membership. For any serious contender, expressing support for that amendment was simply a box that had to be checked, even as it cost my campaign financial backing from some progressives who lived outside the district and didn't understand the region. A more developed position on guns was certainly desirable, but with so many competing demands for time and attention, it wasn't high on my list in August and September.

Then, on October 1, 2017, the day the campaign was scheduled to kick off, a 64-year-old shooter in Las Vegas opened fire from his hotel window and into a crowd attending a music festival. The incident killed 60 people and wounded at least 413. Finding a sensible, commonsense way to address gun violence immediately became a top campaign priority.

Conducting my own research—since there was no one else to whom I could assign the task—I found the work of the Giffords Law Center to Prevent Gun Violence, a nonprofit organization that promotes gun violence prevention and gun safety laws.[10] On my website and in social media posts and public appearances, I drew on the work of Giffords in calling for practical action to prevent gun violence such as banning bump stocks (attachments that allow semi-automatic weapons to function as automatic weapons, capable of shooting up to 800 rounds per minute) and supporting federal gun violence prevention research. I also laid out the rationale for what we needed: "I believe in the Second Amendment, but our first priority—consistent with the core purposes of our Constitution—is to take sensible steps that keep our families and our communities safe from mass gun violence."[11]

My "bold and practical" campaign theme was intended to align with entry into the race as the "jobs and family incomes" candidate, but it soon expanded to reflect my unanticipated status as the race's "gun violence prevention" candidate. That quick evolution was on full display in mid-November 2017, during my first debate appearance with the other Democratic Party candidates; at that event, I drew attention to a Giffords report released the previous day: "Legal and Lethal: Nine Products that Could Be the Next Bump Stock."[12] And my commitment to the issue—as well as disappointment with the positions of both incumbent Rep. Reed and my Democratic opponents—only increased over time, especially in the wake of the school shooting in Parkland, Florida on February 14, 2018, the deadliest mass shooting at a high school in US history.

By the time the Democratic field met for yet another public face-off on March 7, I was out of the race, but a writer covering the event reported that "candidates handled the [gun] issue as cautiously as an AR-15."[13] In the wake of my withdrawal, none of the remaining candidates picked up the mantle of leadership on gun violence. Meanwhile, I followed through with a commitment to speak on the subject at two rallies on March 24, in downtown Geneva and in nearby Seneca Falls, events organized as part of the nationwide March for Our Lives.[14] None of the district's congressional candidates appeared at either event.

Speaking at each event as a parent and concerned citizen, not a candidate, allowed me to connect with the assembled crowd in a way that had been impossible within the structure and limitations of campaign debates and panel discussions. While still respecting the program's tight schedule, I had time to address the topic without a stopwatch counting down the seconds and was able to speak freely. My race had ended, but sensing an ability to reach both the hearts and minds of hundreds of people at a park in Seneca Falls (just steps from the site of its pioneering Women's Rights Convention), that event was, ironically, also the moment I felt most strongly that a campaign under slightly different circumstances might have been able to gain the traction that proved so elusive this time around.

I made my final stand on behalf of gun violence prevention on April 19, 2018—Patriots' Day. That's when my campaign officially closed its books and I donated the balance of my campaign funds—about $10,000—to the Giffords Law Center.

EPILOGUE: CONTINUING THE FIGHT AMID MULTIPLE CRISES

In 2018, nobody could have foreseen the improbable path that returned Donald Trump to the White House in 2025. But here we are. And it's nearly impossible to keep up with his policy changes, including considerable backtracking, since inauguration day.

Claiming to be chosen by God to save America, President Trump's initial flurry of executive orders and public statements in early 2025 provided an audacious display of narcissism and disregard for the rule of law. It was only Trump's third day in office when political analyst Stephen Collinson wrote that the president "is sending almost hourly shockwaves through the government, the legal system, the science community, and around the world."[1]

Convinced his authority is without limit, Trump moved quickly to centralize executive power by eliminating agency watchdogs, silencing public information bureaus, and removing officials who might challenge him or even offer an independent voice.[2] Extreme loyalists with dubious credentials were appointed to top government positions, federal employees believed disloyal were fired, and an unprecedented worker buyout weakened agencies further by enticing 75,000 people to leave government service.[3] Trump also issued pardons, not only for participants in the attack on the US Capitol in January 2021, but also for police officers convicted of serious crimes, pardons many observers described as an effort to intimidate those who might consider speaking out against his actions or holding people in law enforcement accountable for theirs.[4]

Many financially strapped working families voted for Trump because he promised to bring down the price of eggs and reduce other food prices as soon as "Day One."[5] Instead, in just the first few weeks of the new administration, Trump's wide-ranging actions included: attempting to end birthright citizenship spelled out in the US Constitution; renaming the Gulf of Mexico the "Gulf of America"; imposing what most constitutional scholars considered a blatantly unlawful freeze on nearly all federal grants and loans (including foreign aid);[6] calling for immigration sweeps that led to raids on homes, hospitals and other workplaces, and even detention of Native Americans;[7] withdrawing the United States from not just the Paris Agreement on Climate Change, but also the World Health Organization; granting access to the US Treasury payments system and other sensitive government computer networks to a shadowy team led by Elon Musk; targeting the Consumer Financial Protection Bureau for a complete shutdown;[8] and announcing that the United States will "take over" Gaza and develop it into the "Riviera of the Middle East."[9] As for tackling food prices and other sources of inflation: forget it. Trump only added to the problem by slapping tariffs on Mexico, Canada, and China, and promising the same for the European Union and other nations, which would increase the price of food, energy, and consumer goods.[10]

Under the Trump administration, problems facing workers seem to mount daily. The Federal Policy Watch website of the Economic Policy Institute became operational soon after Trump's inauguration and quickly identified a long list of executive, congressional, and judicial moves that will harm working people.[11] As of Labor Day 2025, executive actions on that list included gutting the federal office responsible for studying worker health and safety, suspending regulations that protect coal miners from cancer-causing silica dust, eliminating the collective bargaining agreements that covered many federal workers, and hobbling the National Labor Relations Board, which protects private-sector workers' right to organize unions and engage in collective bargaining.[12] Meanwhile, corporations benefit from the administration's assault on industry regulations, and businesses and the rich enjoy Trump-backed tax cuts tilted heavily in their favor.[13]

Many Democrats—especially state governors—are trying to mount a defense, but their party is largely in disarray. "We have no coherent message," says Representative Jasmine Crockett of Texas.[14] "Democrats are just flatlining," observes Maureen Dowd, a longtime columnist at *The New York Times*.[15]

Several Crises, But Still Fighting

Today, America faces a serious political crisis. Trump's election kicked pluralistic democracy to the curb and replaced it with strongman democracy. And that type of politics and governance can soon become no democracy at all.[16]

While an extended answer to who killed pluralistic democracy might look a lot like the solution to *Murder on the Orient Express* (they all did it), much of the blame must be placed on public officials who allowed economic insecurity among working families to simmer and spread for a half century—choosing instead to ignore or even cynically manipulate its painful consequences. Mainstream economists must also shoulder some of the blame: since the mid-1970s, they enabled those officials by either dismissing worker precarity or insisting on "market-driven" policies that have only made matters worse. In other words, we face a *political* crisis, an *economic* crisis, and an *economics* crisis, and they're all connected.

The political crisis was not nearly as severe in Trump's first term as it is today (except, of course, for his supporters' assault on the US Capitol), but even back then the danger displayed itself unmistakably in his authoritarian impulses, combined with numerous policies that were patently at odds with improving worker well-being. That's why I considered it important to jump into the 2018 congressional race. We needed a constructive, worker-oriented agenda as an alternative to Trump's nihilistic populism and reckless, self-defeating nationalism.

My political vision was inclusive and emphasized common economic challenges. In contrast, many Democratic Party activists tended to focus on racism, sexism, and LGBTQ+ rights, an approach that some voters (who might have otherwise turned away from the GOP) felt didn't give sufficient attention to their most pressing concerns. Meanwhile, donors with deep pockets discouraged Democrats from pursuing an economic message. Don't just take my word for it; ask Jeff Beals, a teacher who, like me, thought he could generate broad political support by running for office with a focus on the economic issues of concern to most Americans. In 2018, Beals ran in the Democratic primary in New York's 19th Congressional District, north of New York City. A friend invited him down to the city to make a fundraising pitch at a dinner party, which Beals later learned included mostly asset managers and others in the financial industry. After the speech, Jeff's friend pulled him aside and chided him for his message, "What the heck are you doing, man? You should have talked about LGBT." Stay away from the economy; that's the compromise often forced on Democrats aiming to mount what the party considered a competitive Congressional race.[17]

Once it became clear I wasn't having much success addressing our country's political and economic problems as a candidate for public office, I took full advantage of the opportunity to address the multiple crises affecting working families through my (unpaid) position as a research fellow at the University at Buffalo. Between leaving CBO in early 2017 and the second Trump inauguration in 2025, I delivered more than two dozen presentations—mostly before academic audiences, including keynote addresses at conferences in Poland and Japan, but also at broader public forums.[18] I also wrote articles and book chapters, at a pace averaging one publication every three months, and edited four books since early 2020.[19] In addition to examining our political, economic, and economics crises and their interrelations, those presentations and publications occasionally addressed other crises involving public health and environmental sustainability.

The main thread of my post-CBO work aims to align economic research with economic reality by focusing on money manager capitalism and its consequences. Building on the foundation of post-Keynesian institutionalism, I explore how an economy dominated by institutional investors produced decades of mounting worker insecurity, sharper income inequality, slower technological progress, and greater economic instability.[20] In addition, I draw attention to how financial sector deregulation and other public policies (from tax breaks to trade policies) enabled the managed-money era to emerge and evolve, leading to a public sector that increasingly places financial and corporate interests before the well-being of workers and the public.[21]

My work in the 2017–2025 period also highlights how the relentless drive for business profits worsened the COVID-19 pandemic and undermines our urgent need to combat climate change. For example, a pair of papers coauthored with Yan Liang, one of my former students from Zhongshan University, shows how some of the dominant business practices of the managed-money era (cutting labor costs, outsourcing jobs offshore, pursuing corporate mergers and acquisitions, and engaging in stock buybacks) not only intensified worker financial insecurity during the pandemic, but also accounted for many shortages of personal protective equipment and other supplies essential to saving lives and combatting the virus.[22] In a similar manner, my work on climate change highlights how short-term financial incentives have disrupted the solar energy industry, reduced the resilience of farming, diverted climate policies in unproductive directions, and weakened support for multinational action on global warming.[23]

In articles addressing the political crisis, I suggest ways to shore up essential components of a free society, including a national commitment to the rule of law and a robust democracy that allows all economic interests a meaningful voice in public decision-making.[24] But my work also draws attention to how worker insecurity weakens support for a law-bound society and fuels the rise of authoritarianism. As John R. Commons observed a century ago, workers demoralized by financial insecurity, overwork, or unemployment tend to lose faith in politics and other social institutions; and he didn't look to the labor movement or even the socialist party to recruit these voters. Instead, he expected someone like Hitler or Mussolini: "I look for a demagogue."[25]

A Product of the Great Unraveling

In the 1990s, Hy Minsky responded to a question about the influences on his career by admitting intellectual debts to a few professors, but also by observing that the real-world shaped his work. "I believe we are all products of our environment," he replied.[26] In the years that shaped Minsky's career, that environment included the New Deal, the Second World War, and the emergence of a postwar managerial era rooted in mass production by large corporations. Broad contours of the environment in which my parents grew into adulthood weren't all that different from Minsky's, but without a college education mom filed invoices and dad worked in a machine shop.

In contrast, the managerial economy began to unravel during my teens, giving way to a managed-money economy that continues to shape our lives today. There's no question that Vernon Briggs, Ray Marshall, Hy Minsky, and other professors influenced my academic and career decisions. But the most essential factor shaping my identity and career path was being raised in a blue-collar family during the nation's postwar boom and then coming of age as that prosperity unraveled.

The managerial era gave factory workers like my dad a chance to support their families in jobs with rising incomes, employer-provided healthcare, and defined-benefit pensions. That economy wasn't perfect. But the hope I shared with many at the time was that constructive public policies would expand opportunity for those who didn't share fully in the era's prosperity, and that a compassionate safety net would ensure security for those unable to support themselves. Helping to shape such policies was the work I first envisioned when considering a policy-oriented career.

Then came the great unraveling, partly a product of the ever-evolving economy but also a result of "free-market" policies that helped solidify the new era. The unraveling began in the 1970s with the financial strain of high inflation and steep interest rates, but that was soon followed by a spreading wave of plant shutdowns that threatened the livelihoods and communities of blue-collar workers. By the late 1980s, worker insecurity involved much more than factory shutdowns, and I decided my career would focus on addressing the country's economic transformation and its consequences for workers.

It quickly turned out that worker insecurity was something I would experience firsthand, not merely investigate in research and public policy explorations. And it remained that way throughout much of my career. In fact, my experiences often paralleled those of the workers for whom I aimed to fight, even if the reasons for my precarity sometimes didn't perfectly match the workforce's most common cases. From those experiences, I encountered precarity in several forms, including long, fruitless job searches; temporary contracts and part-time work for lack of a more stable position; work that made limited use of my education, skills, and experience; barriers to advancement; job uncertainty caused by the rapidly changing economy; job loss following successful completion of a work project; long commutes and extended periods away from home; and pay that sometimes went down, not up, when landing a new position.

That precarity often prevented me from contributing to the cause of advancing workers' interests as fully and effectively as I had hoped. But it also gave me greater empathy for the many others struggling to find enough security to raise their families and lead modest lives. There may have been several hard landings during my career, but I did usually manage to land on my feet. Many others haven't been so lucky.

The consequences of the great unraveling continue today, even when headlines report that the jobless rate is low. For example, in early 2025, CNN presented an interview with Diane Evans (age 59) of Brooklyn, New York. After a 35-year career, Evans was laid off from her job as a human resources executive making over $200,000 per year. Following a relentless search that lasted nearly a year, she took a minimum wage job as a bathroom attendant at a catering hall. "I thought I was going to have money for retirement, and now my job's gone, my money's gone, and starting all over from scratch is scary," said Evans.[27]

Americans like Evans strive to be resourceful and self-reliant, but we *are* products of our environment. The economic environment that emerged after the great unraveling has not been kind to workers. And it has severely tarnished the American Dream.

Lessons Learned from the Front Row

Early in his second presidential term, Barack Obama identified growing inequality and a lack of upward mobility as the "defining challenge of our time." Arguing that the middle class powered early postwar progress, Obama added that further progress was now threatened by erosion of the basic bargain that "if you work hard, you have a chance to get ahead." In short, "the combined trends of increased inequality and decreasing mobility pose a fundamental threat to the American Dream, our way of life, and what we stand for around the globe." The nation's top priority must be to adopt practical public policies that can "restore opportunity and broad-based growth for all Americans," he concluded.[28]

My career provided a front-row seat for observing and analyzing that defining challenge, including understanding how it emerged and exploring what we can do about it. But I've been far from a detached spectator. Sometimes I've actively participated in helping unions and employers save jobs and boost economic security for workers; and at other times, my own career has been caught in the same economic riptide as the working families I've aimed to defend.

Here are several lessons that emerge from my mix of observation and experience. I don't presume they combine to sketch out all the answers; in fact, I'd advise against taking seriously anyone who claims to have them. I believe only that the following items point us in the direction of constructive social change—and hope they can spark a thoughtful, long-overdue public discussion that can move us forward together.

(1) *The erosion of the American Dream is real.* President Obama was right about the challenge we face. The American Dream has been fraying for half a century. Here's some of what's occurred:

- Upward mobility has been eroding for decades. One study finds that nine out of ten people born in 1940 had higher incomes than their parents, while only about five in ten born in 1984 are likely to earn more than their parents.[29] Other studies find that US economic mobility is much lower than in Canada and other developed nations.[30]

- Wage growth has stagnated since the mid-1970s, with average (inflation-adjusted) hourly wages only 10 percent higher in 2017 than in 1973, even as worker productivity more than doubled over the same period.[31] A survey-based report released in early 2025 finds that nearly three out of four workers struggle to afford anything beyond basic living expenses in the face of rising costs and stagnant wages.[32]
- Today, nearly half of US households are unprepared to weather a financial emergency, such as a temporary job loss.[33] Unsteady worker incomes compound the problem of insufficient emergency savings: Employers have increasingly demanded flexible labor (often changing schedules with less than a day's notice), and household earnings have become more volatile since the 1970s, with considerably more households reporting income losses of 50 percent or more within any two-year period.[34]
- The middle-class share of total household income has plunged: The share of income held by the middle class (those earning between two-thirds and double the median household income) has fallen steadily from 62 percent in 1970 to 43 percent in 2022. Over the same period, the share of income held by lower-income households edged down from 10 to 8 percent, while the share held by upper-income households grew from 29 to 48 percent.[35]
- Home ownership, a key indicator of the American Dream for most people, remains out of reach for many. The rate of US home ownership has risen and fallen over the past several decades, but renters headed about one in three households in 2025, roughly the same ratio as in 1980.[36] Looking at trends over a shorter horizon, a report by Redfin found that the number of renter households grew three times faster than homeowner households in 2024: "With home prices at record highs and mortgage rates remaining elevated, renting is increasingly the only viable choice for many young people and families," said economist Sheharyar Bokhari.[37]

Meanwhile, Americans have become increasingly pessimistic. A poll conducted in mid-2025 for *The Wall Street Journal* found that almost 70 percent of US adults believe the American Dream (defined as the idea that "if you work hard, you'll get ahead") doesn't hold true anymore or never did, the highest percentage in nearly fifteen years.[38] The poll found similar results on questions about whether people have a good chance of improving their standard of living and whether life for the next generation will be better than for people today. The standard of living question showed confidence at a record low since the newspaper's polls began in 1987.

It's easy to understand the discontent. Stepping back from all the data, economic reality for most workers from the mid-1970s to the mid-2020s can be summarized as a succession of blows. In the 1970s, they suffered through worsening inflation for nearly a decade and have confronted an increasingly precarious labor market ever since. They also lost their shirt, and in many cases the hope of a secure retirement, when the dot-com boom collapsed. To sustain their families in the face of wage stagnation, they enriched Wall Street by resorting to credit on terms that often turned out to be predatory—and watched in disbelief as banks and large corporations received huge bailouts with scant oversight during both the Great Recession and the pandemic. Then inflation returned, partly due to a failure of the global supply chains that corporations established (with the aid of trade agreements and other policies enacted with bipartisan political support) to replace US workers with cheaper labor abroad. Donald Trump is certainly not the answer to the problems of working families, but it's easy to understand why many Americans have recently felt at the end of their rope.

(2) *Erosion of the American Dream must be seen through the lens of money manager capitalism.* For much of the twentieth century, the individual investors controlling the bulk of US corporate stocks and bonds tended to "buy and hold" financial assets for the long term, which gave corporations the latitude to retain some earnings for business reinvestment (a strategy called "retain and reinvest"). However, as institutional investors began to overshadow individual investors, the aim of money managers to maximize the value of the assets entrusted to them led corporations to pursue the aim of *maximizing shareholder value.* In turn, that caused companies to shift their focus to cost cutting and returning cash to shareholders (a strategy called "downsize and distribute").[39] The economic and human consequences have been far-reaching.

Today, short-term profits, dividend payouts, and stock-market prices are the all-important corporation metrics, and fund managers rely on a variety of methods to achieve the returns they seek. Those methods initially ranged from engaging in high-frequency program trading to pressing for changes to a corporation's top management or board of directors, but private equity firms have increasingly taken companies private while driving change. The overall result has been corporate restructuring, downsizing, offshoring, and all sorts of cost cutting. At the same time, the search by fund managers for quick, high returns provides an eager market for financial innovations ranging from the junk bonds of the 1980s to the mortgage-backed securities of the early 2000s. Those innovations (and the computer-driven trading) have often increased the risk of financial crisis, fueling economic instability.

Business historian William Lazonick describes the rise of managed-money capitalism as corporate America's transition from *creating value* through business reinvestment to *extracting value* by means of predation.[40] That predation has made our lives as consumers more precarious, in areas ranging from air travel to medical and emergency services, by pressuring organizations to scrimp on quality controls, operational capacity, and standards of care.[41] It also has made combating climate change more difficult because many corporations consider the pursuit of profits incompatible with reducing greenhouse gas emissions. However, predation's most tangible effects over the past several decades have hit workers: in the era of money manager capitalism, the economic well-being of workers has become especially precarious.

Rising worker economic insecurity is a defining characteristic of the managed-money era. In fact, managed money and worker insecurity can be considered two sides of the same coin. Lazonick identifies three stages in the evolution of the current era, each increasing the extent to which precarity has spread throughout the workforce:

- *Rationalization* (1980s), characterized by plant closings that "terminated the jobs of high school educated blue-collar workers, most of whom were well-paid union members";
- *Marketization* (1990s), characterized by the end of the career-with-one-company norm, which "placed in jeopardy the job security of middle-aged white-collar workers, many of whom were college educated"; and
- *Globalization* (2000s), characterized by the accelerated movement of even advanced job opportunities offshore to lower-wage nations (especially China and India), a development that "left all members of the US labor force vulnerable to displacement, whatever their educational credentials and work experience."[42]

I'd add another stage: *digitalization* (2010s to the present), characterized by work done on a freelance basis through use of a digital platform, such as a website or smartphone app (applications such as Uber, Lyft, DoorDash, and Instacart). In this stage, workers become independent contractors, who receive no health insurance or other fringe benefits and have an incentive to be always "on call." At the same time, today's workers in jobs across the economy must contend with the threat of being replaced by automation or artificial intelligence—and entry-level employment for recent college graduates has become increasingly precarious.

In the face of that unrelenting economic change, it's extraordinarily difficult for people to adapt as individuals. Many don't have the resources—and others just don't know what to do in such a rapidly shifting environment.[43] While worker insecurity comes in many forms, job loss can be particularly distressing and costly;[44] and responding by turning to self-employment is fraught with its own formidable risks. Most workers are ill-prepared to pursue entrepreneurship in the face of job loss.[45]

In an environment characterized by wave after wave of seismic economic tremors, a nation is only inviting deaths of despair from alcohol, drugs, and self-harm when it refuses to adequately help its citizens adjust—and we've seen ample evidence of such damage in the United States in recent decades.[46]

(3) *The economic benefits of money manager capitalism don't outweigh its costs.* Supporters of the status quo often argue that institutional investors pursue maximum financial gains in the interest of retired teachers and other pensioners—that money managers are merely looking after the financial interests of ordinary Americans.[47] It's true that more than half of American households currently hold stock, either directly or indirectly through retirement funds, mutual funds, or other managed accounts.[48] But it's also true that the distribution of stock ownership is wildly unequal: the richest 10 percent of American households own the vast share of all US stock (nearly 90 percent). Meanwhile, four in ten households have no retirement savings at all, in or out of the stock market.[49] Even if it were true that in the era of managed money "we have met the enemy and it is us," a system that thrives on generating retirement funds for workers by creating severe economic insecurity for that same workforce definitely needs reform.[50]

(4) *Erosion of the American Dream harms more than individuals, communities, and the economy; it also threatens the fabric of American society.* There's no question that erosion of the American Dream in the managed-money era has taken its toll not only on the economic, physical, social, and psychological well-being of workers, but also on their families and the places they call home.[51] In addition, there's ample evidence that rising worker insecurity and inequality have increased economic instability and slowed economic growth.[52] We also know that joblessness, wasted skills, and undeveloped talents represent an unrecoverable loss to the entire nation. But throughout my career I've worried increasingly about something else as well: the fraying foundations of our society.

From the New Deal through the Great Society, America's leaders connected with the public by emphasizing a unity of purpose and commitment to each other. But that social solidarity began to collapse in the Carter era. As economic insecurity began to rise, people turned inward and became less willing to support policies designed to assist others. By the 1980s, gone was attention to social responsibility, replaced at best by the idea of personal responsibility and at worst by "Greed is Good" and a "You're on your own" sentiment.

That shift has affected the college and career decisions of students, resulting in a move away from even the sciences and engineering and toward business, finance, and accounting. Today, top career choices for Ivy League graduates include finance, investment banking, asset management, and management consulting.[53] The destination of choice is Wall Street; public service has been uncool for decades.[54]

An inward turn is only part of what I observe as a threat to our social fabric. That turn has been accompanied by the distrust of public institutions, erosion of social trust, and reduced commitment to social reciprocity. The combination of increased economic insecurity and that distrust has, in turn, contributed to severe political polarization and even undermined support for constitutional democracy and the rule of law.[55]

And if all that isn't enough cause for concern, I also worry about yet another threat to the foundations of American society. The decades-long assault on the American Dream inflicts economic pain in the present, but it also jeopardizes our future by undermining the work ethic, which is the bedrock of any free, prosperous, and flourishing society. If hard work isn't rewarded and legitimate economic opportunities aren't abundant, then we have a recipe for widespread disillusionment, corruption, and social chaos at home, and the United States loses its moral authority in the world.

(5) *But all is not lost. We can find constructive public policies to fashion a new social contract—one that moves us beyond money manager capitalism and into a new era of shared prosperity capitalism.* The policies would necessarily be wide ranging:[56]

- Taxes and regulations that rein in institutional investors and bring corporate objectives and business practices closer in line with the interests of workers, communities, and the nation. Examples: prohibiting stock buybacks; ending preferential tax treatment for the share of fund managers' earnings known as carried interest; and rewarding companies that not only create domestic jobs, but also upgrade workers' skills, offer paths for career advancement, and share profits with all employees;[57]
- Wage and employment policies that give workers a chance to support their families. Examples: substantially raising the federal minimum wage and indexing it to increases in the cost of living; restoring regulations that take employment discrimination seriously; and offering unemployed workers public service jobs that address community needs;[58]
- Education, health, and social policies that not only foster healthy and productive lives, but also enable meaningful opportunities to raise children, balance work and family obligations, and enjoy a secure retirement. Examples: expanding free public education to include community college attendance; requiring employers to provide paid family and medical leave for employees; and making retirement savings plans available to all workers, with employer contributions and an automatic employee opt-in as the default option;[59]
- Labor-relations policies that strengthen our economy by giving workers a voice in economic decisions. Examples: reducing barriers to union organizing and collective bargaining by reforming the nation's labor law;

and providing tax breaks or other incentives to companies that foster employee participation in business decisions, not just in the workplace but also in the boardroom;[60] and

- Industrial and trade policies that promote cutting-edge technologies to enhance human well-being and ensure environmental sustainability. Examples: fashioning a national economic strategy to ensure global leadership in vital sectors, new technologies, and innovation; committing to trade agreements with enforceable labor and environmental standards; and creating a national investment initiative that further upgrades the nation's infrastructure, anticipates the effects of climate change, and makes strategic investments in people and communities.[61]

Of course, public policy isn't enough; the full range of society's institutions have a role to play, including businesses, schools and universities, households, unions, and civic organizations. But government has a central role because only it can coordinate all the pieces and channel society's functioning toward the public interest.[62]

(6) *To make effective use of public policies, we must understand our past: government has deeply influenced economic development throughout US history.* The creative role of government in shaping the economy is often overlooked in the United States, but it's been vital from our earliest days when targeted trade policies, infrastructure investments (originally called "internal improvements"), and government-funded research helped nurture our infant industries and promote economic expansion. Without government to fund, encourage, and coordinate the development of lathes, precision grinders, and other machine tools (as early as the 1790s), the interchangeable parts essential to mass production, national defense, and postwar prosperity would have emerged much more slowly. Without government to amass resources, nurture the creativity of private enterprise, and foster technological breakthroughs, the Apollo project of my childhood would have never existed. And that mission did much more than land humans on the moon; it also paved the way for advances in computers, microelectronics, communications technology, and materials that are essential to our daily lives. The necessity of a similar role for government continues to exist; strategic investments today are essential to prosperity tomorrow.

Government can make mistakes, but inaction can also be a mistake. The best we can do is make informed, strategic, and purposeful decisions—especially as we confront a determined China with its own domestic and global economic strategies. The city of Austin didn't become a high-tech hub without public-private partnerships, including tens of millions of dollars from the state of Texas and hundreds of millions from the federal government. And I've seen the same approach replicated in southeastern Poland, where government-business collaboration and investment produced a prosperous hub for the aerospace industry known as "Aviation Valley."

It would be a huge mistake for the United States to forget that finding a constructive economic role for government has long been a source of its strength.

(7) *Workers deserve a voice in business and government decision-making.* The importance of employers recognizing labor as a source of competitive advantage has never been greater than in the past few decades. In the mid-1990s, against the backdrop of a rapidly changing economy, business professor Jeffrey Pfeffer wrote that firms can achieve success "by working *with* people, not by replacing them or limiting the scope of their activities."[63] He argued that a fully engaged workforce was increasingly necessary because traditional sources of competitive advantage had eroded as capital became increasingly global, business competition intensified, and technological advantages became ever more fleeting.[64]

Although Pfeffer's view was widely held among professors of labor relations, most US corporations chose instead to treat labor as a cost to be minimized or avoided. Their approach generated financial gains, but at a tremendous social cost.[65] Getting our nation off the path of value extraction and back on the path of value creation means reviving the notion of labor as a source of strategic advantage, and that means giving employees a voice at work.[66]

Including the voice of workers in American business decision-making has most often come in the form of union-management collective bargaining, but it can take many forms. Approaches tried with some success include workplace teams, ongoing employee involvement initiatives, problem-solving committees, and even worker representation on corporate boards.[67] Incorporating the voices of workers into the business world hasn't always been easy, and sustaining success can be tricky, but it does happen—I've seen it firsthand.[68] I've even watched managers admit what Harrison and Bluestone wrote in 1988: "Corporate management alone does not hold the secret of how to produce high-quality, competitive products."[69] Including workers' voice in business decisions can yield win-win results for business and labor.[70]

Equally important, but usually receiving less attention, is the need for workers to have a voice in shaping public policy. In the United States, forums allowing labor and management an ongoing voice in policy formation have most often focused on local and regional issues. Industry-oriented commissions in the steel, automotive, and construction sectors also operated during the Carter years, but didn't survive the Reagan era. In its final year, the Carter administration even created a forum for the AFL-CIO to provide workers with a voice on economic policy. Unlike lobbying sessions aimed at influencing specific legislation, ongoing public-private forums seek to generate new ideas through dialogue and even joint research. If government is to take more strategic action to shape the US economy, such forums can help ensure that its decisions are grounded in widespread stakeholder engagement by citizens and experts alike.[71]

(8) *A vibrant democracy is essential to achieving a prosperous future and revitalizing the American Dream.* The unique coordinating abilities, creative power, and social authority of government in human societies demands the rule of law, the separation of powers, and pluralistic participative democracy. That sort of democracy includes citizen participation that goes beyond voting for local and national leaders every few years.

The late US Representative Barbara Jordan described a vibrant democracy as a society in which all of us have not only equal standing under the law, but also an equal *opportunity* and a civic *responsibility* to participate in the public forum.[72] Such a society is essential to ensure that the people decide the public interest and government action aligns with what's decided. As theologian Reinhold Niebuhr recognized nearly a century ago, a robust democracy grounded in the rule of law and separation of powers is "the best way to restrain human egoism and will-to-power."[73] Humanity's "capacity for justice makes democracy possible"; but humanity's "inclination to injustice makes democracy necessary."[74]

(9) *Democracy must be nurtured.* A vibrant democracy requires an informed public, forums that foster thoughtful discussions of public issues, news outlets that present contrasting viewpoints when covering those issues, and mutual tolerance of political opponents. According to political scientists Steven Levitsky and Daniel Ziblatt, authors of *How Democracies Die*, strong constitutional *rules* can help protect democracy, but ultimately only the development of strong democratic *norms* can safeguard it.[75]

Unfortunately, norms and institutions ensuring the requirements for a healthy American democracy have eroded in recent decades, resulting in a sharply polarized nation. Policymaking in the United States certainly has been divisive in earlier times; but starting with the arrival of Newt Gingrich in Congress in the late 1970s, an increasing number of elected leaders in Washington have adopted an extremely combative version of politics. That version often demonizes the political opposition, such as by calling them "corrupt," "sick," and "unpatriotic," and accusing them of "trying to destroy the country."[76] Such politicians have also forged strong ties to an array of media outlets, resulting in an echo chamber for their views, which is often startlingly apparent in a reliance on common talking points and shared language.[77] Meanwhile, it's been nearly forty years since the Federal Communications Commission rescinded the "fairness doctrine" (which required broadcast stations to present contrasting viewpoints) and today's "equal time" or "equal space" requirements on media companies are few and extremely limited.[78]

Federal restrictions aimed at leveling the campaign playing field by limiting the spending of corporations and ultra-wealthy donors have also eroded. In 2010, the Supreme Court decision in *Citizens United v. Federal Election Commission* invalidated campaign finance restrictions on corporations and other organizations, allowing them to engage in unlimited spending on elections, including by means of "dark money" groups that keep their sources of funding secret. "While wealthy donors, corporations, and special interest groups have long spent money on campaigns, their role has ballooned as a result of *Citizens United* and subsequent decisions, resulting in a fusion of private wealth and political power unseen since the late 19th century," writes Daniel I. Weiner of the Brennan Center for Justice.[79] Overturning *Citizens United* would be a first step back in the right direction.

(10) *The choice: predation or collaboration?* This final lesson is also my biggest concern. In recent years, political propaganda has become a suit of armor for economic predation. Peddling a false choice between the need to either turbocharge investor-driven capitalism or succumb to the bondage of socialism is sheer demagoguery and will only lead to economic and social decline. In reality, we can fashion capitalism in various ways—and on close inspection the labels of "capitalism" and "socialism" both become fuzzy.[80] A more accurate choice for society is the one described recently by jazz trumpeter Wynton Marsalis, and only one path is consistent with sustainable prosperity and a revitalization of the American Dream: we either work together in a collaborative pursuit of common ground, mutual gains, and synergy, or we resign ourselves to a predatory world in which the strong exploit and control the weak.[81] As I learned from my return to the world of music in the nation's capital, you can always count on a jazz cat to tell it like it is.[82]

"The Battle Is in Our Hands"

Looking back on a career-long battle on behalf of working families, there's no escaping the limited role that hard work plays in shaping one's destiny. External forces often prevent us from realizing our full potential and restrict what we can achieve. Sometimes economic or social conditions hold us back. And sometimes the difference between a series of extraordinary opportunities and none at all comes down to whether we get one lucky break. Timing is also critical, and even that tends to be beyond our control. For example, after I tried unsuccessfully to land positions with the Clinton and Obama administrations, a union professional who follows my jazz group proposed to recommend me for an economics post with the Biden administration only weeks after my wife, Linda, was diagnosed (in the midst of the pandemic) with a serious medical condition which led me to decline the offer.

There's no question I could have benefited greatly from a couple of well-timed, lucky breaks to serve as stepping-stones early in my career. There was certainly room for more secure employment and greater professional advancement. The same goes for opportunities to make a larger contribution to advancing workers' interests, both directly through work with business, government, and labor, and indirectly through efforts to refashion economics and contribute to public policy discussions. Workers and their families deserve greater security, opportunity, dignity, and respect; I wish I could have contributed more.[83]

Meanwhile, there's surely been an abundance of irony. Encouraged by more than $41 million in support from major foundations, economists at several top universities recently began rethinking economic theory and searching for policy alternatives to free markets in response to wage stagnation, increased inequality, job losses, and community dislocation caused by the economic changes of the past several decades.[84] My reward for focusing on those matters throughout my career was professional marginalization. But even without institutional funding I managed to edit four books to advance economic theory and policy alternatives since the start of the pandemic (three in collaboration with an international team of scholars). And still I persist.

Despite the odds stacked against me, I never stopped fighting for the American Dream, a battle for working families including my own. My pursuit of a career as a maverick economist began with ambitious "shoot for the moon" aspirations, only to quickly hurtle back to earth with a hard landing. But then I clawed my way back, with work that took me from the floor of century-old factories to the gleaming towers of midtown Manhattan and eventually to the US Capitol. Along the way, I helped working men and women pursue innovative workplace and community efforts to save family-supporting jobs and create new ones, wrote timely *BusinessWeek* commentaries that reached a wide readership, and produced economic analyses for federal lawmakers and the public through work at the Congressional Budget Office. In each case, I did my best to bolster economic well-being for workers and their families by helping business, government, and labor to pursue sensible policies that build stronger communities and foster sustainable national prosperity.

Today, I feel fortunate—grateful for my partnership with Linda, for the foundation we were able to provide our daughter, Katie, and for my current situation. Linda's supportiveness and quiet strength helped keep me going through all the rough patches, and her position with the State of New York, combined with our frugality, kept us financially afloat. Katie and her husband have successful careers in Sweden, where family-friendly public policies ease some of the burdens of balancing work responsibilities with raising their young child. Meanwhile, my affiliation with the University at Buffalo keeps me intellectually engaged and provides vital access to excellent library resources; plans are even being made for my jazz quintet, Dial 251, to return to action following its pandemic-driven hiatus.

Thanks to unwavering and indispensable family support and encouragement, my work continues. And it continues in collaboration with others whenever possible. The work continues because there's far too much to be done and too much at stake to stop now.

My work also continues because I feel a moral obligation to carry on. Historian Anne Applebaum is correct: "There is no arc of history, nothing inevitable about either democracy or dictatorship. What happens tomorrow depends on what all of us do today."[85] As I wrote in the introduction to one of my recently edited books, "Economic systems are social entities, not natural systems. The future, regarding both economics and the economy, is in our own (collective) hands."[86] I envision a more prosperous, sustainable, and humane society that's stakeholder-driven, not shareholder-driven, and am committed to working toward it.

People often quote the statement of Dr. King that the arc of the moral universe "bends toward justice"; they usually overlook King's message that progress here on earth depends on us.[87] "We must come to see that human progress never rolls in on the wheels of inevitability. It comes through the tireless efforts and persistent work of dedicated individuals," said King at the National Cathedral in Washington on March 31, 1968.[88] He delivered a similar message three years earlier in Selma, Alabama. Speaking of the struggle for civil rights and social justice, King said: "The battle is in our hands.... The road ahead is not altogether a smooth one. There are no broad highways that lead us easily and inevitably to quick solutions. But we must keep going."[89]

The now deeply faded fortune strip on the wall of my home office had it *half* right. I have made "a good start." There's plenty of evidence of that on my bookshelves and in my 100 boxes. But I don't need to "work harder"; I just need to keep at it. My optimism may have diminished over time, but I still retain hope, I'm still fired up (as my homeroom classmate Sue Winterkorn would probably expect), and I still wield a pen.

NOTES*

Prologue: The American Dream in 100 Boxes

1 Core tenets of the American Dream are generally recognized as including economic opportunity, upward mobility, and the belief that hard work leads to success. However, the extensive literature on the American Dream offers a wide range of interpretations and perspectives. For example, a collection edited by Sandra L. Hanson and John Kenneth White, *The American Dream in the 21st Century* (Philadelphia: Temple University Press, 2011), examines the American Dream through lenses of race, gender, religion, and politics. I offer an analysis grounded in a combination of business history, working-class roots, and personal experience.

Two conceptions of the American Dream feature prominently in my book. One is the personal conception that motivated my career efforts: it aims to meld professional work with public service. The other is a more widely held conception, which not only resonates with my observations of what motivates many Americans, but also corresponds with descriptions often found in public discussions as well as the academic literature. In that version of the American Dream, hard work, diligence, and accomplishment will be rewarded, not by countless riches, but by financial security, increasing economic well-being, an improving quality of life, and the opportunity to help the next generation lead an even better life.

I often refer to that conception as a "modest version" of the American Dream to distinguish it from a more ambitious version envisioning unbounded "rags-to-riches" possibilities. But at the heart of even the modest version is a belief that diligent effort pays off. In fact, presidential candidate Bill Clinton placed the importance of that belief at the center of campaign speeches in 1992. Clinton stressed there was one common idea that he and "millions and millions of Americans" grew up with: The idea that "if you work hard and play by the rules, you'll be rewarded, you'll do a little better next year than you did last year, and your kids will do better than you."

---

*All website addresses were last accessed and confirmed active on October 15, 2025.

Clinton's comments illustrate the long tradition emphasizing a vital connection between work and success. Hanson and White show that many Americans have long held a conception of the American Dream that promises "hard work (not luck) is the path to prosperity" for individuals and society overall. President Barack Obama highlighted a similar view of the American Dream in 2013 when he stressed that America has long strived to deliver, and must continue to work toward, genuine economic opportunity—to ensure that success "depends on effort and merit," not "on being born into wealth or privilege." See, respectively: Gwen Ifill, "Clinton's Standard Campaign Speech," *New York Times*, April 26, 1992, https://www.nytimes.com/1992/04/26/us/the-1992-campaign-clinton-s-standard-campaign-speech-a-call-for-responsibility.html; Hanson and White, *The American Dream in the 21st Century*, 14; and Barack Obama, "Remarks of the President on Economic Mobility," Washington, DC, December 4, 2013, https://obamawhitehouse.archives.gov/the-press-office/2013/12/04/remarks-president-economic-mobility.

Chapter 1. Confident, Optimistic, and Tenacious

1 My mom's parents emigrated from Italy. My dad's parents were born in the United States to Irish immigrants and retained the immigrant identity of the families and neighborhoods (in and near Boston) in which they were raised.

Chapter 2. Work—and the Lure of Public Service

1 Abraham Lincoln, "Letter to John M. Brockman," in *Collected Works of Abraham Lincoln*, vol. 4, ed. Roy P. Basler (New Brunswick: Rutgers University Press, 1953), https://name.umdl.umich.edu/lincoln4.

2 Waltham served as the prototype for industrial cities in the United States. In the early nineteenth century, the Boston Manufacturing Company developed the "Waltham System" of textile production. That system brought the entire manufacturing process under one roof, using a water-driven power loom, the labor of young women from rural areas (who worked 14-hour days, six days a week), and a regimented approach to workforce management. The company later applied that system on a much larger scale in other locations across New England. See Amy Green, "Francis Cabot Lowell and the Boston Manufacturing Company," n.d. Charles River Museum of Industry and Innovation, https://www.charlesrivermuseum.org/fcl-bmc.

3 Angie and her family traveled third class (often called "steerage" because berths were on the ship's lower decks, near propulsion and steering equipment) from Naples, Italy, on the SS *Taormina*, which could transport 60 first-class passengers, 120 second-class passengers, and 2,500 third-class passengers. The trip took roughly ten days. See "SS *Taormina* (1908)," Wikipedia, last modified May 29, 2024, https://en.wikipedia.org/wiki/SS_Taormina (1908); and for a discussion of immigrants' transatlantic

ordeal, see Gillian Houghton, *Ellis Island: A Primary Source History of an Immigrant's Arrival in America* (New York: Rosen Publishing Group, 2004).

4 For details on US immigration from the mid-nineteenth through the mid-twentieth centuries, see "U.S. Immigration Before 1965," History.com, 2021, https://www.history.com/articles/u-s-immigration-before-1965. On the migration from Italy around the start of the twentieth century, see "The Great Arrival," n.d. Library of Congress, https://www.loc.gov/classroom-materials/immigration/italian/the-great-arrival/.

5 "The Great Arrival," Library of Congress. On the Italian immigrant experience, see, for example, Michael La Sorte, *La Merica: Images of Italian Greenhorn Experience* (Philadelphia: Temple University Press, 2003).

6 One of the bedrooms in Angie and Vincenzo's home was designed as a sitting room, which barely accommodated a double bed; three girls slept there together. The house itself fell within one of Waltham's two "redlined" neighborhoods, where residents' low and often unsteady incomes led banks to consider the areas "hazardous" from a lending standpoint. (Angie's parents lived in the other redlined area, and both neighborhoods were home to many Italian immigrants.) Residents of such neighborhoods were often charged high loan rates or even denied access to mortgages and other financial services. This is where my mom was raised and where I lived for the first few years after I was born. Meanwhile, my dad grew up across the city in an area bordering farmland. During his youth, banks considered his neighborhood only marginally better, designating it as undesirable and "definitely declining." See Robert K. Nelson, LaDale Winling, et al., "Mapping Inequality: Redlining in New Deal America," Digital Scholarship Lab, 2023, https://dsl.richmond.edu/panorama/redlining/map/MA/Waltham/areas#mapview=full&loc=15/42.3767/-71.2383.

7 My mother is the source of the quote (from a discussion with the author, July 3, 2025).

8 In high school, my mother worked as a salesclerk at the Grover Cronin department store in downtown Waltham. Many of Cronin's customers were immigrants, but the store wasn't very accommodating. One afternoon, my mom nearly lost her job for responding in Italian to a question from a customer who didn't speak English. The store's floor manager insisted all employees must always speak only English.

9 In the early 1960s, Joe left General Motors to help his younger brother, John, begin a plumbing contracting business. (John, the only sibling of either my mom or dad to attend college, studied mechanical engineering at Tufts University after working for, and receiving mentorship from a Tufts alumnus who owned businesses in Waltham.) Joe stayed with that contracting business for the rest of his career. Joe's older brother, Francis, worked for Raytheon but died in his mid-30s from cancer, possibly a consequence (according to my mom) of exposure to toxic substances while serving in the Navy. Their youngest brother, Vincent, worked as a salesman for a liquor distributor. The oldest of Madeline's sisters, Anna, worked as a hair stylist, and her other sister, Sally, worked as an office clerk for several manufacturers in and around Waltham.

10 Raytheon Company, founded in Cambridge, Massachusetts in 1922, changed its name to the Raytheon Technologies Corporation in 2020 and then to RTX Corporation in 2023. It was headquartered in Waltham from 1941 through 1961, and then again from 2003 until 2022, when the company moved to Arlington, Virginia. In 1945, a Raytheon scientist working with a radar magnetron in Waltham discovered what became the microwave oven; in the 1960s, the company built the Apollo spacecraft guidance computers in Waltham. My brother Frank began his career as an electrical engineer at Raytheon in Northborough, Massachusetts; much of his work supported the factory in Waltham, which closed around the start of the new millennium. For details on the history of Raytheon and its presence in Waltham, see "Raytheon," CompaniesHistory.com, March 12, 2024, https://www.companieshistory.com/raytheon/; "Waltham, Massachusetts," n.d. The Waltham Museum, https://walthammuseum.org/waltham/walthamhistory1.html; Don Seiffert, "100 Years of Raytheon in Mass: A Timeline," *Boston Business Journal*, June 8, 2022, https://www.bizjournals.com/boston/news/2022/06/08/100-years-of-raytheon-in-mass-a-timeline.html; "Where the Microwave Was Invented," Want to Know It?, March 9, 2008, https://wanttoknowit.com/where-was-the-microwave-oven-invented/; Dan Hogan and Will Engel, "Cold War Wayland: Raytheon," 2005, https://www.whshistoryproject.org/1950s/missiles.html; and Paul Ring, "When Waltham Went to the Moon," WickedLocal.com, July 20, 2009, https://www.wickedlocal.com/story/waltham-news-tribune/2009/07/20/when-waltham-went-to-moon/40894648007/.

11 Charlie worked at a machine shop that supplied parts to Raytheon and other manufacturers.

12 John and Helena were roughly the same age as Madeline's father. I don't know much about my father's siblings. His oldest brother died when I was in elementary school; his other brother managed a bowling alley; and his oldest sister and her husband moved in with Helena (and enlarged the house) after my grandfather died. When Charlie died in 2021, the only surviving sibling was his youngest sister, residing in Florida.

13 My father's parents were well acquainted with hardship. When John was a child, the family livery business in Newton was shuttered following his father's death, leaving John's mother to support three young boys on her own. And on the few occasions when Helena discussed her youth, she described her childhood home in Chelsea (a city bordering Boston) as a "rag shack." John died in 1970, just a few years after retiring from his factory job; Helena died in 1985.

14 According to my father, his boyhood home was not connected to the municipal sewer system until after he was discharged from the Marines. At first, the family used an outhouse, which was replaced by a septic system during Charlie's youth. Although the house was tiny and property lots in the area were small, the Whalen family owned a double lot and used much of it to grow vegetables and raise chickens. In fact, my father maintained a vegetable garden on the lot until the late 1960s.

15 Vulcanization is a process that hardens rubber (for tires, the soles of footwear, etc.). It involves adding sulfur to the rubber and then heating the mixture.

16 As an alternative, John could walk 20 minutes and then take two streetcars, but he often walked the longer distance to save trolley fare.

17 In the documentary film "Destination Watertown," local resident Leon Janikian observes that his relatives who worked at Hood Rubber never bothered with the question of whether they liked their jobs: "They were just happy to have a job. [They] were from 'the old country' and they lived through the Great Depression; to have a job was everything." For the interviews, see Roger Hagopian, "Destination Watertown: The Armenians of Hood Rubber," 2010, YouTube, https://youtu.be/ry_bpSibIys. Armenian immigrants constituted a large portion of the Hood workforce, but Hagopian's film stresses that the factory employed workers from various ethnicities; see also Kathleen Moore, "Little Armenia," Boston.com, April 1, 2010, https://archive.boston.com/news/local/articles/2010/04/01/watertowns_hood_rubber_co_served_as_hub_for_armenians_documentary_shows/.

18 For the "New Frontier" convention speech, see John F. Kennedy, "Excerpt, 1960 Democratic National Convention, 15 July 1960," the John F. Kennedy Presidential Library and Museum, https://www.jfklibrary.org/learn/about-jfk/historic-speeches/acceptance-of-democratic-nomination-for-president. For one of several campaign speeches in which Kennedy expanded on the New Frontier theme, see John F. Kennedy, "Speech of Senator John F. Kennedy, Valley Forge Country Club, Valley Forge, PA," October 29, 1960, the American Presidency Project, https://www.presidency.ucsb.edu/documents/speech-senator-john-f-kennedy-valley-forge-country-club-valley-forge-pa.

19 My middle name was chosen as a nod to both families: Charles Joseph was the name of one of my dad's uncles, and Giuseppe, which translates into Joseph, was Angie's father. (In addition, Madeline's brother Joseph drove her to the hospital for my delivery.) My father, meanwhile, had no middle name, which, strictly speaking, means I'm not "Charles Jr."

20 One of my earliest memories of the Highlands house is watching President Kennedy's funeral in November 1963. We watched on a black-and-white television in the room my family called the "den," designed as a dining room but used until the late 1970s as a family room, playroom, and homework room.

21 Adjusting for inflation, the price my parents paid for their house in the Waltham Highlands was equivalent to about $211,000 in 2025. Because house prices in the Boston area have appreciated greatly over the years, the house's current estimated value is about $800,000. My family sold the house in 1983 for $90,000.

22 For the number of employees at Polaroid's peak, see "Polaroid Quits Instant Film," *Sun Journal* [Lewiston, Maine], February 9, 2008, B7–B8. For a look at Polaroid Corporation and its history, see Alan R. Earls and Nasrin Rohani, *Polaroid* (Charleston: Arcadia Publishing, 2005).

23 When I recently mentioned "Heigh-Ho" to my brother, he reminded me that the tune also appears on *Walt Disney's Happiest Songs*, an LP released in 1967. Frank added he was so fond of the album as a child that he bought a copy of it at a yard sale not long ago.

24 A few years after her third son (John) was born, Madeline again returned to work.

25 On one especially memorable camping trip, we traveled to Niagara Falls and rode the "Maid of the Mist" tour boat to the base of the Horseshoe Falls (also known as the Canadian Falls). It was 1969, when the American Falls were "turned off" by the US Army Corps of Engineers for a survey and repairs, but the timing of the visit allowed us a rare glimpse of the gorge. Other camping destinations were much closer to home, except one visit to the nation's capital. The only other places outside New England that I visited before completing high school were New York City, which I attended on a school trip, and Florida (see Chapter 3, note 13).

26 My mother also had another reason for wanting her children to attend college. In the late 1950s, her brother and his girlfriend refused to double date with my parents,

saying it was because Madeline and Charlie didn't have college degrees. Humiliated by the experience, my mom resolved that her children would go to college.

27 For the history of Rosary Academy, see Lara Farrar, "25 Years of Rosary Academy," WickedLocal.com, October 6, 2006, https://www.wickedlocal.com/story/watertown-tab/2006/10/06/25-years-rosary-academy/40659279007/; and Rita Kelly et al., "The History of St. Patrick Parish," n.d. https://watertowncatholic.com/the-history-of-st-patrick-parish.

28 That catechism also states, "Those who find comfort and security in the Catholic faith may be tempted to close themselves off from the world and its complicated problems. But it is impossible for us to come close to Christ without being willing to help Christ save the world." See John J. Hill and Theodore C. Stone, *A Modern Catechism* (Chicago: ACTA, 1964), 272–277. Of course, my parents also modeled the same ethics I absorbed in Catholic school. For example, they were always quick to help others, including delivering meals "to the elderly" even in their mid-80s.

29 Robert Heilbroner and Aaron Singer, *The Economic Transformation of America: 1600 to the Present* (Fort Worth: Harcourt Brace, 1994), 61. This book remains a valuable, reader-friendly history of the American economy, including an insightful look ahead to the early twenty-first century.

30 "Waltham, Massachusetts," The Waltham Museum, https://walthammuseum.org/waltham.

31 "Waltham, Massachusetts," The Waltham Museum, https://walthammuseum.org/waltham.

32 In sharp contrast to the economy of the 1960s, the proportion of workers in goods-producing industries today is close to one in ten (13.6 percent). Proportions are the author's calculations using data from the US Bureau of Labor Statistics, "Current Employment Statistics, Establishment Data, Table B-1," https://www.bls.gov/webapps/legacy/cesbtab1.htm (data extracted September 20, 2025).

33 If anything, workers in my family were overrepresented in goods production.

34 In this book, I use "money manager" capitalism and "managed money" capitalism as synonyms. Both variants were coined by Hyman Minsky, as I discuss in Charles J. Whalen, "Money-Manager Capitalism," in *Handbook of Critical Issues in Finance*, ed. Jan Toporowski and Jo Michell (Cheltenham: Edward Elgar, 2012), 254–262.

Chapter 3. "Who the Hell Do You Think You Are?"

1 In the 1960s and 1970s, baby boomers strained the classroom capacity of the Waltham public schools. As a result, I attended a different school each year from grades five through seven: an elementary school (a half mile from my home), a middle school (a mile from home), and a junior high school (just a few blocks further away than the middle school).

2 It turns out that I was lucky in breaking out of my preassigned public-school track. Despite his equally solid Catholic school academic foundation, my brother's teachers

resisted reassigning him to a more advanced classroom. Frank did get reassigned, but my change was made in weeks, while his took nearly a year.

3 Although my neighborhood was generally safe, several troublemaking youths would occasionally cause disturbances in our backyard late at night (which could be quite a frightening way to wake up in the wee hours). But the most serious incident occurred when a parent of one of the troublemakers returned home drunk from a New England Patriots game and goaded another adult into tossing a softball-size rock through our living room picture window. The rock smashed the huge window and sailed across the entire room (only moments after my mom left the room), leaving a large dent in its rear wall. (I impulsively, and in retrospect somewhat foolishly, chased the culprit, barefoot, and caught him just as the police arrived.) When I left home to attend college, I didn't miss the neighborhood; my parents also had no strong attachment to it and moved to another part of the city in 1983.

4 In addition to constructing jigsaw puzzles, birdhouses, and toy race cars, we built pinhole cameras and developed our own photos.

5 Since Madeline wouldn't agree to a cat or dog, we instead had white mice, gerbils, and eventually rabbits. We raised Dutch rabbits for many years, and my dad would sometimes present a dressed rabbit to Grandma Angie shortly before a holiday. We also hatched chicken eggs and tended to hens for a few years, which provided a regular supply of eggs. It wasn't until I was in college that Madeline relented on having a dog, allowing the family to adopt a miniature schnauzer.

6 I can't recall writing many stories with my own plotlines and characters, but there were some. I remember writing mostly book reports and essays on topics that caught my attention while browsing in the public library, including science fiction and Greek and Roman mythology. Sometimes I even submitted what I wrote to my teachers for extra credit at school. I also recall making sports scrapbooks and writing all sorts of lists with ideas and plans for backyard carnivals, vacations, etc. My parents certainly thought I did a lot of writing; throughout my youth, they'd often say, "He always has a pencil in his hand" or "Give him a pen and paper and he's happy as can be."

7 My parents also purchased two encyclopedia sets: *Encyclopedia Britannica* and the more youth oriented *The New Book of Knowledge*. I don't recall many other books in the house until I started bringing them home, creating a family library that continued to grow over the years.

8 I believe my dad brought the pages of "Kids' Fun News" to work and came home with about a dozen photocopies for me to sell. The newspaper had a run of two or three issues.

9 One afternoon in early 1973—shortly after representatives of North Vietnam, South Vietnam, and the United States reached a peace agreement in Paris—Congressman Drinan made an after-school public appearance at my junior high school, and I was one of the few students who chose to attend. During the question-and-answer period, I raised my hand and found the courage to ask about his confidence in the agreement. The next day, a local newspaper story on the event described my question and Drinan's answer. At age 12, it was my first encounter with a politician beyond viewing the mayor who marched in the city's Easter parade, and the newspaper story was the first time I was mentioned in the paper beyond the Little League box score.

The next time I saw Fr. Drinan was in January 2006, in Washington, DC. I recognized him in the registration hall of the annual meeting of the Association of American Law Schools and briefly thanked him for his service and inspiration. He was warm and appreciative, and I was grateful for the chance meeting. Drinan died the following January.

10 In the late 1960s and early 1970s, three-quarters of the viewing public watched an evening news broadcast; CBS drew the largest audience of the era's three major networks. For a discussion of the nightly news during that period, see Andie Tucher, "Walter Cronkite: Witness to History," American Masters Digital Archive, April 18, 2006, https://www.pbs.org/wnet/americanmasters/archive/interview/andie-tucher/.

11 At nine years old, I was the youngest *Boston Globe* paper carrier when I began my route. The newspaper's minimum age for carriers was ten, but the *Globe* agreed to assign me the route because my dad ensured that I'd get the job done. In addition to the *Globe*, public broadcasting (radio and television) became an increasingly important source of news for my family in the 1970s.

12 Many journalists and writers were first inspired by delivering newspapers in their youth. For example, Christopher Daly, a journalism professor with experience at the Associated Press and *The Washington Post*, writes that delivering *The Boston Globe* sparked his interest in news reporting: "I started to get interested in the contents of all those papers.... This was, no doubt, the genesis of my lifelong career in journalism." Christopher B. Daly, "Not All Change Is Progress: Why *The Globe* Should Bring Back Paperboys (And Girls)," WBUR Cognoscenti, January 6, 2016, https://www.wbur.org/cognoscenti/2016/01/06/boston-globe-delivery-woes-christopher-b-daly.

13 It's possible my parents anticipated that delivering newspapers would dovetail with my voracious appetite for reading, but they were mainly interested in my learning about the responsibilities of paid work, managing money, and dealing with people outside a school environment. Interacting regularly with my customers and *The Boston Globe* business office did make me more comfortable and confident around adults, even if I occasionally needed some gentle prodding from my dad or external rewards from the newspaper company.

The most memorable instance of that gentle prodding came when the local *Globe* business office inadvertently shortchanged me by thirty-eight cents. Getting into the car with my dad afterward, I said that I'd realized the error but hadn't asked for the mistake to be corrected. He agreed it was only a small amount, but then added, "It's their error and your money. It won't take long to fix; I'll wait here." The office manager recognized the error right away and handed me the extra change with no hassle; the lesson I learned about politely and confidently speaking up for myself continues to stick with me (and has been passed on to my daughter).

Meanwhile, the *Globe* encouraged me to be bold when, in 1972, it offered paper carriers a chaperoned weekend trip to Orlando, Florida, (with visits to Walt Disney World and NASA) for selling fifteen newspaper subscriptions within a certain amount of time. The day I heard about the contest, I walked my route and knocked on the door of every family that didn't already subscribe to the paper. At first, I was extremely nervous, but then I got into a rhythm—and as my dad pointed out, the worst that could happen was the person answering the door wouldn't be interested in subscribing.

After two days of relentlessly knocking on doors, I was the first *Globe* carrier—across its entire home-delivery market—to reach fifteen subscriptions. Months later,

I joined a few dozen other boys at Logan Airport (I don't recall any girls) and took my first-ever airline flight, from Boston to Orlando, on a DC-9 operated by Eastern Airlines. About a year later, the *Globe* offered 12-speed, Italian racing bicycles to carriers enrolling ten new subscribers; that was a "piece of cake," and I used the bike during high school and college.

14 Instruments purchased through the school music program were returnable only during a brief trial period.

15 Frank Ellsworth Olds, founder of F.E. Olds, was a skilled craftsman (a machinist, like my dad) who began his musical instrument business by designing trombones and repairing band instruments in the 1910s. According to R. Dale Olson, who worked for several decades as director of research at Olds, the company was a "one tolerance shop," which meant "all brass instruments were crafted to the same close tolerances, regardless of price or market niche." Today, Olds trumpets are valued by professional musicians and collectors, and the student-model Ambassadors continue to be recognized as excellent horns. See Dale R. Olson, "F.E. Olds and Sons, Inc.—A Short History," n.d. https://www.robbstewart.com/olds-catalogs.

A much larger US instrument maker, G.C. Conn, also ran into difficulties in the late 1960s and 1970s. Conn emerged in the 1870s, in Elkhart, Indiana, and a decade later about 40 percent of the world's band instruments were made by skilled workers in Elkhart. But in the 1960s and 1970s, Conn—and the community of Elkhart that depended on its jobs—was hurt severely by mounting Wall Street pressures, ill-conceived plant relocations and outsourcing, changing consumer preferences (including a shift from band instruments to guitars), cuts to school music programs (because of budgetary belt-tightening), and less expensive imported instruments. In fact, the tragic saga of the US band instrument industry encapsulates much of the rise and decline of US manufacturing and its effects on American communities. For more on Olds, Conn, and the history of the US band instrument industry, see "F.E. Olds," Wikipedia, October 23, 2024, last modified January 8, 2025, https://en.wikipedia.org/wiki/F._E._Olds; and "Conn-Selmer, Inc." n.d. Company-Histories.com, https://www.company-histories.com/ConnSelmer-Inc-Company-History.html.

16 The Greater Boston area was a vibrant radio market in the 1970s, partly because of the many colleges and universities in the region. Meanwhile, the Boston Symphony Orchestra offered a concert series that provided short lectures and matinee concerts for young people in the region; my brother Frank and I attended that series for two seasons. Both the radio and live performances contributed greatly to expanding my musical horizons.

17 On October 22, 1974, a friend and I took a commuter train from Waltham to Boston's North Station to see the band Chicago at the adjacent Boston Garden. A married couple seated next to me was amused to see two young teenage boys at their first rock concert (I was in ninth grade). In the high school years that followed, I often took advantage of the Boston area's vibrant live music scene, attending performances by artists including Herbie Hancock, Phil Woods, and Jean-Luc Ponty, as well as groups ranging from the Stan Kenton Orchestra to the British rock band Yes.

18 In the mid-1970s, Aerosmith was among the most popular rock bands in the Greater Boston area, so it certainly didn't hurt my interest in trumpet when the opening track on the group's *Get Your Wings* album (released in 1974), featured horn lines by the Brecker brothers (Randy on trumpet and Michael on saxophone).

Aerosmith also piqued my interest in straight-ahead rock and roll. In early 1975, when I was in ninth grade, Aerosmith began renting a warehouse as rehearsal space in Waltham, next to railroad tracks that I used regularly as a shortcut to and from junior high school. Over time, the building also became a recording space (dubbed the Wherehouse) where the band recorded *Rocks* (1976), and I remember hearing afternoon rehearsals of new material when I walked home from school. One afternoon, I even got the courage to climb down the slope from the tracks, walk around the concrete structure, and peek at the building from the front. The band was taking a break, but the open warehouse doors revealed a stage with a large Oriental rug flanked by stacks of amplifiers and cases of sound equipment—quite an after-school find for a young teenage boy.

Aerosmith occasionally sublet its Waltham rehearsal space to other bands, and in late 1975 the band Boston rented the stage to perform for record company executives, who insisted on seeing the group play a live set before agreeing to a recording contract. Tom Scholz, founder of the band, was an MIT graduate who worked at Polaroid on the same "instant motion pictures" research project as my dad until sales of Boston's first album skyrocketed. The success of local bands such as Aerosmith and Boston, which played its first public show at Waltham's high school football field (a few blocks from my home, three days after release of its debut album in August 1976), further inspired me to play music, including branching out to learn bass guitar in tenth grade, and at least occasionally dream of music as a full-time career.

19 Waltham had three junior high schools: Central, Kennedy, and South Junior High; the latter served the Italian neighborhood where Grandma Angie lived as well as other southside neighborhoods that continued to attract newcomers as in earlier decades.

20 When the Kennedy principal made the "heathen" remark, I was standing next to my music teacher, a newcomer to the school district, and she was appalled. Everyone else in the auditorium seemed unfazed. The event included a performance by a citywide youth orchestra, for which I played first-chair trumpet; not bad for a heathen.

21 In the mid-1970s, enrollment at the public high school in the city of Brockton was slightly larger than at Waltham High School. In the 1960s and 1970s, other public-school systems in communities larger than Waltham, such as the adjacent city of Newton, operated more than one high school to accommodate the baby boom cohort and overall regional population growth. In the 1970s, the population of Waltham was 60,000, and the population of Newton was 90,000; Brockton was almost as large as Newton, but much less affluent. (Newton was and remains one of the most affluent communities in the state; Waltham's household income level has historically been below the state average; and Brockton has tended to rank toward the low end of the statewide income distribution.)

22 In the summer before starting college, I worked a single day at Polaroid. My dad arranged for me to apply for a summer job there, but it didn't materialize until about a week after I started working at Proteon Associates, an engineering firm of about a dozen people (founded by a pair of MIT graduates) that hired me on the recommendation of a friend. I felt obliged to go to Polaroid because my dad lobbied for me and the pay was a bit higher than at Proteon; but I found it miserable—far more unpleasant than loading boxes the previous summer in a brake factory.

At Polaroid, I worked a punch press the entire day. (I later learned that my grandfather Whalen manned a punch press for years at the Quincy Shipyard.) It was set up in the corner of a storeroom adjacent to the top of a stairwell. On one side of the press was a bucket full of metal discs (spare parts) and on the other side was an empty bucket. My job was to place each disc into the punch press (one at a time), stamp it, and then place it in the empty bucket. I received a new bucket of discs every couple of hours, which was the only time I saw anyone else all day. During my lunch break, I sat in the stairwell, ate a peanut butter sandwich, and washed it down with milk from a Thermos.

The next day, I told the CEO at Proteon the situation. He raised my pay a bit above the rate offered by Polaroid, and I spent the rest of the summer at Proteon working with engineers and technicians who designed and built marine distress buoys, roadside emergency call boxes, and other communications equipment for state and federal agencies. To be sure, the Polaroid job offered a paycheck and the nation's manufacturing sector was full of repetitive jobs, but it was also a long way from résumé-building summer work experience; in fact, it made no use of any skills of a college-bound, high-school graduate—even working in the mail room would have at least used my ability to read. I was lucky to have the Proteon job as an alternative.

23 Ferrante, of course, was the real powerhouse. In addition to serving as director of bands for Waltham High School, he taught at the University of Massachusetts Lowell for thirty-five years and performed on clarinet and saxophone throughout the Boston area as recently as 2023 (in his late eighties).

24 In addition to playing trumpet, I played keyboards briefly with a local cover band and bass guitar during occasional basement jam sessions with friends.

25 The pit orchestras often included professional musicians. For example, I performed on a few occasions alongside trumpeter Herb Pomeroy, a legendary figure on the Boston jazz scene. In the 1950s, Pomeroy led a successful big band that inspired Chick Corea (who grew up in Chelsea, Massachusetts). Pomeroy also taught Bill Chase (founder of the jazz-rock band Chase, best known for the hit single, "Get It On"), worked as a professor at Berklee College of Music, and founded the MIT Festival Jazz Ensemble. Herb was warm and encouraging; if I had chosen to pursue a music career, he would have been the perfect mentor.

26 Attending the summer music program at the University of New Hampshire (prior to my junior and senior years) expanded my network of friends during high school.

27 After graduating from Berklee, Doug toured with Stanley Turrentine and later with Phyllis Hyman and Rachelle Ferrell. Bobby followed in the footsteps of Dexter Gordon and other African American jazz musicians and left the states to make his career in Copenhagen; he became well-known to the Danish public as the bandleader on "Meyerheim," a television program similar to "The Tonight Show."

28 The 100 boxes that surround me as I write this memoir began as a collection of two-pocket folders in which I stored articles distributed by Mr. Macy as well as clippings from *The Boston Globe*. Looking back on what was saved during my years in high school, college, and graduate school, I'm astonished at just how much I was trying to learn and follow in the world of public affairs. After recently reviewing the articles from Macy's class, I decided to track him down and contact him: today, he's a professor of sociology at Cornell University.

29 The Massachusetts Student Advisory Council (SAC) is organized in a similar manner today; one main difference is that each school is now required to elect two representatives to their regional council, which provides more student input into statewide education decisions; see "Student Advisory Council," Massachusetts Department of Elementary and Secondary Education, February 16, 2024, https://www.doe.mass.edu/sac.

30 While my high school treated SAC as an extracurricular activity, the Massachusetts Department of Education has always advised that academic credit be granted for SAC participation. See "Questions and Answers Relative to the Regional and State Advisory Councils," Massachusetts Department of Education, 1976 (author's personal copy); and "Students on School Boards in Massachusetts," Sound Out, April 7, 2015, https://soundout.org/2015/04/07/students-on-school-boards-in-massachusetts/.

31 For example, Chapter 622 of the General Laws of Massachusetts, enacted in 1971, prohibits public-school discrimination based on race, color, sex, religion, or national origin; and the Title IX amendment to federal education law, passed in 1972, prohibits sex-based discrimination in any school or education program that receives funding from the federal government.

32 The number of students represented by SAC in the late 1970s comes from Richard E. Cohen, "Student Advisory Council, 1977–1978: Mid-Year Report," distributed by the Massachusetts Student Advisory Council, 1977 (author's personal copy).

33 It's no surprise that I followed the Red Sox and Bruins in the late-1960s and early 1970s: the Red Sox played in the World Series in 1967, and the Bruins won the Stanley Cup in 1970 and 1972. My Uncle Joe (Cannistraro) sometimes took me to a Red Sox or Bruins game, and on a few occasions Frank and I traveled by bus with our mom to see an afternoon game at Fenway Park (from the bleachers, where seats cost $1.00). In 1968, the local newspaper announced that Red Sox players Mike Andrews and Rico Petrocelli were to appear at a gas station "grand opening" in Waltham. I brought my baseball glove for them to sign. At the event was also a young member of the Bruins, so he signed my glove as well; it was Bobby Orr, who became one of the greatest professional hockey players of all time.

34 In addition to hockey, downhill skiing was a winter sport I occasionally enjoyed as a high school student. To my parents, skiing, tennis, and golf were sports for "rich kids," but I learned to ski from the father of a high school student I met at summer music school and my brother Frank learned on school-sponsored outings. Still, I never skied more than a few times a season, and it's now been a couple of decades since I've been on the slopes.

35 I never gave serious consideration to limiting my college choices to schools that I could attend by commuting and living at home. I envisioned college as a place where I'd be surrounded by others who liked to read books and explore ideas; and by the time high-school graduation arrived, I was keen to leave Waltham.

36 Loventhal grew up on Long Island (Mineola, New York) and attended the University of Michigan, where he played football and aspired to compete in the National Football League. After a knee injury ended Bob's football dreams in his sophomore year, he transferred to Brandeis University in Waltham and created the city's youth football program.

37 The high school refused to be more specific about the class ranking.

38 During the meeting with my assigned counselor, I recalled that most colleges required a letter of recommendation from each applicant's guidance counselor. But I decided not to worry about that and let the rest of each application speak for itself.

39 "Shooting for the moon" was a popular expression at the time, which I preferred to interpret as "having ambition that aims realistically high" (such as the national goal of reaching the moon by the end of the 1960s). Of course, others interpret it as "striving for the impossible."

40 Robert F. Hoxie, *Trade Unionism in the United States* (New York: D. Appleton, 1917), 4.

41 To be sure, it was impossible to grow up in the United States during the 1960s and 1970s and not recognize that people of color experienced deeply rooted prejudice and institutional racism, not just in the southern United States but also in Northeastern cities such as New York and Boston (where the issue of desegregation busing tore the city apart for years in the 1970s). Still, I grew up thinking that the bulk of the nation aimed to overcome the racial divide. Looking back, I see both that I was overly optimistic about the nation's ability to address racial issues and that I glimpsed but failed to appreciate the depth and significance of the socioeconomic (class) divisions all around me—rifts, within and across communities, that extended beyond race and that would affect me (indeed, were already affecting me) more than I recognized as a teenager.

42 Public schools weren't the only institutions in society to perpetuate a socioeconomic hierarchy; universities and corporations did as well. For example, although at least a half-dozen students in my high school graduating class had the qualifications to submit a competitive application to Harvard University, only one student, whose father was a college professor in the Boston area, received an unhurried admissions interview in his own home. All other applicants were interviewed, back-to-back, in the high school's guidance office, at 15-minute intervals. (The student with the home interview was the only applicant to receive a letter of admission.) And it's difficult to believe that the solitary and repetitive summer job offered to me by Polaroid was the same work that would have been offered to the college-bound child of an engineer, manager, or junior executive. In fact, it's a fair bet that someone in the human-resources department thought the machine-shop worker's son was lucky to be offered any job at all.

Moreover, the parallel presence of stratification in education and industry was no accident. Research on the evolution of education in the United States—by experts Ray Marshall (my PhD adviser) and Marc Tucker—demonstrates that public education since the dawn of the twentieth century focused not on minds to be developed, but instead on a workforce to be molded in accordance with the needs of large employers. Those needs included basic proficiency in English (reading and writing) and rudimentary vocational skills (which meant "shop classes" for males and typing or bookkeeping for females), but especially punctuality, obedience to authority, and acceptance of social hierarchy. In a book (published in 1992) based on a major research study of education and the US economy, Marshall and Tucker write that nearly all the nation's public schools in the early twentieth century embraced "an anti-intellectual conception of their purpose," which allowed mastery of basic skills to become the de facto standard of American schooling. That produced a "symbiotic relationship" between American industry and schools that persisted even as the new millennium approached.

Marshall and Tucker explain that educational administrators justified their approach by insisting that intelligence was inherited and fundamentally unalterable, and that most people were not fit for serious academic work or other "intellectual" activity. Meanwhile, the administrators assumed that intellectually gifted students would be nurtured in private schools—or perhaps in the equally elite schools of affluent public-school districts offering a similarly supportive environment for student learning. The best that students in less-affluent public schools could hope for was entry into their schools' extremely small, highly selective advanced-placement course tracks, but the obstacles facing those students were often formidable.

In short, Marshall and Tucker find that US public education in the twentieth century served mainly to sort children according to their parents' education. As a result, children from low-income backgrounds had little chance of economic mobility through educational achievement: "Teachers had low expectations for such children, and those expectations were, of course, fulfilled, because these children were seldom challenged to produce their best," write Marshall and Tucker. (What comes immediately to mind here is the public-school experience of my dad, who came from a low-income background and, when reflecting on his school days, reported that his teachers repeatedly told him he was "stupid." That was far from the case: as a highly skilled machinist, he was the go-to person when engineers had a practical problem at Polaroid, and at age 54 he turned a wooded city lot into a pair of rent-generating townhouses despite having no prior homebuilding experience.)

In that type of educational system, I was destined to be a maverick: the expectations I received and internalized from my parents and parochial-school teachers were fundamentally at odds with the public-school worldview. For the research, analysis, and quotes presented here, see Ray Marshall and Marc Tucker, *Thinking for a Living: Education and the Wealth of Nations* (New York: Basic Books, 1992), especially 20–25.

43 Even my performance on national standardized tests (without the help of expensive test-prep courses) reinforced the conclusion that I could hold my own against other students my age, regardless of family background.

44 I returned to Waltham during school breaks and for summer work but never gave serious consideration to returning there to live after college.

Chapter 4. Seeking Practical Solutions in an Age of Limits

1 Martin Luther King Jr. "Remaining Awake Through a Great Revolution," National Cathedral, Washington, DC, March 31, 1968; published in US Congress, 90th Congress, second session, *Congressional Record* 114 (April 9, 1968): 9395–9397. Over time, I began to question the idea that developments tend toward justice here on earth, but that only underscored the need for persistent work by dedicated individuals.

2 The average price increases are my calculations, based on data from the US Bureau of Labor Statistics, using "Consumer Price Index, 1913–," n.d. Federal Reserve Bank of Minneapolis, https://www.minneapolisfed.org/about-us/monetary-policy/inflation-calculator/consumer-price-index-1913-.

3 The average rates of unemployment are my calculations, based on data from the US Bureau of Labor Statistics, "(Seas) Unemployment Rate," https://data.bls.gov/timeseries/LNS14000000.

4 The inflation rate even surpassed 11 percent in 1974 and 1979; and the unemployment rate reached 9 percent in May 1975; see "Consumer Price Index, 1913–," Federal Reserve Bank of Minneapolis, and US Bureau of Labor Statistics, "(Seas) Unemployment Rate."

5 Barry Bluestone, Bennett Harrison, and Lawrence Baker, *Corporate Flight: The Causes and Consequences of Economic Dislocation* (Washington: Progress Alliance, 1981), 13.

6 Bluestone, Harrison, and Baker, *Corporate Flight*, 15 (emphasis in original).

7 When Carter took office, the nation's unemployment rate was 7.5 percent and the inflation rate was 5.2 percent. Data for January 1977 are from US Bureau of Labor Statistics: for the unemployment rate, see "(Seas) Unemployment Rate"; the inflation rate is calculated by the author using "Table 24. Historical Consumer Price Index for All Urban Consumers (CPI-U)," https://www.bls.gov/cpi/tables/historical-cpi-u-201710.pdf.

8 Jimmy Carter, televised national address from the White House, "Energy and the National Goals: A Crisis of Confidence," July 15, 1979, American Rhetoric: Top 100 Speeches, https://www.americanrhetoric.com/speeches/jimmycartercrisisofconfidence.htm.

9 On the media reaction to Carter's speech, see Frank Gannon, "Days of Malaise," *Wall Street Journal*, June 20, 2009, W9. Gannon and others recall that the initial reaction to the speech was positive, but public sentiment soon turned on Carter and many news commentators derided the speech.

10 The United States lost ground on the trade front as businesses in Japan and Europe recovered in the postwar era and began competing successfully against American firms, especially those engaged in manufacturing. The country lost ground in international finance because control of the value of the US dollar was eroded by the globalization of finance. And the nation's energy security began to erode with creation of the OPEC oil cartel and then the Iranian Revolution. (OPEC refers to the Organization of the Petroleum Exporting Countries, which was founded in 1960 but began oil production cuts and embargoes to the United States and other nations in the mid-1970s.)

11 Inflation, high interest rates, and high energy prices were key elements in the undoing of the Carter administration (in addition to the Iran hostage crisis). Many Democrats—even union members—turned against Carter when inflation and interest rates soared, and although they didn't necessarily accept Ronald Reagan's supply-side argument for tax cuts, political consultants found that workers felt they could use whatever extra money they could get. For an examination of the "Age of Limits," see Carl W. Biven, *Jimmy Carter's Economy: Policy in an Age of Limits* (Chapel Hill: University of North Carolina Press, 2002); and for an insightful discussion of that era's politics, see Rowland Evans and Robert Novak, "A Blue-Collar Setback for Carter," *The Boston Globe*, August 5, 1980, 11.

The Evans and Novak article is particularly interesting because it highlights the shift of the "overwhelmingly Democratic blue-collar voters of Waltham"—my hometown—from support for Carter to an embrace of Reagan. According to that article, national pollster Patrick Caddell focused on Waltham because he saw it "as prototypical of blue-collar precincts" that had long been Democratic strongholds but seemed to be turning away from Carter. Over time, residents of such precincts became known as Reagan Democrats. I often said I didn't need a poll or focus group to know where blue-collar workers were leaning because I just had to listen to my neighbors; it seems Caddell would have agreed.

Chapter 5. Studying Work

1 The legislation authorizing Cornell ILR is excerpted in a brochure I received as a prospective student: Office of Resident Instruction, *Cornell University Announcements: ILR at Cornell* (Ithaca: Cornell University, January 7, 1977), 8.

2 On the field of industrial and labor relations encompassing all aspects of the world of work, see Bruce E. Kaufman, *The Origins and Evolution of the Field of Industrial Relations in the United States* (Ithaca: ILR Press, 1993), 104; Office of Resident Instruction, *Cornell University Announcements: ILR at Cornell*, 3; and Kathryn Stamm, "'Roundabout Route' Brings Alexander Colvin PhD '99 to Become New ILR Dean," *Cornell Daily Sun*, July 8, 2019, https://www.cornellsun.com/article/2019/07/roundabout-route-brings-alexander-colvin-ph-d-99-to-become-new-ilr-dean.

3 Perhaps the most well-known practitioner-oriented faculty member in the history of Cornell ILR was Frances Perkins, Secretary of Labor to President Franklin Roosevelt, who taught at the school from 1957 until her death in 1965.

4 On the "only college" of its kind in the 1970s and early 1980s, see Office of Resident Instruction, *Cornell University Announcements: ILR at Cornell* (Ithaca: Cornell University, July 7, 1980), 8. For a contemporary view, see "About the ILR School," Cornell University, 2025, https://www.ilr.cornell.edu/current-students/credit-internships/sponsors.

5 Other courses taken during my first two years at Cornell included two "freshman seminars" (required of every first-year undergraduate) and a few electives. For seminars, I chose a course on American political theory and another on American literature, the first because of my interest in public policy and the second because I thought my prior exposure to literary classics of all sorts was inadequate. The electives included an introduction to energy resource economics (taught in the College of Agriculture and Life Sciences)—the nation was, after all, dealing with an energy crisis—and a course on the American presidency (taught in the College of Arts and Sciences), as well as ILR electives in American labor and politics (an advanced labor history course) and union organizing. I also received course credit for participating in university bands and for "military science" courses (including a course in leadership theory) taken as part of the Army ROTC program; I offer a further discussion of my participation in Cornell bands and ROTC in the next chapter.

6 Prior to being recruited to work for the Federal Mediation and Conciliation Service, Jim Foss served as director of industrial relations at the Quincy Shipyard (General Dynamics Corporation) where my grandfather Whalen worked many decades earlier.

7 The Cornell ILR course in "economic security" used a similar (choice theory) perspective to analyze social insurance policies.

8 I later learned that Galenson was much more of a labor historian than a contemporary labor economist. In fact, he held a Cornell ILR appointment in the department of international and comparative labor relations in addition to the department of labor economics. Galenson and I eventually crossed paths a few years later, as I describe in Chapter 7, not long after I discovered a remarkable coincidence involving Galenson and my PhD adviser.

9 For an early discussion of the importance of workers to the wealth of nations, see Adam Smith, *An Inquiry into the Nature and Causes of the Wealth of Nations* (New York: Modern Library, [1776] 1935), 734.

10 In the early postwar decades, the policy realm focusing on human resource development was called "manpower policy" (today, many use the term "workforce development"). In fact, the Manpower Development and Training Act of 1962 was the federal legislation that funded pathbreaking employment and training initiatives. The term "human resources" began to replace "manpower" around the time I started my undergraduate work. To work most effectively, such policies had to be complemented by serious efforts to fight labor market discrimination, and many human resource policies even included outreach and placement efforts targeted to demographic groups underrepresented in high paying jobs. For more on human resource economics, see Charles J. Whalen, "Human Resources: The Key to Institutional Economics After the Great Recession," in *The Global Financial Crisis: What Have We Learnt?* ed. Steven Kates (Cheltenham: Edward Elgar, 2011), 204–217; Vernon M. Briggs, "Human Resource Development and the Formulation of National Economic Policy," *Journal of Economic Issues* 21, no. 3 (September 1987): 1207–1240; and Sar A. Levitan, Garth L. Mangum, and Ray Marshall, *Human Resources and Labor Markets: Employment and Training in the American Economy*, 3rd ed. (New York: Harper & Row, 1981).

11 After taking the human resource economics course with Professor Briggs (a labor economist), he became my informal faculty adviser and supervised a research project I conducted on immigration policy in my final semester at Cornell. Later, he served as an external member of my doctoral dissertation committee, and we remained in contact until he passed away in late 2023. In contrast, Professor Mueller (an economic sociologist) left Cornell before I completed my degree.

12 Commons (1862–1945) was a pioneer in the areas of labor history and labor-market policies as well as institutional economics. He is also credited with creating—on an institutionalist foundation—the field of industrial relations in the United States, by establishing it as a field of specialization at the University of Wisconsin in 1920; see Kaufman, *The Origins and Evolution of the Field of Industrial Relations in the United States*, 10.

13 The institutionalist foundation of human resource economics is a key element that distinguishes it from a narrower study of human resources called "human capital theory," an approach most often associated with Gary Becker and grounded in choice theory. For a discussion and evaluation of human capital theory in the context of a survey of several approaches to labor markets, see Levitan, Mangum, and Marshall, *Human Resources and Labor Markets*, Chapters 229–297; and for critiques of human capital theory from an institutionalist perspective, see Briggs, "Human Resource Development and the Formulation of National Economic Policy," 1210–1213; and Michael J. Piore, "The Importance of Human Capital Theory to Labor Economics—A Dissenting View," in *Industrial Relations Research Association Series: Proceedings*

of the Twenty-Sixth Annual Winter Meeting, ed. Gerald Somers (Madison: Industrial Relations Research Association, 1974), 251–258.

14 As the name suggests, "neoclassical" economics (which I use synonymously with "choice theory" and modern "price theory") builds on an earlier tradition often called the "classical" school of economics. For the observation that neoclassical theory provides "only an introduction" to studying the real world, see Alfred Marshall, *Principles of Economics* (London: Macmillan, 1898), 516. Despite Marshall's acknowledgment of the limitations of price theory, those limitations were put aside in his analytical work, even when considering labor markets, where human factors add further complications not found in other markets; see Paul J. McNulty, *The Origins and Development of Labor Economics* (Cambridge: The MIT Press, 1984), 125–126.

15 The role of government is pervasive even in the most heavily market-oriented economies. That's because government defines the nature of private property and determines the acceptable shape of competition. For an institutionalist examination of the ever-present role of government in the economy, which means there's no such thing as a "free market," see A. Allan Schmid, "Government, Property, Markets … In That Order … Not Government Versus Markets," in *The Fundamental Interrelationships Between Government and Property*, ed. Nicholas Mercuro and Warren Samuels (Stamford: JAI Press, 1999), 233–237; and for a broader discussion of the shortcomings of neoclassical theory, see Charles J. Whalen, "A Reason to Look Beyond Neoclassical Economics: Some Major Shortcomings of Orthodox Theory," *Journal of Economic Issues* 21, no. 1 (March 1987): 259–280.

16 For a further discussion of institutional economics, including a brief historical overview and survey of contemporary applications, see Charles J. Whalen, *Institutional Economics: Perspectives and Methods in Pursuit of a Better World* (London: Routledge, 2022). Price theorists have fashioned various patches with the aim of making neoclassical theory relevant to labor markets, but John Dunlop, who taught labor economics and industrial relations at Harvard University, dismissed them as providing no help in dealing with reality; see John T. Dunlop, "Industrial Relations and Economics: The Common Frontier of Wage Determination," in *Industrial Relations Research Association Series: Proceedings of the Thirty-Seventh Annual Meeting*, ed. Barbara Dennis (Madison: Industrial Relations Research Association, 1985), 9–23.

17 The ILR school's department of personnel and human resource management, eventually renamed the department of human resource studies, was a hybrid unit with two distinct areas of teaching and research: management of human resources within an organization (such as a corporation or government agency) and public policies affecting the development and use of human resources within a community, state, or nation. My interest was in the public policies.

18 A strength of Mayhew's course was that he presented a variety of economic theories and emphasized how changing just a few assumptions can generate analyses with entirely different conclusions.

19 Other electives I took in my junior and senior years at Cornell included: ILR courses in organizational leadership, dispute resolution, and public-sector collective bargaining (which seemed important because union density was greatest in that sector); a department of government survey course on political theory; and an interdisciplinary university course called "America and the World Community."

20 Actually, the ILR school emphasized the importance of writing even in its admissions process. When I applied to Cornell ILR, applicants were required to participate in an on-campus interview and complete an on-site timed essay.

21 My other undergraduate research papers addressed a wide range of topics, including: the consequences of foreign labor ("guestworker") programs; the failure of American unions to achieve labor law reform; the role of labor-management consultants in defeating union organizing drives; the impact of a Massachusetts property tax cap on Boston police and firefighters; and, for a department of government course on the presidency, an evaluation of a proposal that aimed to improve policy development by reforming how US Cabinet secretaries are selected.

Chapter 6. Cornell Through a Wider Lens

1 Senator Edward M. Kennedy, "Address to the Democratic National Convention, New York City, August 12, 1980," the John F. Kennedy Presidential Library and Museum, July 21, 2021, https://www.jfklibrary.org/learn/about-jfk/the-kennedy-family/edward-m-kennedy/edward-m-kennedy-speeches/address-to-the-democratic-national-convention-new-york-city-august-12-1980.

2 An irony of President Reagan's response to the air traffic control workers is that their union was one of the few that endorsed Reagan over Carter. Although many defended Reagan's action by pointing out that federal workers did not have the right to strike, the prohibition hadn't been enforced in other instances, such as during a postal workers' strike in 1970. Firing the PATCO workers also left unaddressed their public-safety concerns over long work hours; in fact, the firings only made work schedules more demanding for the remaining controllers.

3 For the impact of President Reagan's firing of air traffic controllers, see Charles J. Whalen, "Echoes of a Broken Strike," *Washington Post*, August 5, 2006, A19; and Michael Barera, "The 1981 PATCO Strike," UTA Libraries Blog, September 2, 2021, https://libraries.uta.edu/news/1981-patco-strike.

4 For discussions of the Reagan administration's effect on workers, see Harry Anderson and Diane Weathers, "The NLRB: Labor's Love Lost," *Newsweek*, May 21, 1984, 70; Joseph P. Fried, "Raymond J. Donovan, 90, Labor Secretary Who Quit Under a Cloud, Is Dead," *New York Times*, June 7, 2021; and Stacey Hirsh, "Reagan Presidency Pivotal for Unions," *The Baltimore Sun*, August 21, 2019, https://www.baltimoresun.com/2004/06/08/reagan-presidency-pivotal-for-unions/.

5 Ronald Reagan, "Inaugural Address, 1981," Ronald Reagan Presidential Library & Museum, https://www.reaganlibrary.gov/archives/speech/inaugural-address-1981.

6 Reagan's tax cuts were justified by the argument that lower tax rates would generate more than enough tax revenue to "pay for themselves" by boosting economic growth (based on the "Laffer Curve," first sketched on the back of a napkin by economist and Ford administration policy consultant Arthur Laffer). However, that idea was unsound; see David A. Stockman, *The Triumph of Politics: The Inside Story of the Reagan Revolution* (New York: Avon Books, 1987). For a more recent view, see Rebecca Shabad, "Budget Director: 'Tax Cuts Do Not Pay for Themselves,'" *The Hill*, August 25, 2015, https://thehill.com/policy/finance/251946-gop-appointee-tax-cuts-do-not-pay-for-themselves/.

7 For a look at the value of employment and training programs in the 1970s, see Vernon M. Briggs, "The Revival of Job Creation Programs in the 1970s: Lessons for the 1980s," in *Industrial Relations Research Association Research Series: Proceedings of the Thirty-Fourth Meeting*, ed. Barbara Dennis (Madison: Industrial Relations Research Association, 1982), 258–265.

8 On Reagan's cuts to jobs programs, see Ronald Smothers, "CETA Cutbacks Leaving Thousands Unemployed," *New York Times*, April 11, 1981, 1. When Reagan took office, the US unemployment rate was at 7.4 percent. The rate exceeded 10 percent each month from September 1982 through June 1983, reaching a post–Great Depression high of 10.8 percent in November 1982, the highest rate until the COVID-19 pandemic pushed joblessness even higher for a brief period in 2020; see US Bureau of Labor Statistics, "(Seas) Unemployment Rate."

9 The Reagan administration also tried to prevent about 20,000 workers from beginning their jobs with the federal government in early 1981. People who were offered federal jobs after the 1980 presidential election but before Reagan's inauguration found themselves without work in early 1981 because President Reagan imposed a federal hiring freeze on inauguration day and made it retroactive to November 5, the day following the election.

I vividly recall the negative effects of that freeze on the newly hired workers, some of whom bought and sold houses only to find themselves without a federal job, because it nearly affected me. In fall 1980, I applied for a field examiner position with the National Labor Relations Board (NLRB), which was to begin in early 1981 and substitute (in the form of a paid internship) for my spring semester. Positions were available in several cities, and I requested the Boston office, which would allow me to keep expenses low by living at home. However, I was instead offered a position in Brooklyn, New York, and declined the offer. In early 1981, the person who accepted the position I refused found himself with a lease on an apartment in New York City, no NLRB job, and no lodging to return to in Ithaca for the spring term.

A lawsuit on behalf of the affected workers was eventually decided in favor of the appointees, but the suit was not settled until mid-August and did not automatically entitle money damages or other court-ordered relief. See Laura A. Kiernan, "Job Freeze by Reagan Is Upheld," *Washington Post*, February 26, 1981; and the Associated Press wire story, "Reagan's Hiring Freeze Loses a Court Decision," *New York Times*, August 13, 1981.

10 It's worth recalling that President Reagan did not begin the shift to market-based policy solutions and away from the use of government as a meliorative force. For example, President Carter ushered in a wave of industry deregulation and appointed Paul Volcker to head the Federal Reserve. Under Volcker's leadership, the central bank pursued a punishingly tight monetary policy consistent with the "monetarist" views of economists opposed to economic policy activism. But Reagan broadened Carter's effort to cut regulations and reappointed Paul Volcker in 1983, which served as an endorsement of high interest rates and tight money to fight inflation. Reagan's budgets also slashed non-defense spending.

11 For a summary of the perspective on government held by the most prominent Marxist economist in the United States during the second half of the twentieth century, see Paul Sweezy, "The Radical Theory of the State," in *Problems in Political Economy*, ed. David M. Gordon, (Lexington: D.C. Heath, 1971), 24–29; and for an article on

radical economics that received much attention in the 1970s and early 1980s, see Martin Bronfenbrenner, "Radical Economics in America: A 1970 Survey," *Journal of Economic Literature* 8, no. 3 (September 1970): 747–766.

12 Despite sidestepping much radical economics, I found considerable value in the writings of Michael Harrington, who is said to have inspired the War on Poverty with his book *The Other America* (New York: Macmillan, 1962), and who founded the Democratic Socialists of America in 1982. Instead of a traditional Marxist's world without markets, Harrington envisioned a democratic, mixed economy (that is, markets combined with an unapologetic, active role for government)—a full-employment society that advanced human well-being and achieved its ends via policy reforms that Harrington often described as being "on the left wing of the possible." At Cornell, I read about Harrington and purchased his book *Decade of Decision* (New York: Touchstone, 1980), which argued convincingly that America's economic problems were "structural" and required much more than the right mix of macroeconomic policies. It's a view that has always dovetailed with my institutionalist perspective and continues to influence how I think about the economy. In the mid-1980s, I heard Harrington speak in Austin, Texas, and he signed my copy of *Decade of Decision*: "With hope, Mike Harrington." He died in the summer of 1989, and in the aftermath of the fall of the Berlin Wall, which occurred a few months later, I examined his final book, *Socialism: Past and Future* (New York: Arcade, 1989), with my students as part of an economics seminar I taught at Hobart and William Smith Colleges.

13 I knew Galbraith, Dunlop, Thurow, Piore, and Marshall from their academic work, but I also knew Galbraith from his occasional essays in *The Boston Globe* (several of which I recall reading on my front steps as a paperboy), Thurow from his regular column in *Newsweek*, and Marshall from news coverage of his work in the Carter administration.

14 I also found myself a slow reader of academic material.

15 In addition to performing with Cornell bands, I also wrote a few reviews of jazz albums for the university newspaper. Although Cornell had a jazz ensemble, it operated as a club, rather than as part of the university's music department, and my recollection is that its auditions weren't widely publicized. As for composer Samuel Pellman, he taught at Hamilton College until a tragic accident took his life in 2017.

16 Speaking to me about making a military commitment in exchange for tuition assistance, my dad said: "There are lots of ways to engage in public service. The military is just one. If you want to go to law school, you'll find a way to get there without a military obligation. And if you graduate from law school and decide that working as a military lawyer is what you want to do, you can walk in anytime and sign up with the degree in hand." He wanted me to be in control of my career options as much as possible. In addition, although Charlie was proud of his military service, I also believe he saw much (involving how authority was exerted and how people often treated each other) that made him uncomfortable about being in the military.

17 Mom complained about me being in college instead of "working for a living," but she was also the one who saw college as a vital necessity since as long as I can remember.

18 My parents were OK with me taking an unpaid winter internship in Boston with the Department of Manpower Development because it was for just a few weeks in the middle of January, and I could live at home. They were also fine with me applying

for a paid internship with the National Labor Relations Board (discussed in note 9). But Madeline wouldn't hear of me working without pay for several months on Capitol Hill or elsewhere. She simply couldn't understand it when I explained that my classmates and their families considered such work a "résumé-building" investment. To her, that was the nonsense talk of the affluent for only "rich people" could afford to work without getting paid.

19 In the early 1980s, a small but intriguing graduate program in industrial relations was gaining prominence within the MIT Sloan School of Management, largely through the efforts of Thomas Kochan, a professor who moved from Cornell ILR to MIT in 1980. I would have considered applying there, but at the time the program only admitted students after at least one year of full-time, post-undergraduate work experience.

20 Most Cornell ILR electives were open to both graduate students and undergraduates. The difference was often just the course number used for enrollment (sometimes graduate students would be required to submit an additional research paper). In other cases, a course would be listed only at the graduate level, but undergraduates could enroll with the professor's permission or after merely fulfilling the course prerequisites.

21 I received some guidance from Professor Briggs, but he didn't encourage me to go to Texas, even though he taught there for many years before relocating to Cornell in 1978. I know his relocation involved reasons for leaving Austin as well as the attraction of Cornell, but we never discussed the details.

22 Because I developed a good relationship with Ken Mayhew (and even proctored his labor economics examinations), I considered applying to pursue graduate work under his supervision at Pembroke College in Oxford. However, I thought it would be best to stay in the states and focus on US economic institutions and policies. In retrospect, I believe studying in the UK would have been a better idea than I realized at the time. I probably made too much of the loss of a focus on institutional features of the American economy—and too little of well-established "across the pond" academic networks and the high regard US academic institutions have for Oxford scholars.

23 In addition to my own recollections, I rely here on a Boston University department of economics "Graduate Programs" brochure from 1981, which I retained all these years.

24 I didn't consider studying economics at Harvard or MIT largely because I didn't earn an undergraduate degree in economics and both programs were heavily oriented toward neoclassical theory despite the existence of a few unconventional faculty members at both universities. For the same reason, I didn't consider studying at Princeton with Henry Farber, a labor economist (and alumnus of the Cornell ILR master's degree program) who impressed me when he participated in a Cornell seminar on job loss in early 1981. The programs at BU and the University of Texas were different: unlike most other graduate curriculums in economics, the BU and Texas programs offered both a strong dose of conventional economic theory and several applied courses that were policy focused and institutionalist in orientation.

25 BU's Institute on Employment Policy was much like the Ray Marshall Center; I wouldn't be surprised to learn that both were established with the same sort of federal assistance as part of the nation's commitment to employment and training research in the 1960s and 1970s. On the Ray Marshall Center, see "Ray Marshall Center: About Us," n.d. https://raymarshallcenter.org/about-us/.

26 Much of the UT attention to institutional economics can be traced to the influence of institutionalist Clarence Ayres, who began teaching in Austin in 1927 and remained there until his retirement in 1968. The university featured a pluralistic economics department when Ayres arrived, but the department housed several institutionalists and stood out as exceptionally eclectic into the mid-1980s owing to the powerful influence of Ayres's teaching, writing, and commitment to free inquiry.

While I chose UT because it appeared to fit well with my interests, I later learned that academics often weigh department rankings above all else. When I was a university student, mainstream economists didn't rank the Texas economics department within their "top 10," but John Kenneth Galbraith visited the campus when I was at UT and said he told President Johnson in the 1960s that Austin offered "the most interesting economics department in the United States" and that he continued to hold that view. According to a survey of economics department rankings from the mid-1990s (about a half-dozen years after I completed my doctorate), the rank of the UT economics department ranged from 11th (a publication-based ranking) to 38th (a survey-based ranking); see Richard Dusansky and Clayton J. Vernon, "Rankings of U.S. Economics Departments," *Journal of Economic Perspectives* 12, no. 1 (Winter 1998): 157–170.

27 President Kennedy called Cohen "Mr. Social Security," and others later called him "The Man Who Built Medicare." In 1988, a year following Cohen's death, the Social Security Administration Building in Washington, DC, was renamed the Wilbur J. Cohen Federal Building. In the end, I didn't study with Cohen or Barbara Jordan, which I regret. I was even too shy to visit them during office hours, though I did have a chance to talk with Jordan when she visited Hobart and William Smith Colleges to receive an award in 1993.

28 In the 1980s, a Texas tourism agency ran an advertisement with the tag line, "Texas: It's like a whole 'nother country!"—which prompted me to joke that I chose UT because I had always wanted to study abroad. There was some truth to it; a chance to study abroad would have been nice, and I did consider studying in Texas the next best thing.

29 When I studied at UT, its graduate tuition for out-of-state students was about $100 per credit hour.

30 My Uncle Joe was among those who worried that my shooting for the moon amounted to aiming beyond my reach and would lead to disappointment. Joe never discouraged me directly; and he admired my grit and determination so much that he volunteered in November 1977 to drive me the six snowy hours to my ILR School interview in Ithaca. But it was apparent that Joe was world weary and not optimistic about what I could achieve; he thought the deck was stacked against me and didn't want to see me hurt. He felt I put too much stock in personal ambition, hard work, and academic achievement, all of which he considered no match for the professional connections and wealth my family lacked.

31 Disparaging Cornell's state-sponsored schools ignores the fact that many of them rank among the top in the world in their disciplines. But then even pointing that out provides evidence of the attention to hierarchical divisions pervasive in higher education.

32 One source of the resentment some Cornellians felt toward students at other Ivy League schools was the belief that professors at those universities often graded on a higher curve than Cornell professors; Cornell students felt the disparity in grading practices placed them at a disadvantage when competing for graduate school admissions and employment opportunities. Regardless of whether that concern had any merit, it underscored the sense that Cornell was a place where many people were acutely aware of stratification and social competition.

33 There certainly weren't country club memberships in my family. My dad never even stepped on a public golf course. In my parents' world, golf (like tennis and skiing) was for "rich people."

34 Ehrenreich recognized that "fear of falling" was a perennial fear among the "middle class," but her 1989 book stressed that the insecurity of college-educated workers intensified in the 1980s; see Barbara Ehrenreich, *Fear of Falling: The Inner Life of the Middle Class* (New York: Pantheon, 1989).

35 In 1993, when I tried unsuccessfully through multiple avenues to land a position with the Clinton administration, I thought of my friend's uncle (who said I'd probably never get a chance to play a role in public policy) and then recalled the eerie coincidence that he was from Park Ridge, Illinois—hometown of Hillary Rodham Clinton.

36 For a discussion of my day in front of a punch press, see Chapter 3, note 22.

Chapter 7. The Making of a Maverick Economist

1 I used that Smith-Corona to type all my graduate research papers except the dissertation, which I composed on an Apple Macintosh Plus (purchased in 1986) that still works.

2 Throughout graduate school, I kept the sheet of paper with my academic plan of work. As I completed each requirement, I marked a check beside that item on the list.

3 Dan eventually settled in Chicago. We stayed in touch and occasionally got together when I visited his city for academic conferences (he died in 2020).

4 Although it isn't discussed in previous chapters, I had two roommates at Cornell. (I later lived in a single room within a small on-campus residential community.) In my first year, I roomed with Bill Yanavitch (who grew up south of Ithaca in a small community along the Pennsylvania border and whose dad worked a factory job at Ingersoll Rand), and in my second year I roomed with John Tai (who lived near Washington, DC, where his dad was a scientist and his mom worked as a translator for Voice of America). Yanavitch was an ILR student who wanted to become a corporate manager of human resources; when we were last in touch, that's exactly what he was doing at a manufacturing firm headquartered in central New York. The last time I saw Tai, he and his girlfriend paid me a surprise visit in Austin during the mid-1980s; they were engineers headed to Silicon Valley to take part in that region's information technology boom.

5 Over the years, I've continued to play tennis occasionally with my wife, but I still find it hard to pick up a racquet without remembering that my parents called it a "rich kids' sport."

6 Although I studied calculus in high school, it was not part of my undergraduate curriculum and I wanted to refresh my familiarity with the subject before beginning math-oriented graduate courses in economic theory.

7 My parents took an out-of-character leap into the business world partly because several of my dad's coworkers purchased rental properties years earlier and often encouraged him to do the same. Also, when my parents bought their own home in the 1960s, my grandfather Whalen criticized my dad for purchasing a single-family home instead of a duplex. Another consideration was that my parents believed such investments would boost university financial aid packages for their children because the calculation of such aid seemed to penalize households without debt. Still another factor was that dad had the mechanical skills to handle most of the handyman work and mom had the bookkeeping skills needed to manage the properties' financial records.

By the end of the 1980s, my parents added a second duplex to their properties by building it. In the mid-1980s, the city of Waltham constructed a road alongside my parents' fourplex, which enabled my dad to construct a duplex behind the fourplex. It was ready for occupancy in mid-1989.

8 During one class, Professor Liebhafsky asked us to explain what was wrong with an analysis, published in a top-ranked journal, on the economics of church attendance (which, it turns out, was coauthored by one of the neoclassical labor economists who taught at Cornell ILR during my undergraduate years). The problem wasn't in the math or the equations—it was in the assumptions. The analysis treated church attendance as an investment of time that yields benefits (after death) over eternity, and even included the assumption that churchgoers know when they will die—information considered vital to making the most "efficient" church attendance decisions.

9 Professor Gordon, who saw a world characterized by imperfect knowledge and widespread uncertainty, put a continual reappraisal of ends and means at the center of pragmatic problem-solving. At the start of his course, Gordon distributed to each student a free copy of his *Institutional Economics: The Changing System* (Austin: University of Texas Press, 1980). Nevertheless, he insisted that even institutionalism should be scrutinized.

While Gordon's institutional economics course closely followed the outline of his book, he required that we also read books by other institutionalists and his syllabus offered a long list of suggestions. That's how I came to read Commons's *Legal Foundations of Capitalism* (New York: Macmillan, 1924) and Galbraith's *Economics and the Public Purpose* (Boston: Houghton Mifflin, 1973). After I submitted several dozen pages of notes on *Legal Foundations*, Gordon wrote that he hoped they'd prove useful in other contexts—and it turns out I recently gave them a fresh look when asked to write a journal article to commemorate that book's centenary.

10 During the Second World War, Gordon served with distinction in Army counterintelligence. He served in North Africa, Sicily, Italy, France, and Germany, earning five battle stars as well as a Bronze Star for "meritorious service in direct support of combat operations" in France and Germany. After his military discharge, Gordon's faculty reappointment in Austin was approved personally by the head of the Board of Regents overseeing the state university system; see "In Memoriam: Wendell C. Gordon," Memorial Resolution of The University of Texas at Austin, 1997.

11 I first visited San Antonio shortly after arriving in Austin in 1982, travelling there with one of my temporary suitemates. It was a brief visit, with obligatory stops at the Alamo and Riverwalk, but I was struck that San Antonio is much older than Austin (and Dallas) and that appealed to me. My initial visit (prior to establishment of the Missions National Historic Park) gave me only a glimpse of the city's eighteenth-century mission churches and the trail connecting them, but I had the chance to explore that trail at a more leisurely pace years later with my wife and daughter. For me, the still-active churches on that trail are the city's true gems.

12 Professor Helburn retired at the peak of his career to work as a full-time arbitrator, and we have stayed in contact over the years. In the late 1990s, my family and I traveled to China, where I taught as a Fulbright professor. Because Helburn had been to China in the 1980s, he put me in touch with some of the friends he made there. I was fortunate to meet a few of them during my Fulbright year, including the head of the country's steel ministry who gave my family a personal tour of Beijing's Forbidden City.

13 Howard Wachtel, an economist at American University, taught the industrial policy course, and Dan Luria, an economist with the United Auto Workers, and Jack Russell, a Michigan-based public-policy consultant, taught the reindustrialization workshop. A Progressive Planning Program scholarship made possible my participation in the Cornell summer program.

14 Sandy Darity did his doctoral work at MIT, where he also hosted a late-night radio show as "The Sandman." When I told him I grew up in the Boston area and was a jazz fan who attended several MIT music events, he mentioned his show and I recalled listening to it during my high school days.

15 See, for example, Barry Bluestone and Bennett Harrison, *The Deindustrialization of America: Plant Closings, Community Abandonment, and the Dismantling of Basic Industry* (New York: Basic Books, 1982).

16 *Business Week* editors, "The Reindustrialization of America," *Business Week*, June 30, 1980, 56–138; Robert H. Hayes and William J. Abernathy, "Managing Our Way to Economic Decline," *Harvard Business Review* 58, no. 4 (July–August 1980): 67–77.

17 In the early and mid-1980s, I dove deeply into the literature on national industrial policies, and one of the first books on the subject that caught my attention was Ira C. Magaziner and Robert B. Reich, *Minding America's Business: The Decline and Rise of the American Economy* (New York: Harcourt Brace Jovanovich, 1982). I also found Reich's historical and structural account of the American economy, laid out in his *The Next American Frontier* (New York: Times Books, 1983), consistent with my own emerging views.

18 Darity was critical of the economic mainstream, but he was also well versed in conventional macroeconomics. At MIT, his dissertation committee included two Nobel prize winners: Robert Solow and Paul Samuelson.

19 Post-Keynesian economics emerged in the 1970s as an alternative to two competing strands of standard macroeconomics, one represented by Keynesians such as Paul Samuelson, and the other by monetarists such as Milton Friedman. The post-Keynesian alternative, which contains several elements also found in institutional economics, argues the best way to develop a useful macroeconomics is to reconnect with essential and overlooked ideas of John Maynard Keynes.

20 Two other labor economists left the university around this time; two newcomers eventually replaced them, but Marshall taught my labor courses.

21 Like Marshall's LBJ School seminar, his labor economics seminar also offered a mix of economic theory, history, international comparisons, and policy analysis. Each course focused on a different set of topics, but the methods of analysis used to examine them were similar.

22 My paper for Marshall's seminar provided a nice coda to the Walter Galenson story because the paper cited some of Galenson's research on labor relations and industrial policy in Japan; I certainly didn't foresee that in my early days at Cornell.

23 A paper I wrote for my first course with Professor Marshall in 1982 was also well received (it addressed aspects of immigration policy), but it was not nearly as ambitious as the later paper.

24 Although labor, public economics, and macroeconomics were my specialty fields, I didn't take the macro field exam because only two specialty exams were required for my degree. Macroeconomics nicely complements my focus on worker issues. In fact, John R. Commons saw labor economics and macroeconomics as inseparable because he recognized the business cycle (a macroeconomic phenomenon) as a major source of economic trouble for workers, and Keynes stressed that the macroeconomic context (the overall demand for goods and services) determines a nation's employment level.

25 The chairman of the economics department in Chapel Hill offered to let me transfer my course credits, but he also insisted that I sit for his department's core comprehensive examinations, despite having already passed my core exams in Austin. Although I decided to stay in Texas, Sandy continued to offer valuable research suggestions and we remain in contact.

26 Professors McDonald and Hill turned out to be good choices because aspects of my dissertation touched on each of their areas of specialization. Also, both were sympathetic to institutional economics, especially Hill, who served in the 1960s as the first editor of the *Journal of Economic Issues*, a major outlet for institutionalist research.

27 In 1982, I conducted research for LBJ School professor Norton Grubb on public policies addressing youth unemployment in nations belonging to the Organisation for Economic Cooperation and Development (OECD). Starting the following year, I began tutoring economics to University of Texas undergraduates. For a while, I tried to find part-time or summer work in Austin that related to my policy interests (such as with SER-Jobs for Progress, a nonprofit that provided employment and training programs) but was offered only unpaid internships. I stuck with tutoring because it provided good pay and a flexible schedule.

28 My dissertation committee had no objection to a project based on case studies of consensus-building forums and their role in community economic problem-solving; and I received considerable assistance from employment relations researchers at MIT's Sloan School who were familiar with such institutions. But several mainstream economists at the University of Texas thought the work wasn't really "economics." In fact, upon hearing about my research idea, one economics professor (who had recently earned his doctorate at Harvard) said there was no reason for economists to study such mechanisms because "if they were necessary and truly useful, they would

emerge spontaneously without prompting from academic investigation and public policy."

Much of the applied research on such institutional innovations had been conducted in departments of industrial relations, but the work was thoroughly within the research tradition of institutional economics, and John Dunlop, one of the world's leading labor economists, championed such work. Still, skepticism toward my project from the young Texas faculty members struck me as a warning about the sort of reception my work might face on the academic job market. With that in mind, I decided to modify my project, trying to head off criticism by carefully laying out the case for such work and grounding it explicitly in institutionalism.

29 The day following my dissertation defense, Massachusetts Governor Michael Dukakis announced that Senator Lloyd Bentsen would be his running mate in the 1988 presidential election, evoking the Kennedy-Johnson ticket of 1960 and sparking much discussion of a new "Boston-Austin axis." For a moment, it looked like I was onto something by making the unusual move from the Boston area to Austin for graduate school, especially with Bentsen flashing the UT "Hook 'em Horns" sign in an Associated Press photo taken just after the announcement; see John Council, "Dukakis Taps Bentsen, Evokes Victory of 1960," *The Daily Texan*, July 13, 1988, 1. But Vice President George H.W. Bush (a Texan with his own ties to the Northeast) defeated Dukakis, and a few years later (in 1994) Bush's son defeated incumbent Ann Richards in the Texas gubernatorial race, which, in retrospect, signaled a major and long-enduring shift in that state's politics away from the Democratic Party.

30 Charles J. Whalen, *Beyond Neoclassical Thought: Economics from the Perspective of Institutionalists and Post-Keynesians*, doctoral dissertation, Department of Economics, The University of Texas at Austin, 1988. Published originally in Ann Arbor, Michigan, by UMI (University Microfilms International), now known as ProQuest.

31 The Buffalo area labor-management committee examined in my dissertation covered Buffalo and the rest of Erie County, New York, while the Beaumont committee encompassed Beaumont, Port Arthur, and surrounding communities.

32 In the mid-1980s, I followed news reports about the Catholic Church's analyses of capitalism, but I didn't know of Professor Wilber's involvement with the US bishops until the mid-1990s, when he contributed a chapter to a book I edited (that book, *Political Economy for the 21st Century*, is discussed in Chapter 11). For a discussion of the US bishops' pastoral letter, see Rembert G. Weakland, "Report from the *Ad Hoc* Committee on the American Economy," *Crisis Magazine*, January 1, 1984, https://www.crisismagazine.com/vault/report-from-the-ad-hoc-committee-on-the-american-economy. In addition, for a book by Wilber and one of his colleagues that not only draws on institutionalism and post-Keynesianism, but also builds on principles of Catholic social thought, see Charles K. Wilber and Kenneth P. Jameson, *An Inquiry into the Poverty of Economics* (Notre Dame: University of Notre Dame Press, 1983).

Chapter 8. Texas People and Politics

1 Jane Manchester, the Cornell classmate who taught me tennis, was also part of the small circle.

2 Because Venezuela is an oil-rich nation, several students came from that country to study resource economics at the University of Texas, where the research of several professors focused on the oil and gas industries. In fact, during the 1980s the economics graduate program in Austin attracted students from around the world, including a Chinese student (which was rare at that time) and several from South Korea. Cornell was also diverse, but the group of students studying graduate-level economics in Austin was much more diverse than the student body of Cornell's ILR School during my undergraduate days.

3 A couple of months after we began rooming together, John Quinn's father died of a heart attack at home near Chicago. In 2008, John, then a professor at Hope College (located in Holland, Michigan) died of a heart attack at age 45 while jogging on campus during his lunch break. Quinn and I had been in touch just a few weeks earlier and were looking forward to getting together for a visit.

Quinn was quiet and mild-mannered, but he had a classmate from the University of Notre Dame who stopped by our apartment late one evening—a young military officer passing through Austin on his way to begin a new posting—and that friend was not similarly well-behaved. The soldier, who had been drinking, saw a copy of Karl Marx's *Capital* on a table in the apartment (I was writing a critique of Marxist economics as an appendix to my dissertation) and threatened to break down the door to my bedroom and kill me. John removed him from the apartment. Even after accounting for the alcohol, it showed me just how much passion Marx continues to stir.

4 While living in Austin, I was an avid reader of several news and opinion journals, such as *The New Republic*, which introduced me to the writings of Robert Kuttner (who, in 1990, cofounded the progressive journal *The American Prospect*, to which I became an early subscriber). I was so impressed with Kuttner's book *The Economic Illusion: False Choices Between Prosperity and Social Justice* (Boston: Houghton Mifflin, 1984) that I wrote him a short note, which kicked off years of occasional exchanges and led to his participation in a panel discussion on rising worker insecurity that I organized in the mid-1990s for a meeting of the Eastern Economic Association.

In addition to *The New Republic*, I was an enthusiastic reader in the 1980s (and beyond) of *Challenge: The Magazine of Economic Affairs*, published by M.E. Sharpe, which in the 1990s published my first book. I liked *The New Republic* and *Challenge* because both offered a range of policy viewpoints.

5 In January 2019, Jamie Galbraith graciously delivered the introduction to my presidential address before the institutional economists' Association for Evolutionary Economics.

6 While in Texas, I also occasionally indulged my interest in live music. For example, I attended several shows by Austin guitarist Eric Johnson. In addition, I enjoyed the jazz-fusion music of Mitch Watkins, who led his own Austin-based band and played with Passenger, a Texas group that became Leonard Cohen's backing band.

7 Professor Marshall was an adviser to the Mondale campaign. In fact, if Mondale had won the presidency, Marshall would likely have returned to Washington. Since I hadn't yet completed my graduate program when Ronald Reagan began his second term, I sometimes thought the silver lining to his reelection was that I didn't lose my dissertation adviser. However, Marshall's graduate students worked with him during the Carter era, so we probably would have found a workable solution.

8 See Seth Kantor, "Bentsen Off Fence, On Mondale's Side at Austin Reception," *Austin American-Statesman*, May 4, 1984, 1. A few years later, Ann Richards delivered the keynote address at the Democratic National Convention (in 1988) and then ran successfully to serve as governor of Texas (in 1990).

9 Personal letter from Walter Mondale to the author, January 15, 1985.

10 Today, Doggett, a Democrat, is a member of the US Congress. He was defeated in the 1984 US Senate race by Phil Gramm, an extremely conservative member of Congress, who worked previously as a Texas A&M University economics professor and switched from the Democratic Party to the Republican Party in 1983.

Chapter 9. Early Accomplishments, But Limited Options

1 Carol Petersen, an economics graduate student a few years ahead of me in the Austin doctoral program, was a member of AFEE and encouraged me to read its journal, which led me to join the organization in 1983.

2 Whalen, "A Reason to Look Beyond Neoclassical Economics."

3 To ensure a sharp contrast between AFEE papers and the work of conventional economists, the conference organizer invited papers providing historically grounded accounts of real-world economic change. For my contribution on business-labor engagement in Western New York, see Charles J. Whalen, "Consensus Mechanisms and Community Economic Development: The Buffalo Experience," *Journal of Economic Issues* 21, no. 2 (June 1987): 763–774.

4 Eichner had a longstanding interest in institutionalist approaches to labor economics and labor-management relations, but his work gravitated increasingly toward macroeconomics over time. As a result, he was even more interested in my research when he learned I was drawn to the macroeconomics of Hyman Minsky. It turns out that Eichner helped prepare a collection of Minsky's essays for publication as *Can It Happen Again? Essays on Instability and Finance* (Armonk: M.E. Sharpe, 1982) and encouraged me to consider publishing a book on Minsky (for M.E. Sharpe) after completing my dissertation.

Eichner also discussed the idea with Sandy Darity, who wrote to me after talking with Eichner and suggested that we collaborate on a Minsky book after the dissertation. However, Eichner died unexpectedly (at age 50) in February 1988, only about a year after the conference at which we met; and there was no time for a book when I began teaching immediately after completing my PhD.

5 Charles J. Whalen, "The Minsky-Simons Connection: A Neglected Thread in the History of Economic Thought," *Journal of Economic Issues* 22, no. 2 (June 1988): 533–544.

6 For the "new classical" macroeconomics that emerged in the 1980s, see Robert E. Lucas, *Studies in Business-Cycle Theory* (Cambridge: The MIT Press, 1981). On the aim and (anti-Keynesian) core assumptions of that approach to business cycles, Lucas writes:

> [Much of the theory] is simply an attempt to understand and make more explicit the implicit model underlying the policy proposals of Henry Simons, Milton Friedman, and other critics of activist aggregative policy. By seeking an equilibrium account of business cycles [which means that unemployment is treated as voluntary], one accepts *in advance* rather severe limitations on the scope of governmental countercyclical policy which might be rationalized by the theory.
>
> (Lucas, *Studies in Business-Cycle Theory*, 234–235, emphasis in original)

In contrast, my *JEI* article demonstrates that Henry Simons (who died in 1946) did not treat unemployment as voluntary and that his model was quite different from the one developed by Lucas (who, in 1985, won the Nobel Memorial Prize in economics).

7 The Allied Social Science Associations (ASSA) includes several academic associations in economics and related fields (including industrial relations); it meets annually for a three-day period. The American Economic Association is the dominant group within the ASSA.

8 I organized my first industrial relations session in collaboration with Marianne Koch, a PhD student at Columbia University. That session was the second in a series of annual "doctoral student consortiums" sponsored by the Industrial Relations Research Association (IRRA), and those consortiums, always organized by doctoral students, are still held each year. (To reflect changes in the field of labor and industrial relations, IRRA changed its name to the Labor and Employment Relations Association in 2005.) Given the difficulty I would soon have in finding steady work as a professor, it's ironic that I organized one of my first professional panels on the topic of starting and maintaining a career in academia.

9 The idea for a conference session on Minsky's economics (which is where I delivered my Minsky-Simons research paper) emerged during a discussion with Sandy Darity, who encouraged me to pursue it. In addition to my paper, the session featured papers by Darity (and coauthor Bobby Horn), Mike Lawlor (of Wake Forest University), and Marc Jarsulic (who taught at the University of Notre Dame and recently served as chief economist at the Center for American Progress, perhaps the country's most prominent think tank oriented toward the Democratic Party). Minsky's ideas would have been of interest to AFEE members, and many other economists, even without the October 1987 stock-market drop, but a much wider group of economists and social scientists were interested in hearing from Minsky in the wake of that financial turmoil because financial crises and economic instability were at the heart of his research.

10 Most public-policy schools seeking economists advertised for someone with teaching and research interests involving applications of conventional microeconomics; opportunities to teach the sort of courses Ray Marshall offered at the LBJ School were just not available.

11 Other unconventional economists in my cohort ran into the same difficulty that year. See, for example, L. Randall Wray, "In Memoriam: Gladys Foster (1921-2021)," *Journal of Economic Issues* 55, no. 4 (December 2022): 1194. While all of us who began our careers by highlighting the shortcomings of the economic mainstream and exploring alternative directions diminished our chances of being hired in an economics department, liberal-arts colleges (and a few universities) tended to offer at least some room for diversity of thought among economists. As the article by Wray suggests, direct assistance by graduate professors often proved indispensable in that tough job market.

12 The colleges in Geneva were originally two separate institutions, Hobart College for men and William Smith College for women, with contiguous campuses. Today, they operate as one institution, but each retains its identity and traditions. When I worked at HWS, its official (but rarely used) name was The Colleges of the Seneca.

13 Linda tried to find work in Austin when her Dallas internship ended in the summer of 1983—and nearly landed a nutrition education position with a local school district. She was one of two finalists, and the position seemed perfect for her, but the hiring team said (in an apparent violation of federal law) it decided to offer the position to the other finalist since that applicant was married. Unable to land a position in Austin, Linda accepted an opportunity to direct the federal Women, Infants, and Children (WIC) program in two Southern Tier counties within the state of New York. Based in the village of Bath, the position was too good to pass up. Linda's parents were born and raised in Bath, and many of her relatives still resided in the area.

In late 1986, Linda and I were married, and I finished my dissertation from Bath. We rented a one-bedroom apartment on the second floor of a Victorian home located a block from the village square and a five-minute walk from Linda's office. The apartment was modestly furnished, but in Austin I slept on a futon and used cardboard boxes and plywood to fashion bookshelves and a coffee table, so for me it was a major improvement. Also, Bath was about an hour's drive from Ithaca, where Linda's parents lived and where I could use the Cornell libraries.

14 As I will discuss in Part Four ("Colleges of the Seneca"), I learned quickly that a non-tenure-track position was far from a move that "gets your foot in the door." In retrospect, given John Dunlop's interest in labor-management consensus building, I should have asked my dissertation chair, Ray Marshall, to help me arrange a post-doctoral position at Harvard with Dunlop, which is what Walter Galenson helped arrange when Marshall completed his own dissertation. I'm sure the idea occurred to me back then and that I dismissed it because there seemed too little time to work out such an arrangement once it became clear my search for a tenure-track post hadn't been fruitful. In retrospect, however, it's an alternative I should have at least explored—and I certainly wish someone had warned me that taking a non-tenurable post came with a considerable downside, including the risk of career damage.

Chapter 10. A City and Nation Transformed

1 When I began graduate school, Austin's status as a technology hub was emerging; by the time I defended my dissertation in mid-1988, it had arrived. In mid-1984, *The Economist* captured the transformation taking place in Austin with an article that appeared under the headline: "Austin Discards Its Dungarees," *The Economist,* May 26–June 1, 1984, 34. Even then, much of Texas was still dependent on oil and when oil prices plummeted in 1982, parts of the Austin economy took a hit, including many local financial institutions. But huge public-private partnerships in microelectronics, computer technology, and semiconductors during that decade cemented the city's place as the "tech hot spot" it remains today. See "The Town That Won the Pennant: A Short History of Austin's Economic Development," Austin Environmental Directory,

2003, https://www.environmentaldirectory.info/a-short-history-of-austins-economic-development/; "Sematech Joins MCC Research Center in Calling Austin Its Home: Texas Capital Fast Becoming High-Tech Capital," *Los Angeles Times*, January 18, 1988, https://www.latimes.com/archives/la-xpm-1988-01-19-fi-36854-story.html; and Sebastian Herrera, "35 Years Ago, MCC 'Planted a Flag' for Austin as a Tech Hot Spot," *Austin American-Statesman*, October 12, 2018, https://www.statesman.com/story/business/technology/2018/10/12/austin-is-tech-hot-spot-it-wasnt-always-this-way/9527918007/.

2 For an examination of the overall decline in US manufacturing employment in the 1980s (and beyond), see Kevin Bahr, "U.S. Manufacturing Employment: A Long-Term Perspective," University of Wisconsin-Stevens Point, January 29, 2025, https://blog.uwsp.edu/cps/2025/01/29/u-s-manufacturing-employment-a-long-term-perspective/. For a discussion of Polaroid's decline, see "Polaroid Corporation," Wikipedia, December 13, 2024, https://en.wikipedia.org/wiki/Polaroid_Corporation. It must also be kept in mind that income losses from employment cuts ripple through a community, resulting in additional job reductions.

3 For conventional economists' perspectives on the American economic problems of the 1980s, see, for example, Robert Z. Lawrence, "The Myth of U.S. Deindustrialization," *Challenge* 26, no. 5 (November 1983): 12–21; Charles L. Schultze, "Industrial Policy: A Dissent," *The Brookings Review* 2, no. 1 (Fall 1983): 3–12; and Martin Feldstein, "Counterrevolution in Progress," *Challenge* 31, no. 4 (July 1988): 42–46. Schultze and Feldstein chaired the Council of Economic Advisers for Presidents Carter and Reagan, respectively.

4 For example, see Ray Marshall, *Unheard Voices: Labor and Economic Policy in a Competitive World* (New York: Basic Books, 1987).

5 Bennett Harrison and Barry Bluestone, *The Great U-Turn: Corporate Restructuring and the Polarization of America* (New York: Basic Books, 1988).

6 Harrison and Bluestone, *The Great U-Turn*, 12–13. As mentioned by Harrison and Bluestone, much corporate restructuring was enabled by new transportation and communications technologies. Also, for my discussion of the era of managerial capitalism, see the final section of Chapter 2.

7 Harrison and Bluestone, *The Great U-Turn*, viii.

8 Harrison and Bluestone organized their policy strategy around the following themes, all of which remain relevant today: industrial policy, workplace democracy, a strong labor movement, infrastructure investment, a rebuilt and extended social safety net, prudent government regulation, and managed (what many now call "strategic") international trade; see Harrison and Bluestone, *The Great U-Turn*, 182–193.

9 See Michael Harrington, *The New American Poverty* (New York: Penguin Books, 1984). As discussed in Chapter 6, note 12, Harrington's *The Other America* is said to have inspired the War on Poverty, and his *Decade of Decision* highlighted the structural economic transformation that began to take shape in the United States during the 1970s. For Harrington, America's existing faces of poverty (highlighted in *The Other America*) could be found in Appalachia and other long-neglected communities and regions; the economic transformation of the 1970s and 1980s produced the new poverty.

10 Here too my father's experience dovetailed with that of countless others. When his employer (Polaroid) filed for bankruptcy in 2001, my dad and others who worked for that company saw promised pensions and other retirement benefits vanish except for certain benefits guaranteed by the Pension Benefit Guaranty Corporation (PBGC). Prior to creation of the PBGC in 1974, workers often found themselves without any pension when plants closed. PBGC offers protection guarantees for defined-benefit pensions; it doesn't protect defined-contribution plans against market fluctuations.

11 On the anticipated spread of worker insecurity, see Harrington, *The New American Poverty*, 62–64.

12 On the industrial policy of the Reagan administration, see Harrington, *The New American Poverty,* 239. In 1983, in response to Democrats' calls for an industrial policy, President Reagan created the President's Commission on Industrial Competitiveness. Two years later, that commission, headed by John A. Young (CEO of Hewlett-Packard) released a two-volume report, *Global Competition: The New Reality* (Washington: US Government Printing Office, 1985). That report combined a recognition of the nation's need to strengthen its competitive performance with a call for policies to improve the ability of capital "to flow freely to its most productive uses." It also called for government to "take the lead in highlighting the importance of competitiveness and … [in nurturing] an effective consensus-building dialogue among leaders in industry, labor, government, and academia" (*Global Competition*, Vol. 1, 2–3). The Reagan administration focused on policy changes that allowed capital to flow freely, but the rest of the commission's competitiveness agenda was largely ignored and economic polarization only intensified.

13 The notion of building the economy "from the middle out" (or "from the bottom up and the middle out") began to garner considerable attention in the early 2010s; see, for example, Eric Liu and Nick Hanauer, "The True Origins of Prosperity," *Democracy: A Journal of Ideas*, Summer 2013, https://democracyjournal.org/magazine/29/the-true-origins-of-prosperity/. But Harrington and other progressives clearly had this vision and agenda several decades earlier.

14 To complement an economic agenda centered on full employment, Harrington also called for a living wage, healthcare for all, and a national commitment to affordable housing, all of which dovetailed with his jobs focus; see Harrington, *The New American Poverty,* 230–255.

15 Harrington's discussion of public investments emphasized investments in infrastructure, rail transportation, and renewable forms of energy; see Harrington, *The New American Poverty,* 241–242.

16 Some might argue Harrington had a naïve vision, but in fact constructive action by government (including major investments in education and training) and the coordination of public and private action provided essential foundations for Austin's emergence as a high-tech mecca. (The same is true for Greater Boston.) In the case of Austin, Harrington would have probably called for giving more attention to affordable housing, training and jobs programs for unemployed and low-wage workers, and community involvement in policy decision-making. But the region's use of public action to spur knowledge-based development in emerging industries seems broadly consistent with the role of government outlined in *The New American Poverty.*

17 On the possibility of building a "majority movement" around rising economic insecurity, see Harrington, *The New American Poverty*, 62.

18 I was certainly not alone in feeling anxious about America's future. Several observers of the political economy of the 1980s—see, for example, Bertram Gross, *Friendly Fascism* (Boston: South End Press, 1980) and Robert Lekachman, *Greed Is Not Enough* (New York: Pantheon 1982)—worried about the possible emergence of undemocratic planning, authoritarianism, despotism, or "friendly fascism." Also, US Representative James Weaver of Oregon wrote in the mid-1980s of his fear that rising economic insecurity would cause jobless workers to "become intensely bitter." He continued: "Already unemployed steelworkers are getting angry enough to threaten people on the street. A fireside chat will not comfort them. They may well demand harsh remedies, remedies that only a despot can promise"; see James Weaver, "The Sky Is Falling." *The New Republic*," May 13, 1985, 19–20.

Unemployed workers most often directed their anger and frustration toward family members or inward in the form of self-destructive behavior (such as turning to alcohol, drugs, or suicide), but Weaver's broader point, that frustration was becoming intense, was on target. And the presidential campaigns of Patrick Buchanan and Donald Trump later indicated there was indeed reason to worry that rising economic insecurity would lead in a direction that was not at all progressive. For evidence that even Michael Harrington saw the possibility of an authoritarian future, see his *The Next America* (New York: Holt, Rinehart and Winston, 1981).

Chapter 11. Real-World Economics

1 My paper was prepared for a session organized by AFEE, which met during the annual meeting of the Allied Social Science Associations.

2 The job opening at HWS during my first year was a tenure-track position, but, alas, not in my fields; among the applicants were two non-tenure-track HWS faculty members who had been teaching there for a few years while finishing their PhD.

3 According to a report by the American Association of University Professors (published as I began my final year at HWS), "There is little evidence to support those who hope that their accomplishments off the tenure track will result in consideration for a tenure-eligible appointment." Instead, when a tenure-line position becomes available even in their own department, the teaching experience of non-tenure-track faculty members tends to be "interpreted as evidence of failed promise when measured against new PhDs who are just entering the job market." See American Association of University Professors, "The Status of Non-Tenure-Track Faculty," *Academe* 79, no. 4 (July–August 1993), 39–46.

4 At various times in my career, I suggested to my wife that I'd someday write a memoir with the title *Striking While the Irony Is Hot*. It does seem irony is everywhere.

5 For a survey of segmented labor markets in the postwar era of managerial capitalism, see Bennett Harrison and Andrew Sum, "The Theory of 'Dual' or Segmented Labor Markets," *Journal of Economic Issues* 13, no. 3 (September 1979): 687–706. Over the past few decades, many jobs long considered primary labor-market positions have experienced an erosion of their advantages over jobs in the secondary markets, but the primary-versus-secondary distinction remains relevant in academia and beyond.

6 Located in the Finger Lakes region of New York, HWS was within an hour's drive of my wife's workplace, the home of her parents, and the libraries of Cornell University.

7 Between fall 1988 and spring 1994, I taught two courses in each of the colleges' 10-week trimesters except fall 1991, when I took advantage of the opportunity to take a one-term research leave (available to all full-time members of the faculty upon completing three years of teaching). In addition to my classroom teaching, I usually supervised one or two independent study students each term. During my research leave, I was a visiting research fellow at Cornell ILR, which provided full access to Cornell University libraries.

8 In fact, I relied heavily on a textbook only when teaching macroeconomic theory, a course organized around core concepts and analyses that my students needed to understand before advancing to other courses in the economics major.

9 Class discussions were structured around a series of questions and grounded in each day's assigned readings. The discussion format ensured that students took an active role in analyzing course material in class.

10 One student, for example, wrote on their end-of-term student evaluation form that "Professor Whalen inspired and encouraged me to work to my potential, by believing in me—sometimes even more than I initially believed in myself."

11 My deindustrialization seminar was first offered in spring 1991. It was so popular that I offered it again each year until my contract expired. It was certainly timely. In fact, in May 1992, Senator Daniel P. Moynihan delivered the Commencement address at HWS and even his presentation addressed the changing economy, its adverse effects on workers and communities, and the need for constructive public policy action to assist working families. According to historian Clark Davis (1998), "Americans began to feel the pinch of corporate belt-tightening in the 1970s, but it was not until the early 1990s that wholesale layoffs became standard practice and generated significant anger"; see Clark Davis, "Downsizing Becomes Normal," Origins: Current Events in Historical Perspective, April 1998, https://origins.osu.edu/history-news/downsizing-becomes-normal.

12 Diane E. Herz, "Worker Displacement Still Common in the Late 1980s," *Monthly Labor Review* 114, no. 5 (May 1991), 3–9. For discussions of rising worker insecurity in the early- and mid-1990s, see, for example, Philip Mattera, *Prosperity Lost* (New York: Addison-Wesley, 1990); Donald L. Bartlett and James B. Steele, *America: What Went Wrong?* (Kansas City: Andrews and McMeel, 1992); and Katherine S. Newman, *Declining Fortunes: The Withering of the American Dream* (New York: Basic Books, 1993).

13 For discussions in the early 1990s of threats to the US economy and national security owing to moving technology and jobs overseas, the increasing foreign ownership of US-based firms, and foreign lobbying of US policymakers, see, for example, Martin Tolchin and Susan J. Tolchin, *Selling Our Security* (New York: Alfred A. Knopf, 1992); Laura D'Andrea Tyson, "They Are Not Us: Why American Ownership Still Matters," *American Prospect* 1, no. 4 (Winter 1991), 37–49; and Pat Choate, *Agents of Influence* (New York: Alfred A. Knopf, 1990).

14 During the presidential administration of George H.W. Bush, Michael Boskin, Bush's chair of the Council of Economic Advisers, dismissed concerns about US manufacturing jobs going overseas and was widely reported to have said "it doesn't make any difference whether American companies produce potato chips or semiconductor chips." Although Boskin denied making the comment, it succinctly expressed the view of most of that era's US economists.

In fact, economist Paul Krugman (who later moderated his views while writing as a columnist for *The New York Times*) viciously attacked progressives and other supporters of industrial policy and strategic trade policies in several books and articles in the 1980s and 1990s. In a careful review of such criticism, economic journalist Robert Kuttner noted that Krugman and other orthodox economists eventually conceded there was room for active government policies *in theory*, but also that they then argued the policies would fail *in practice* owing to the likely negative consequences of political pressures on policymaking. Kuttner concluded: "Orthodox economists long criticized advocates of industrial policy for practicing economics without a license, but in their retreat to the claim that strategic trade can work but not here, they now practice political science without a license"; see Robert Kuttner, *The End of Laissez-Faire* (New York: Alfred A. Knopf, 1991), 122.

15 A short time before the end of my HWS faculty appointment, a business leader (an executive at a large, high-technology corporation based in Rochester, New York) delivered a public lecture on campus during which he dismissed concerns about corporate downsizing and instead painted a bright picture of the job prospects for soon-to-be college graduates. He told the assembled students, "You have nothing to worry about. Your future is bright. You are smart. You are skilled. The ones that need to worry are those in their mid-30s, not you." Many of my students recognized that they too would be in their mid-30s before too long.

16 My colleagues in the HWS capstone courses came from the disciplines of anthropology, history, sociology, and political science. Another economist, whose research focused on worker-run enterprises, also took part in the course on capitalism and socialism. Each of the courses enrolled 100 students. After my first lecture for the "Me Generation" course, a colleague sent me a congratulatory note: "You did an excellent job in getting us off to a fine start. You raised all kinds of neat issues relevant to the course [and] I appreciate the transition you made to the Me Generation." After the "Capitalism and Socialism" course ended, a colleague in that course complimented me for inspiring and engaging students and for presenting "complex material in an accessible and even entertaining manner, yet without compromising scholarly rigor." (The comments of those two colleagues are contained in documents I compiled when creating a teaching portfolio at the conclusion of my HWS contract. The portfolio and accompanying documents remain in my personal files.)

17 Although American economic history wasn't one of my graduate fields of specialization, my dissertation committee included Forest Hill, an economic historian.

18 I wasn't discouraged by Professor McClelland's remarks about graduate students at top-tier university economics departments having no interest in history. I understood that there were no economic history jobs at major research universities. But undergraduate programs at liberal arts colleges had a different aim, and reviving a course in US economic history seemed a perfect way to better integrate economics into the broader HWS (liberal arts) curriculum. The time also seemed right considering growing public

interest in understanding economic changes taking place within the United States and around the world, changes that demanded a historical perspective.

Since then, interest in economic history within academia has blossomed, and much of that attention has focused on the evolution of capitalism since the Second World War—with interest picking up first among non-economists (historians, sociologists, labor scholars, etc.) but eventually even among some economists. In fact, attention to history among economists seemed to emerge most quickly at the most prestigious universities, where faculty members have the liberty to be trendsetters instead of followers.

19 Some of the readings I assigned in my HWS American economic history course derived from material in Professor McClelland's syllabus, but my HWS course was also influenced by Stuart Bruchey's *Enterprise: The Dynamic Economy of a Free People* (Cambridge: Harvard University Press, 1990). Bruchey, who taught economic history at Columbia University, dispelled the myth of an America built on rugged individualism and instead demonstrated how government deeply influenced economic development throughout US history. In addition, his references offered a treasure trove of research material and sources. Although I taught American economic history only once at HWS, I revamped the course for delivery during my 1998–1999 Fulbright professorship in China and have occasionally considered updating the material and fashioning it into a book.

20 Charles J. Whalen, "Institutional Economics," in *Survey of Social Science: Economics,* vol. 3, ed. Frank N. Magill (Pasadena: Salem Press, 1991), 1090–1097.

21 Charles J. Whalen, "John R. Common's Institutional Economics: A Re-examination," *Journal of Economic Issues* 23, no. 2 (June 1989): 443–454.

22 Charles J. Whalen, "Stabilizing the Unstable Economy: More on the Minsky-Simons Connection," *Journal of Economic Issues* 25, no. 3 (September 1991): 739–763; Charles J. Whalen, "Saving Capitalism by Making It Good: The Monetary Economics of John R. Commons," *Journal of Economic Issues* 27, no. 4 (December 1993): 1155–1179; Charles J. Whalen, "Schools of Thought and Theories of the State," in *The Stratified State*, ed. William M. Dugger and William T. Waller (Armonk: M.E. Sharpe, 1992), 55–85; Charles J. Whalen, "Structural Change and the Compulsive Shift to Institutional Analysis," in *Institutional Economics and the Theory of Social Value*, ed. Charles M.A. Clark (Boston: Kluwer Academic Publishers, 1995), 179–194; and Charles J. Whalen and Linda B. Whalen, "Institutionalism: A Useful Foundation for Feminist Economics?" in *The Economic Status of Women Under Capitalism: Institutional Economics and Feminist Theory*, ed. Janice Peterson and Doug Brown (Aldershot: Edward Elgar, 1994), 19–34.

23 The original draft of my chapter on feminism and institutionalism—coauthored with my wife, Linda—included a section outlining the elements of a feminist-institutionalist agenda on public policy in addition to a section exploring the institutionalist foundations of feminist economic theory. The policy discussion, largely omitted from the final version by the editors so the chapter would fit better into the book, included an exploration of the need to challenge society's corporation-driven values by restructuring work in ways that would make progressive family policies available to all employees, in the interest of women, men, families, and their communities. That discussion (still hinted at in the final version) highlighted the need for an ongoing pursuit of women's rights in the workplace and beyond, but it also sought to build on feminist ideals to redirect society beyond the traditional corporate bottom line and toward universal human values.

At the time (early 1990s), that policy view was just beginning to emerge in feminist circles, but by the end of the 1990s it had become part of the feminist mainstream, as I learned directly from feminist icon Betty Friedan. In late 1999, Friedan was a visiting professor at Cornell's ILR School and I was among the ILR faculty working in Buffalo, where Friedan spent an afternoon and delivered an evening public lecture. In our one-on-one afternoon discussion and again in her lecture, Friedan drew on expertise as a social activist, as well as experience as a parent and grandparent, to stress the need for feminists to pursue a new social revolution by shifting the agenda "from women's rights to how jobs are structured for both men and women." See Linda Myers, "Betty Friedan's New Agenda: Apply Feminist Ideals of Equality, Fairness to Men as Well as Women," *Cornell Chronicle*, December 1, 1998, https://news.cornell.edu/stories/1998/12/friedans-new-agenda-fairness-men-too.

24 Bill Dugger, whom I met in Austin in the mid-1980s (see Chapter 8), played a leading role in fostering that community of institutionalist researchers.

25 While at HWS, I also secured publication of (and wrote an introduction to) a historically important memorandum that Henry Simons composed and circulated during the Great Depression; it appeared as "Henry Simons's Banking and Currency Reform," in *Research in the History of Economic Thought and Methodology, Archival Supplement* 4, ed. Warren J. Samuels (Greenwich: JAI Press, 1994), 23–49. In addition, I contributed two research notes (essays in response to the work of others) to the *Journal of Economic Issues*, one of which was reprinted in a research volume by Edward Elgar Publishing while I was still at HWS. My 1988 article on Minsky and Simons was also reprinted, twice: in research volumes by publishers Elgar and Routledge. Taken together, my publications show that I maintained a high degree of scholarly engagement at HWS while also teaching many courses.

26 Rexford G. Tugwell, *The Trend of Economics* (New York: Alfred A. Knopf, 1924).

27 On *The Trend* as a manifesto of maverick economists, see Tugwell, *The Trend of Economics*, vii–xi. According to economist Martin Bronfenbrenner, institutional economics "seemed likely to assume a commanding position in American economic thought" only once: in the years immediately following publication of Tugwell's book; see Martin Bronfenbrenner, "Early American Leaders—Institutional and Critical Traditions," *The American Economic Review* 75, no. 6 (December 1985): 20.

28 Charles J. Whalen, *Political Economy for the 21st Century: Contemporary Views on the Trend of Economics* (Armonk: M.E. Sharpe, 1996).

29 John Charles Pool and Ross M. LaRoe, "Summer Reading Ideas for Economist Buffs," *Democrat and Chronicle/Times-Union* [Rochester, New York], June 3, 1996, B2.

30 The first two interview teams on which I served were to fill tenure-track positions in the field of quantitative economics. (Both of those positions became available as the department gradually replaced non-tenure-track positions with tenure-eligible positions; and mine, the department's last remaining non-tenure-track slot, was next in line.) My third interview team reviewed candidates to fill a vacancy created by the death of the department's environmental economist.

31 My tenure-review committee work involved writing a report on the scholarship of a colleague, based on assessments from department colleagues and external reviewers. I was chosen because my research and teaching fields overlapped with those of the professor under review. It was an easy assignment because all the reports on the professor's scholarship were highly favorable.

32 I also assisted colleagues in bringing to campus authors Barbara Ehrenreich, Christopher Lasch, and Ruth Sidel, whose visits were arranged in conjunction with my team-taught courses.

33 One book review covered a three-volume set on institutional economics; another was an article-length review essay on a 500-page book about the economic notion of the "invisible hand." My other reviews examined books on industrial policy, labor relations, and macroeconomics. Since then, I've continued to write about one or two book reviews each year.

34 Paxon's political involvement began at the age of 15, when he volunteered for Jack Kemp's first congressional campaign. At age 23, he began his political career, serving, in turn, as a county, state, and federal legislator.

35 I sent my letter to Doug Call about a week after he entered the congressional race. I was familiar with regional issues and knew several public- and private-sector leaders at the western end of the district because of my PhD research; and I was familiar with the eastern end of the district because I worked at HWS for four years and studied in nearby Ithaca as an undergraduate. Meanwhile, the most pressing national economic issues were at the heart of my teaching and writing. In addition, I followed the rise of Rep. Paxon because he was one of several young Republicans who held more extreme, limited-government views than the Republican moderates (such as Barber Conable and Frank Horton) who represented much of central and western New York for decades.

36 Doug entered the congressional race at the request of his friend, US Representative Louise Slaughter, who represented an adjacent district that included the city of Rochester. Slaughter didn't want to see Paxon run unopposed. But the smart money knew it was better to stay on the sidelines. In fact, Kevin Gaughan, a Buffalo-area Democrat who opposed Paxon in 1990, withdrew from the 1992 race a month before Doug decided to jump in (before new district maps were set). Gaughan argued the decision was "painful, but realistic" because the redistricting delays made it "impossible to mount an effective campaign"; see George Borrelli, "Gaughan Withdraws from Race," *Buffalo News*, June 3, 1992, B4.

37 Paxon was skilled at self-promotion and self-preservation. For example, his congressional office consistently spent more on taxpayer-funded direct mail than nearly all others. See, for example, Jerry Zremski, "Franking Bill of $191,693 Puts Paxon Third in House," *Buffalo News*, March 25, 1992, D7. And in what many observers considered an attempt to make state lawmakers think twice before eliminating Paxon's district or forcing him to run against an incumbent, Paxon donated $60,000 to the New York State Senate Republican Campaign Committee and promised an additional $10,000 per year for the decade ahead; see Douglas Turner, "Paxon's $100,000 Pledge Defended," *Buffalo News*, March 19, 1991, A1. Paxon also helped organize fundraisers for key Republican state legislators.

38 At the start of Doug's campaign, Rep. Slaughter's campaign provided Doug with research on Paxon, which her team accumulated when it appeared that redistricting

might result in a merger of the Slaughter and Paxon districts. That material jump-started our own work.

39 Despite the many hours I devoted to the Call campaign, the political work never interfered with my teaching or other HWS obligations. In fact, the campaign experience boosted my understanding of the economic challenges faced by working families, businesses, and local governments across the district, which increased my effectiveness in the classroom. At the same time, the campaign gave me an opportunity to translate academic research into practical policy ideas.

40 For example, the *Buffalo News* editorial board wrote of Call: "He thrives on solving problems through consensus and innovation"; see "For Congress: Houghton, Gorski, Call and LaFalce," *Buffalo News*, October 18, 1992, G10.

41 For some editorial board endorsements of Doug Call, including criticism of Bill Paxon, see "For Congress: Houghton, Gorski, Call and LaFalce," *Buffalo News*; "Our Choices for Congress," *Democrat and Chronicle* [Rochester, New York], October 26, 1992, 6A; "House of Representatives," *Times-Union* [Rochester, New York], October 22, 1992, 10A; "For Congress: Call," *Daily Messenger* [Canandaigua, New York], October 22, 1992, 2C. Also, see Douglas Turner, "Paxon Votes Against 4 Breast Cancer Bills," *Buffalo News*, January 21, 1992, D1.

42 For a comparison of campaign spending, see Jerry Zremski, "Paxon Campaign Costliest in WNY," *Buffalo News*, February 16, 1993, B1. Paxon's tab for taxpayer-funded direct mail in just the first quarter of 1992 was close to what Call raised and spent during his entire campaign; see Jerry Zremski, "Paxon Again Leads WNY Group in Use of Congressional Franking," *Buffalo News*, June 24, 1992, A7.

43 I didn't attend the AARP event, but Doug insisted that when asked about the plan he said only that he would consider it. The sole newspaper report on the event makes no mention of the matter, focusing instead on the appearance of Paxon's mother as a surrogate for the incumbent; see Jonathan Goldstein, "A Different Paxon Stumps Locally," *Daily Messenger* [Canandaigua, New York], September 18, 1992, 1A, 15A.

44 According to HWS policies, full-time faculty contracts extending beyond six years had to be accompanied by tenure, which ensures a continuous appointment except in extreme cases such as professional misconduct. Since I never held a tenure-eligible appointment, the college's policies meant I could not teach beyond the sixth year.

45 It was also difficult to carry on academic research (which often takes several years to see through to completion) when job contracts spanned only two years.

46 A couple of years after I left the colleges, one of my former colleagues emailed me to mention that the economics department at HWS ranked in the top ten among national liberal arts colleges based on research productivity over the period 1989–1994, which covers most of the time I was at the colleges. He also noted that I contributed significantly to that achievement; in fact, my contributions put me among the department's top contributors. For the revised, published version of the paper ranking economics departments during that period (which ranks HWS 12th), see James E. Hartley and Michael D. Robinson, "Economics Research at National Liberal Arts Colleges: School Rankings," *Journal of Economic Education* 28, no. 4 (Autumn 1997): 337–349.

47 The quote "of very high quality" (in all areas of work at HWS) comes from the comprehensive, third-year review document submitted by the Department of

Economics to HWS on May 28, 1991 (author's personal copy). The report incorporates findings of a student subcommittee, which reviewed all the evidence including course materials, student evaluations, and a survey of all my former students, and concluded, "We strongly believe that Professor Whalen has been and continues to be an excellent teacher."

48 In this chapter, I focus on family matters that directly involved my household. However, my youngest brother (John) chose, by sheer coincidence, to attend Hobart College (attracted in good part by its sailing team) and studied there from 1988 through 1992, graduating with a major in geoscience. He visited my family occasionally, but we rarely crossed paths on campus.

49 Until Katie was born, Linda directed the WIC nutrition program in Steuben and Allegany Counties, a position located within Cornell Cooperative Extension.

50 "Patches"—an extraordinarily gentle, basset-beagle mix—was part of the family for sixteen years.

51 Based in Rochester, Linda oversaw more than a dozen WIC programs within the state health department's Western Region.

52 The HWS administrators in place when the economics department's position request was rejected were not the same as when I was hired. HWS had recently hired a new president and provost. The refusal to add a tenure-eligible position in economics might have been a financial decision, but the economics major was one of the most popular areas of study on campus and my courses generated solid enrollment numbers, often at or even slightly above the class-size maximums set by the colleges (I found it difficult to turn away interested students when my courses exceeded enrollment limits).

53 The labor economist who was turned down for tenure had been hired into a tenure-track slot in 1988, the same year I was hired at HWS. Prior to receiving the tenurable appointment, that economist taught in a non-tenure-track capacity at HWS; when she moved into the tenure-track slot, I was given her non-tenurable slot. We were recruited based on the same position announcement and taught some of the same courses. (The tenure review case mentioned here is the same as discussed in note 31; the adverse tenure decision had nothing to do with scholarship.)

54 In its 1991–1992 search to fill the newly available tenure-track position, HWS did not grant me a job interview. At the same time, it granted an on-campus interview to one of my PhD adviser's current doctoral students who fulfilled the colleges' requirement for an ethnic minority. My adviser, whom I still relied upon for letters of recommendation, was understandably confused by the situation.

55 The HWS tenure-track position announcement appeared in the fall 1991 "Job Openings for Economists," published by the American Economic Association (photocopy; author's personal files). It advertised for the same fields as the position announcement that brought me to HWS in 1988.

56 I must credit that administrator with providing a demeaning, revealing, muddled, and diversionary answer in so few words. (For a discussion of the labor-market significance of networks, see Chapter 13.)

57 Linda Ray Pratt, "Exploitation or Equity Off the Tenure Track?" *Footnotes: A Publication of the American Association of University Professors* (Fall 1991), 1. Another article published that same fall, which explored the labor-market challenges facing many white males, also underscored that I was not alone: see Charlene Marmer Solomon, "Are White Males Being Left Out?" *Personnel Journal* 70, no. 11 (November 1991): 88–94.

58 My feeling of being exploited came not from inequitable compensation (my pay and benefits were comparable to tenure-track colleagues) but from not having a chance at a tenurable post. Yet one aspect of my job did strike me as purposefully humiliating: throughout my appointment, my office was in a different building from that of my economics colleagues. For the first few years, my office was in a building that housed the modern languages and classics faculty. Then, around the time it was clear my position would not become tenurable (and the rest of the economics department moved into a newly renovated building), I was given an "office" on the top floor of the colleges' administration building, which was actually a theater costume closet. Instead of expecting students to find that isolated and bleak office, I held afternoon office hours at a table in the campus café, where we'd share a box (or two) of popcorn that I poured over spread napkins. Those office hours were a huge hit with my students; in fact, I often arrived at the designated time to find a box of warm popcorn and the napkins already spread.

Chapter 12. The Six-Year Search—Including a Huge Near Miss

1 The HWS president who arrived in 1991 encouraged faculty-student dinners, but Linda and I were already hosting them each semester. Toward the end of my years at the colleges, we also hosted an end-of-year picnic for my students.

2 In addition to searching on the academic job market, I sought (without success) policy work in Washington, DC, on the staff of Democratic legislators and in newly formed organizations such as the Council on Competitiveness and the Competitiveness Policy Council.

3 In fact, some institutionalists and post-Keynesians confided that, because of their non-mainstream views, they were isolated from the rest of their colleagues in their own department.

4 The pressure to hire women and minorities was especially strong in the labor field, a specialization that tended to attract more women than many other areas within economics.

5 While others I met at conferences also tried to help me find work, John Henry (who taught at California State University, Sacramento) and Warren Samuels (who taught at Michigan State University) seem to have tried especially hard. Meanwhile, I searched vigorously, using all my professional contacts to spread the word—while also trying to avoid becoming a nuisance.

6 By all accounts, Professor Marshall's letters praised my work and described me as among the best doctoral students of his career.

7 After Robert Reich was nominated as Secretary of Labor, several news stories reported that Marshall was preparing Reich for his new job, so I sent my résumé to Reich at

Harvard and expressed interest in working for him at the Labor Department. He sent a nice, handwritten reply, but it didn't lead to a job offer.

8 I did receive two academic job offers, but one seemed less than solid and the other was in England. During my third year at HWS, I was selected as the top faculty candidate for an economics position at a nearby women's college, but the salary offer was far below the market rate, the teaching load was higher than at HWS, and the institution's future was uncertain (in fact, it has since been shuttered). In addition, at that time a tenurable line at HWS still appeared to be a real possibility. I took the advice of one of my graduate-school professors and declined the offer. A year later, thanks partly to a recommendation from John Henry, I received an offer of a position in the UK at Staffordshire University (in Stoke-on-Trent), which was posted outside the usual US job-market channels. But my family was reluctant to move abroad, so I renewed my HWS contract for the final time and kept searching stateside.

9 At the request of the director of the Levy Institute, I even served as a reviewer of research fellowship proposals submitted to the institute by other economists as early as 1993.

10 Meanwhile, HWS hired a succession of labor and political economists who fulfilled the administration's notion of diversity but didn't remain in upstate New York for long. At one point, the department hired one of my former students, who wrote to thank me for having prepared her so well for her career—and mentioned using my syllabus as a guide to teaching the "Political Economy" course in which she had been my student (see Chapter 24).

Chapter 13. Perseverance and Accomplishments Are Not Enough

1 Looking young has been with me throughout my career. In fact, at a conference in 2007, another attendee thought I was a graduate student and asked me how my dissertation was proceeding. I tactfully avoided mentioning that it was completed in 1988.

2 During my final years at HWS, one incident that struck me as especially callous came from a member of the faculty who recruited me in 1988. In a moment of frustration, I wondered aloud whether my situation warranted a discrimination lawsuit. Without hesitation, the reply was that people are always free to sue: "That's why the Colleges has lawyers."

3 On another occasion, an HWS economist laughed at me for including one of my own papers alongside an article by John Maynard Keynes in a course reading list. The point of my work was to show that some of Keynes's thinking aligned with, and may have even been borrowed from, the work of John R. Commons, a pioneering institutionalist. In the years since then, important links between Commons and Keynes have become widely recognized in the economics profession, and my research contributed to that growing literature; see Charles J. Whalen, "John R. Commons and John Maynard Keynes on Economic History and Policy: The 1920s and Today," *Journal of Economic Issues* 42, no. 1 (March 2008): 225–242. In fact, the connection

between Commons and Keynes has even been mentioned by Robert Skidelsky, author of the definitive biography of Keynes, who writes that Commons was an important but not always acknowledged influence on Keynes; see Robert Skidelsky *John Maynard Keynes*, vol. 2 (New York: Viking Penguin, 1994), 229.

4 A decades-long body of academic literature highlights the crucial role of professional guidance, mentorship, and indeed "sponsorship" in launching the careers of PhD students. For example, one study on academic career success, by Susan Cameron and Robert Blackburn, indicates that "while merit is part of the picture, social selection on any of a number of ascriptive variables plays a role in selection for initiation into a profession [including academia]. In the literature, the process of this initiation is often termed 'sponsorship.'" The study highlights sponsorship from senior faculty members, often a student's major professor or dissertation chair, across several dimensions of support, including financial, publication, personal/emotional, and job placement (including "direct assistance in obtaining the first faculty appointment").

Recognizing the importance of mentoring graduate students, some universities offer mentoring guidelines. For example, guidelines published by the Graduate Council at University of California, Davis state that while the major professor will be a student's primary mentor, all faculty have a responsibility to mentor graduate students and that faculty mentoring is broader than advising a student on degree requirements. It must also include "guiding students through professional development," and must be considered "an integral part of the graduate experience."

For illustrative research and references on this subject, see Susan W. Cameron and Robert T. Blackburn, "Sponsorship and Academic Career Success," *Journal of Higher Education* 52, no. 4 (July–August 1981): 369–377; Lewis Z. Schlosser, et al., "Advisor–Advisee Relationships in Graduate Training Programs," *Journal of Career Development* 38, no. 1 (February 2011): 3–18; Stephanie M. Mazerolle, et al., "An Analysis of Doctoral Students' Perceptions of Mentorship During Their Doctoral Studies," *Athletic Training Education Journal* 10, no. 3 (July–September 2015): 227–235; Cheryl E. Ball, "Be a Good Job Mentor," *Inside Higher Ed*, October 20, 2013, https://www.insidehighered.com/advice/2013/10/21/essay-how-be-good-mentor-academic-jobs; and UC Davis Graduate Council, "Mentoring Guidelines," Department of Economics, UC Davis (guidelines approved Jun 24, 1999), https://economics.ucdavis.edu/mentoring-guidelines.

5 A reviewer of my book proposal suggested that responsibility for my career difficulties falls entirely in my lap: the result of my decision to adopt an unconventional approach to economics instead of simply conducting a mainstream dissertation research topic. The reviewer acknowledges that academia mirrored other sectors of the economy in its trend toward non-tenure-track faculty since the 1970s, but also maintains my troubles did not reflect that broader trend and instead stemmed from pursuing unorthodox research. In short, had I merely delivered a neoclassical PhD dissertation, the reviewer believes my entire career would have been prosperous and secure: I should have known better, or perhaps I did and still chose to make a reckless decision.

Academia has indeed mirrored the rest of the economy in its move toward increasing reliance on non-tenure-track positions. In higher education, such job holders, both full-time and part-time, are described as contingent faculty: In fall 2022, 68 percent of faculty in US colleges and universities held contingent appointments, compared with about 47 percent in fall 1987, according to a recent report by the American Association of University Professors (AAUP). The report also identifies a common thread in the explanations: economic and administrative pressures are "presented—in good economic times and bad—as justification for a constantly increasing reliance on part- and full-time non-tenure-track appointments." Regardless of the reason I fell into a contingent position, there's no question that my own career was caught up, from the very start, in one of the same trends affecting the American workers whose interests I intended to advance through my work. (For the report on contingent faculty, see AAUP "Contingent Appointments and the Academic Profession," 2024, https://www.aaup.org/reports-publications/aaup-policies-reports/topical-reports/contingent-appointments-and-academic; for an earlier report, see AAUP, "The Status of Non-Tenure-Track Faculty.")

To be sure, I was aware that pursuing my research interests didn't make me an attractive candidate to the mainstream economics departments at most major universities. Today, thanks to Frederic Lee's *A History of Heterodox Economics* (London: Routledge, 2009), everyone can read about difficulties faced by unconventional economists in the final decades of the twentieth century. As a graduate student, I learned about those difficulties as they happened to those who preceded me; but I also saw reasons to believe I could fit myself into an academic niche.

In graduate school, I took several steps to maximize my options as an unconventional economist. For example, I aimed to cast a net wide enough to encompass interdisciplinary fields such as industrial relations and public policy, which are eclectic and more open to diverse perspectives and methods. I pursued coursework, research, and professional activities with an eye to standing out as an attractive candidate for the few positions usually available each year at the handful of universities and much larger number of colleges open to my brand of economics. And I chose a PhD adviser with a distinguished reputation among academics and practitioners in the fields of labor economics, industrial relations, and public policy. Perhaps I was overly optimistic about landing a position by pursuing the dissertation path I followed, but I did receive support and encouragement from individuals and organizations along the way.

There's also an element of irony in the suggestion that I should have pursued a different dissertation. The distinguishing feature of my work as an economist—my major contribution to the profession—is a research stream that develops and advances a constructive alternative to conventional economics. That alternative originated with my PhD dissertation; pursuit of a different doctoral thesis would have put my career on an entirely different research track.

6 On contest mobility and sponsored mobility, see William M. Dugger, *Corporate Hegemony* (Westport: Greenwood Press, 1989), 75–80.

7 Dugger, *Corporate Hegemony*, 76.

8 There's also path dependence in the secure, primary labor market. But in that case, what happened in the past (securing a good job at the start of one's career) provides a foundation that opens doors to new and expanded opportunities.

9 On feminism and work restructuring, see Chapter 11, note 23, which discusses Whalen and Whalen, "Institutionalism: A Useful Foundation for Feminist Economics?"

10 In their third-year review of my performance, the economics faculty also noted my active scholarly engagement and innovative research. Still, my mom would say, "You can't eat compliments; tributes don't put food on the table." (My personal files include copies of the HWS performance reviews conducted in years two, three, and four of my faculty appointment.)

11 My teaching portfolio was prepared at a workshop in mid-June 1994, under the guidance of a mentor with extensive expertise in faculty assessment. After reading my portfolio draft—which provided the requisite experience summary, reflective narrative, and evidence of teaching effectiveness—my mentor said that she found it an extraordinary portfolio, adding: "And it's astonishing that you're not in therapy after what you've been through!" The leader of the workshop (from Pace University) was also impressed by the portfolio. In a note to me following the workshop, he wrote: "It is a gem! Clear, thoughtful, and very well-written, it's been added to my pile of exemplary portfolios." (Letter to the author from Peter Seldin, July 1, 1994.)

12 Students often wrote that I prepared them especially well for business school because my institutionalist approach has much in common with the strategic management approach found in graduate business programs. Over the years, I lost touch with most of my students, but I'm still in occasional contact with one of the first students I taught at HWS, who later earned an MBA degree.

13 See Ali Tahir, "Professor's Leaving Is a Great Loss," *The Herald* [Hobart and William Smith Colleges, Geneva, NY], May 6, 1994, 9. The HWS administration was less gracious about my exit from the colleges than the students. When my contract expired, I visited the campus library to swap my faculty library card for a Geneva city resident card. Without offering an explanation, the head librarian refused to issue me a resident borrower card. Whatever the reason, it certainly wasn't a graceful move by the institution. It took about a year, but the library eventually issued me a Geneva resident card. In the meantime, Linda registered for her own local resident card and borrowed whatever books I needed for my ongoing research projects.

14 Charles J. Whalen, "Professor Whalen Thanks Students for Years at HWS," *The Herald* [Hobart and William Smith Colleges, Geneva, NY], May 13, 1994, 6.

15 On quiet strength, see Meaghan McMahon, "Why We Need More Quiet Strength," Pioneer Network, December 2, 2020, https://www.pioneernetwork.org/why-we-need-more-quiet-strength/.

Chapter 14. Budget Sideshows and the Silent Depression

1 Campaigning for president in 1992, Bill Clinton stressed the need for an investment-oriented agenda (including, for example, greater attention to worker education and training programs) and a focus on addressing the challenges facing America's middle class. However, Clinton's policy attention shifted to deficit reduction and fiscal belt-tightening even before his inauguration, an orientation that intensified when the GOP took control of Congress after the 1994 midterms.

2 It might have been possible for Linda to transfer to a New York State Department of Health position in Albany (about an hour drive from the Levy Institute), but there was no reason to move the family eastward from Geneva while my Levy Institute appointment remained temporary.

3 In 1969, the US federal debt was $354 billion, 36 percent of the nation's gross domestic product (GDP). In 1992, the federal debt was just over $4 trillion, 61 percent of GDP. See Kimberly Amadeo, "U.S. National Debt by Year," The Balance, July 10, 2024, https://www.thebalancemoney.com/national-debt-by-year-compared-to-gdp-and-major-events-3306287.

4 During my first few months at the Levy Institute, prior to working on the balanced budget amendment, I devoted much of my time to studying proposals on biennial budgeting. In fact, my first contribution to the institute's Working Papers series examined the legislative history of federal proposals and deliberations on two-year budgeting from the 1970s through the early 1990s; see Charles J. Whalen, "Should the U.S. Government Adopt a Biennial Budget?" Working Paper No. 128, November 1994, Levy Economics Institute of Bard College.

5 Charles J. Whalen, "Fiscal Irresponsibility: The Balanced Budget Amendment of the 'Contract with America.'" Working Paper No. 132, January 1995, Levy Economics Institute of Bard College.

6 Charles J. Whalen, "We Couldn't Live with a Balanced Budget," *New York Times*, December 22, 1994, A18; and Charles J. Whalen, "Budget Straitjacket Can't Replace Political Will," *USA Today*, January 13, 1995, A8.

7 My work on the balanced budget proposal drew not only on my graduate work and HWS teaching in the field of public economics, but also on my experience as issues director for Doug Call's congressional campaign, which included writing and speaking about economic policy issues in public (nonacademic) forums.

8 Beyond the New Deal, deficit spending by the federal government in the Second World War (which resulted in a debt-to-GDP ratio of 119 percent in 1946) funded military purchases that enabled success in that conflict; see Amadeo, "U.S. National Debt by Year."

9 For Minsky's view on the need for a balanced budget over the business cycle, which was also the view of John Maynard Keynes, see Hyman P. Minsky, *Stabilizing an Unstable Economy* (New Haven: Yale University Press, 1986), 336–339.

10 Charles J. Whalen, "Statement on the Balanced Budget Amendment," in Subcommittee on the Constitution, US House Judiciary Committee, *Balanced Budget Constitutional Amendment* (Washington: US Government Printing Office, 1995), 234–236.

11 Edwin Chen and Michael Ross, "Balanced Budget Amendment Falls Short in Tight Senate Vote," *Los Angeles Times*, March 3, 1995, https://www.latimes.com/archives/la-xpm-1995-03-03-mn-38285-story.html.

12 Charles J. Whalen, "Assessing the Constitutional Route to Federal Budget Balance," *Public Policy Brief*, No. 20 (April 1995), Levy Economics Institute of Bard College.

13 For example, see my "Budget Needs Discipline, Not Balance," *Los Angeles Times*, December 8, 1995, B9; "Tearing into the Deficit," *Time*, June 12, 1995, 7; and "Budget Amendment Offers Toxin, Not Tonic," *Challenge* 38, no. 3 (May–June 1995): 50.

14 Charles J. Whalen, "The Case Against a Balanced Budget Amendment," *Social Policy* 25, no. 3 (Spring 1995): 45–48; and Charles J. Whalen, "Budget Deficits: Dead Ends and Sensible Directions," *Social Policy* 26, no. 3 (Spring 1996): 38–45. The social workers' association that invited me to its annual meeting in the mid-1990s is known today as the Social Welfare Action Alliance.

15 Panetta, a Democrat from California, served as a member of Congress (including four years as chairman of the House Budget Committee); later in the Clinton administration he served as director of the Office of Management and Budget (OMB) and chief of staff at the White House. Rivlin served nearly a decade as the first director of the nonpartisan Congressional Budget Office (CBO), later as deputy director of OMB (1993–1994), and then as that agency's director (1994–1996). Domenici, a Republican from New Mexico, served in the Senate; he chaired the Senate Budget Committee for several years in the 1980s and returned to that post when his party took control of the Senate in 1995. Other supporters of biennial budgeting, who submitted or cosponsored such proposals in that era, included Senator William Roth (R-Delaware), Representative Lee Hamilton (D-Indiana), and Representative Ralph Regula (R-Ohio).

16 National Performance Review, *From Red Tape to Results: Creating a Government that Works Better and Costs Less* (Washington: US Government Printing Office, 1993), 17; see also "Vice President's Reinvention Initiatives: Reinventing Government," n.d. Clinton White House archives, https://clintonwhitehouse4.archives.gov/WH/EOP/OVP/initiatives/reinventing_government.html.

17 The New Jersey budget office produced its survey in response to Governor Christine Todd Whitman's interest in the possibility of moving her state to a biennial budgeting cycle.

18 Charles J. Whalen, "Biennial Budgeting for the Federal Government: Lessons from the States," *Policy Studies Review* 14, nos. 3–4 (Winter 1996): 303–322. My research on biennial budgeting was also summarized in an op-ed essay in early 1996: "Two-Year Budget Might Restore Sanity in Washington," *Star-Ledger* [Newark, New Jersey], February 1, 1996, A21.

19 My work on biennial budgeting led to three written statements for congressional hearings and two oral presentations as a hearing witness:

- "Statement on Biennial Budgeting," in *Concurrent Resolution on the Budget for Fiscal Year 1998: Hearings* (Washington: US Government Printing Office, 1997), 115–134, written statement prepared for a hearing before the Committee on the Budget, US Senate (February 13, 1997);
- "Statement on S. 261, Biennial Budgeting and Appropriations Act," in *S. 261: Biennial Budgeting and Appropriations Act* (Washington: US Government Printing Office, 1997), 23–25 and 78–81, written statement and in-person testimony before the Committee on Governmental Affairs, US Senate (April 23, 1997); and
- "Statement on Biennial Budgeting," in *Biennial Budgeting: A Tool for Improving Government Fiscal Management and Oversight* (Washington: US Government Printing Office, 2000), 275–279, 362–365, written statement and in-person testimony before the Committee on Rules, US House of Representatives (March 16, 2000).

20 On the "third deficit," see David Alan Aschauer, *Public Investment and Private Sector Growth: The Economic Benefits of Reducing America's "Third Deficit"* (Washington: Economic Policy Institute, 1990). In addition to core public infrastructure (including highways, mass transit, airports, electrical and gas facilities, and water and sewer systems), most other non-military public capital identified by Aschauer fell into two broad categories: conservation and resource development, and hospitals and educational buildings.

21 For details on the public investment slowdown and its relation to weakened economic performance, see Aschauer, *Public Investment and Private Sector Growth*, 1–2.

22 A broadly conceived federal capital budget might include assets funded by the US government but operated by states and localities. While tracking such public investment would certainly provide useful information, I opted for starting with a narrower framework in the paper submitted to the Levy Institute. A final, slightly revised version was submitted in July 1996: Charles J. Whalen, "Paving the Way for a Sensible Discussion of Federal Capital Budgeting: What Is a Capital Expenditure?" Submitted to the Levy Institute and circulated among its scholars and fellows on April 3, 1996; revised version July 31, 1996 (author's personal copy).

23 Edward V. Regan, Letter to the author, July 3, 1996. "Paving the Way" was never released as an institute Working Paper. After I left the institute, David Aschauer was appointed as a Levy Institute resident scholar, bringing to Blithewood his work on the relationship between public capital and employment, output, and economic growth, but to my knowledge the institute has not pursued further work on capital budgeting. Meanwhile, interest in capital budgeting waned in Washington as much attention shifted to deficit reduction during the mid-1990s.

24 Alice Rivlin, quoted in Robert Pear, "Clinton Aide Criticizes G.O.P. Plans for Tax Cuts," *New York Times*, November 16, 1994, A16. A few months later, Federal Reserve Board Chairman Alan Greenspan (first appointed by President Reagan) also warned against dynamic scoring, arguing that its use in federal budget calculations could harm the government's credibility with financial markets; see James Risen, "Greenspan Warns Against 'Dynamic Scoring' in Budget," *Los Angeles Times*, January 11, 1995, https://www.latimes.com/archives/la-xpm-1995-01-11-mn-18740-story.html.

25 The nation's jobless rate decreased from an average of 7.5 percent in 1992 to around 5.5 percent in the mid-1990s, according to the author's calculations using data from the US Bureau of Labor Statistics, "(Seas) Unemployment Rate."

26 According to Peterson, most economists and policymakers overlooked the disturbing reality of an ongoing economic crisis rooted in a 25-year downward trend of wages and family incomes. Peterson called this trend the "silent depression" because it occurred below the radar of most economists, who tend to measure national economic well-being by tracking output (gross domestic product), employment, and inflation. The mid-1990s is when Robert Reich, President Clinton's Secretary of Labor, often quoted a worker who said he didn't want to hear about how many jobs were being created in the economy because "I have three of them, and I'm not all that impressed." For wage stagnation in the 1990s, see, for example, Lawrence Mishel and David M. Frankel, *The State of Working America, 1990–91 Edition* (Armonk: M.E. Sharpe, 1991), 95–98; and Wallace C. Peterson, *Silent Depression: Twenty-Five Years of Wage Squeeze and Middle-Class Decline* (New York: W.W. Norton, 1994), 28–48.

27 Charles J. Whalen, "The Anxious Society: Middle-Class Insecurity and the Crisis of the American Dream," Levy Economics Institute *Report*, October 1995, 9–11.

28 For a newspaper story that cited my work on economic insecurity, see Robert Keefe, "Economy a Big Issue on This Big Day," *St. Petersburg Times*, March 12, 1996, 1A published on the day of the GOP presidential primary in Florida.

29 In the *Bard Journal* article, I tied policymakers' inattention to economic insecurity to the need for a new approach to economics that could highlight such issues; see Charles J. Whalen, "Economics Must Change: Workforce Insecurity and the Need for a New Political Economy," *Bard Journal of Social Science* 5, nos. 1–2 (Summer 1996): 34–40. In that way, I connected my research on economic insecurity to my attempts (which began in graduate school) to refashion economics. While at the Levy Institute (and later at Cornell ILR in Buffalo), I also organized conference panels and made presentations at professional meetings on topics related to reforming economics and advancing alternative perspectives on economic theory and policy.

30 The Broadway Democrats is the official Democratic club in the Upper West Side and southwest Harlem; and today the National Jobs for All Coalition (NJFAC), a full-employment advocacy organization, is called the National Jobs for All Network (NJFAN). I served on the NJFAC executive committee during most of 1996 (until my new job in Buffalo made it increasingly difficult to attend monthly meetings downstate) but remain on the NJFAN advisory board. I also spoke on rising economic insecurity during a seminar at the State University of New York College at Brockport in April 1996.

31 Minsky's attention to growing financial instability in the managed-money era foreshadowed the dot-com boom and collapse as well as the global financial crisis of 2007–2009. In fact, Minsky warned several times in the 1990s about the growth of asset securitization, which was at the heart of the global crisis.

32 Among the panel's discussants was Heather Boushey, then a graduate student at The New School. Boushey served recently on President Joe Biden's Council of Economic Advisers.

33 Hyman P. Minsky and Charles J. Whalen, "Economic Insecurity and the Institutional Prerequisites for Successful Capitalism," *Journal of Post Keynesian Economics* 19, no. 2 (Winter 1996): 155–170.

34 Before the Minsky-Whalen article was published, nearly all of Minsky's attention to money manager capitalism could be found only in book chapters and working papers.

35 Charles J. Whalen, "The Age of Anxiety: Erosion of the American Dream," *USA Today: The Magazine of the American Scene* 125, no. 2616 (September 1996): 14–16.

36 Findings are the product of work by Nitin Nohria of Harvard Business School; see Karen Pennar, "Economic Anxiety," *Business Week*, March 11, 1996, 50–52.

37 See Bill Montague, "Feeling the Squeeze," *USA Today*, February 19, 1996, 1A.

38 Findings are the product of a US Census Bureau study; see G. Paschal Zachary, "Census Bureau Confirms Eroding Wages," *Wall Street Journal*, January 25, 1995, A2.

39 Polly Callaghan and Heidi Hartmann, *Contingent Work: A Chart Book on Part-Time and Temporary Employment* (Washington: Economic Policy Institute, 1991), 3–4.

40 Council of Economic Advisers, *Economic Report of the President* (Washington: US Government Printing Office, 1996), 314, 330.

41 US Department of Labor, "Employment Cost Index—December 1995," US Bureau of Labor Statistics, February 13, 1996, https://www.bls.gov/news.release/archives/eci_02131996.pdf.

42 For family incomes, see John Cassidy, "Who Killed the Middle Class?" *The New Yorker*, October 16, 1995, 113–124; for the findings of Graef Crystal on the gap between workers and CEOs, see Don L. Boroughs, "Winter of Discontent," *US News & World Report*, January 22, 1996, 47–54.

43 Between 1950 and 1990, money managers (pension funds, mutual funds, and other institutional investors) saw the fraction of US corporate equities under their control grow from 8 percent to 60 percent. Over the same period, pension funds increased their share of total business equities from less than 1 percent to almost 39 percent, while their fraction of corporate debt rose from 13 percent to 50 percent. See, respectively, Michael E. Porter, "Capital Disadvantage: America's Failing Capital Investment System," *Harvard Business Review* 70, no. 5 (September 1992): 65–83; and Teresa Ghilarducci, *Labor's Capital: The Economics and Politics of Private Pensions*. (Cambridge: MIT Press, 1992), 117.

44 In contrast with the views of Reich and Kennedy, Senator Coverdell's article fingered government spending, taxes, and regulation as the source of our economic problems and identified balancing the federal budget as the key to reforming government. For the entire feature, see "What's Killing the American Dream?" *USA Today: The Magazine of the American Scene* 125, no. 2616 (September 1996): 14–25.

Chapter 15. End of the Line

1 For examples of newspaper stories citing me on budget matters, see Jennifer Oldham, "The Budget Battle; Deficit and Debt: A Primer," *Los Angeles Times*, January 6, 1996, 1D; and Collette Baxley, "Balanced Budget Plans Called 'Wishful Thinking,'" *The Post and Courier* [Charleston, South Carolina], February 25, 1996, 14.

2 The "television in every room" remark was reported to me by institute staff and scholars. I've occasionally wondered whether Leon Levy, founding chairman of the Levy Board of Governors, was a source of complaints about my work on rising insecurity, since he was a pioneer in institutional investing and my insecurity research linked increasing worker anxiety to emergence of an economic era dominated by fund managers. Perhaps not, but at least one board member objected to the work. The irony is that my research was inspired by and drew upon the work of two of the institute's most distinguished scholars, Minsky and Godley.

3 Some members on the institute's Board of Governors may have thought rising worker insecurity was imaginary, but Stephen Roach, chief economist at Morgan Stanley, understood it was real. In my article with Minsky, we quoted from a *New York Times* op-ed in which Roach wrote: "Recovery or not, the 1990s are still all about downsizing, longer workdays, white-collar shock and relatively limited opportunities for new employment"; see Stephen S. Roach, "Who Should Worry About the Economy," *New York Times*, June 16, 1995, A2. In fact, job growth following the recession of 1990–1991 was so unusually sluggish that economists dubbed it the "jobless recovery," and the phenomenon occurred again after the recessions of 2001 and 2007–2009; see Natalia

A. Kolensikova and Yang Liu, "Jobless Recoveries: Causes and Consequences," Federal Reserve Bank of St. Louis, April 1, 2011, https://www.stlouisfed.org/publications/regional-economist/april-2011/jobless-recoveries-causes-and-consequences. Moreover, business journalists at *Fortune* certainly thought money managers were the key players to watch in the economy, and that corporate restructuring was being driven by pressure from institutional investors, consistent with the Minsky-Whalen view; see Joe Spiers, "The Profits Flowed," *Fortune*, April 29, 1996, 260–261; and Ronald B. Lieber, "Who Owns the 500?" *Fortune*, April 29, 1996, 264–270.

4 The Levy Institute eventually recognized the importance of studying worker and household insecurity, at least in the context of the COVID-19 pandemic. See "Levy Economics Institute Receives $80,000 Grant to Explore Links Between Public Spending and Economic Insecurity," Levy Economics Institute Press Release, February 10, 2022, https://www.levyinstitute.org/wp-content/uploads/2024/02/pr_2_10.pdf.

5 There may have indeed been something to the argument that administrators are "sheep." Over the years, I was invited twice to return to work at the Levy Institute. The first call came when I was in a tenured position at Utica College and in the process of negotiating an appointment with the Congressional Budget Office (CBO); I might have even accepted the Levy invitation, but it again involved only a temporary appointment (to write a book on Minsky). Over a half-dozen years later, the call came again, asking whether I could be lured away from CBO and back to Blithewood. I responded that although I couldn't be "lured away" because I just left CBO (only a few weeks earlier) and was serving as a research fellow at the University at Buffalo, I would be happy to return to the institute. But the institute never followed up with an offer.

6 The term "extension" refers to work that extends or applies academic research into the world of practitioners. The term first emerged in the context of county agricultural extension agents who were affiliated with state universities and assisted farmers by keeping them informed of university research findings. I was aware of the professional gulf (characterized partly by differences in career opportunities and access to institutional resources) that often separated "extension faculty" and "resident faculty," not only from my observations as a student at Cornell ILR, but also from discussions with my father-in-law, who began his career as an agricultural extension agent and later held an industrial extension faculty appointment with Cornell's agricultural college in Ithaca. The gulf between these two faculty groups is not universal, and some universities bridge the gap by creating extension professorships. But there were no positions of that sort at Cornell ILR in Buffalo.

7 In addition to Minsky, I worked with several excellent colleagues at the Levy Institute, especially Oren Levin-Waldman. We continue to share our work and have collaborated on several occasions.

8 Even my attention to biennial budgeting proved ahead of the curve. In 2015, President Barack Obama and Congress reached an agreement on a two-year budget deal, and President Donald Trump and Congress did the same in 2019.

9 Katie was in kindergarten and first grade while I was at the Levy Institute. I recall arranging to come home early at the end of one week in time to pick her up at the close of school. She was so thrilled that she excitedly told her friends several times during the day, "Daddy's coming home from the institute and he's going to pick me up!" When I arrived, she was closely guarded by a nervous teacher's aide who hesitantly explained, "I thought the 'institute' was a hospital…."

Chapter 16. Saving Good Jobs and Creating New Ones in the Face of Globalization

1 Buffalo's "Queen City" nickname reflects its long standing as the second most populated city in the state of New York.

2 As described in note 6 in the previous chapter, the term "extension" refers to work that extends or applies academic research into the world of practitioners. ILR Extension delivers programs and services to labor and management, as well as joint programs for both parties. Its work aims to foster high performance workplaces, effective leadership, harmonious employment relations, and employee engagement in workplace and enterprise decisions.

3 Because the Cornell position and I were a bit of an awkward match from the outset, Linda and I decided that the family would continue to live in Geneva while I learned how the job would work out in practice. If it worked out well, we would have eventually moved to the Buffalo area and Linda would have transferred her state position from Rochester to Buffalo. My ILR Extension teaching evaluations and performance reviews were always highly favorable, but, as described in this chapter (as well as in Chapter 18), I found the position wasn't a good fit.

However, working in Buffalo enabled me to offer my daughter Katie two rare opportunities. The first occurred shortly after I began the ILR position. In late September 1996, I learned that President Clinton would make a public appearance at the Greater Buffalo International Airport on his way to Chautauqua, New York, where he prepared for his first presidential debate with Senator Bob Dole. I arranged for Katie to miss a day of school, and on October 3, Katie, Linda, and I attended Clinton's airport appearance, arriving early enough to find a spot along the rope line. After Clinton spoke, we each shook his hand, and he signed a campaign shirt and poster for Katie.

The other opportunity involved Coretta Scott King, whom I knew Katie admired. Upon hearing that King would be the keynote speaker at a YWCA luncheon in Niagara Falls on Saturday, June 7, 1997, I purchased a pair of tickets for us. Before the event, several people lined up to say hello to King; Katie joined them, but King was escorted away before the two could meet. I was watching from a distance and when King's aide noticed, she said there'd be a chance for Katie to meet King after the event. True to her word, the aide arranged for Katie to meet one-on-one for a few minutes with Mrs. King, in a side room blocked to the public (including me) by a pair of Niagara Falls policemen. I never learned the name of the aide, but I remain grateful that she made the effort to let Katie connect with Mrs. King.

4 To engage participants, the AIS program was heavily discussion oriented, incorporating interactive technological tools as well as realistic and thought-provoking workplace scenarios performed by professional actors.

5 Upon being tasked with creating a strategic planning course for the United Steelworkers and American Brass, I felt the need to pursue my own crash course on using such planning to successfully achieve organizational change. In addition to reading

Leading Change by John P. Kotter (Boston: Harvard Business School Press, 1989) and *The Fifth Discipline: The Art and Practice of the Learning Organization* by Peter Senge (New York: Doubleday, 1990), I enrolled in a graduate-level evening course on Organizational Change offered by Cornell ILR Extension's Buffalo Labor Studies program (in fall 1996). The course, taught by a Rochester-based business consultant, was structured around a series of real-world case studies and a reading list that included *Recreating the Workplace* by Steven R. Rayner (Essex Junction: Oliver Wight, 1993). That course proved useful in preparing me to develop the brass industry course and an accompanying 80-page strategic planning casebook and resource guide. I also drew on lessons from the organizational-change course in 1998, when developing a pilot workplace education program for the electric industry.

6 While the brass factory in Buffalo survived the shutdown threat, a sister facility in Kenosha, Wisconsin (which did not participate in the Cornell industry education program) was shuttered in the late 1990s.

7 Before working with ILR Extension, my own research on labor-management cooperation in Buffalo (conducted as a graduate student in the 1980s) contributed to literature on collaborative labor relations; see Whalen, "Consensus Mechanisms and Community Economic Development." I also wrote a pair of book reviews on new labor-relations developments: Charles J. Whalen, "Review of *The New Unionism: Employee Involvement in the Changing Corporation*, by Charles C. Heckscher," *Journal of Economic Issues* 23, no. 3 (September 1989): 918–923; and Charles J. Whalen, "Review of *The New American Workplace*, by Eileen Appelbaum and Rosemary Batt," *Journal of Economic Issues* 29, no. 1 (March 1995): 310–313.

8 For examples of research published by Cornell ILR extension faculty, see Sally Klingel and Ann Martin, *A Fighting Chance: New Strategies to Save Jobs and Reduce Costs* (Ithaca: ILR Press, 1988); Susan Woods, et al., *Case Studies in Cooperative Labor-Management Relations: Examples in Western New York* (Buffalo: Cornell University School of Industrial and Labor Relations, 1991); and Lois Gray, et al., "Union-Management Training Programs in the Public Sector: The New York Experience," in *Joint Training Programs: A Union-Management Approach to Preparing Workers for the Future*, ed. Louis A. Ferman, et al. (Ithaca: ILR Press, 1991), 95–112. Those publications were part of a burgeoning literature on innovative approaches to work and employment relations, which also included, for example, William N. Cooke, *Labor-Management Cooperation: New Partnerships or Going in Circles?* (Kalamazoo: W.E. Upjohn Institute for Employment Research, 1990); Lawrence Mishel and Paula Voos, *Unions and Economic Competitiveness* (Armonk: M.E. Sharpe, 1992); Lauri Bassi, "Workplace Education for Hourly Workers," *Journal of Policy Analysis and Management* 13, no. 1 (Winter 1994): 55–74; Thomas A. Kochan and Paul Osterman, *The Mutual Gains Enterprise* (Boston: Harvard Business School Press 1994); Michelle Kaminski, et al., *Making Change Happen: Six Cases of Unions and Companies Transforming Their Workplaces* (Washington: Work and Technology Institute, 1996); and Jeffrey Pfeffer, *The Human Equation* (Boston: Harvard Business School Press, 1998).

9 In fact, Gompers said:

> We want more schoolhouses and less jails; more books and less arsenals; more learning and less vice; more constant work and less crime; more leisure and less greed; more justice and less revenge; in fact, more of the opportunities to cultivate

our better natures, to make manhood more noble, womanhood more beautiful, and childhood more happy and bright. These in brief are the primary demands made by the Trade Unions in the name of labor. These are the demands made by labor upon modern society and in their consideration is involved the fate of civilization.

(Samuel Gompers, "What Does Labor Want?" speech before the International Labor Congress, Chicago, Illinois, August 28, 1893, published in the Samuel Gompers Papers, https://gompers.umd.edu/1893%20more%20speech.htm)

10 In pursuit of a new fee-based program for the Institute for Industry Studies (which depended for years on income from a UAW-Ford education program that was beginning to wind down), I created and delivered a pilot workforce education program in early 1998 for the electric industry, which at the time was being transformed by deregulation and a wave of industry mergers. Participants in the pilot sessions were managers from Niagara Mohawk Power Corporation and union leaders from the International Brotherhood of Electrical Workers Local 97, which represented employees at Niagara Mohawk's power plant in Niagara Falls, New York. However, Niagara Mohawk itself soon became an acquisition target (by National Grid) and the education program never rolled out at the plant.

11 During my time with Cornell ILR Extension in Buffalo, I participated in events and projects sponsored by the University at Buffalo (the "State of the Region" project), Erie County Center for Cooperative Growth, New York State Department of Labor, area union labor councils, the AFL-CIO's Working for America Institute, US Representative Amory Houghton (a "Business-Education Roundtable"), Western New York Manufacturers Network, and the local chapter of the Industrial Relations Research Association. I also served on the program planning committee of the Western New York Employee Involvement Council, organized a regional conference on the importance of manufacturing (in partnership with the Federal Reserve Bank of New York Buffalo Branch), and testified at a hearing on challenges facing working families (convened in Buffalo by US Representative John LaFalce). Since many events occurred in the evening, I frequently stayed in the area overnight, usually at an inexpensive hotel near the Buffalo airport. In addition, because I was the only economist at Cornell ILR Extension in Buffalo, I was expected to stay abreast of regional economic trends and field reporter inquiries about the employment consequences of Western New York business developments.

12 In addition to delivering ILR marketing presentations and making cold calls (over one period during my second year at Cornell I called or met with representatives of over 100 organizations), I was tasked with developing and updating IIS marketing brochures, experience summaries, and other promotional materials. Meanwhile, I regularly received notes and phone calls from Lionel Nosenchuk, a former Doug Call campaign coworker, urging me to write a book on rising worker insecurity and the erosion of the American Dream. Lionel, who was familiar with my articles on economic insecurity, began urging me to write such a book after hearing me on a radio broadcast of a forum convened by Rep. LaFalce to discuss the challenges facing workers. Lionel lost his job to corporate downsizing and believed economic insecurity demanded much more attention from policymakers.

13 I have an especially vivid memory of sitting on the floor of a gymnasium (after a pick-up basketball game) at the UAW education center in Michigan and listening to assembly line workers tell me about their work, their run-ins with difficult supervisors, the challenges of balancing work and family obligations, and how (and why) they still managed to find time for community service such as serving on their local school board. I was getting paid to teach, but I was learning at least as much (about real-world work and employment relations) from the workers I met through IIS programs.

14 In 1997, I also began several years of participation in conferences attended by law professors and "socio-economists" working at the intersection of economics and sociology. It started when a former colleague from HWS introduced me to Robert Ashford, a law professor at Syracuse University who advocated the expansion of employee stock ownership. Robert organized workshops at annual gatherings of the Society for the Advancement of Socio-Economics and the Association of American Law Schools (AALS), and during my first two years at Cornell ILR Extension I delivered brief presentations and commentaries at those meetings in July 1997, January 1998, and July 1998.

At an AALS event that took place during my final year at Cornell ILR (January 2000), I met the Rev. Dr. Virgil Wood, a civil rights leader who worked with Dr. King and stressed King's notion of the need to fashion a "beloved community" grounded in a more just economy; see Virgil A. Wood, *In Love We Trust: Lessons I Learned from Martin Luther King* (Silver Spring: Beckham Publications, 2005). For about a dozen years thereafter, Wood and I stayed in contact, and I incorporated his ideas into a course on government's role in the economy that I taught several years later at Utica College. Meanwhile, my interaction with law school professors led eventually to my appointment in 2017 as a research fellow in the Baldy Center for Law and Social Policy, located within the University at Buffalo Law School.

15 Charles J. Whalen, "Creating Competitive Advantage Through Industry Education," *Forward Thinking* (newsletter of the National Labor Management Association) 1, no. 5 (1998): 1–2.

16 Charles J. Whalen, "Money-Manager Capitalism and the End of Shared Prosperity," *Journal of Economic Issues* 31, no. 2 (June 1997): 517–525; and Charles J. Whalen, "Economic Insecurity and the Problem-Solving Approach of John R. Commons," in *Industrial Relations Research Association Series: Proceedings of the Fiftieth Annual Meeting*, ed. Paula B. Voos (Madison: Industrial Relations Research Association, 1998), 320–327.

17 I enjoyed teaching "Labor and the American Economy" (in 1998 and again in 2000) and learned much from interacting with the course's students, who often shared employment experiences that dovetailed with the course material. In addition, it was clear the students were interested in the subject. In fact, at the end of the term several students asked for additional reading suggestions so they could learn even more about the economy.

18 Linda also took a leave of absence from her position with the New York State Department of Health.

Chapter 17. "The Future Will Be Chinese"

1 On the rising influence of China, see Martin Jacques, "Welcome to China's Millennium," *The Guardian*, June 23, 2009, https://www.theguardian.com/commentisfree/2009/jun/23/china-martin-jacques-economics.

2 On toymaker Mattel, see M. Eric Johnson, "Mattel, Inc: Vendor Operations in Asia," Case #1-0013, Tuck School of Business at Dartmouth, February 14, 2000, https://digitalstrategies.tuck.dartmouth.edu/wp-content/uploads/2016/10/1-0013.pdf. US manufacturers weren't outsourcing only to China; jobs were also going elsewhere in Asia and around the world, including Mexico; see Chris Kraul, "Toy Makers Expanding Production in Mexico," *Los Angeles Times*, January 16, 1991, https://www.latimes.com/archives/la-xpm-1991-01-16-fi-275-story.html. In fact, Mexico became even more attractive to manufacturers once the North American Free Trade Agreement took effect in 1994.

3 On China's aim to dominate the "knowledge economy," see, for example, Ding Li, "Knowledge Economy Is on the Way," *Beijing Review* 41, no. 35 (August 31–September 6, 1998): 11–13; and on the tremendous growth in university enrollments in China that accompanied its focus on such an economy, see Yinmei Wan, "Expansion of Chinese Higher Education Since 1998: Its Causes and Outcomes," *Asia Pacific Education Review* 7, no. 1 (July 2006): 19–31. The irony here is that my dissertation adviser, Ray Marshall, and other progressive American economists like Lester Thurow, stressed for years that the future wealth of nations would depend on "brainpower" industries (such as biotechnology, microelectronics, and telecommunications) and that the goal of US economic and industrial policy should be a knowledge-intensive economy that puts us on the leading edge of key, emerging technologies (such as those related to renewable energy). On more than one occasion, I heard Thurow say: "China has their list of industries to promote. If we can't come up with our own, we can borrow theirs."

4 English speakers often referred to Guangzhou (and sometimes Guangdong) as "Canton," and the dialect, people, and cuisine of that broad region of South China (including Hong Kong) have long been called "Cantonese."

5 Alas, the Trump administration ended the Fulbright program with China in 2020.

6 Administrators of the Fulbright program also told me they lobbied for my appointment in Guangzhou because I was traveling with a child and air pollution was worse in many other cities on China's list of available teaching locations.

7 As is customary in China, I place Chinese family names before given names throughout the chapter.

8 In China, I taught US economic history by drawing on the history course I taught at Hobart and William Smith Colleges, except this time I structured the course around the stages of capitalism found in Minsky's theory of US capitalist development. Meanwhile, the main themes of my 1996 book, *Political Economy for the 21st Century*, provided the starting point for my graduate seminar. Both of my Lingnan courses touched on economic aspects of work and employment, but labor economics was one of the few fields that China did not want taught by Fulbright professors (apparently to avoid attention to unions and labor movements). Most students had a good command of English, not just because it was part of their educational curriculum, but also because students often met informally to practice their English.

9 When Lingnan opened as a college on the Zhongshan University campus in the late 1980s, it quickly moved to connect with university economics and business programs in the United States, Europe, and Australia. For example, a short time before I arrived in Guangzhou the college signed a partnership agreement with the

Carlson School of Management at the University of Minnesota. Intended as a nod to Lingnan's past as a university, the college's official name appears a bit awkward at first glance: "Lingnan (University) College."

10 I've sometimes thought about the residents who were displaced from their shacks when luxurious housing developments were constructed in the area surrounding the university's North Gate. They were probably among the countless number of migrants who came to Guangzhou from rural villages, workers who would never have a chance to live in the sort of development that displaced them.

11 The quads were well manicured, but the baseball field was, understandably, a bit overgrown owing to lack of use. Basketball was popular in China at the time, but baseball was not well known.

12 Because of Guangzhou's subtropical location, our apartment building featured air conditioning; but it was not heated, which made for a few weeks of cold nights in the winter.

13 A surprising difference between Beijing and Guangzhou in 1998 was that streets in Beijing were often filled with bicycles, while mopeds and motorcycles dominated Guangzhou, which locals attributed to the city's growing affluence (owing to economic and trade reforms that began in South China). Over time, the motorcycles were increasingly replaced by automobiles.

14 My bold response to the visa dilemma did come with a price: on the same day the extended-stay visas arrived we also learned that Katie would not be allowed to attend the (Chinese) primary school on campus, even though it was a provision spelled out in my university appointment. With the help of administrators at Lingnan College, our workaround to that obstacle enabled Katie to participate in daily after-school activities at the school, including dance, art, and sports programs. Since we always intended the primary school experience as a supplement to home schooling by Linda, the after-school arrangement was a fine compromise.

15 I can't recall whether the GITIC lecture was presented by a university professor or local government official. I recall that one of each was introduced at the start of the event, but the situation quickly became chaotic when I was spotted in the audience. The student who was to translate the talk for me during the event later typed and emailed me her lecture notes (so much for state secrets!), but the notes don't identify the speaker. For a discussion of the GITC shutdown in fall 1998 and its subsequent collapse in early 1999, see Maggie Farley, "Chinese Investment Firm GITIC Collapses," *Los Angeles Times*, January 12, 1999, https://www.latimes.com/archives/la-xpm-1999-jan-12-fi-62726-story.html.

16 The trip to Xian was one of my family's few sightseeing getaways of the academic year. Another was to Yangshuo, known for its dramatic karst mountain landscape along the Li River. We also visited Beijing (including the Great Wall) and Shanghai for Fulbright events, and made several trips to Hong Kong, accessible from Guangzhou by train in about two hours.

17 As soon as Peter Jennings's image appeared and the nightly news show began, the sound and visuals were replaced with an eerie static and snowy screen.

18 For a US news report on the protests across China after the NATO bombing, see Vince Morris, "U.S. Diplomats: 'We're Hostages' as Protests Rage in China," *New York*

Post, May 10, 1999, https://nypost.com/1999/05/10/u-s-diplomats-were-hostages-as-protests-rage-in-china/.

19 Alas, much of the "one country, two systems" policy that protected residents' freedoms in Hong Kong has been cast aside in the past few years.

20 I found it remarkable to come from upstate New York to the other side of the globe and learn that a good number of my Chinese students shared the same professional ambition as many of my American students at HWS: to become an asset manager. But it did clearly underscore the relevance of my approach to economics (building on the work of Minsky), which emphasizes that we're living in the increasingly globalized era of money manager capitalism. For a discussion of Deng Xiaoping's market-oriented reforms and his statement that "to get rich is glorious," see Tony Walker, "'To Get Rich Is Glorious': How Deng Xiaoping Set China on a Path to Rule the World," The Conversation, July 9, 2021, https://theconversation.com/to-get-rich-is-glorious-how-deng-xiaoping-set-china-on-a-path-to-rule-the-world-156836.

21 Before leaving China, I introduced my badminton-playing student (who I can only recall by his Anglicized name, James Jin) to the Guangzhou Rams touch rugby squad. The following year, I returned to China to present a lecture and attend the graduation of my Lingnan undergraduates, and decided to participate in a rugby scrimmage on the night of my arrival. When I reached the rugby pitch, James was there to greet me. It turns out, James hadn't been to a scrimmage in months, but he heard I'd be attending the graduation—and guessed correctly where he'd find me that evening.

22 To be sure, one needed to read reports on China's factory conditions to learn the full story, but the faces I saw tended to suggest exhaustion and even despair, and I occasionally observed workers lined in orderly rows within factory courtyards. For examples of reports on conditions within factories in South China, see Anita Chan, "Regimented Workers in China's Free Labour Market," *China Perspectives*, January–February 1997, 12–16; and China Labor Watch, *An Investigation into Four Toy Sweatshops* (New York: China Labor Watch, 2016), https://chinalaborwatch.org/an-investigation-into-four-toy-sweatshops/.

For a more recent examination of Chinese factory conditions, focusing on clothing factories on the outskirts of Guangzhou, see Laura Bicker, "The Truth Behind Your $12 Dress: Inside the Chinese Factories Fueling Shein's Success," BBC, January 13, 2024, https://www.bbc.com/news/articles/cdrylgvr77jo. It's also worth noting that seeing far more women than men at the factories reminded me of the original Waltham system of factory production, which involved hiring mainly female production workers—young women from the countryside, just as in China—and housing them in factory dormitories.

23 On pollution in China, see Chuanjiao Xie, "Pollution Makes Cancer the Top Killer," *China Daily*, May 21, 2007, https://www.chinadaily.com.cn/china/2007-05/21/content_876476.htm.

24 The telethon (the brainchild of a foreign teacher at Zhongshan University) aimed to fund goods and services for children with special needs, but the need for a telethon in a socialist country struck me as odd. In response to an invitation to participate, Katie carefully choreographed her performance to the theme from *The Sound of Music*.

25 Katie and several Chinese friends on campus experienced no language barrier because her friends had lived for some time in English-speaking countries, usually

while their parents pursued graduate degrees and began academic careers. One of the girls (whose English name was Elise) was born in the United States and had only recently moved to China, so she and Katie developed a particularly strong bond.

Another of Katie's closest friends in China was Elizabeth, the daughter of an official at the Australian consulate. Katie and Elizabeth met when I joined the touch rugby squad of the Guangzhou Rams, an organization formed by Australian expats. Elizabeth and her family lived across town in Guangzhou's Friendship Hotel, and the girls often arranged to get together on weekends for swimming and overnights.

26 I became acquainted with Renmin University's Dean Dong Keyong through an American professor of industrial relations, who stressed that Renmin University (located in Beijing) was perhaps the most politically connected university in China when it comes to shaping public policy. In fall 1998, I participated in a conference in Beijing at Dong's invitation and he later accepted my invitation to lecture at Lingnan College.

In Beijing, Dong introduced me to several business leaders and government officials working in the human resources field, including a pair from TCL Corporation (a major Chinese telephone and consumer electronics firm) and the head of workforce development for the government in Shenzhen. The managers from TCL jointly delivered a Lingnan guest lecture at my invitation; the Shenzhen official hosted my family during a visit to his city and we later reciprocated when his family came to the United States.

I also traveled from Guangzhou to Beijing in 1998 to participate in a workshop with government officials and representatives of the Kelso Institute, a small American think tank devoted to promoting the pioneering employee stock ownership ideas of Louis Kelso. I attended at the invitation of Louis's partner, Patricia Kelso, who was introduced to me by law professor Robert Ashford at a socio-economics event in the United States. At the time of the Beijing workshop, China was beginning to privatize many state-owned enterprises, so policymakers had considerable interest in employee stock ownership. For information on Louis Kelso and the Kelso Institute, see https://kelsoinstitute.org.

27 The young students and I developed a routine. Using lined paper, we wrote a word in English near one edge of the page and the corresponding word in Chinese (using the *pinyin* romanization) near the other edge, leaving room in the middle for drawing relevant pictures and Chinese characters. We began with colors, then animals, and food, and gradually expanded the vocabulary in other practical directions.

My "schoolyard Chinese" wasn't nearly as extensive or sophisticated as the Chinese learned by the many American scholars who visited Zhongshan University. But it did prove useful daily, as well as at a dinner event where the host stumped everyone else by ordering an unusual type of meat-filled dumplings: it appears "donkey" doesn't get much attention in Chinese language courses at US universities.

28 In China, I appeared in a television advertisement for a hair-care product and briefly as a judge in a documentary on the history of Macao.

29 I suppose the Levy Institute's willingness to fly me from China to Bard College in April 1999 is evidence that "nobody wants you until someone else wants you." It was my first invitation to participate in a conference at the institute since my appointment there ended in mid-1996.

30 While in China, my family kept a journal of our adventure on a laptop computer, and Linda kept an extensive diary in the hope of finding time later to prepare a travelogue. But once we returned home, work and family responsibilities of the moment always took precedence and the book remains unwritten.

31 When I returned to China a year later to attend the graduation of my undergraduate students, William (who was then a Lingnan graduate student) was at the airport waiting for me.

Chapter 18. Union Engagement in Regional Development

1 The discussion of the US economy in 1999 draws on data from multiple sources. For real output growth, see US Bureau of Economic Analysis, "Gross Domestic Product: Third Quarter 1999 (Final)," December 22, 1999, https://www.bea.gov/sites/default/files/2019-04/gdp399f.pdf; it shows a preliminary real GDP growth rate of 4.8 for the third quarter of 1999 and later upward revisions. For the unemployment and inflation rates, see US Bureau of Labor Statistics, "(Seas) Unemployment Rate" and "Table 24. Historical Consumer Price Index for All Urban Consumers (CPI-U)." For business cycle expansions, see National Bureau of Economic Research, "U.S. Business Cycle Expansions and Contractions," https://www.nber.org/research/data/us-business-cycle-expansions-and-contractions. For federal budget deficits and surpluses, see FRED Economic Data, https://fred.stlouisfed.org/series/FYFSD.

2 Economic research published in early 1999 indicated that the Buffalo region was indeed failing to share fully in the nation's prosperity. For example, personal income in that region grew only half as fast as the nation for at least a decade; see George P. Palumbo and Mark P. Zaporowski, "The Economic Outlook for the Buffalo Region," *Western New York Economic News* 2, no. 2 (1999): 1–8. That lagging prosperity occurred despite unions in the region receiving national recognition for labor-management partnerships; see, for example, Lou Jean Fleron et al., *Champions at Work: Employment, Workplace Practices, and Labor-Management Relations in Western New York* (Buffalo: Western Region of Cornell University School of Industrial and Labor Relations, 2000), 46 and 54.

Adding to workers' worries and frustration were developments in US trade policy in the 1990s, such as enactment of the North American Free Trade Agreement, which took effect in 1994, and the agreement in 1999 to admit China into the World Trade Organization (WTO). See, for example, Robert E. Scott, "The High Price of 'Free' Trade," Economic Policy Institute Briefing Paper, 2003, https://files.epi.org/page/-/old/briefingpapers/147/epi_bp147.pdf. Some of that frustration boiled over in late 1999 during protests at the WTO Ministerial Conference in Seattle.

3 Labor unions in WNY continued to pursue labor-management cooperation at the workplace and enterprise levels even as they pursued new strategies at the dawn of the new millennium.

4 As discussed in Chapters 7 and 9, I analyzed the WNY labor-management committee in the 1980s as part of my dissertation and in a related academic article.

5 According to the EDG, its objectives were as follows:

- Create a strong, diversified economy with living-wage jobs for all and quality standards of living in WNY;
- Strengthen a highly skilled workforce as a competitive regional advantage;
- Secure a voice for organized labor in economic development in the region;
- Mobilize organized labor to seize and expand opportunities for partnership with regional job-creation efforts, building on mutual interests;
- Actively promote progressive, constructive labor relations throughout WNY, and publicize the successes as a regional advantage; and
- Coordinate and build labor cohesion in regional economic development efforts, learning from one another. (Buffalo AFL-CIO Council, "News Release: Buffalo AFL-CIO Announces Formation of Western New York AFL-CIO Economic Development Group," June 25, 1999, Buffalo, New York, author's copy)

6 A longtime union leader in WNY, Lipsitz would later serve as president of the Western New York AFL-CIO Labor Federation.

7 The EDG members supported their belief that the region's workforce was "world class" by citing numerous achievements, awards, and recognition from the business community, including a statement from General Motors that its WNY engine plant was the most productive anywhere.

8 See Carlos Tejada, "Work Week," *Wall Street Journal*, September 26, 2000, A1. For the reaction of EDG chairman Donovan to the Champions study, see Charles J. Whalen, "Social Unionism in Western New York: The Case of the Economic Development Group," *Labor Studies Journal* 35, no. 4 (December 2010): 548.

9 Before being assigned to lead the regional study, I participated in the initial EDG-BNE meetings and played a small role in forming the Champions Network.

10 For the final Champions at Work report, see Fleron et al., *Champions at Work*.

11 The NPP produces more electricity than any other power plant in the state of New York.

12 The Federal Energy Regulatory Commission approved the NPP application; NPP facilities have operated under a new 50-year license since September 2007.

13 For more on initiatives of the EDG, see Whalen, "Social Unionism in Western New York: The Case of the Economic Development Group," 540–565.

14 A few years after leaving Cornell, I read a book about unemployment among white-collar workers, which mentioned that those jobless workers are often offered sales jobs and that even among salespersons the cold call is something "most people would do almost anything to avoid having to make." It seems cold calling is a nearly universal signal to workers with university degrees that they've fallen out of the primary labor market and into the world of what Barbara Ehrenreich calls "survival jobs." Perhaps that's why I was so uncomfortable engaging in such calls at Cornell; it's as though I somehow intuited that cold calling meant crossing a bright line; see Barbara Ehrenreich, *Bait and Switch: The (Futile) Pursuit of the American Dream* (New York: Owl Books, [2005] 2006), 180.

15 It turns out that the Institute for Industry Studies didn't survive many more years after I left Cornell, partly because its UAW-Ford auto industry program came to an end. Around the same time, some of the state's regional ILR extension offices were shuttered or downsized, and the number of faculty and staff in the Buffalo regional office was greatly reduced.

16 Before traveling to China, serving in ILR Extension involved occasional inconveniences such as covering my own expenses when traveling to testify in Washington at congressional hearings, even as the university touted my activities in news releases. (See, for example, Darryl Geddes, "Cornell Economist to Testify Before US Senate Committee April 23," Cornell University News Service, April 21, 1997.) Later, serving within ILR Extension also seemed to limit my ability to build on the professional and institutional relationships I established through my Fulbright work.

17 As a Fulbright alumnus, I also had access to programs and resources that would have supported forging institutional ties between Chinese universities and Cornell ILR. And it would have been the perfect time for such a pioneering effort because, despite China's emerging importance, there was no China expertise on the ILR resident faculty and little attention to China in the ILR curriculum. Meanwhile, the Council for International Exchange of Scholars, which administers the Fulbright Scholar Program, was keen to have my continued involvement in Fulbright-related activities. In fact, when I returned from my year in China, the Council appointed me to a three-year position on its Senior Scholar Program Review Committee for China, Taiwan, and Hong Kong.

18 A stark indication of Cornell ILR's apparent lack of interest in China occurred in 2000, when Dean Dong of Renmin University (an institution with exceptionally strong ties to China's policymakers) wrote to the ILR dean and mentioned an upcoming trip to the United States that would include several weeks in New York City, where the ILR School maintains an office for its dean. Dong asked for the chance to meet with the ILR dean in the downstate Cornell office, but the ILR dean replied he had no plans to travel to the city during that period. Dong responded that he would travel to Ithaca to meet the ILR dean at any time during his stay in the states. The ILR dean answered that he was not available for a visit, even in Ithaca. Dong hoped I could serve as an intermediary between the two deans, but, alas, he soon learned I had no influence in Ithaca.

When Dong came to the United States, I met with him for lunch in New York City and asked about his current activities. He had come to the states to meet with financial experts at some of the nation's top banks, in conjunction with a Chinese government project to consider creating private savings accounts as part of that country's retirement system. When I shook my head at the enormity of that undertaking, Dong mentioned that another ongoing project aimed to revamp the pension system for China's teachers, covering everyone from primary school faculty through university professors. Looking at me across the table, Dong used his hands to form the Chinese symbol for "ten," emphasizing how even that project was enormous in scope: "Ten-million teachers, Charles!" Dong's inability to meet with the ILR dean was unquestionably a major lost opportunity for Cornell.

19 *BusinessWeek* listed its position advertisement in the American Economic Association's monthly jobs bulletin, alongside university faculty positions, and the ad indicated a preference for an economist with a PhD.

20 *Business Week* was a McGraw-Hill company with an 80-year history until late 2009, when it was bought by Bloomberg and renamed *Bloomberg Business Week*. Prior to that sale, the magazine's offices were in the McGraw-Hill Building, part of the Rockefeller Center complex, on Sixth Avenue (also known as Avenue of the Americas) between 48th and 49th Streets.

Chapter 19. Viewing the Economy from the 43rd Floor

1 In the wake of my appointment at *Business Week*, economists at Hobart and William Smith Colleges even invited me to visit campus (in May 2001) as the external examiner of research by a student in the colleges' Honors Program.

2 I was an avid reader of economic journalism since my Cornell days. For details on Silk and Wolman, see Caroline Schaberg, "Leonard Silk: 1918–1995, *Business Week, The New York Times*," Society of American Business Editors and Writers, March 2013, https://ahbj.sabew.org/lives/03292013leonard-silk-1918-1995-business-week-the-new-york-times/; and Jonathan LaMantia, "Bill Wolman: 1927–2011, *Business-Week*," Society of American Business Editors and Writers, March 2013, https://ahbj.sabew.org/lives/03302013bill-wolman-1927-2011-businessweek/. See also Leonard Silk, "Yes, Virginia, Institutionalists Do Exist," *Journal of Post Keynesian Economics* 12, no. 1 (Autumn 1989): 3–9, on the importance of an institutionalist outlook toward economics. Silk's remarks were presented at the annual meeting of the American Economic Association in December 1988, my first year of teaching as an economics professor. After the meeting, I wrote to Silk and requested a copy of his remarks, which he kindly provided along with a note of encouragement.

3 My apartment in New York was located on East 55th Street, between First and Second Avenues, about a 25-minute walk from the offices of *Business Week*.

4 I stopped working for the magazine in mid-September 2001, but my final *Business-Week* article was published at the end of November 2001. When I began at *Business-Week*, Katie was 10 years old and finishing fifth grade. When I left the magazine, she was nearly 12 and beginning seventh grade.

5 Charles J. Whalen, "Is the Fed Fighting a Phantom Menace?" *Business Week*, May 29, 2000, 174–176. I hoped to delay my start at *Business Week* for a few months to complete the Champions at Work research project, but the best I could negotiate was a start in early May. That provided just enough time to tie up some loose ends with the research and recruit Howard Stanger, a labor-relations specialist and professor of business at Buffalo State College, to complete the project with Lou Jean Fleron (the Cornell ILR regional director) and the rest of the Cornell ILR team in Buffalo.

6 For my first commentary, see Charles J. Whalen, "How Much Further Can the Fed Push?" *Business Week*, June 12, 2000, 51.

7 Each "Economic Trends" story contained only about three or four paragraphs, which demanded very tight writing.

8 For two of my contributions on tax cuts, see Charles J. Whalen, "Give Taxpayers a \$250 Rebate," *Business Week*, February 19, 2001, 28; and Charles J. Whalen, "A Better Way to Use All That Dough," *Business Week*, February 26, 2001, 30–31.

9 George W. Bush first proposed a tax-cut package as a presidential candidate during the election season of 2000. It included no rebate provisions. At the time, Bush justified the package by pointing to projections that showed federal budget surpluses "as far as the eye can see"—a much different economic climate than the early 1990s, when fears of skyrocketing and endless federal deficits were so great that the topic featured prominently in the 1992 presidential campaign of Ross Perot. But shortly after Bush's inauguration in 2001, his original tax-cut package (still without rebates) was introduced to buoy a rapidly slowing economy. Then came my article and other calls for tax rebates. In the end, the administration and Congress passed a package that included rebates, which were eventually considered vital to stabilizing the economy and preventing a more severe recession. In fact, I attended an economics conference in early 2003 during which a Treasury Department official stressed that rebates were the key to the economy's quick recovery.

10 My article on the North American Free Trade Agreement (NAFTA) was one of the few I wrote at the request of *BusinessWeek*'s editor in chief. It staked out a middle ground between conventional economists who considered increased international economic integration unquestionably good and free-trade critics (including Ross Perot) who argued NAFTA would be a complete disaster for the US economy. My nuanced article acknowledged job losses but found not nearly as much damage as critics had feared, mainly due to the counterbalancing effects of a strong US economic expansion. Still, I recognized this was a complex topic that deserved more attention; and I was fortunate a few years later to have the chance to revisit NAFTA and other trade agreements from several angles as editor of *Perspectives on Work*.

11 According to my article on stadium construction, the right message from communities to team owners boils down to three words: "Build it yourself." See Charles J. Whalen, "Time for the Stadium Boom to Go Bust?" *BusinessWeek*, November 20, 2000, 150.

12 Writing on developments in economic theory and methods, I covered the following: the burgeoning field of behavioral economics (which integrates findings from psychology into economic analyses); the statistically oriented research of two Nobel prize-winning economists, James Heckman and Daniel McFadden; and the evolutionary economics of Joseph Schumpeter, originator of the notion of "creative destruction," an economic concept that became immensely popular during the high-tech boom occurring a half century after his death. See Charles J. Whalen, "Putting a Human Face on Economics," *BusinessWeek*, July 31, 2000; Charles J. Whalen, "A Couple of Nobel Prizes for Practicality," *BusinessWeek*, October 23, 2000; and Charles J. Whalen, "Today's Hottest Economist Died 50 Years Ago," *BusinessWeek*, December 11, 2000.

13 One book I reviewed for the magazine examined the sources of postwar US economic expansion (*The Great Boom*, by business historian Robert Sobel); the other book featured key economic writings by John Kenneth Galbraith (*The Essential Galbraith*).

14 Charles J. Whalen, "The Finest Scenery Under Heaven," *BusinessWeek*, September 4, 2000, 130E2–130E4, Lifestyle Supplement to the international edition.

15 Charles J. Whalen, "Can Teamwork Rescue a Rust-Belt City?" *BusinessWeek*, December 4, 2000, 22E4–22E6.

16 An advantage of working at the magazine was that I tended to leave my writing at the office and felt no urge or need to write on weekends—at least until near the end, when my *BusinessWeek* work gave me the idea for an academic article, which I wrote partly to demonstrate that I could still contribute to professional journals. Until joining *BusinessWeek*, I wrote regularly on nights and weekends since graduate school (although the weekend work did ease up while at the Levy Institute), and Linda proofread nearly all my finished work. During my time at the magazine, however, I usually put the writing aside on weekends, and Linda enjoyed a break from proofreading.

17 There was never going to be less writing and editing at *BusinessWeek*, but the job certainly became easier with experience.

18 I also worried that some senior members of the magazine's editorial team wanted me to take over for Gene Koretz, who edited the "Economic Trends" page and was expected to soon retire. That page, which I was asked to cover on an increasingly frequent basis, offered a terrific opportunity to work on my writing. But it was much less satisfying, and sometimes a bit frustrating, to summarize the work of university and think-tank economists rather than produce news analyses and commentaries for the magazine. Koretz retired about a month after I left *BusinessWeek*.

19 During my first year at *BusinessWeek*, I interviewed for two academic jobs. One was at an innovative new engineering school (located near Boston) that cast a wide net for a broadly trained social scientist. The other was at a university in Texas, which sought to fill an endowed position in its business program, but decided ultimately to search for someone specializing in small-business entrepreneurship. I also met with Maureen Steinbruner, president of the nonpartisan Center for National Policy (CNP), in the hope of finding a way to work with that organization, but CNP had no position to offer.

20 After an early round of *BusinessWeek* layoffs, I ran into Peter Coy (at the annual meeting of the American Economic Association), who said he mentioned to Mike Mandel that perhaps it was fortunate my family hadn't moved to New York. According to Peter, Mike responded: "Charles was very productive; he would have been spared." Yet more cutting was to follow, and by the time the magazine became *Bloomberg BusinessWeek*, even Mike was gone. Dozens of extraordinary, experienced writers and editors lost their jobs in those years, and many of them struggled to find work because the employment of journalists contracted nearly everywhere at the same time. For a news story on *BusinessWeek* layoffs in 2001, see "Business Week Cuts Jobs, Some Operations," *Los Angeles Times*, November 8, 2001, https://www.latimes.com/archives/la-xpm-2001-nov-08-fi-1510-story.html.

Chapter 20. "This Is Terrorism"

1 Had I exaggerated the possibility that I was in a building that could be the target of a broader set of terrorist attacks? Perhaps. However, two media outlets in Rockefeller Center (NBC and *New York Post*) were among several targets in the anthrax attacks that occurred only weeks after the twin towers fell.

2 I was fortunate that Linda contacted Katie's school because news of the terrorist attack was spreading in the school, and some classrooms were beginning to follow the events on television.

3 Mayblum and I talked as he walked toward a midtown hotel where rooms were arranged for him and his colleagues. The next day, Mayblum typed his account on a laptop, perhaps partly inspired by having shared it with me, and emailed it to family, friends, and colleagues. The email (which mirrored the account he shared with me) went viral; it was republished in newspapers, and Mayblum was interviewed by several news outlets. Two decades later, his account is still reprinted on anniversaries of the attack. See, for example, Fritzie Andrade and Sara Frazier, "From the Archives: Survivor Recalls His Viral 9/11 Email," NBC News, September 10, 2021, https://www.nbcchicago.com/news/local/from-the-archives-survivor-recalls-his-viral-9-11-email-2/2609904/.

4 Diane Brady and Charles Whalen, "Snapshots of a City Under Siege," *BusinessWeek Online*, September 12, 2001.

5 Brady and Whalen, "Snapshots of a City Under Siege."

Chapter 21. Picking Up the Pieces

1 I can't recall whether Stern or others used the "think and do" label to describe what he had in mind. The "do" part of Stern's foundation certainly never aimed to advance a public policy agenda or advocate specific policies; it sought only to demonstrate, by example, the value of enabling people to engage in thoughtful discussions about public issues. But what Stern envisioned fits the "think and do" label in that he wasn't content to bring fellows together to merely think and write about how citizens and experts might participate in policy-related discussions. He also wanted fellows to directly engage people by facilitating citizen-expert dialogues on vital issues of public concern. Over time, the foundation has also taken its principles into community settings and classrooms, with work that includes training facilitators.

2 For the jobless rate, see US Bureau of Labor Statistics, "(Seas) Unemployment Rate." On jobless recoveries, see Kolensikova and Liu, "Jobless Recoveries: Causes and Consequences."

3 For example, business journalist Joe Spiers noted in the mid-1990s that employee headcounts in industry after industry were reduced while profits increased. He wrote, "Indeed, the driving force of this five-year-old business expansion has been corporate restructuring." See Joe Spiers, "The Profits Flowed," *Fortune*, April 29, 1996, 260–261.

4 Introduced in the early 1990s as an extreme version of corporate restructuring, business reengineering soon became a generic label for making change in organizations. See "Reengineering," *Inc.* February 6, 2020, https://www.inc.com/encyclopedia/reengineering.html.

5 For a compelling analysis of workplace trends that increased worker precarity and continued apace in the new millennium, see David Weil, *The Fissured Workplace* (Cambridge: Harvard University Press, 2014). Outsourcing illustrates the expansion and eventual pervasiveness of these trends: it began with work involving the production of component parts in manufacturing, but then it spread to other corporate

functions, including janitorial services, customer service, information technology support, human resources, and even product design.

6 In 1995, Sarah Horowitz (a Cornell ILR alum), responded to the spread of project-based work by founding Working Today, a nonprofit created to assist freelance writers and other temporary, part-time, and independent workers; see Bob Herbert, "Strength in Numbers," *New York Times*, November 3, 1995, A29. In 2001, Working Today created the Freelancers Union, to provide group-rate health insurance to those "gig economy" workers. For a look at the pervasiveness and adverse social consequences of the "gig economy," see Sarah Kessler, *Gigged: The End of the Job and the Future of Work* (New York: St. Martin's, 2018).

Chapter 22. Perspectives on Work

1 *PoW* settled into a semiannual pattern after producing three large issues in its inaugural year (1997).

2 For a time, Robert Taylor, a former labor writer at the *Financial Times*, served as *PoW* book review editor. But I also wrote book reviews (about one review essay per year), covering topics including meritocracy versus nepotism, balancing efficiency and equity in the workplace, the brainpower behind everyday work, restoring the American Dream in a high-risk economy, and how labor issues are framed in the corporate media.

3 In addition to the work of the *PoW* editorial advisory board, I benefited from the services of the University of Illinois Press, which copy edited and published *Perspectives on Work*. The publication required little marketing because *PoW* was distributed for free as an IRRA member benefit, although I always believed its content would interest a much wider audience.

4 For editing the online issues, known as the *Perspectives on Work Online Companion*, LERA paid me an additional $1,000 per issue.

5 The *PoW* feature on "the new world of work" after September 11, 2001, examined transportation security issues, workplace crisis management, and even the labor-management partnership behind the recovery and cleanup at the World Trade Center.

6 In addition to a broad feature on workers' rights across the globe, I organized another on workers' rights in China, motivated partly by observations from my Fulbright year, but also by having met Tiananmen protest leader Han Dongfang while at *BusinessWeek*. Han was exiled to Hong Kong, where he founded China Labour Bulletin (CLB), a nonprofit dedicated to promoting and defending workers' rights in China. The CLB research director composed an article for the *PoW* feature on China, and a reprint of it remained on the CLB website until the organization shut down in June 2025 (one of dozens of civil society groups to disband since Beijing imposed a security law in 2020 that restricts civil liberties); see Robin Munro, "Perspectives on Work: Labor Unrest and Denial of the Right to Organize in China," China Labour Bulletin, November 26, 2004, https://web.archive.org/web/20231221143806/https://clb.org.hk/en/content/perspectives-work-labor-unrest-and-denial-right-organize-china.

Chapter 23. The Future of Retirement

1 The quote from Stern's unpublished memo comes from Natalie Hopkinson, *Julius "Jay" Stern (1913–2009): A Biography*, 2nd ed. (Parkersburg: Interactivity Foundation, 2010), 29–30, which provides a concise biography of Stern as well as a history of the emergence of IF. As Hopkinson's biography documents, Stern's decision to walk away from the Wood County bank and give his shares to the US government was finalized on the day John Hinckley Jr. attempted to assassinate Ronald Reagan in 1981, so Stern's unusual action was noted by only a few financial reporters. Also limiting a public discussion of Stern's action and his belief in the need for monetary and banking reform was an enduring unwillingness to speak publicly about the matter.

2 The Stern Brothers holding company owned a variety of stocks, but also land rich in oil, gas, and coal (especially the latter); see Hopkinson, *Julius "Jay" Stern (1913–2009)*, 24–25.

3 See Hopkinson, *Julius "Jay" Stern (1913–2009)*, especially 4, 34–38. Stern had no children; IF was his legacy.

4 Since the days of John R. Commons in the early twentieth century, institutionalists have consistently stressed that even business decisions are often best when they draw upon widespread input, not just from managers and expert advisers, but also from workers all the way down the organizational chart. The same philosophy motivated much of the work of the extension division at Cornell ILR.

5 For Stern's suggestion to the editor of the *American Mercury*, which probably occurred shortly after the end of the Second World War, see David G. Williams, *Plenary Review: A Macro-Policy Approach to Improve Public Policy* (Morgantown: Think About ... Press, 1992), 138.

6 The discussion process summarized in this chapter was sketched by IF fellows, working in conjunction with Stern and Byrd, in 2002. I believe IF's core process for examining areas of concern remains essentially the same today, but key elements of that process are also now applied to promote conversations in a variety of settings; see "Interactivity Foundation: What We Do," 2025, https://www.interactivityfoundation.org/what-we-do/.

7 When I worked at IF, the two panels were referred to as the "citizens" and "experts" panels. In my experience, the line between "experts" and other "citizens" is often blurry in the real world, especially when one seeks to place "those of practical bent" into the "citizens" category, as Stern often did. For "those of practical bent," see Stern quoted in Hopkinson, *Julius "Jay" Stern (1913–2009)*, 4.

8 During my work at IF, panelists weren't paid but were reimbursed for travel and other expenses associated with their panel work; they also received a small honorarium at the conclusion of the project.

9 Discussing the IFDP with my father-in-law, a career-long community educator and facilitator with Cornell Cooperative Extension, he pointed out that IF's process resembles the "Alternatives and Consequences" model of public issues education, developed and used by extension agents in many parts of the country. For that approach to exploring public issues, see Richard Barrows, *Public Policy Education*

(Ames: Iowa State University, North Central Region Extension Publications, 1983); and Alan J. Hahn, *Resolving Public Issues and Concerns Through Policy Education* (Ithaca: Cornell Cooperative Extension, 1988).

10 Two IF fellows were philosophers and the other was a political scientist whose research focused on democratic theory and political philosophy.

11 Stern's interest in an IF project on the financial system became increasingly understandable to me as I learned about his background from discussions with Byrd and other Stern associates during visits to Parkersburg.

12 An IF project related to the financial system could have explored the subject of corporate governance and finance in the wake of the accounting scandals that contributed to the recession of 2001, but the perfect time for a fresh examination of the broader financial system would have been in the aftermath of the global financial crisis of 2007–2009. Alas, until then it seemed to me the topic didn't have sufficient resonance with most Americans, and the "experts" tended to cling to theories that suggested such crises couldn't happen. In the crisis's aftermath, there was—at least for a short period—great interest in looking ahead, preventing future crises, assessing and rethinking financial regulation, and creating a "new financial architecture" to ensure economic stability across the global economy.

13 See President's Commission to Strengthen Social Security, *Strengthening Social Security and Creating Personal Wealth for All Americans* (Washington: President's Commission to Strengthen Social Security, 2001), https://www.ssa.gov/history/reports/pcsss/Final_report.pdf.

14 The backdrop to the IF retirement security project also included Americans' increasing life expectancy, inadequate retirement savings for most households (most workers between the ages of 25 and 64 had no retirement savings account in 2000), financial gains and losses of the dot-com bubble and collapse, and even corporate scandals that caused employee retirement savings to suffer huge losses at Enron, WorldCom, and Global Crossing. See, for example, Christian E. Weller and Jeffrey B. Wenger, "The Retiree Health Insurance Crisis Leaves Workers Between a Rock and a Hard Place," *Perspectives on Work* 9, no. 2 (Winter 2006): 20–22; Elizabeth A. Myers and John J. Topoleski, "A Visual Depiction of the Shift from Defined Benefit to Defined Contribution Pension Plans in the Private Sector," Congressional Research Service, December 27, 2021, https://www.congress.gov/crs-product/IF12007; and Christian E. Weller, "Retirement Out of Reach," Economic Policy Institute Briefing Paper, August 2002, https://files.epi.org/page/-/old/briefingpapers/129/bp129.pdf.

15 Since Stern took pride in working six days a week until he died in 2009 at age 95, other IF fellows suggested that my decision to work on a "retirement" project was probably a misstep. However, the time Jay devoted to IF also illustrated the nation's need for thoughtful reflection on what it means to "work" and "retire." Each of the retirees on the retirement security panel used their time in socially constructive and intellectually gratifying ways, while other panelists over age 65 were not "retired" but worked for the joy of it. Their experiences highlight the richness of the topic of the future of retirement security, which is deeply intertwined with the subject of financial security, the definition of living a rewarding life, and even the question of whether the public interest may be best served by enabling seniors to "give back" to their communities through creative pursuits after a long working life.

16 From my home in New York's Finger Lakes Region, I began panelist recruitment by seeking recommendations from professional associations (such as the New York Employee Benefits Conference), financial services professionals, educators (especially those specializing in retirement-related fields), union representatives, religious leaders, business leaders in the field of human resource management, and administrators of nonprofit service agencies and community organizations. The recommended individuals were informed of the project and asked about their interest in participating, but they were also asked to suggest names of other possible panelists; the goal was to deepen and expand the network across the Rochester metropolitan region. For a discussion and application of the network approach that inspired my IF panel recruitment, see Joel Savishinsky, *Breaking the Watch: The Meanings of Retirement in America* (Ithaca: Cornell University Press, 2000), a book offering a broad range of perspectives on retirement in America. The IF panelists were encouraged to read Savishinsky's book, the publication of which was well-timed for the IF project.

17 The retirement project panel agreed to meet monthly for a little longer than a year, which included time for a review of the final report and a discussion of IF's reaction and plans for the final product. From my discussions with panelist candidates during the recruitment period, that project length seemed about as long a commitment as I could ask. Also, I expected at least a couple of people would withdraw over the course of that period, which is why I began with fourteen panelists, rather than twelve. It was sometimes hard to decide whether to place a particular person into the so-called "experts" panel or the "citizens" panel, but I tried to populate one group with panelists who had professional ties to retirement issues and the other with panelists who viewed the topic from a more personal perspective. And I tried to avoid using the terms "experts" and "citizens"—after all, who is more of an expert on retirement than an ordinary citizen trying to get by after a long work life?

18 Charles J. Whalen, "The Future of Retirement Security in the United States," prepared for the Interactivity Foundation, Parkersburg, West Virginia, January 21, 2004 (author's personal copy).

19 Several prominent economists raised significant concerns about the recommendations of the president's commission, arguing that diverting payroll taxes into private accounts would worsen Social Security finances in both the short and long terms (requiring a huge transfer of funds from general revenues), reduce benefits substantially for many workers, and diminish retirement security by subjecting retirees to the uncertainties of the stock market. See, for example, Peter A. Diamond and Peter R. Orszag, "Reducing Benefits and Subsidizing Individual Accounts: An Analysis of the Plans Proposed by the President's Commission to Strengthen Social Security," Center on Budget and Policy Priorities and The Century Foundation, June 2002, https://www.cbpp.org/sites/default/files/archive/6-18-02socsec.pdf.

20 In one of life's interesting coincidences, the President's Commission to Strengthen Social Security included one of my former Cornell ILR professors who taught labor economics.

21 My view on the retirement security project report was that the panel followed the IF process faithfully and produced a valuable, timely report; further discussion in small-group settings was appropriate, but the report stood on its own and deserved to be released as the product of the panel's hard work. Anything less seemed a disservice to the panelists after their commitment to the project for over a year. However, the

outcome wasn't entirely surprising. I had done my homework on the foundation's history and tracked down participants in IF projects from the foundation's earlier years. (A folder on what I found remains in my personal IF files.) On the matter of what the foundation called "going public" with project reports, one participant condensed what I found into a single sentence: "I can't say anything that will be optimistic." Still, I had hoped for a different result.

22 Reviewing past versions of the Interactivity Foundation website, I find two IF project reports mentioned in March 2006: one on privacy rights and another on healthcare (with a focus on depression); see "Our Staff Work Reports," Interactivity Foundation, March 17, 2006, https://web.archive.org/web/20060317013050/http://www.interactivityfoundation.org/Our%20Staff%20Work%20Reports.htm. According to the website, those projects completed panel discussions in June and September 2004, respectively; I don't recall any project in my cohort producing a final report before my IF employment concluded at the end of June 2004.

23 Adolf G. Gundersen, *How Will We All Retire? Policy Possibilities for Public Discussion* (Parkersburg: Interactivity Foundation, 2010), described on its cover as: "Edited by Adolf G. Gundersen, Fellow of the Interactivity Foundation, Based on Project and Public Discussions facilitated by Charles Whalen and Adolf Gundersen."

24 See Ehrenreich, *Bait and Switch* (first published in 2005). In an earlier work, Ehrenreich exposed how workers in service jobs requiring little education and training face widespread economic insecurity and mistreatment; see Barbara Ehrenreich, *Nickle and Dimed: On (Not) Getting By in America* (New York: Metropolitan Books, 2001).

25 Ehrenreich, *Bait and Switch*, 2, 202–211, 237.

26 Ehrenreich, *Bait and Switch*, 2, 216–217.

27 Ehrenreich, *Bait and Switch*, 245–246.

28 Ehrenreich, *Bait and Switch*, 210.

29 There's also an equally nagging question: What can I do differently in the future?

30 "Underemployment" involves working in a job that doesn't fully use one's skills or experience. (The Champions at Work research project was an exception to the general thrust of my ILR Extension work.) I exclude my Fulbright year in China from the ILR Extension period; that year involved a very different experience than my ILR work (and my only opportunity to teach graduate students).

31 In the two decades since my departure from IF, it appears the foundation has produced a solid track record, partly by collaborating with universities, community groups, and other organizations.

32 Steady work and economic security during one's career don't require the same job year after year. Rather, they ideally mean a career ladder that increases opportunities and responsibilities as work experience increases. They also require that a lost job can be replaced with an economically comparable one.

33 My dad passed away in August 2021. When he became ill during retirement, he relied on the healthcare benefits available to him as a military veteran. Without those benefits, he and my mom would have likely faced financial hardship. What people often overlook is that retiree health benefits were not a gift; they were deferred compensation, involving a tradeoff of lower pre-retirement paychecks for greater

retirement security. Breaking that benefits promise represents the breaking of a social contract; one could also argue it amounts to wage theft.

34 In *Bait and Switch*, Ehrenreich provides a powerful case for a serious IF-style project on rising economic insecurity. She writes that our society would greatly benefit from, and sorely lacks, "settings for a wide-ranging discussion, leading, perhaps, to some kind of action" on worker insecurity and how business is run in America; see Ehrenreich, *Bait and Switch*, 217–225. In fact, the foundation conducted an IF project touching on worker insecurity in the mid-2010s, see Mark Amadeus Notturno, *The Future of Employment: Policy Possibilities for Public Discussion* (Parkersburg: Interactivity Foundation, 2015).

Chapter 24. Recharged and Reengaged

1 On my travels from Geneva: east refers to the Levy Institute in the Hudson Valley, west to Cornell in Buffalo, and south to *BusinessWeek* in New York City as well as IF in West Virginia. Having mentioned Patches, I should add that Pepys, the orange tabby I adopted during graduate school in Austin, passed away shortly before the start of our Fulbright year, and that Katie adopted an orange tabby of her own, named Tiger, soon after we returned to the states from China. Tiger and I got along fine, but Katie and Linda were Tiger's favorite humans, which is understandable since I was away so often during his first few years.

2 Returning to the Finger Lakes allowed me to also return to ice hockey, which I hadn't played since high school. I started by playing with others my age once a week but eventually played year-round in three different leagues. I continued to play regularly until I began working in Washington, DC, in September 2010.

3 I attribute Katie's exceptional study habits and record of academic performance to Linda, who has a gentle touch but also consistently devoted hours each week to working with Katie on schoolwork; on exam days, Linda regularly slipped a mock quiz onto the breakfast table.

4 In the pit orchestra, Katie performed on violin and I played trumpet, having brushed up just enough to share the experience with my daughter.

5 Webb Institute students pursue a tuition-free double major in naval architecture and marine engineering. Katie selected Webb over an impressive list of institutions, including Wellesley College, Barnard College, and even Cornell University, which offered her admission with the special designation of Presidential Research Scholar. Ironically, her first choice was Yale, which placed her on the admissions "waiting list," as was the case with me three decades earlier.

Katie managed to incorporate her interest in history into the Webb program in several ways, including taking an elective course with an archeologist, working for the Bermuda Maritime Museum between semesters, helping to create a Webb course on marine forensics and maritime archeology, and using her senior thesis to analyze the Civil War–era *Sub Marine Explorer*. She also surprised me by writing a paper on the offshoring of engineering jobs for her first-year course on the engineering profession. I admired her for exploring the topic but also found it heartbreaking to see her confronting that issue before her career even took flight.

6 Although I hadn't taught American students in a conventional academic setting since 1994, I taught "Labor and the American Economy" to working adults in the Buffalo Labor Studies Program as recently as spring 2000, and I taught a few hundred university students in China during the 1998–1999 academic year.

7 Der Hovanesian departed from *BusinessWeek* soon after it was sold to Bloomberg. Today, she works as an analyst for an international asset management firm.

8 The precarious financial condition of Wells College meant the faculty was considerably overworked and underpaid relative to professors at many other colleges and universities, realities that long hindered faculty recruitment and retention. To support their families, some Wells professors even taught elsewhere on an adjunct basis.

9 I've always found organizing conference sessions a great way to stay engaged with important developments in economics and industrial relations; and that engagement only increased in 2006, when I began a four-year stint as co-chair of LERA's Labor Markets Interest Section.

10 In the early 2000s, my academic work appeared not just in economics journals, but also in journals in the fields of management studies, labor studies, and labor-management relations. However, it was my op-ed on the air traffic controllers' strike that pleased my mom the most; that's because the newspaper paid me a few hundred dollars for the essay (which the paper distributed widely via syndication). See Charles J. Whalen, "Echoes of a Broken Strike," *Washington Post*, August 5, 2006, A19.

11 For my article on erosion of automatic stabilizers, see Charles J. Whalen and Jeffrey B. Wenger, "Destabilizing an Unstable Economy," *Challenge* 45, no. 6 (November 2002): 70–92; and for the attention it received in *The New York Times*, see Jeff Madrick, "Let's Hear from Those Who Feel Government Has a Role in Stabilizing the Economy," *New York Times*, August 8, 2002, C2. Madrick edited *Challenge*, which explains how he wrote about the Whalen-Wenger paper before its publication.

12 Art Wheaton and Charles J. Whalen, "Using Industry Education to Facilitate Changes in Organizational Culture," *Perspectives on Work* 12, nos. 1–2 (Summer 2008): 15–19.

13 Charles J. Whalen, "Union-Driven Economic Development Initiatives and Community Solidarity in Western New York," *Ephemera: Theory and Politics in Organization* 7, no. 3 (August 2007): 403–418. That paper appeared as the lead article in a special issue on Solidarity and Business Development; it was first presented at a meeting of the Academy of Management. During the same period, I collaborated with a former Levy Institute colleague on a different worker-related topic: Oren M. Levin-Waldman and Charles J. Whalen, "The Minimum Wage Is a Middle-Class Issue," *Challenge* 50, no. 3 (May 2007): 59–71.

14 Charles J. Whalen, "Social Unionism in Western New York: The Case of the Economic Development Group," *Labor Studies Journal* 35, no. 4 (December 2010): 540–565; and Charles J. Whalen, "Union Engagement in Western New York Economic Development: An Institutional Analysis," in *Advances in Industrial and Labor Relations*, vol. 18, ed. David Lewin, et al. (Leeds: Emerald, 2011), 177–213.

15 For an article that focuses on one round of call center job losses in Buffalo, but also mentions other rounds, see Fred O. Williams, "846 to Lose Jobs in Call Center Closing," *Buffalo News*, January 9, 2003, A1.

16 See Timothy A. Fay, "The Carrier Move from Syracuse," *Perspectives on Work* 8, no. 2 (Winter 2005): 4–6.

17 David Moberg, a labor journalist, offered an exception to the superficial coverage of offshoring with a story on the shutdown of the Maytag factory in Galesburg, Illinois (the city's largest employer). Moberg began his story by quoting Aaron Kemp, a union safety official who had a temporary job counseling other laid-off workers at two-thirds his old pay: "I wanted to work a decent job and earn a decent wage, with decent benefits, so I can raise my kids, give them a decent education, and maybe take them out to Pizza Hut on a Friday night. I don't need a Mercedes, just a ho-hum existence, and now … it seems hard to even do that." See David Moberg, "Maytag Moves to Mexico," *In These Times*, December 29, 2004, https://inthesetimes.com/article/maytag-moves-to-mexico. Research conducted later by students at Knox College found that 70 percent of workers retrained after losing jobs at Maytag were hired into lower-paying jobs; see Andrea Houlihan, "Maytag Project: No Quick Fix for Lost Jobs," Knox College, March 14, 2011, https://web.archive.org/web/20210830225505/https://www.knox.edu/news/maytag-survey-results/no-quick-fix-for-lost-jobs.

18 Jyoti Thottam, "Is Your Job Going Abroad?" *Time*, March 1, 2004, 86.

19 See Charles J. Whalen, "Sending Jobs Offshore from the United States: What Are the Consequences?" *Intervention: European Journal of Economics and Economic Policies* 2, no. 2 (November 2005): 33–40.

20 Whalen, "Sending Jobs Offshore from the United States"; and Charles J. Whalen, "Offshoring: Still a Threat to Workers," *Working USA: The Journal of Labor and Society* 8, no. 6 (December 2005): 717–719.

21 Charles J. Whalen, "Broaden Public Discussion to Include All Retirement Options," *Democrat and Chronicle* [Rochester, New York], January 31, 2005, A13; Charles J. Whalen, "Social Security: A View from Beyond the Beltway," *Challenge* 48, no. 4 (July 2005): 5–10; and Charles J. Whalen, "The Future of Retirement Security in the United States: Laying the Groundwork for Public Discussion," *Journal of Economic Issues* 39, no. 3 (September 2005): 777–791.

22 Schumpeter supervised Minsky's dissertation at Harvard.

23 Charles J. Whalen, "Integrating Schumpeter and Keynes: Hyman Minsky's Theory of Capitalist Development," *Journal of Economic Issues* 35, no. 4 (December 2001): 805–823. For a related article on Schumpeter, see Charles J. Whalen, "The Age of Schumpeter," in *Global Business and Economics Review–Anthology 2002*, ed. Demetri Kantarelis (Worcester: Business and Economics Society International, 2002), 194–202.

24 See Charles J. Whalen, "Money-Manager Capitalism: Still Here, But Not Quite as Expected," *Journal of Economic Issues* 36, no. 2 (June 2002): 401–406; Charles J. Whalen, "Post-Keynesian Institutionalism and the Anxious Society," in *Assessing the Evolution and Impact of Alternative Institutional Structures*, ed. Sandra Batie and Nicholas Mercuro (London: Routledge, 2008), 273–299; and Charles J. Whalen, "Toward 'Wisely Managed' Capitalism: Post-Keynesian Institutionalism and the Creative State," *Forum for Social Economics* 37, no. 1 (2008): 43–60. The *Forum* article on "wisely managed" capitalism was selected as that journal's best paper of the year. For yet another product of this research stream, see David A. Zalewski and Charles J. Whalen, "Financialization and Income Inequality: A Post Keynesian Institutionalist Analysis," *Journal of Economic Issues* 44, no. 3 (September 2010): 757–777.

25 Charles J. Whalen, *Reforming Capitalism for the Common Good: Essays in Institutional and Post-Keynesian Economics* (Cheltenham: Edward Elgar, 2022).

26 Jacob Powell, Review of *Reforming Capitalism for the Common Good*, by Charles J. Whalen, *Review of Keynesian Economics* 11, no. 3 (July 2023): 427–429.

27 Charles J. Whalen, *New Directions in the Study of Work and Employment: Revitalizing Industrial Relations as an Academic Enterprise* (Cheltenham: Edward Elgar, 2008); and Charles J. Whalen, *Human Resource Economics and Public Policy: Essays in Honor of Vernon M. Briggs Jr.* (Kalamazoo: W.E. Upjohn Institute, 2010).

28 Charles Wilber's comments appear inside the front cover of Charles J. Whalen, *Financial Instability and Economic Security After the Great Recession* (Cheltenham: Edward Elgar, 2011).

29 Charles J. Whalen, "The U.S. Credit Crunch of 2007," *Public Policy Brief No. 92*, Levy Economics Institute, October 2007, 7–23.

30 Charles J. Whalen, "Understanding the Credit Crunch," *Challenge* 51, no. 1 (January 2008): 91–109; and Charles J. Whalen, "The Credit Crunch: A Minsky Moment," *Studi e Note di Economia* 13, no. 1 (March 2008): 3–21.

31 Here's an excerpt from my former student's email: "I have amazing memories of your Political Economy class, and learned much from you—and in fact, took off from your syllabus when I taught the same this year. You really were an excellent teacher … one that made students think." (Author's personal copy.)

32 Faculty administrators at other institutions advised me against managing a department and academic programs without tenure, but the president wouldn't budge. And I wasn't comfortable walking away from an academic post not too far from home that came with at least a chance of professional and economic security.

Chapter 25. Utica College

1 Utica, New York, is about 55 miles east of Syracuse. Utica College changed its name to Utica University in 2022.

2 Letter from Linda Garceau to the author, October 2009 (personal files).

3 At AACSB conferences, including a plenary session at the annual meeting in 2009, I heard corporate leaders and analysts tell similar stories of how investors and lenders pressured companies to offshore their operations.

4 Marks's visit was timely. On the day he visited campus, he appeared (via satellite) as a guest of Glenn Beck on CNN. Following what was, as expected, a highly contentious interview with Beck, Marks delivered his evening lecture at the college.

5 For the notion of an "innovation nation," see John Kao, *Innovation Nation: Why America Is Losing Its Innovative Edge, Why It Matters, and What We Can Do to Get It Back* (New York: Free Press, 2007). Some of my Utica students were so intrigued with Kao's vision that they sought to invite him to campus. Although Kao was unavailable, he was flattered by the invitation and sent a few autographed copies of his book.

6 My Utica College contract required that I teach just one course per semester (because of my administrative responsibilities), but I willingly taught the research proposal course as a fall semester overload because it met just once a week and dovetailed with the spring research course. Meanwhile, the "Government and Economic Life" course, created in the early years of the college by an institutional economist, fit with my teaching and research experience in public economics, economic history, and political economy, all of which examined the role of government in the economy.

7 In addition to my own teaching at Utica College, I regularly delivered a guest lecture to first-year management students, offering writing tips based on my work at *BusinessWeek*. A version of my lecture was published as Charles J. Whalen, "Writing: Work? Fun? Both!" *Perspectives on Work*, Spring 2008, online edition, https://web.archive.org/web/20100610060010/http://www.lera.uiuc.edu/Pubs/Perspectives/onlinecompanion/Sp08-Whalen.html.

Chapter 26. "We're All Minskyites Now"

1 There are at least two reasons why deregulation reduced the power and authority of central banks and government regulators: it limited the scope of their regulatory framework and risked creating global financial crises that could be addressed only through coordinated international action. For Minsky's prescient views on the dangers of securitization, see, for example, Hyman P. Minsky, "Global Consequences of Financial Deregulation," *Marcus Wallenberg Papers on International Finance* 2, no. 1 (October 1986): 1–19; and Hyman P. Minsky, "Schumpeter: Finance and Evolution," in *Evolving Technology and Market Structure: Studies in Schumpeterian Economics*, ed. Arnold Heertje and Mark Perlman (Ann Arbor: The University of Michigan Press, 1990), 51–74.

2 For a discussion of how conventional economists were surprised by the global financial crisis, see Charles J. Whalen, "Post-Keynesian Institutionalism After the Great Recession," *European Journal of Economics and Economic Policies: Intervention* 10, no. 1 (Spring 2013): 12–27.

3 See Justin Lahart, "In Time of Tumult, Obscure Economist Gains Currency," *Wall Street Journal*, August 18, 2007, A1.

4 For the comments of Fed Chair Bernanke on the urgency of emergency legislation, see Andrew Ross Sorkin, et al., "As Crisis Spiraled, Alarm Led to Action," *New York Times*, October 1, 2008, https://www.nytimes.com/2008/10/02/business/02crisis.html.

5 Robert Pollin, "We're All Minskyites Now," *The Nation*, November 17, 2008, 5–6.

6 Lawrence H. Summers, "A Conversation on New Economic Thinking," Institute for New Economic Thinking, April 8, 2011, https://web.archive.org/web/20250219111628/https://larrysummers.com/commentary/speeches/brenton-woods-speech/.

7 For a discussion of Krugman's attempt to reread Minsky, see Charles J. Whalen, "Minsky Goes to Buffalo—and Takes on the Economics Establishment," *Forum for Social Economics* 40, no. 2 (2011): 276–278.

8 See Janet L. Yellen, "A Minsky Meltdown: Lessons for Central Bankers," *FRBSF Economic Letter* Number 2009-15, May 1, 2009.

9 See Charles J. Whalen, "An Institutionalist Perspective on the Global Financial Crisis," in *Macroeconomic Theory and Its Failings*, ed. Steven Kates (Cheltenham: Edward Elgar, 2010), 235–259; and Charles J. Whalen, "A Minsky Perspective on the Global Recession of 2009," in *Minsky, Crisis and Development*, ed. Daniela Tavasci and Jan Toporowski (London: Palgrave, 2010), 106–126. The chapter for Kates also led to a follow-up chapter that looked beyond the economic recovery: Charles J. Whalen, "Human Resources: The Key to Institutional Economics After the Great Recession."

10 Charles J. Whalen, "Economic Policy for the Real World," Levy Economics Institute *Policy Note*, No. 2010-1 (July 2010): 1–5.

11 See Whalen, "Post-Keynesian Institutionalism After the Great Recession"; and Whalen, "Money-Manager Capitalism." The global financial crisis led to other research products as well as two public policy sessions organized for LERA; see, for example, Charles J. Whalen, "Beyond the Recovery: Keeping Jobs and Working Families at the Center of the Nation's Economic Agenda: Discussion," in *Labor and Employment Relations Association Series: Proceedings of the 62nd Annual Meeting*, ed. Françoise Carré and Christian Weller (Champaign: Labor and Employment Relations Association, 2010), 165–166.

Chapter 27. Moment of Truth

1 Letter from Frank Bostyn, AACSB International, to Charles J. Whalen, January 14, 2010. (The author retains an electronic copy.)

2 Memo from Charles Whalen and Herb Rau to Utica College provost and dean of Business and Justice Studies on IACBE, March 2010 (author's personal copy).

3 Report from Charles Whalen to Utica College on AACSB International, International Conference and Annual Meeting, April 27, 2010 (author's personal copy).

4 Author's personal notes of meeting, May 12, 2010.

5 Letter from Charles J. Whalen to Dr. Judith Kirkpatrick, June 7, 2010, with accompanying list of "Business and Economics Department Activities and Accomplishments Since January 2008" (author's personal copies).

6 After my departure from HWS, the colleges converted from trimesters to semesters and the faculty teaching load fell to five courses per year.

7 Although congressional Democrats took the lead in appointing Elmendorf (because the Democratic Party controlled the House and Senate at the time), the appointment process is a joint and cooperative one involving leaders from both parties; the position is intended to be decidedly nonpartisan.

Chapter 28. In the Shadow of the Capitol

1 Although CBO offered me the job in June 2010, I negotiated a September start to finish *Financial Instability and Economic Security After the Great Recession* and allow some summer family time.

2 For example, see Charles Whalen, "The Economic Outlook," in *The Budget and Economic Outlook: Fiscal Years 2011 to 2021* (Washington: Congressional Budget Office, 2011), 27–52; and Charles Whalen, *A Macroeconomic Analysis of the President's 2017 Budget* (Washington: Congressional Budget Office, 2016).

3 For examples of reports on CBO's methods, see Charles Whalen, *How CBO Analyzes the Effects of Changes in Federal Fiscal Policies on the Economy* (Washington: Congressional Budget Office, 2014); and Charles Whalen and Alexander Arnon, *How CBO Projects Income* (Washington: Congressional Budget Office, 2013). For a discussion of uncertainties affecting CBO's economic projections, see Charles Whalen, "Uncertainties in the Economic Outlook," Congressional Budget Office Blog, September 7, 2016, https://www.cbo.gov/publication/51967.

4 Because I wanted to expand my CBO contributions beyond the writing aspects of my job and deeper into the work of macroeconomic analysis, I participated in a week-long "applied econometrics" refresher course offered by the National Association of Business Economists in May 2014. I wasn't aiming to jettison my role as MAD's go-to writer, only to better equip myself to more fully engage in CBO's economic research.

5 Mark Lasky and Charles Whalen, *What Accounts for the Slow Growth of the Economy After the Recession?* (Washington: Congressional Budget Office, 2012).

6 To be precise, the contribution of investment to the economy's slow recovery came through its effect on a category of assets called capital services: "The flow of services available from capital assets—such as equipment, structures, inventories, and land—grew more slowly in the current recovery because net investment (relative to the existing stock of those assets) was much lower during this recession than in others." See "What Accounts for the Slow Growth of the Economy After the Recession? Infographic," Congressional Budget Office, November 14, 2012, https://www.cbo.gov/publication/43712.

7 One reason for the slow economic recovery was a decline in defense purchases by the federal government, combined with sluggish spending by state and local governments owing to slow growth in tax revenues and federal grants.

8 David Brauer and Charles Whalen, *The Slow Recovery of the Labor Market* (Washington: Congressional Budget Office, 2014).

9 The labor market report identified three reasons for a lower rate of labor force participation: long-term population trends (primarily the aging of the population); recession-related weakness in employment prospects and wages; and discouragement that led unemployed workers to drop out of the labor force. Population trends accounted for half of the participation rate decline, and employment prospects and worker discouragement accounted for the other half; see Brauer and Whalen, *The Slow Recovery of the Labor Market*, 1.

10 Douglas W. Elmendorf, "Confronting the Nation's Fiscal Policy Challenges," Testimony of the director of the Congressional Budget Office before the Joint Select Committee on Deficit Reduction, US Congress, September 13, 2011, 1, 26, 34.

11 I also learned much from Kim Kowalewski, deputy to the head of MAD, who worked in the agency since 1989 and reviewed every report before it left the division. I often learned by working alongside Kim just as I'd done with Seymour Zucker at *BusinessWeek*.

12 Charles J. Whalen and Felix Reichling, "The Fiscal Multiplier and Economic Policy Analysis in the United States," *Contemporary Economic Policy* 33, no. 4 (October 2015): 735–746.

13 Charles Whalen and Felix Reichling, "Estimates of the Frisch Elasticity of Labor Supply: A Review," *Eastern Economic Journal* 43, no. 1(January 2017): 37–42.

14 Bill Clinton, interviewed by Aaron Task, "President Bill Clinton: Yes, the American Dream Is Under Assault," Yahoo Finance, September 19, 2011, https://finance.yahoo.com/blogs/daily-ticker/president-bill-clinton-yes-american-dream-under-assault-231659873.html.

15 For the three articles focusing on contributors to PKI, see Charles J. Whalen, "Pluralism: Lifeblood of Post-Keynesian Institutionalism" [an article highlighting the work of W. Robert Brazelton], *International Journal of Pluralism and Economics Education* 6, no. 1 (Spring 2015): 68–81; Charles J. Whalen, "Wallace C. Peterson: A Post-Keynesian Institutionalist," *Journal of Economic Issues* 50, no. 2 (June 2016): 584–593; and Charles J. Whalen, "Institutionalism and the 'Common Man' Through the Lens of Philip Klein: Business Cycles, the Public Sector, and Keynes's Economics," *Journal of Economic Issues* 51, no. 4 (December 2017): 1094–1113.

For two other articles prepared on my own time while employed by CBO (each composed in response to a specific request), see Charles J. Whalen, "Core Concepts of Institutionalist Public Finance," *Forum for Social Economics* 42, no. 4 (November 2013): 359–379; and "Post-Keynesian Economics: A Pluralistic Alternative to Conventional Economics," *International Journal of Pluralism and Economics Education* 7, no. 1 (Spring 2016): 23–38.

16 Some of the praise for CBO's work found its way into news stories, but sometimes it came via email. For example, Larry Mishel, then president of the Economic Policy Institute, sent me an email in early 2013, commenting on a report I coauthored on national income. In part, he wrote, "This is the first time I've seen an analysis [of income shares] that's not superficial, and I really appreciate all the references. We're undertaking an assessment of the literature around declining labor's share in advanced countries, so this is very helpful."

17 During my daughter's first visit to CBO, Doug also welcomed her to come along with his entourage to Capitol Hill and observe a hearing.

Chapter 29. The Other DC

1 For details about Gessford Court, see Capitol Hill Restoration Society, "Gessford Court Walking Tour Handout," May 8, 2019, https://chrs.org/gessford-court-walking-tour/; see also Elizabeth Festa, "D.C.'s Gessford Court Is a Little Alley Oasis," *Washington Post*, March 20, 2010, F1.

2 In addition to public jam sessions, I met on Monday nights with a CBO colleague's husband and his friends for casual basement jams.

3 The Modern Jazz "200" series of Dial Records appeared on 10-inch long-playing records. Charlie Parker was featured on Dial 201, 202, 203, and 207, and Dizzy Gillespie on Dial 212. Meanwhile, "2-5-1" also refers to a chord progression common in jazz and popular music, so we became: Dial 251 (pronounced "two-five-one") and

I added "for Jazz" partly to emphasize we're a jazz group, but also because the longer name reminded me of the Alfred Hitchcock film, *Dial M for Murder*. The band eventually earned its subliminal connection to the film title by gaining a reputation for delivering "killer" sets.

4 I always paid the band before taking a cut for myself; if tips were paltry, I went home without a share. In retrospect, it's astonishing we played for so little, but for me the education was priceless.

5 The wood paneling and wall sconces of Mr. Henry's upstairs jazz lounge look the same today as on the cover of Roberta Flack's debut album, *First Take* (1969).

6 I met Leonhardt through DC's Different Drummers, where he directed both the big band and the small jazz combo.

7 It was also my responsibility to maintain a list of reliable substitutes who could fill in when band members couldn't make a gig.

8 A "listening room" is a serious jazz venue where the crowd keeps talking to a minimum and the music is the center of attention. When I began working at CBO, there were three listening rooms in DC: Twins Jazz, Bohemian Caverns, and Blues Alley in Georgetown. Bohemian Caverns closed in 2016, and Twins didn't survive the pandemic shutdown, leaving Blues Alley the only remaining venue of this sort.

9 Michael J. West, "Ambitious and Rewarding Show from Jazz Sextet Dial 251 Honors Two Music Legends," *Washington Post*, September 26, 2016, C4.

10 The phrase comes from Michael West's description of the Dial 251 sextet, but straight-ahead jazz with a shot of R&B is also an apt description of hard bop. See West, "Ambitious and Rewarding Show."

Chapter 30. The Personal and the Political

1 I hadn't intended to pursue research on trends in national income. Shortly after arriving at CBO, I was assigned to the original incomes project to help a colleague translate the agency's projections into a widely accessible report. Then that economist left the agency, as did her replacement some months later, and the project became mine (with technical assistance from an assistant analyst who knew the computer code used to run CBO's macroeconomic model). My paper on the decline in labor's share of income emerged as an offshoot of the larger incomes project, mirroring the way I built on CBO fiscal policy reports to produce a paper on fiscal multipliers.

In another offshoot of the incomes project, I reviewed the literature on how income inequality affects economic growth. My research reflected growing interest in that subject within CBO, the economics profession, and the policymaking community. I delivered two internal reports on the subject, in June 2013 and March 2014, but an assignment for a full-scale CBO report on the topic never materialized.

2 See Rebecca Shabad, "Budget Director: 'Tax Cuts Do Not Pay for Themselves.'"

3 Another economist who worked in the fiscal policy unit when I arrived at the agency was nominally a member of the unit when I departed, but the focus of his work shifted to economic projections a few years prior to my departure.

4 As fate would have it, the first Dial 251 gig cancelled because of COVID-19 was the Gala Dinner of the World Vaccine Congress, scheduled for April 2020.

5 While all my Dial 251 bandmates are extremely talented, Bryan is an extraordinary jazz musician, who could always be counted on to deliver finely crafted solos. Bryan studied music performance as an undergraduate and then majored in jazz studies as a graduate student. A high point of my own jazz education was the privilege of playing on the front line alongside him for more than five years.

6 See Kenneth M. Casebeer and Charles J. Whalen, "Taking Interdependence and Production More Seriously: Toward Mutual Rationality and a More Useful Law and Economics," *University of Miami Law Review* 66, no. 1 (Fall 2011): 141–156. That article highlights two essential realities often overlooked in law and economics: human interdependence and the need to produce goods and services before they can be exchanged.

7 See "Tracking Congress in the Age of Trump: Tom Reed, 117th Congress," FiveThirtyEight, updated January 13, 2021, https://web.archive.org/web/20250306200215/https://projects.fivethirtyeight.com/congress-trump-score/tom-reed/.

8 When I eventually entered the congressional race, I expressed support for healthcare for all, not Medicare for All, and identified several constructive policy proposals that would get us there without relying on the plan favored by Senator Sanders. Support for Medicare for All worked against the eventual Democratic Party nominee in the district's general election, and Vice President Kamala Harris pivoted from her earlier support for the proposal during the 2024 presidential campaign.

9 Following my withdrawal from the race, a resident from the heart of the district sent me a handwritten note to thank me for my campaign. She wrote, in part: "I applaud your courage and determination. Every time you spoke or posted online, you helped us better understand how much more can be done in Washington. You helped promote a more progressive and inclusive platform for Democrats."

10 The Giffords Law Center was founded by former Congresswoman Gabby Giffords, who was shot during a public appearance in a suburb of Tucson, Arizona, on January 8, 2011. The gunman hit 19 people, killing six. In 2013, Giffords and her husband Mark Kelly established a political action committee called Americans for Responsible Solutions. It merged with the public interest Law Center to Prevent Gun Violence in 2017, producing the Giffords Law Center, an organization with a lobbying arm and research arm as well as a political action committee.

11 In my campaign I stressed that although the Second Amendment protects gun ownership, the *essential purposes* of the Constitution, as laid out clearly in its Preamble, are: "to insure domestic tranquility, provide for the common defense, promote the general welfare, and secure the blessings of liberty for ourselves and our posterity"—none of which are possible in a society with an ever-present threat of mass gun violence. The position I took on the Second Amendment and gun violence anticipated the approach taken by Governor Tim Walz when accepting the Democratic Party's nomination for Vice President in August 2024: "I believe in the Second Amendment, but I also believe our first responsibility is to keep our kids safe." See "Full Transcript of Tim Walz's Speech at the Democratic National Convention," *New York Times*, August 22, 2024, https://www.nytimes.com/2024/08/22/us/politics/tim-walz-dnc-speech-transcript.html.

12 David Chipman and Lindsay Nichols, "Legal and Lethal: Nine Products That Could Be the Next Bump Stock," Giffords, November 15, 2017, https://giffords.org/wp-content/uploads/2017/11/Giffords-Lethal-and-Legal-1.pdf.

13 Robert Lynch, "A Crowded Field in a Crowded Room," Ithaca.com, March 7, 2018, https://www.ithaca.com/opinion/editorials/a-crowded-field-in-a-crowded-room/article_deb14822-2794-11e8-b82f-cb335b1f249b.html.

14 See Charles Whalen, "Why I Marched Last Weekend," Ithaca.com, March 28, 2018, https://www.ithaca.com/opinion/guest_opinions/why-i-marched-last-weekend/article_1e7bd6c6-3298-11e8-abc7-0f007111706a.html.

Epilogue: Continuing the Fight amid Multiple Crises

1 Stephen Collinson, "Trump Is Imposing MAGA Rule on the Government Hour-by-Hour," CNN.com, January 23, 2025, https://www.cnn.com/2025/01/23/politics/maga-rule-government-trump-analysis/index.html. According to Peter M. Shane, a legal scholar at New York University, "We are well past euphemism about 'pushing the limits,' 'stretching the envelope,' and the like.… [The array of legal constraints Trump has violated amounts to] programmatic sabotage and rampant lawlessness"; see Charlie Savage, "Trump Brazenly Defies Laws in Escalating Power Grab," *New York Times*, February 6, 2025, A17.

2 Laura Barron-Lopez, "Trump Fires Inspectors General Across Federal Agencies," PBS News Hour, January 29, 2025, https://www.pbs.org/newshour/classroom/daily-news-lessons/2025/01/trump-fires-inspectors-general-across-federal-agencies.

3 Garrett Haake and Megan Lebowitz, "White House Says About 75K Federal Workers Accepted 'Deferred Resignation' Offer," NBC News, February 12, 2025, https://www.nbcnews.com/politics/white-house/white-house-says-75000-accepted-federal-buyout-trump-rcna191971. In a more recent tally, at least 148,000 federal employees left government voluntarily or involuntarily as of July 21, 2025, owing to President Trump's efforts to shrink the federal workforce; see Sean Michael Newhouse, "At Least 148,000 Federal Employees Have Left Government Under Trump, Good Government Group Says," *Government Executive*, August 1, 2025, https://www.govexec.com/workforce/2025/08/least-148000-federal-employees-have-left-government-under-trump-good-government-group-reports/407171/.

4 Collinson, "Trump Is Imposing MAGA Rule …"; Dean Jackson and Justin Hendrix, "Nine Experts on the Impact of President Trump's Pardons and Commutations for January 6 Offenders," Just Security, February 3, 2025, https://www.justsecurity.org/107288/nine-experts-pardons-january-6/; Sasha Abramsky, "Trump's January 6 Pardons Were a Green Light to Far Right Paramilitaries," Truthout, February 3, 2025, https://truthout.org/articles/trumps-january-6-pardons-were-a-green-light-to-far-right-paramilitaries/. More recently, President Trump deployed National Guard troops to Los Angeles to quell protests against federal immigration raids.

5 See Alicia Wallace, "Trump Pledged to Bring Down Food Prices on Day One. Instead, Eggs Are Getting More Expensive," CNN.com, January 28, 2025, https://

www.cnn.com/2025/01/28/economy/trump-inflation-price-promises/index.html; and Domenico Montanaro, "Prices Were a Key Issue in 2024, But Trump Makes Clear They're Not His Top Priority," NPR, February 1, 2025, https://www.npr.org/2025/02/01/nx-s1-5282353/trump-economy-prices-inflation.

6 Elena Moore, "Federal Judge Issues Restraining Order Blocking Federal Spending Freeze," NPR.org, February 3, 2025, https://www.npr.org/2025/02/03/nx-s1-5285687/trump-federal-spending-freeze. For a more recent development, see Ann E. Marimow, "Supreme Court Lets Trump Cut Billions in Aid," *New York Times*, September 27, 2025, A1.

7 Alaa Elassar, "Navajo Nation Leaders Raise Alarm over Reports of Indigenous People Being Questioned and Detained During Immigration Sweeps," CNN.com, January 27, 2025, https://www.cnn.com/2025/01/27/us/navajo-detained-ice-indigenous-immigration-trump/index.html.

8 Christopher Rugaber, "Trump Administration Orders Consumer Protection Agency to Stop Work, Closes Building," Associated Press, February 9, 2025, https://apnews.com/article/trump-consumer-protection-cease-1b93c60a773b6b5ee629e-769ae6850e9.

9 Lex Harvey, "Key Takeaways from Trump's Plan to 'Take Over' Gaza," CNN.com, February 5, 2025, https://www.cnn.com/2025/02/05/middleeast/takeaways-trump-gaza-proposal-intl-hnk.

10 It's difficult to keep track of the tariff situation because President Trump seems to change his mind on the matter daily, but administration officials now acknowledge taming inflation will take more time; see Alan Rappeport and Colby Smith, "With High Prices Persisting, Trump Tempers Tone on Slaying Inflation," *New York Times*, February 13, 2025, B1.

11 "Federal Policy Watch," Economic Policy Institute, https://www.epi.org/policywatch/. See also Celine McNicholas, et al., "100 Ways Trump Has Hurt Workers in His First 100 Days," Economic Policy Institute, April 25, 2025, https://www.epi.org/publication/100-days-100-ways-trump-hurt-workers/.

12 With executive action in March and August 2025, President Trump revoked bargaining rights for more than 1 million federal workers—almost 85 percent of federal workers represented by unions. See Aurelia Glass, "The Trump Administration Ended Collective Bargaining for 1 Million Federal Workers," Center for American Progress, October 1, 2025, https://www.americanprogress.org/article/the-trump-administration-ended-collective-bargaining-for-1-million-federal-workers/; and Erich Wagner, "A Fresh Executive Order Aims to Ban Unions at More Federal Agencies," *Government Executive*, August 28, 2025, https://www.govexec.com/workforce/2025/08/fresh-executive-order-aims-ban-unions-more-federal-agencies/407774/.

13 Alicia Parlapiano, et al., "Everything in Trump's Big Tax and Spending Law, and How Much It Will Cost or Save," *New York Times*, July 22, 2025, https://www.nytimes.com/interactive/2025/06/30/upshot/senate-republican-megabill.html; James Myall, "How Trump's 'Big Beautiful Bill' Further Enriches the Rich and Immiserates the Poor," Maine Center for Economic Policy, July 8, 2025, https://www.mecep.org/blog/how-trumps-big-beautiful-bill-further-enriches-the-rich-and-immiserates-the-poor/.

14 Rep. Jasmine Crockett, quoted in Lisa Lerer and Reid J. Epstein, "'We Have No Coherent Message': Democrats Struggle to Oppose Trump," *New York Times*, February 3, 2025, A1.

15 Maureen Dowd and Patrick Healy, "Maureen Dowd on Trump the Narcissist, Act II," *New York Times*, January 30, 2025, https://www.nytimes.com/2025/01/30/opinion/trump-power-narcissism.html. For a more recent view, see Ezra Klein, "It's Simple: Stop Enabling Trump's Power Grab," *New York Times*, September 7, 2025, SR6.

16 At the annual meeting of the Association of American Law Schools in January 2012, I recall an attendee chiding panelists for failing to recognize that many citizens have no interest in participatory democracy: "Many people don't care at all about democracy. They want a strongman to fix things." The only problem is that a strongman without accountability decides for himself where fixes are needed, what fixes are required, and when things are fixed. In such a system, there is also no check on presidential corruption.

17 "It's My Party and I'll Try If I Want To," This American Life, Episode 649, June 22, 2018, https://www.thisamericanlife.org/649/transcript. Recalling his discussion with a Democratic congressman, Robert Reich makes a similar point in a memoir: "'We're owned by them. Business,' Representative Marty Sabo, the chairman of the House Budget Committee, matter-of-factly explains. 'That's where the campaign money comes from now. In the 1980s, we gave up on the little guys.'" See Robert B. Reich, *Locked in the Cabinet* (New York: Knopf, 1997), 93.

18 Presentations included the presidential address to AFEE (2019), remarks on receipt of AFEE's Veblen-Commons Award (2024) for contributions to institutional economics, and keynote addresses at economics conferences in Poland (2017) and Japan (2019). I consider each of those occasions as a high point in my career, especially receipt of the Veblen-Commons Award; I remain in awe of that award's cavalcade of earlier recipients, including John Kenneth Galbraith, Wendell Gordon, Ray Marshall, Robert Heilbroner, and Hyman Minsky. For publications based on those presentations, see, respectively: Charles J. Whalen, "Institutional Economics and Chock-Full Employment: Reclaiming the 'Right to Work' as a Cornerstone of Progressive Capitalism," *Journal of Economic Issues* 53, no. 2 (June 2019): 321–340; Charles J. Whalen, "Telling It Like It Is: Reflections of a Maverick Economist," *Journal of Economic Issues* 58, no. 2 (June 2024): 360–377; Charles J. Whalen, "Understanding Financialization: Standing on the Shoulders of Minsky," in *Alternative Approaches to Economic Theory*, ed. Victor A. Beker (London: Routledge, 2020), 185–206; and Charles J. Whalen, "Post-Keynesian Institutionalism: Past, Present, and Future," *Evolutionary and Institutional Economics Review* 17, no. 1 (January 2020), 71–92.

19 See Whalen, *Reforming Capitalism for the Common Good*; Charles J. Whalen, *Institutional Economics: Perspectives and Methods in Search of a Better World* (London: Routledge, 2022); Charles J. Whalen, *A Modern Guide to Post-Keynesian Institutional Economics* (Cheltenham: Edward Elgar, 2022); and Charles J. Whalen, *Fashioning Prosperous, Sustainable and Humane Societies: Beyond Precarity* (Cheltenham: Edward Elgar, 2025).

20 See, for example, Whalen, "Understanding Financialization."

21 See, for example, Charles J. Whalen, "Post-Keynesian Institutionalism and the Failure of Neoliberalism," *Journal of Economic Issues* 55, no. 2 (June 2021): 469–476. See also

Yan Liang and Charles J. Whalen, "Money Manager Capitalism and the Coronavirus Pandemic," in *A Modern Guide to Post-Keynesian Institutional Economics*, ed. Charles J. Whalen (Cheltenham: Edward Elgar, 2022), 101–103.

22 Charles J. Whalen and Yan Liang, "Money Manager Capitalism and the Coronavirus Pandemic: A Post-Keynesian Institutionalist Analysis of Inadequate Industrial Capacity," *Journal of Economic Issues* 56, no. 2 (June 2022): 508–551; and Yan Liang and Charles J. Whalen, "Money Manager Capitalism and the Coronavirus Pandemic," 89–120. The Liang-Whalen chapter also shows that the pandemic's adverse effects on workers fell disproportionately on women and people of color.

23 See, for example, Charles J. Whalen, "Toward Real Sustainability: Incorporating Insight from Ecological Economics into Post-Keynesian Institutionalism," in *A Modern Guide to Post-Keynesian Institutional Economics*, ed. Charles J. Whalen (Cheltenham: Edward Elgar, 2022), 358–388; and Charles J. Whalen, "Green Investment, Institutions, and Ecological Sustainability," in *Conceptualising an Alternative Political Economy of Sustainability*, ed. Arturo Hermann (London: Routledge, 2025), 218–231. Also, for an example of research on environmental sustainability conducted in collaboration with my daughter (who holds a PhD in industrial environmental economics), see Charles J. Whalen and Katherine A. Whalen, "Circular Economy Business Models: A Critical Examination," *Journal of Economic Issues* 54, no. 3 (September 2020): 628–643.

24 See, for example, Charles J. Whalen, "The 'Middle Way' of John R. Commons: Pursuing Reasonable Value in an Age of Unreason," *Journal of Economic Issues* 54, no. 4 (December 2020): 1161–1173.

25 For the "demagogue" quote, see John R. Commons, "Is Class Conflict in America Growing and Is It Inevitable?" *American Journal of Sociology* 13, no. 6 (May 1908): 763. For a broader discussion of Commons's views on the political consequences of worker discouragement, see Charles J. Whalen, "Reasonable Capitalism, Worker-Oriented Policies, and the Future of American Democracy," *Journal of Economic Issues* 58, no. 4 (December 2024): 1089–1090.

26 Minsky, quoted in Dimitri B. Papadimitriou, "Minsky on Himself," in *Financial Conditions and Macroeconomic Performance: Essays in Honor of Hyman P. Minsky*, ed. Steven Fazzari and Dimitri B. Papadimitriou (Armonk: M.E. Sharpe, 1992), 25. See also Hyman P. Minsky, "Beginnings," *Banca Nazionale del Lavoro Quarterly Review*, no. 154 (September 1985): 211–221.

27 "'I've Never Seen Anything Like This': Former HR Executive on Today's Job Market," CNN Business, February 6, 2025, https://www.cnn.com/2025/02/06/business/video/job-market-white-collar-ny-digvid.

28 Barack Obama, "Remarks of the President on Economic Mobility."

29 Raj Chetty, et al., "The Fading American Dream: Trends in Absolute Income Mobility Since 1940," *Science* 356, no. 6336 (April 24, 2017): 398–406.

30 See, for example, Raj Chetty, "Improving Opportunities for Economic Mobility: New Evidence and Policy Lessons," in *Economic Mobility*, ed. Federal Reserve Bank of St. Louis (St. Louis: Federal Reserve Bank of St. Louis, 2016), 35–42.

31 Jay Shambaugh, et al., "Thirteen Facts About Wage Growth," Brookings, September 25, 2017, https://www.brookings.edu/articles/thirteen-facts-about-wage-growth/. A more recent analysis by the Economic Policy Institute (EPI) compares hourly compensation (wages plus benefits) in the periods 1948–1979 and 1979–2025 (through mid-year 2025). It finds compensation grew at average annual rates of 2.1 percent in the first period and 0.6 percent in the second period. The EPI analysis also finds that worker productivity has grown 2.7 times as much as compensation since 1979. See "The Productivity-Pay Gap," Economic Policy Institute, September 3, 2025, https://www.epi.org/productivity-pay-gap/. In both the Brookings and EPI analyses, wage growth calculations rely on hourly earnings of production and nonsupervisory workers in the private sector; the calculations adjust for inflation.

32 Bryan Robinson, "The Wage Crisis of 2025: 73% of Workers Struggling," *Forbes*, February 12, 2025, https://www.forbes.com/sites/bryanrobinson/2025/01/24/the-wage-crisis-of-2025-73-of-workers-struggling/.

33 According to an annual survey by the Federal Reserve, 55 percent of adults reported having emergency savings to cover three months of expenses in the event of a financial challenge such as a job loss; see "Report on the Economic Well-Being of US Households in 2024–May 2025," Board of Governors of the Federal Reserve System, June 12, 2025, https://www.federalreserve.gov/publications/2025-economic-well-being-of-us-households-in-2024-savings-and-investments.htm.

34 See Whalen, "Post-Keynesian Institutionalism and the Failure of Neoliberalism," 470–471.

35 Rakesh Kochhar, "The State of the American Middle Class," Pew Research Center, May 31, 2024, https://www.pewresearch.org/race-and-ethnicity/2024/05/31/the-state-of-the-american-middle-class/. (Shares do not total 100 percent due to rounding. Lower-income households are defined as those with incomes less than two-thirds of the median; upper-income households have incomes more than double the median.)

36 US Census Bureau, "Homeownership Rate in the United States," FRED, Federal Reserve Bank of St. Louis, https://fred.stlouisfed.org/series/RHORUSQ156N (data available through the second quarter of 2025).

37 For the Redfin report and quote by Sheharyar Bokhari, see Mark Worley, "The Number of Renter Households Is Growing Three Times Faster Than Homeowner Households," Redfin News, January 2, 2025, https://www.redfin.com/news/renter-household-growth-q3-2024/.

38 Lindsay Ellis and Aaron Zitner, "Americans Lose Faith That Hard Work Leads to Economic Gains," *Wall Street Journal*, September 1, 2025, https://www.wsj.com/economy/wsj-norc-economic-poll-73bce003.

39 On maximizing shareholder value, see Whalen, "Understanding Financialization," 186; and William Lazonick and Mary O'Sullivan, "Maximizing Shareholder Value: A New Ideology for Corporate Governance," *Economy and Society* 29, no. 1 (February 2000): 13–35. A recent study indicates that 68 percent of US equities were held by institutional investors at the end of 2022. (The three largest asset management companies are BlackRock, Vanguard, and State Street.) The same study finds a rapid growth in the global asset management industry in recent decades; it also indicates that institutional investors use various approaches to achieve their goals. For that study, see Wolfgang Drobetz, et al., "Beyond Ownership: The Role of Institutional

Investors in International Corporate Governance," *Corporate Governance: An International Review* 33, no. 5 (September 2025): 1024–1038.

40 Lazonick refers to money manager capitalism as the "new economy business model." See William Lazonick, "Corporate Financialization and Socioeconomic Precarity: Processes, Consequences, and Remedies," in *Fashioning Prosperous, Sustainable and Humane Societies: Beyond Precarity*, ed. Charles J. Whalen (Cheltenham: Edward Elgar, 2025), 269–282. For an analysis of the turn away from creating value within the manufacturing sector, see Suzanne Berger, "How Finance Gutted Manufacturing," *Boston Review*, March 1, 2014, https://www.bostonreview.net/forum/suzanne-berger-finance-gutted-manufacturing/.

41 For example, see Gretchen Morgenson and Joshua Rosner, *These Are the Plunderers: How Private Equity Runs—and Wrecks—America* (New York: Simon and Schuster, 2023); and Luke Goldstein, "Boeing 737 Max Incident a By-Product of Its Financial Mindset," *American Prospect*, January 9, 2024, https://prospect.org/2024/01/09/2024-01-09-boeing-737-max-financial-mindset/.

42 For a description and brief discussion of each stage of spreading worker precarity, see Lazonick, "Corporate Financialization and Socioeconomic Precarity," 281.

43 Over the past few decades, not all worker retraining has paid off: some people trained for a new line of work only to find their new jobs offshored. For example, see Thottam, "Is Your Job Going Abroad?"

44 The earnings consequences of job loss are often substantial, but there are also other important costs. The costs are especially significant when permanent layoffs affect workers with long tenure on the job. Research shows that such job loss leads to large and persistent earnings losses, as well as to outcomes including "less stability in earnings and employment, worse health outcomes, higher mortality, [and] lower educational achievement by the children of displaced workers"; see Steven J. Davis and Till Von Wachter, "Recessions and the Costs of Job Loss," *Brookings Papers on Economic Activity* (Fall 2011), especially 2, 27–34. For more on the earnings consequences of job loss, see, for example, Henry S. Farber, "Employment, Hours, and Earnings Consequences of Job Loss: US Evidence from the Displaced Workers Survey," *Journal of Labor Economics* 35, no. S1 (2017): S235–S272; Henry S. Farber, "What Do We Know About Job Loss in the United States? Evidence from the Displaced Workers Survey, 1984–2004," *Economic Perspectives* 29, no. 2 (May 2005): 13–28; Daniel Cooper, "The Effect of Unemployment Duration on Future Earnings and Other Outcomes," Working Papers No. 13-8, Federal Reserve Bank of Boston, January 13, 2014, https://ideas.repec.org/p/fip/fedbwp/13-8.html; and Michael Greenstone and Adam Looney, "Unemployment and Earnings Losses: A Look at the Long-Term Impacts of the Great Recession on American Workers," Brookings, November 4, 2011, https://www.brookings.edu/articles/unemployment-and-earnings-losses-a-look-at-long-term-impacts-of-the-great-recession-on-american-workers/.

45 Starting a successful business requires not only resources, but also entrepreneurial skills that are seldom taught in US schools. One in five US businesses doesn't survive its first year, and only about half (51.6 percent) survive five years. See US Bureau of Labor Statistics, "Establishment Age and Survival Data, Total Private, Table 7," https://www.bls.gov/bdm/us_age_naics_00_table7.txt.

46 Research on deaths of despair by Anne Case and Angus Deaton connects rising mortality rates to economic forces "that have eaten away at the foundations that characterized working-class life as it was half a century ago." They emphasize how the pain of workers' economic losses leads to deeper, more personal losses of "meaning, dignity, and pride," and how those accumulated losses bring on despair; see Anne Case and Angus Deaton, *Deaths of Despair and the Future of Capitalism* (Princeton: Princeton University Press, 2020), 7–8.

47 See, for example, the view of a private equity lobbyist quoted in Sanford M. Jacoby, *Labor in the Age of Finance* (Princeton: Princeton University Press, 2021), 177.

48 The household stock ownership figure was about 54 percent in 2017, rising to 62 percent in 2025; see Jack Caporal, "How Many Americans Own Stock?" The Motley Fool, September 22, 2025, https://www.fool.com/research/how-many-americans-own-stock/.

49 The wealthiest 10 percent of American households owned 87.1 percent of all US stock in early 2025; see Caporal, "How Many Americans Own Stock?" For households with no retirement savings, see "What Percentage of Americans Have a Retirement Savings Account?" Gallup, June 2, 2025, https://news.gallup.com/poll/691202/percentage-americans-retirement-savings-account.aspx.

50 "We have met the enemy …" is the famous line from cartoonist Walt Kelly's comic strip, *Pogo*.

51 See, for example, Jennie E. Brand, "The Far-Reaching Impact of Job Loss and Unemployment," *Annual Review of Sociology* 41, no. 1 (2015): 359–375; Steven Greenhouse, *The Big Squeeze: Tough Times for the American Worker* (New York: Alfred A. Knopf, 2008); and Jeffrey Pfeffer, *Dying for a Paycheck* (New York: Harper Business, 2018).

52 For an early analysis of how worker insecurity and inequality increase economic instability and slow economic growth, see Barry Bluestone and Bennett Harrison, *Growing Prosperity: The Battle for Growth with Equity in the Twenty-First Century* (Boston: Houghton Mifflin, 2000). For more recent analyses, see Joseph E. Stiglitz, *The Price of Inequality: How Today's Divided Society Endangers Our Future* (New York: W.W. Norton, 2012); and Christian E. Weller and Emek Karakilic, "Wealth Inequality, Household Debt, and Macroeconomic Instability," in *A Modern Guide to Post-Keynesian Institutional Economics*, ed. Charles J. Whalen (Cheltenham: Edward Elgar, 2022), 121–143.

53 See, for example, "Finance, Consulting, and Tech are Gobbling Up Top Students," *The Economist*, December 19, 2024, https://www.economist.com/christmas-specials/2024/12/19/finance-consulting-and-tech-are-gobbling-up-top-students. Silicon Valley also has its allure among today's recent university graduates, but even there the attraction is often the venture capital industry, and increasingly fintech (which focuses on integrating new technologies into the realm of finance), suggesting a blurring of Silicon Valley and Wall Street.

54 See, for example, Ron Suskind, *Confidence Men: Wall Street, Washington, and the Education of a President* (New York: Harper, 2011), 474–475.

55 Institutional economist Wallace Peterson expressed a similar concern about economic insecurity and sociopolitical polarization in the mid-1990s, warning that wage stagnation and rising inequality had become "the raw material for a bitter, divisive conflict in America"; see Peterson, *Silent Depression*, 92. More recently, columnist David Brooks (drawing on the work of William A. Galston) wrote that dark passions—anger, hatred, resentment, fear, and the urge to dominate—"now pervade the American psyche, and thus American politics." His conclusion: "[I]n order to repress dark passions and arouse good ones, leaders need to create conditions in which people experience social mobility." Without that, he argued, people "will fight like scorpions in a jar." See David Brooks, "The Era of Dark Passions," *New York Times*, September 19, 2025, A22.

56 The policy areas listed are intended to be illustrative, not comprehensive. For a compatible policy agenda, see "A Real Agenda for Working People," Economic Policy Institute, June 2018, https://files.epi.org/2017/real-workers-agenda.pdf; see also Josh Bivens and Adam S. Hersh, "The US Approach to Globalization Has Gone from Bad to Worse Under Trump," Economic Policy Institute, May 29, 2025, https://www.epi.org/publication/the-u-s-approach-to-globalization-has-gone-from-bad-to-worse-under-trump-how-to-construct-a-progressive-policy-agenda-instead/.

57 Stock buybacks weren't even legal until 1982; before then, they were considered a form of stock market manipulation by the US Securities and Exchange Commission.

58 The best way to support working families is by achieving and sustaining a robust, full-employment economy that offers family-supporting wages. Such an economy also helps job seekers who lack social networks or face other labor-market disadvantages. In addition, unions, community colleges, and local nonprofits can help those job seekers by investing in worker skills, cultivating mentoring relationships, and fostering career development; our nation needs to strengthen (and ensure access to) those labor market intermediaries, which offer an important alternative to temporary agencies that tend to channel workers into jobs with low wages and few benefits. See, for example, Chris Benner, et al., *Staircases or Treadmills? Labor Market Intermediaries and Economic Opportunity in a Changing Economy* (New York: Russell Sage Foundation, 2007).

59 Instead of aiming to privatize US education, the nation needs to pursue the goal of a world-class public education system that educates all students to high standards. Other examples of education and health-related policies worth pursuing include: (a) enhancing regional and sectoral workforce development and adult education programs, building on successes and emphasizing lifelong learning; (b) restoring, simplifying, and expanding college loan repayment programs for graduates working in vital fields and communities; (c) teaching the fundamentals of business planning and entrepreneurship to high school students; (d) providing income-based subsidies to ensure safe and affordable pre-school and after-school care for children; (e) restoring and enhancing worker safety and health protections; and (f) rolling back federal cuts to Medicaid spending (cuts enacted in July 2025) and adopting a proposal by Senator Brian Schatz (D-Hawaii), which would expand health insurance coverage by allowing Americans to buy into Medicaid. For more on constructive approaches to education and workforce development, see chapters by Ray Marshall as well as Robert W. Glover and Christopher T. King in Whalen, *Human Resource Economics and Public Policy*, 187–252; for more on expanding health insurance through Medicaid, see Jeff Stein and Sarah Kliff, "Sen. Schatz's New Health Care Idea Could Be the Democratic Party's Future," *Vox*, August 22, 2017, https://www.vox.com/policy-and-politics/2017/8/22/16171160/schatz-health-care-medicaid.

60 Survey research shows that nearly half of nonunion workers (48 percent) would join a union if they could; see Margaret Poydock, et al., "16 Million Workers Were Unionized in 2024," Economic Policy Institute, January 28, 2025, https://www.epi.org/publication/millions-of-workers-millions-of-workers-want-to-join-unions-but-couldnt/.

61 To better advance US industrial, trade, and technology policies, I'd also reestablish the Office of Technology Assessment, a research agency that Congress created in the early 1970s and which operated until 1995. It examined new technologies, assessed their effects, and analyzed policy alternatives. The office produced valuable studies on industrial competitiveness; today, it could make a meaningful contribution to a much-needed national conversation on a wide range of technology-related issues including the use of artificial intelligence.

Also, trade policy can include the strategic and judicious use of tariffs as part of a broader national economic and industrial strategy. In contrast, the Trump administration's approach to tariffs has been much more indiscriminate, with policy objectives that appear incoherent and haven't been well articulated. See Todd N. Tucker, "How Should Progressives Respond to Trump's Tariff Threats?" Roosevelt Institute, February 13, 2025, https://rooseveltinstitute.org/publications/how-should-progressives-respond-to-trumps-tariff-threats/.

62 One might argue that President Joe Biden aimed to pursue a worker-oriented agenda similar to the policy agenda I have in mind; I think he was on the right track. However, pursuit of his agenda was hampered by ineffective communication, overshadowed by political distractions, and limited by less than full support from his party combined with slim margins of control in the Senate in 2021–2024 and House in 2021–2022 (Republicans gained control of the House in 2023). Meanwhile, the Clinton and Obama eras had significant disappointments from a worker-oriented perspective, even while making advances with important legislation such as the Family and Medical Leave Act of 1993 and the Patient Protection and Affordable Care Act. See, for example, Nelson Lichtenstein, "A Fabulous Failure: Clinton's 1990s and the Origins of Our Times," *American Prospect*, January 29, 2018, https://prospect.org/2018/01/29/fabulous-failure-clinton-s-1990s-origins-times/; and Zachary D. Carter, "Obama Called Inequality 'The Defining Challenge of Our Time.' He Didn't Do Much About It," HuffPost, January 5, 2017, https://www.huffpost.com/entry/obama-income-inequality_n_5866836ce4b0de3a08f808dd.

63 Jeffrey Pfeffer, *Competitive Advantage Through People* (Boston: Harvard Business School, 1994), 16, emphasis in original.

64 Pfeffer, *Competitive Advantage Through People*, 6–26.

65 Evidence even suggests that employment downsizing isn't the cure-all executives often believe. For example, a study of 6418 cases over the period 1982–2000 finds no significant, consistent evidence that workforce downsizing led to improved financial performance in the two-year period following an employment change. In fact, companies with stable employment, and even those that increased employment, often experienced better performance than downsizers, according to the study's authors, Wayne F. Cascio and Clifford E. Young. Other studies find similar results, suggesting that employees and managers can work together to deliver both financial returns and employment security. See, for example, Wayne F. Cascio and Clifford E. Young, "Financial Consequences of Employment-Change Decisions in Major U.S. Corporations, 1982–2000," in *Resizing the Organization: Managing Layoffs, Divestitures, and Closings*, ed. Kenneth P. DeMeuse and Mitchell Lee Marks (San Francisco: Jossey-Bass, 2003), 131–156; and Jody Hoffer Gittell, "Layoffs and Organizational Resilience: Lessons for Workers, Managers, and Investors," *Perspectives on Work* 10, no. 1 (Summer 2006): 6–8.

66 An important reason business leaders have long chosen to cut labor costs instead of partnering with labor is that management theories carried over from the industrial era stress a rigid hierarchy in which CEOs plan, managers manage, and workers do what they're told. After all, the dominant theories of intelligence and education saw a sharp gulf between knowledge workers and manual workers, leading to the belief that most workers don't have the innate ability to do more than follow orders and perform routine tasks. But those theories have been discredited. The hand-brain distinction is false, and more recent research highlights the underappreciated cognitive demands of modern blue-collar and service work. See Marshall and Tucker, *Thinking for a Living*; and Mike Rose, *The Mind at Work* (New York: Viking Penguin, 2004).

67 In the United States, worker representation on corporate boards has been limited, as is evidence that the representation has significantly affected outcomes for companies and workers. Still, the US experience contains at least some indication that meaningful and lasting employee participation is possible because of worker representation on corporate boards, and the European experience offers considerable evidence that employee board-level representation can benefit companies and workers. See, for example, Kirstin R. Wever, "Toward a Structural Account of Union Participation in Management: The Case of Western Airlines," *ILR Review* 442, No. 4 (July 1989): 600–609; Larry W. Hunter, "Can Strategic Participation Be Institutionalized: Union Representation on American Corporate Boards?" *ILR Review* 51, No. 4 (July 1998): 557–578; Michael Gold, "'Taken on Board': An Evaluation of the Influence of Employee Board-Level Representatives on Company Decision-Making Across Europe," *European Journal of Industrial Relations* 17, no. 1 (2011): 41–56; and Laurent Belsie, "Worker Representation on Company Boards Raises Investment," The Digest, National Bureau of Economic Research, February 1, 2020, https://www.nber.org/digest/feb20/worker-representation-company-boards-raises-investment?page=1&perPage=50. See also "A Seat at the Table: Worker Voice and the New Corporate Boardroom," Aspen Institute Business and Society Program, August 23, 2021, https://www.aspeninstitute.org/publications/new-corporate-boardroom/.

68 For a still relevant discussion of obstacles to workplace changes that incorporate the voice of employees in business decision-making, see Eileen Appelbaum and Rosemary Batt, *The New American Workplace* (Ithaca: ILR Press, 1994), 146–160. For a successful case of organizational change that I've observed firsthand, see Fleron et al., *Champions at Work*, 52–54; and Wheaton and Whalen, "Using Industry Education to Facilitate Changes in Organizational Culture."

69 Harrison and Bluestone, *The Great U-Turn*, 185.

70 For a recent book contributing to a revival of interest in treating employees as a valuable business asset, see Stephan Meier, *The Employee Advantage: How Putting Workers First Helps Business Thrive* (New York: Public Affairs, 2024).

71 For a discussion of tripartite (business, labor, and government) forums during the Carter era, see Marshall, *Unheard Voices*, 233–249. For an examination of how and why labor's voice often gets overlooked in public discussion of issues involving business and the economy, see Christopher R. Martin, *Framed! Labor and the Corporate Media* (Ithaca: ILR Press, 2004).

72 Barbara C. Jordan, "1976 Democratic National Convention Keynote Address," New York, July 12, 1976, https://www.americanrhetoric.com/speeches/barbarajordan1976dnc.html.

73 Reinhold Niebuhr, *The Children of Light and the Children of Darkness: A Vindication of Democracy and a Critique of Its Traditional Defense.* With an introduction by Gary Dorrien (Chicago: University of Chicago Press, [1944] 2011), xx.

74 Niebuhr, *The Children of Light and the Children of Darkness*, xxxii.

75 Steven Levitsky and Daniel Ziblatt, *How Democracies Die* (New York: Crown, 2018).

76 Steven Levitsky and Daniel Ziblatt, "How a Democracy Dies," *The New Republic*, December 7, 2017, https://newrepublic.com/article/145916/democracy-dies-donald-trump-contempt-for-american-political-institutions.

77 For a discussion of the common language used by the Trump administration and Fox News, see Stuart A. Thompson, "For Trump and Fox News, New Policies Are Simply 'Common Sense,'" *New York Times*, February 15, 2025, B1. This is particularly important because Fox News Channel is the most-watched cable network and has been the most-watched television news channel for more than 22 years; attracting over 50 percent of the cable news viewing audience; see "Fox News Channel Finishes 2024 with Highest Audience Share in Nearly a Decade," Fox News Press Release, December 31, 2024, https://press.foxnews.com/2024/12/fox-news-channel-finishes-2024-with-highest-audience-share-in-nearly-a-decade-as-it-marks-nine-years-as-cables-most-watched-network. Hearing the administration and Fox News attack experts and describe Trump's outrageous actions as a "restoration of common sense," reminds me of the widespread anti-intellectualism in my extended family and hometown during my youth, where people with college degrees were often mocked for having "book smarts but no common sense."

78 See Eric N. Holmes, "The Equal Time Rule for Political Candidates: Constitutional Context," Legal Sidebar, Congressional Research Service, October 7, 2024, https://www.congress.gov/crs-product/LSB11239. As this book goes to press, the Trump administration appears to be pressing the Federal Communications Commission to reinterpret and aggressively enforce the "Equal Time Rule" in ways that many consider selective and partisan.

79 Daniel I. Weiner, "Citizens United Explained," Brennan Center for Justice, January 29, 2025, https://www.brennancenter.org/our-work/research-reports/citizens-united-explained.

80 Minsky often said: "Capitalism comes in as many varieties as Heinz has of pickles" (a reference to the "57 Varieties" slogan), and today there's considerable literature on the varieties of capitalism. Minsky also highlighted the fuzziness of capitalism and socialism; see, for example, Minsky, "Beginnings," 221.

81 Wynton Marsalis, Interview with Tom Power, CBC Radio, January 25, 2021, https://www.cbc.ca/radio/q/monday-jan-25-2021-wynton-marsalis-and-yulissa-campos-1.5886218/wynton-marsalis-on-segregation-jazzocracy-and-activism-through-instrumental-music-1.5886220. In the interview, Marsalis describes the contest between cooperation and predation as unending: the choice between them is one we confront every day.

82 The social choice laid out by Marsalis reminds us that the challenges we face today involve much more than public policy. As David Brooks writes, the current global trend toward the predatory world of authoritarian strongmen "is more than a set of policies—it's a culture," which its opponents can't possibly fight "by offering some tax credits." Brooks suggests there's a long road ahead for those wishing to turn things around: "Cultural and intellectual change comes first—a new vision. Social movements come second. Political change comes last." Yet he also sees a lesson in the alliance formed by Populists and Progressives at the turn of the twentieth century, which "made social mobility—the American Dream—the core of its vision" in the face of that era's challenges. (David Brooks, "America Needs a Mass Movement—Now," *The Atlantic*, October 14, 2025, https://www.theatlantic.com/magazine/archive/2025/11/autocracy-resistance-social-movement/684336/.) In short, the current challenges are formidable, but there's also a reason for hope—and to believe we're on the right track when centering our efforts on revitalizing the American Dream.

83 America tends to value ordinary workers in a crisis, and then only temporarily (for example, rescue workers during a disaster, and healthcare and delivery workers in a pandemic). However, I was raised to value workers every day, not just for what they contribute to society and their families, but also for their inherent worth as human beings. It should not take a crisis for us to think seriously about what we value, how we value, and who we value. For a related perspective, see Bruce Nussbaum, "Real Masters of the Universe," *BusinessWeek*, October 1, 2001, 55.

84 Steve Lohr, "Are Free-Market Ideas Stale? Some Scholars Think So," *New York Times*, February 17, 2022, B4.

85 Anne Applebaum, quoted in Francis Fukuyama, "The Long Arc of Historical Progress," *Wall Street Journal*, April 29, 2022, https://www.wsj.com/arts-culture/books/the-long-arc-of-historical-progress-11651244262.

86 Charles J. Whalen, "Introduction to the History, Contours, and Frontiers of Post-Keynesian Institutional Economics," in *A Modern Guide to Post-Keynesian Institutional Economics*, ed. Charles J. Whalen (Cheltenham: Edward Elgar, 2022), 23.

87 King, "Remaining Awake Through a Great Revolution," 9397.

88 King, "Remaining Awake Through a Great Revolution," 9395.

89 Martin Luther King Jr. "Our God Is Marching On!" Remarks before a crowd at the Alabama State Capitol in Montgomery, March 25, 1965, Stanford University, The Martin Luther King, Jr. Research and Education Institute, https://kinginstitute.stanford.edu/our-god-marching.

INDEX